THE LIFE OF
SIR WILLIAM FAIRBAIRN

The Life of SIR WILLIAM FAIRBAIRN, Bart

PARTLY WRITTEN BY HIMSELF

Edited and completed by WILLIAM POLE

A Reprint with an introduction by
A.E. MUSSON

DAVID & CHARLES REPRINTS

ISBN 0 7153 4890 6

First published in 1877 by Longmans Green and Company
This reprint published in 1970

© 1970 Introduction by A.E. Musson

Printed in Great Britain by
Stephen Austin & Sons Limited Hertford
for David & Charles (Publishers) Limited
Newton Abbot Devon

INTRODUCTION TO 1970 EDITION

SIR WILLIAM FAIRBAIRN was one of the great engineers of the nineteenth century, and his *Life*, together with the many books and articles which he wrote on engineering, have long been a mine of information for students of industrial history. Not merely did he play a leading role in many of the civil and mechanical engineering developments of his day – in millwork, construction of waterwheels and steam engines, bridge building, locomotive manufacture and iron shipbuilding – but he was also an outstanding propagator of engineering science, keenly interested in technical education, and, in his later years, almost entirely absorbed in writing about the industry in which he had so many achievements to his credit. Moreover, Fairbairn was a student of industrial history and was well aware of the revolutionary effects which engineering developments were having upon areas such as Lancashire,[1] so that his *Life* and other writings have more than a narrowly technical interest.

There is no doubt that in his lifetime Fairbairn was one of the chief agents and eyewitnesses of the Industrial Revolution – the changeover from manual to mechanical methods of production. Looking back, in his presidential address to the British Association meeting at Manchester in 1861, he declared that when he first came to that city in 1814 'the whole of the machinery was executed by hand. There were neither planing, slotting, nor shaping machines; and, with the exception of very imperfect lathes, and a few drills, the preparatory operations of construction were effected entirely by the hands of the workman.'[2] This statement is borne out by other contemporary witnesses, such as James Nasmyth, that equally famous Scottish engineer who also settled near Manchester: 'Up to within the last thirty years', he wrote in 1841, 'nearly every part of a machine had to be made and finished . . . by mere manual labour; that is, on the dexterity of the *hand* of the workman, and the correctness of his *eye*, had we entirely to depend for accuracy and precision in the execution of such machinery as was then required . . .'[3] Consequently, iron machinery could only be constructed inaccurately and at great expense. Samuel Smiles similarly stressed this early dependence on manual labour with hammer, chisel, and file, except for some 'ill-constructed lathes with some drills and boring machines of a rude sort'.[4]

Fairbairn and Nasmyth were not, however, the first engineers in Manchester, and engineering developments were already well under way when they first arrived there. Firms such as those of Bateman & Sherratt, Thomas C. Hewes, Peel & Williams, and many others had already become of considerable size and were producing waterwheels, steam engines, textile machinery, etc, on a large scale, as the revolution in the cotton industry gathered pace.[5] In 1820, when Fairbairn and Lillie had just started up in Mather Street, their works were assessed for poor rate at only £8 annual value, compared with figures ranging from £100 to £440 for established concerns such as those just mentioned.[6] And it is clear that some of these older firms were already, in the late eighteenth century, using power-operated lathes and drills and were working to gauge. In other areas, too, great ironfounding and engineering firms had earlier been developing: in the Midlands, for instance, one need only refer to such well-known men as the Darbys, Boulton and Watt, and John Wilkinson, or in London to Bramah, Maudslay, and others. Fairbairn himself, as the introductory remarks in his *Life* demonstrate, was well aware of the debt owed to these engineering pioneers.

Nevertheless, there is no doubt that these early developments were dwarfed by the revolutionary progress in engineering later in Fairbairn's life. In addition to the continuing transformation of the cotton, iron and other industries and further developments in waterwheels and steam engines, there was now a revolution in transport with the construction of steam-powered railway locomotives and ships, all of which stimulated revolutionary changes in machine-tool manufacture. These greatly impressed a Parliamentary committee in the early 1840s, which reported that 'tools have introduced a revolution in machinery, and toolmaking has become a distinct branch of mechanics, and a very important trade, although twenty years ago it was scarcely known.'[7] This statement was based on evidence given by engineers such as William Jenkinson, of Jenkinson & Bow, manufacturers of cotton-spinning machinery in Salford, another firm which was already well established before Fairbairn came to Manchester: 'What used to be called tools were simple instruments . . . such as hammers and chissels and files; but those now called tools are in fact machines . . . made at a very great cost, from £100 up to £2,000 each; I consider that the tools have wrought a great revolution in machine-making.'[8] He further pointed out that such machine-tools were now 'self-acting, and go on without the aid of the men', so that 'machinery is made by almost labourers', employed at much lower rates than those of the skilled workmen formerly required.

Engineering was also tending to become increasingly specialised. This was noticeable very early in the making of textile machines, on account of the rapidly-growing size of the market in the cotton industry, but it also developed in other branches. Jenkinson, in 1841, divided the engineering industry into three sections: 'the manufacture of steam-engines, mill gearing, hydraulic presses, and such other heavy machinery, I should call one class; the next, and a separate branch, I should say, was tool-making; and the third I should call [textile] machine-making, with its various branches of spindle and fly-making, and roller-making.'[9] Fairbairn was to acquire his fame mainly in the first branch, in heavy engineering: first of all in millwork, beginning with shafting and gearing, then prime movers (waterwheels and steam engines), and finally whole mill structures, but not apparently the textile machinery which went into them, for which he probably sub-contracted with specialist textile-engineering firms. His experience in cast and wrought-iron construction and in making steam engines led him naturally into the manufacture of railway loco-motives and bridges and steamships. For all this heavy engineering work, of course, he required and made machine-tools, which he also appears to have supplied to customers, but he did not become a specialist in this branch of engineering, like his Man-chester contemporaries, Roberts, Nasmyth and Whitworth. One must not exaggerate the degree of specialisation in this period – all these firms engaged in general engineering work, in addition to their specialised activities – but it was certainly developing more strongly.

Unfortunately, the records of Fairbairn's business (account-books, letters, etc) appear to have been destroyed, so that it is impossible to reconstruct the firm's history in any detail. We have to rely mainly on Fairbairn's *Life* and his other published works, supplemented by scraps of information in contemporary news-papers, books, etc. Some aspects of his early life deserve particular emphasis. Firstly, of course, he was a Scot, like so many other outstanding engineers of the Industrial Revolution, including Watt, Rennie, Telford, Nasmyth, etc. Perhaps the Scottish system of parish education contributed to this engineering pre-eminence, or perhaps Presbyterian emphasis on practical self-help. Another significant feature of Fairbairn's early career is that, on being apprenticed at fifteen years of age to John Robinson, millwright, of Percy Main colliery, Northumberland, he not only acquired sound practical experience of steam engines and mining operations, but also continued his studies every evening, with the aid of South Shields subscription library, on a self-imposed programme including arithmetic, algebra, geometry, trigonometry and mensuration, together with literature and history, while he also developed an interest in 'mechanical philosophy' and astro-nomy. And after his apprenticeship ended and he moved to London (where he worked, among other places, at Penn's famous Greenwich workshop), he continued these studies and also came into contact with the Society of Arts and Alexander Tilloch, editor of the *Philosophical Magazine*. Still later, after travelling and working in south-western England and in Dublin, and then settling in Manchester towards the end of 1813 – thus, like many other itinerant millwrights of the time, greatly extending his practical engineering experience – he carried on with his studies in natural philosophy, geometry and algebra, as well as history, etc, with the 'examples of Franklin, Ferguson and Watt always before me'.[10] These scientific-technical interests, in fact, he continued to sustain and develop throughout his career, as his *Life* and other publications strikingly demonstrate.

This testimony can be added to an ever-growing body of evidence on the links between science and technology in the Industrial Revolution.[11] Many, perhaps most, of the leading engineers of that period were not, as is so often imagined and stated in books on the subject, simply illiterate practical crafts-men, devoid of any education or theoretical knowledge. The eighteenth-century millwright, it is true, as Fairbairn says, had a wide practical experience: he was 'a kind of jack-of-all-trades, who could with equal facility work at the lathe, the anvil or the carpenter's bench. . . . He could handle the axe, the hammer, and the plane with equal skill and precision; he could turn, bore, or forge. . . .' But he was also generally 'a fair arithmetician, knew something of geometry, levelling and mensuration, and in some cases possessed a very competent knowledge of practical mechanics. He could calculate the velocities, strength and power of machines; could draw in plan and in section . . .'; indeed millwrights were commonly regarded as men of 'superior attainments and intellectual power'.[12] Such a man was Fairbairn himself: an outstanding example of 'self-education'.

This broad practical experience and education gave Fairbairn a firm grasp of general engineering, both applied and theoretical, and enabled him eventually to engage in a wide range of engineering developments. But, as he himself pointed out, the general skill of the millwright was gradually being replaced by more specialised techniques: 'The introduction of the steam engine, and the rapidity with which it created new trades, proved a heavy blow to the distinctive position of the millwright, by bringing into the field a new class of competitors in the shape of turners, fitters, machine-makers, and mechanical engineers.'[13] As works like Fairbairn's and others grew in size and as 'self-acting' machine-tools were introduced, more narrowly specialised workers were required, often (as we have previously noted) semi-skilled operatives, minding machines. Thus Fairbairn, while paying tribute to the traditional millwrights, helped to bring about their demise.

After his millwright's training in Northumberland and his later itineraries, Fairbairn acquired invaluable experience in Manchester, first in the employment of Adam Parkinson, who had been established as a millwright and machine-maker since the later eighteenth century, and who had become particularly notable as a manufacturer of calico-printing machinery;[14] then, after two years with Parkinson, he worked for Thomas Hewes, who, since the early 1790s, had developed one of the most outstanding millwright-engineering concerns in Manchester,[15] in which Fairbairn acquired extensive knowledge of millwork, waterwheels, etc, in the years 1816–17. Indeed it is clear that some of the revolutionary engineering developments later attributed to

Fairbairn should really be credited to Hewes. This can be illustrated, for example, in regard to millwork, the branch of engineering in which Fairbairn first established himself, in partnership with James Lillie, after leaving Hewes in 1817. Fairbairn's *Life* gives the impression that he was the first to introduce light wrought-iron shafting and smaller pulleys in place of the earlier cumbrous wooden shafts and drums (see pp 113–15), but he appears, in fact, to have been preceded in these developments by Hewes and also by Peel and Williams.[16] Similarly, in mill construction generally, Fairbairn appears to have been following in the footsteps of Hewes, who had previously been building iron-framed mills, complete with waterwheels, millwork, and machinery, in many parts of the country. In the manufacture of waterwheels, Fairbairn did indeed give credit to his former employer, particularly for his introduction of the 'suspension wheel', 'an entirely new system in the construction of water-wheels, in which the wheels attached to the axis by light wrought-iron rods, are supported simply by suspension', the mill-drive being taken from gearing fitted round the inner circumference of the wheel, instead of from the axle as previously.[17] Fairbairn carried forward these improvements, introducing others of his own such as ventilated buckets in waterwheels, and he certainly played a leading role in extending the 'revolution' in mill construction, so that he and Lillie could soon justifiably claim to be 'the leading millwrights of the district' (see p 114).

The application of iron in waterwheels, millwork, etc, was furthered by the experimental researches in which Fairbairn collaborated with Eaton Hodgkinson, the Manchester mathematician who later became professor of mechanical engineering at University College, London.[18] Hodgkinson developed special interests in the strength of materials, especially cast and wrought iron, and in their industrial applications, for example in beams, pillars, bridges, etc. Fairbairn provided him with research facilities at his works and himself participated enthusiastically in these investigations, the results of which were published in a series of papers to the Manchester Literary and Philosophical Society, the British Association and the Royal Society. Fairbairn's contribution, it is clear, was not simply that of patron; he played an active part and obviously had a good grasp of both the practical and theoretical problems involved. These investigations were closely related to much of his later engineering work. They were immediately applied, for example, in the building of an iron bridge for the new Liverpool–Manchester Railway over Water Street and also in the construction of factories at Macclesfield and elsewhere.[19]

Fairbairn and Lillie's initial successes with millwork for Adam and George Murray and then for McConnel & Kennedy, leading Manchester cotton-spinners (see pp 112–15), followed by these later developments, soon led to a rapid influx of orders, not only from British manufacturers, but also from the Continent, and by the early 1830s they were, according to Andrew Ure, 'celebrated over the world'.[20] Before their time, Ure stated, the science of mill architecture was little understood, and mills were built by those who were 'often utterly ignorant of statics or dynamics, or the laws of equilibrium and impulse.' But Fairbairn investigated the materials, sizes and proportions of the various components of millwork and was soon able to undertake the entire construction of large textile factories.[21]

> The capitalist has merely to state the extent of his resources, the nature of his manufacture, its intended site, and facilities of position in reference to water or coal, when he will be furnished with designs, estimates, and offers of the most economical terms, consistent with excellence, according to a plan, combining elegance of external aspect, with solidity, convenience, and refinement in the internal structure. As engineer he [Fairbairn] becomes responsible for the masonry, carpentry, and other work of the building, for the erection of a sufficient power, whether of a steam-engine or waterwheel, to drive every machine it is to contain, and for the mounting of all the shafts and great [gear] wheels by which the power of the first mover is to be distributed.

Two of the most outstanding of such factories were Orrell's mill at Stockport, driven by twin steam engines, and Ashworth's at Egerton, power by 'a gigantic waterwheel of sixty feet diameter, and one hundred horses' power'.[22]

Fairbairn himself took considerable pride in his waterwheel constructions, which demonstrate the continued importance of waterpower long after development of the steam engine. He refers particularly in his *Mills and Mill Work* to the four great breast-wheels, each 50 feet in diameter and $10\frac{1}{2}$ feet wide and each developing 120 horsepower, which were built in 1824–7 for Buchanan & Finlay's celebrated cotton mills at Catrine in Ayrshire,[23] followed by similar wheels for the same proprietors' Deanston mills. On the Continent, similarly, Fairbairn and Lillie erected large waterwheels for Hans Caspar Escher's cotton mills at Zurich, which led to numerous other orders for mills in Switzerland, France, and other countries.[24]

The equipping of these great mills involved, of course, the production of large quantities of shafting and gearing, for which mass-production methods were developed. Andrew Ure was probably referring to Fairbairn's works when he stated:[25]

> One millwright establishment in Manchester turns out from three to four hundred yards of shaft-gearing every week, finely finished, at a very moderate price, because almost every tool is now more or less automatic, and performs its work more cheaply and with greater precision than the hand could possibly do.

Perhaps, as has already been suggested, too much credit has been given to Fairbairn for these developments, and not enough to earlier engineers such as Hewes – Ure did, indeed, admit that the revolution in millwork 'had commenced . . . before their [Fairbairn and Lillie's] time'[26] – but there is no doubt that their activities in this branch of engineering were most impressive.

This rapid growth of business necessitated expansion of their works capacity. After starting up at the end of 1817 in a small shed in High Street, with a single lathe, powered by a muscular Irishman (see p 112), Fairbairn and Lillie moved in the following year to an old building in Mather Street, and then, a few years later, to Canal (or Cannel) Street, Ancoats. Fairbairn states (see p 129) that their business continued to be conducted in Mather Street until the orders for the Catrine waterwheels were received, but according to a surviving lease[27] they first acquired property in Canal Street in 1821; they were certainly established there by 1825.[28] This works, or its later extensions, were apparently built on the site – perhaps in some of the buildings – of an earlier firm, Bassett & Smith's iron foundry, Shooter's Brook, Ancoats Lane, which was already established there in the 1790s.[29] By 1830 Fairbairn and Lillie had apparently accumulated a balance of £40,000 and were employing 'upwards of 300 hands'.[30] In the following year, however, a large part of the works and its contents were destroyed by fire, damage being estimated at £7,000 to £8,000, though the premises had only be insured for £4,000.[31] Since the latter figure was about the same as the estimated valuation of Peel, Williams & Co's Soho Foundry in 1820,[32] we can see how rapidly Fairbairn and Lillie's works had expanded to become one of the biggest engineering concerns in Manchester.

INTRODUCTION TO 1970 EDITION   xiii

This rapid expansion was soon resumed after the fire. Up to this time they had concentrated almost entirely on millwork and waterwheels, but were now beginning to venture into new fields, such as the manufacture of steam engines and the building of iron steamships. Here again, Fairbairn combined practical engineering with applied science, conducting trials in 1830–1 of small iron steamboats on the Forth & Clyde Canal and on the Rivers Irwell and Mersey, with results worked out mathematically.[33] His tests on the strength of iron frames, ribs, plates and rivets for shipbuilding were closely related to his experiments on iron beams and pillars in factory and bridge construction, and just as he played a leading role in revolutionising millwork, so too he pioneered in the development of iron steamships. The first such ship, built by Aaron Manby, had only been launched in 1821, and there was still great uncertainty as to the suitability of iron for ship construction, while marine engines were still in their early stages of development.

Fairbairn's first boats were made in sections at the Manchester works, and the *Manchester Guardian* proudly proclaimed the town's emergence as a shipbuilding centre.[34] But these were all fairly small, flat-bottomed, stern paddlewheelers, for use on canals and rivers, or along the coast; larger vessels could not be built at Manchester. Lillie was, in fact, very dubious about this extension of the firm's activities, as well as about a cottonmill venture at Egerton, so in 1832 the partnership was dissolved, Fairbairn continuing with the Canal Street works on his own. He was then able, in 1835, to establish a shipbuilding concern at Millwall on the Thames, where in the next thirteen years 'upwards of a hundred vessels' were built, both for home and overseas customers, including the Admiralty (see Chapter XIX). But this concern eventually proved unprofitable and had to be sold in 1848, with losses totalling over £100,000. There were many pioneering difficulties to cope with, there was fierce competition, and the Thames was a less favourable location for iron shipbuilding than Merseyside, Clydeside, etc, while Fairbairn's personal attention was divided between Manchester and London.

The Manchester business, however, continued to expand successfully. In addition to carrying on his earlier millwork and waterwheel construction, Fairbairn also developed a large manufacture of steam engines and boilers, which were increasingly required for industrial motive power.[35] He soon achieved an outstanding reputation in boilermaking, in which he patented several important inventions such as the riveting machine (1837) and the Lancashire boiler (1844) and in which he also carried out further scientific-experimental investigations into strengths of plates and rivets and the causes of boiler explosions, publishing papers on this subject in the following years; he played a leading role in the establishment of the Manchester Steam Users' Association (1854), which pioneered in the introduction of safety measures, inspection and insurance for boilers and steam engines.[36]

Fairbairn's experience in iron construction and in steam engine and boiler making led him naturally into the building of railway locomotives, which he began about 1838. In this field, too, he was soon among the leading firms in the country and developed a very large manufacture, as railways were rapidly extended. According to his *Life* (see pp 316–17), more than 600 locomotives were built at the Manchester works, for both home and foreign railways. But E. L. Ahrons, who made a detailed investigation of Fairbairn's locomotive building, found this figure much too high: he listed 392 locomotives built by the firm between 1839 and 1862, and estimated that 'by the time the works closed [after Fairbairn's death in 1874] they had constructed rather more than 400 locomotives', of which about ninety per cent were built for United Kingdom railways and the remainder for various European, Indian and colonial railways.[37] Although later research has shown that Ahrons' list was incomplete, it appears that 'the missing ones cannot well have been more than twenty-five or so'.[38]

Fairbairn also continued to construct iron bridges, many of them for railways, his most famous and most controversial being the Britannia (Menai) and Conway wrought-iron tubular bridges, built in conjunction with Robert Stephenson. By 1870 he claimed to have built nearly a thousand on this principle, with spans varying from 40 to 300 ft (see Chapter XIII). He also built a large number of cranes, especially those of a wrought-iron tubular construction, which he patented (1850). In all these works he carried out further experimental researches, stemming from his early interest in strength of materials, based on similarly scientific procedures and making considerable use of applied mathematics.

In all these engineering activities Fairbairn continued to push into export markets, undertaking extensive journeys abroad, as described in his *Life* (see Chapters VIII, XI, XIV, XXI). A speaker at an Anti-Corn-Law meeting in Bolton in 1839, referring to the exportation of machinery, even went so far as to say that 'Mr. Fairbairn, of Manchester, did little [for sale in] England; and the men at his works are constantly employed in making machinery to be sent abroad'.[39] This was a great exaggeration, but Fairbairn undoubtedly did develop a large export trade. An outstanding example was his work for the Turkish government in the early 1840s, including the construction of iron furnaces, forges, and rolling mills, engineering workshops and machine-tools, a large woollen mill, mainly of iron construction, powered by a 100 hp waterwheel, together with steam-powered cotton and silk mills.[40] Similarly, he erected a large water-powered spinning and weaving factory at Gefle in Sweden,[41] and also carried out engineering work in Russia, visiting both these countries personally. But he also continued his millworking activities in England, of which the huge steam woollen mills built in the early 1850s for Titus Salt at Saltaire, near Bradford, were the supreme example.[42]

The immense expansion in the range of Fairbairn's engineering production and trade was, of course, accompanied and made possible by a remarkable growth of the Manchester works. A vivid impression of its size, mechanised methods and products is conveyed in the description by a visitor there in 1839, which is of such interest as to merit quotation at length:[43]

One of the principal establishments in Manchester in these departments [steam-engine making and general engineering] is that belonging to William Fairbairn, Esq., situate in Canal-street, Great Ancoats-street. To persons unacquainted with the nature of working in iron, an admission into these works affords, perhaps the most gratifying spectacle which the town can present of its manufacture in metal. Consequently, almost every person of distinction visiting the town contrives to procure an introduction to the proprietor before leaving it. In this establishment the *heaviest* description of machinery is manufactured, including steam engines, waterwheels, locomotive engines, and mill gearing. There are from 550 to 600 hands employed in the various departments; and a walk through the extensive premises, in which this great number of men are busily at work, affords a specimen of industry, and an example of practical science, which can scarcely be surpassed. In every direction of the works the utmost *system* prevails, and each mechanic appears to have his peculiar description of work assigned, with the utmost economical subdivision of labour. All is activity, yet without confusion. Smiths, strikers, moulders, millwrights, mechanics, boiler makers, pattern makers, appear to attend to their respective employments with as much regularity as the working of the machinery they assist to construct.

In one department mechanics are employed in building those mighty machines which have augmented so immensely the manufacturing interests of Great Britain, namely, steam engines. All sizes and dimensions are frequently under hand, from the diminutive size of 8 horses' power, to the enormous magnitude of 400 horses' power. One of this latter size contains the vast amount of 200 tons or upwards of metal and is worth, in round numbers, from £5,000 to £6,000.

The process of casting metal is conducted here on a very large scale. Castings of 12 tons weight are by no means uncommon: the beam of a 300 horses' power steam engine weighs that amount. Fly-wheels for engines, and waterwheels, though not cast entire, are immense specimens of heavy castings. A fly-wheel, for an engine of 100 horses' power, measures in diameter 26 feet, and weighs about 35 tons. In this establishment some of the largest waterwheels ever manufactured, and the heaviest mill-gearing, have been constructed; one waterwheel, for instance, measuring 62 feet in diameter. The average weekly consumption of metal in these works in the process of manufacturing, owing to the quantity of wrought-iron used, and the immense bulk of the castings, is 60 tons or upwards, or 3,120 tons annually.

The preparation of patterns – wood facsimiles of the castings – is a very costly process. Every piece of machinery, before it can be cast, must be constructed in wood; and these *patterns*, as they are termed, are made to form in sand, the mould into which the liquid ore [actually pig iron] is poured. Fifty men are daily employed in making patterns. The patterns, which are part of the proprietor's *stock in trade*, are worth many thousand pounds. After being used, the most important are painted and varnished, and laid carefully aside, in a dry room, to be ready for use when machines may accidentally get broken, or to aid in the construction of new ones. The patterns are made frequently of mahogany.

A most curious machine is employed for the purpose of *planing iron*; and, by means of its aid, iron shavings are stripped off a solid mass of metal with, apparently, as much ease as if it were wood, and with the greatest regularity and exactness.[44] Not the least interesting department of these works is that appropriated to boiler-making. Boilers, for steam engines, are composed of a number of plates of wrought-iron, about three-eighths of an inch in thickness. They are riveted together, with rivets about three-quarters of an inch in diameter, holes to receive which are punched through the plates, by a powerful, yet simple, machine, with as much facility as if the resistance was mere air. The process of riveting was, on the *old method*, an extremely noisy one; but a new plan is adopted here, and by it the work is performed silently, and much more efficiently. Some time ago about 50 boiler-makers were employed by Mr. Fairbairn. They 'struck', as it is termed, because their employer infringed, as they considered, upon their privileges, by introducing a few labourers, not in 'The Union', to perform the drudgery connected with the work. On this occurring, Mr. Fairbairn and Mr. Robert Smith invented a machine which super-seded the labour of 45 out of the 50 of his boiler-makers. The work is performed by the machine much quicker, more systematically, and, as before said, without noise.[45]

This extensive concern forwards its manufactures to all parts of the world. The stranger is told, on enquiry, that *this* article is for Calcutta, *that* for the West Indies; this for St. Petersburgh, that for New South Wales: and there are, besides, men belonging to it *located* in various parts of Europe, who are employed, under the direction of Mr. Fairbairn, in superintending the erection of work manufactured on these premises.

Many of the hands employed receive from £2 to £3 weekly wages, and scarcely any, except common labourers, receive less than 25s per week.[46] From these facts, some idea of the capital necessary to conduct a concern of this description may be imagined.

In addition to the above, Mr. Fairbairn has an establishment at Millwall, London, where upwards of 400 hands are employed in the manufacture of steam engines, and in the building of iron steam boats and other vessels constructed of the same material.

In the Manchester establishment, Mr. Fairbairn and Mr. Eaton Hodgkinson have conducted various important experiments, which have been published from to time in the 'Transactions of the Manchester Philosophical Society', and in the 'Reports of the British Association'.

This account emphasises the rapidly-increasing growth and specialisation of the labour force in Fairbairn's works. The 300 or more 'hands' of 1830 had apparently grown by the end of that decade to 550–600 in Manchester and 'upwards of 400' at Millwall. Indeed, these figures may well have been underestimates of the actual number employed. In Fairbairn's *Life* the total number of men at the two works is said to have risen to over 2,000 by about 1840 (see p 339), whereas other contemporary evidence puts it at 'between one and two thousand' around that date.[47]

This rapid growth in the number of employees was accompanied by growing labour problems, particularly associated with the increasing introduction of 'self-acting' machine tools. Fairbairn's invention of the riveting machine, patented in 1837, following a boilermakers' strike, is illustrative of these developments, and of his resistance to restrictive trade union demands. In his early days, as a workman in London, Fairbairn had run foul of the Millwrights' Society of London (see pp 89–90), on account of their restrictions on entry into the trade. These and other skilled craftsmen were struggling to maintain their craft status and to safeguard their manual skills threatened by mechanisation, which, as we have seen, enabled mass-production methods to be introduced, at much lower costs, employing cheaper semi-skilled labour. Early in the development of the Canal Street works, Fairbairn and Lillie experienced a 'turn-out' of millwrights against their taking on an additional apprentice, and they therefore advertised for forty to fifty workmen 'unconnected with the "Manchester Millwrights' Club" '.[48] In 1845, however, we find Fairbairn addressing a boilermakers' delegate meeting in Manchester, in a spirit of compromise and moderation, though he continued to oppose strict apprenticeship regulations and any

idea of fixing prices and wages.[49] Differences on these principles
led to the great engineers' strike in 1851–2, after foundation of
the Amalgamated Society of Engineers.[50] Fairbairn refused to
accept trade union limitations on employment of apprentices and
on the manning of machines; he would not tolerate any such curbs
on employers' authority, or any 'socialist doctrines'. It is also
clear that he was a strict disciplinarian. A fellow engineer
described him as 'the most punctual man he had ever met',
working rigidly regular hours and believing in 'strict adherence
to business subjects during business hours'.[51] His works were
notable for their 'system' and 'regularity' (see above p xv), and
Fairbairn himself declared:

> I strictly prohibit on my works the use of beer or fermented liquors of
> any sort, or of tobacco. I enforce the prohibition of fermented liquors
> so strongly that, if I found any man transgressing the rule in that
> respect, I would instantly discharge him without allowing him time
> to put on his coat. . . . I wish to have an orderly set of workmen;
> and . . . I am decidedly of opinion that it is better for the men them-
> selves and for their families. . . . I have provided water for the use of
> the men in every department of the works.[52]

At the same time, Fairbairn did a great deal to encourage
skilled craftsmen to improve themselves by means of technical
education (though it might be said, of course, that in doing so he
was also motivated by a desire to improve the quality of his own
labour force). In the mid-1820s he played a leading role in
establishing the Manchester Mechanics' Institute, to which he
also lectured,[53] and he was one of the founders of the Manchester
School of Design in the late 1830s;[54] he also participated in an
attempt to establish an 'Institution of Practical Science' in the
city.[55] In addition to helping in the foundation and management
of these institutions, he frequently gave lectures both to them
and to other groups of intelligent working men. Many of these
lectures are gathered in his *Useful Information for Engineers* (1856,
1860, 1866).

Perhaps the most remarkable feature of Fairbairn's career was
this intense interest in 'mechanical science' or 'practical science' –
his constant efforts at combining science and technology. As he
himself confessed, he was imbued with 'a strong desire to distinguish myself as a man of science' (see p 157), and to remove 'the
anomalous separation of theory and practice'.[56] These scientific-
technological interests were amply demonstrated in his active

membership of various scientific and engineering societies and in the enormous volume of his publications on structural engineering.

Soon after he had established himself in Manchester he became a member of the Literary and Philosophical Society, to which he read several papers and of which he eventually became president in 1855–60.[57] He also spoke frequently at meetings of the British Association, over which he presided in 1861; he was president of the Mechanical Section in 1853 and 1862, and in his addresses on all these occasions he particularly emphasised the progress and importance of 'mechanical science'. Mention has already been made of his outstanding scientific-technological researches in collaboration with Eaton Hodgkinson on strength of materials, especially cast-iron beams and pillars, which were published in the Manchester Society's memoirs and the British Association reports. In 1850 he was elected a Fellow of the Royal Society and subsequently delivered several papers on different subjects of mechanical science; in 1860, therefore, he was awarded one of the society's gold medals, 'for his various experimental enquiries on the properties of the materials employed in mechanical construction, contained in the "Philosophical Transactions", and in the publications of other scientific societies.' He joined the Institution of Civil Engineers in 1830, and in 1847 was among the founding members of the Institution of Mechanical Engineers, of which he was elected president in 1854–5 and to whose *Transactions* he contributed many papers.

In addition to these and many other papers, mostly concerned with strength of materials (especially cast and wrought iron) and with steam engines and boilers, Fairbairn published many books, among which the following were outstanding: *On the Application of Cast and Wrought Iron to Building Purposes* (1856, 1857, 1864); *Iron: its History, Properties and Processes of Manufacture* (1861, 1865, 1869); *Treatise on Mills and Mill Work* (1861–3, 1864–5); *Treatise on Iron Shipbuilding* (1865). In all this literature, as in his own engineering constructions, there was a blend of practical engineering and applied science, the necessity for which he constantly reiterated. On account of the limitations of his own theoretical and mathematical knowledge (though this was considerable), he frequently secured the assistance of scientific men such as Eaton Hodgkinson and later Thomas Tate, mathematics master at Battersea Training College, and W. C. Unwin, subsequently professor of engineering at the Royal East Indian Engineering College, Cooper's Hill. He also enjoyed contacts and friendships with many other scientists, both British and foreign, who clearly held him in high esteem. His scientific-technological eminence was recognised by the award of honorary degrees at Edinburgh (1860) and Cambridge (1862), and earlier, in 1852, by his election as a corresponding member of the National Institute of France, not only on account of his practical engineering achievements, but also, as Poncelet, the great French engineer, put it, for his *récherches expérimentales entreprises à vue d'éclairer la science de construction*.

After about 1853, in fact, Fairbairn withdrew from active management of the business, leaving it to his sons, and concentrated on his writing and consultancy work. The firm was later converted into a limited company, but, with his withdrawal, appears to have lost its early pioneering drive and was wound up after his death in 1874.[58] It may be, as Ahrons suggested, 'that the firm had too many irons in the fire'. Fairbairn's death also coincided with the onset of a serious trade depression following the boom of the early seventies. It also appears that, in his later life, Fairbairn was perhaps too much concerned with being a public figure and establishing his status as a scientist and writer, while his sons were less able men. Nevertheless, his life forms a remarkable chapter in the history of British engineering.

A. E. MUSSON

1 See, for example, his account of 'The Rise and Progress of Manufactures and Commerce, and Civil and Mechanical Engineering in these Districts', in T. Baines, *Lancashire and Cheshire, Past and Present* (1867).
2 He made a similar statement in Baines, op cit, Vol II, pt ii, p cliv: 'fifty years ago, tools and all other descriptions of machinery were chiefly made by hand. Blacksmiths' forges, stocks and dies, and lathes for turning metal and wood were in existence, but were very imperfect in construction . . . and void of those motions which constitute the slide-rest and self-acting machine. Planing, slotting and paring machines were unknown; and the machine for cutting the teeth of [gear] wheels was only just making its appearance.'
3 J. Nasmyth, 'Remarks on the Introduction of the Slide Principle in Tools and Machines employed in the Production of Machinery', in R. Buchanan, *Practical Essays on Mill Work* (3rd edn, revised by G. Rennie, 1841), pp 393–418.
4 S. Smiles, *Industrial Biography* (1863), p 180.
5 See A. E. Musson and E. Robinson, 'The Origins of Engineering in Lancashire', *Journal of Economic History*, June 1960, and 'The Early Growth of Steam Power', *Economic History Review*, 2nd ser Vol XI, no 3 (1959); see also A. E. Musson, 'An Early Engineering Firm. Peel, Williams & Co, of Manchester', *Business History*, Vol III, no 1, Dec 1960.
6 Manchester Poor Rate Book, 1820 (Manchester Central Reference Library, M9/40/2/85).
7 *Select Committee on Exportation of Machinery, Parliamentary Papers*, 1841, Vol III, Second Report, p vii.
8 Ibid, First Report, Q 1,314.
9 Ibid, First Report, Q 1,299.
10 Franklin was Benjamin Franklin, the famous American philosopher, and Ferguson was James Ferguson, another natural philosopher, well known in the eighteenth century, who made notable contributions to the general diffusion of scientific and technical knowledge in lectures and publications. Franklin and Ferguson, and also Watt, were to a considerable extent 'self-educated'.
11 See A. E. Musson and E. Robinson, *Science and Technology in the Industrial Revolution* (Manchester, 1969).
12 W. Fairbairn, *Treatise on Mills and Millwork* (1861–3), Vol I, pp v–vi.
13 Ibid, Vol I, pp vi–vii.
14 Musson and Robinson, *Science and Technology*, p 442.
15 Ibid, pp 69–71, 98–9, 445–7.
16 Ibid, pp 446–7, 462–3, 481.
17 Fairbairn, *Mills and Millwork* (2nd edn, 1864–5), part I, p 120, and also in Baines, *Lancashire and Cheshire*, pp cxliv–cxlv. See also *Manchester Guardian*, 19 May 1827 and 11 February 1832.
18 Musson and Robinson, *Science and Technology*, pp 77, 117–18, 481.
19 *Manchester Guardian*, 15 and 22 May 1830.
20 A. Ure, *Philosophy of Manufactures* (1835), pp 32–7.
21 Ibid, p 33.
22 Ibid, pp 33–5, 109–12. See also ibid, p 220, for Fairbairn and Lillie's construction of ventilating fans for cotton mills, and pp 266 and 273 for their improvements in silk-throwing mills.
23 Op cit (2nd edn, 1864–5), pp 91–2, 129–32. See also below, pp 121–3. The building of these 'four enormous waterwheels' was referred to in the *Manchester Guardian*, 19 May 1827, in an address by Benjamin Heywood to the Mechanics' Institution. They were built on Hewes' 'suspension' principle.
24 See below, pp 123–9. For Escher's relations with Fairbairn, see W. O. Henderson, *Industrial Britain under the Regency* (1968), pp 2–7.
25 Ure, op cit, p 37.
26 Ibid, p 36.

xxii REFERENCES

27 Dated 19 October 1821, kindly loaned by Mrs E. Brickell.
28 *Manchester Guardian*, 19 February 1825.
29 Musson and Robinson, *Science and Technology*, p 453.
30 See below, p 129. On p 314, however, a balance of £30,000 is stated.
31 *Manchester Guardian*, 13 August 1831. In addition to a considerable part of the premises, 'a very great number of patterns' and a large quantity of timber had been destroyed or damaged. But the foundry had been preserved and it was 'expected that little interruption of the business will take place'.
32 Musson, 'An Early Engineering Firm', p. 13.
33 See his *Remarks on Canal Navigation, illustrative of the advantages of the use of Steam as a Moving Power on Canals* (1831) and his later *Treatise on Iron Shipbuilding* (1865).
34 For example, on 26 February and 2 April 1831 (the *Lord Dundas*, built for the Forth–Clyde Canal and tried out on the Irwell); 5 May 1832, quoting from the *Glasgow Chronicle* (referring to the *Cyclops*, built twelve months earlier, and a new one, the *Manchester*, both for the Forth–Clyde Canal and coastal trade); 16 March 1833 (*La Reine des Belges*, built for the Ostend–Bruges canal); 4 April 1835 (iron steamboats for the Ouse and Humber trade between Selby and Hull).
35 Marine engines were also made in Manchester, eg the 600 hp engines for the naval frigates *Megaera* and *Odin*, referred to in *Manchester Records* (1868), under date 17 June 1846, in connection with a visit to the works by Ibrahim Pasha, Viceroy of Egypt.
36 See below, Chapter XVI. See also *A Century's Progress* (British Engine, Boiler & Electrical Insurance Co Ltd, 1954).
37 E. L. Ahrons, 'Short Histories of Famous Firms, No II, W. Fairbairn and Sons, Manchester', *The Engineer*, 20 February 1920, pp 184–5. See also ibid, p 357, for an additional French locomotive.
38 P. C. Dewhurst, *The Locomotive*, 15 March 1930, pp 80–1, in an article referring to a Brazilian locomotive by Fairbairn.
39 *Manchester Guardian*, 27 April 1839. See also p xvi.
40 See below, Chapter XI, and also *Manchester Guardian*, 22 March and 20 December 1843, and Fairbairn's 'Description of a Woollen Factory erected in Turkey', *Min Proc Inst Civ Eng*, Vol III (1843), pp 125 ff.
41 See P. Carlberg, 'Personal Contacts between the Manchester area and Gefle in Sweden a Hundred Years Ago', *Lancs & Chesh Antiq Soc Trans*, Vol LXX (1960), pp 57–63, including a photograph of the huge waterwheel, 43 ft in diameter and 11 ft wide.
42 See below, pp 327–8. A more detailed description is given in Fairbairn's work *On the Application of Cast and Wrought Iron to Building Purposes* (1854).
43 Love and Barton, *Manchester As It Is* (1839), pp 210 ff. For a sketch of the inside of Fairbairn's works in 1861, showing steam-engine beams, cylinders, and boilers, together with a Fairbairn crane and plate-punching machine, see W. H. Chaloner and A. E. Musson, *Industry and Technology* (1963), plate 123.
44 The metal-planing machine was a comparatively recent innovation, having first been invented apparently between 1815 and 1820, by various engineers. Nasmyth (op cit, 403–4) stated in 1841 that it 'has done more within the last 10 or 15 years for reducing the cost, and for extending the use of perfect machinery, than . . . all the improvements in mechanism for the last century.' Professor R. Willis, writing about machine-tools in *Lectures on the Results of the Great Exhibition* (1852), pp 291–320, similarly testified that it was 'the greatest boon to constructive mechanism since the invention of the lathe'. It replaced the previous laborious, imprecise, and very costly manual process of chipping and filing to produce plane metal surfaces.

45 In a footnote, it was pointed out that trade unions, by their 'impotent tyranny', their 'insolent and foolish conduct' in strikes aimed at restricting employment and raising wages, were stimulating the introduction of labour-saving machinery, such as the boiler-riveting machine and the self-acting mule.

46 Another footnote stated that the total weekly wages-bill was nearly £1,000.

47 As stated in the *Report on the Sanitary Condition of the Labouring Population of Great Britain* (8vo edn, 1842), p 250. Fairbairn was giving evidence on drink and sobriety among the working classes.

48 *Manchester Guardian* and *Manchester Gazette*, 19 February 1825.

49 *Manchester Guardian*, 22 March 1845.

50 See below, pp 322-7. For the general background, see J. B. Jeffereys, *The Story of the Engineers* (1946), Chapters I and II.

51 A. C. Dean, *Some Episodes in the Manchester Association of Engineers* (Manchester, 1938), p 119, quoting from the Association minutes, 23 February and 9 March 1878, statement by Mr Rawlinson.

52 See above, ref 47, for the source of this statement. Fairbairn considered that alcoholic drink made men less efficient in their work, and that it wasted their money and damaged their health.

53 M. Tylecote, *The Mechanics' Institutes of Lancashire and Yorkshire before 1850* (Manchester, 1957), pp 34, n 7, 43, 129-30. He is said to have been 'the first Secretary of the Mechanics' Institution in Cooper Street'. Dean, op cit, p 120, statement by Mr Walthew.

54 *Manchester Guardian*, 21 February 1838 and 6 September 1843.

55 Ibid, 27 and 30 March 1839.

56 Presidential address to the British Association, Manchester, 1861.

57 He also enjoyed informal 'philosophical and scientific discussions' at home in the evenings, with friends such as Eaton Hodgkinson, the mathematician, Bennet Woodcroft, scientific adviser to the Patent Office, and James Nasmyth, the engineer (see below, pp 155-6).

58 Many of the works buildings, however, are still standing today, having been occupied for many years by Messrs Parker (Ancoats) Ltd, a timber firm.

SIR WILLIAM FAIRBAIRN, BART.

LONDON : PRINTED BY
SPOTTISWOODE AND CO., NEW-STREET SQUARE
AND PARLIAMENT STREET

London, Longman & Co.

THE LIFE

OF

SIR WILLIAM FAIRBAIRN, BART.

F.R.S., LL.D., D.C.L.

CORRESPONDING MEMBER OF THE NATIONAL INSTITUTE OF FRANCE
MEMBER OF THE INSTITUTION OF CIVIL ENGINEERS
HONORARY ASSOCIATE OF THE INSTITUTION OF NAVAL ARCHITECTS
CORRESPONDING ASSOCIATE OF THE ROYAL ACADEMY OF SCIENCES, TURIN
ETC.

PARTLY WRITTEN BY HIMSELF

EDITED AND COMPLETED

BY

WILLIAM POLE, F.R.S.

MEMBER OF COUNCIL OF THE INSTITUTION OF CIVIL ENGINEERS

WITH PORTRAIT

LONDON
LONGMANS, GREEN, AND CO.
1877

PREFACE.

IT WAS NOT without some hesitation that I undertook, at the request of the family of the late SIR WILLIAM FAIRBAIRN, a task which, under ordinary circumstances, would have been better performed by a more practised writer. It was, however, considered that, from the peculiar nature of his occupations and pursuits, justice could hardly be done to his biography, except by some one familiar with the technical and scientific subjects it must so largely treat of; and it was on this ground alone that I felt justified in accepting the proposal.

The autobiography which forms the earlier part of the history bears on its first page the following remark :

This memoir was written at the request of some highly respected friends, who were desirous that I should leave on record the events of what they were pleased to call an eventful and useful life. To this I consented, on condition that it should not be published till after my death ; and then only in case my executors and friends should think it would be for the benefit of those who have to encounter similar difficulties in life.

As most of the account of my early life was written from memory during a voyage, the narrative will require careful revision and condensation, including such omissions as in the judgment of my friends may be deemed necessary.

W. F.

MANCHESTER : *March* 17, 1851.

My work in regard to this has been simply to carry out the revision directed by the author.

For the remainder of the biography, which records the important labours of the last thirty or forty years of his life, my data have been derived from his published works and memoirs ;—from an immense mass of his correspondence and papers put into my hands ;—from information furnished to me by relatives and friends ;—and from facts within my own knowledge. I take this opportunity of expressing my thanks to all those who have so kindly given me their aid.

I have thought it would add to the interest of the work to give a notice, more complete than has hitherto appeared, of the profession to which SIR WILLIAM FAIRBAIRN belonged ;—one which, although so recent in its origin, has acquired in the present day a magnitude and importance most remarkable.

In regard to the general selection of the matter that appears in the following pages, I have been guided by the judgment and wishes of the family ; for the literary and technical treatment I alone am responsible.

W. P.

ATHENÆUM CLUB, LONDON:
December 1876.

CONTENTS.

CHAPTER I.

ON THE PROFESSION OF ENGINEERING GENERALLY.

CHAPTER II.

MECHANICAL ENGINEERING.

CHAPTER III.

FROM BIRTH TO THE END OF RESIDENCE AT KELSO.

AGE, TO 14. 1789-1803.

CHAPTER IV.

FIRST EMPLOYMENT AND APPRENTICESHIP.

AGE 14-21. 1803-1810.

CHAPTER V.

CHAPTER VI.

CHAPTER VII.

CHAPTER XIII.

THE CONWAY AND BRITANNIA TUBULAR BRIDGES.

1845-1849.

CHAPTER XIV.

BRIDGE OVER THE RHINE AT COLOGNE.

1849-1852.

CHAPTER XV.

SCIENTIFIC HONOURS.

AGE 61–64. 1850–1853.

CHAPTER XVI.

STEAM BOILERS AND MATTERS CONNECTED THEREWITH.

1844–1874.

CHAPTER XVII.

MR. HOPKINS'S EARTH EXPERIMENTS.

1851–1857.

CHAPTER XVIII.

THE MANCHESTER MANUFACTURING BUSINESS.

CHAPTER XIX.

THE MILLWALL SHIP-BUILDING FACTORY.

CHAPTER XX.

IRON ARMOUR.

AGE 73–79. 1861–1867.

CHAPTER XXI.

MISCELLANEOUS MATTERS.

AGE 61–80. 1850–1869.

CHAPTER XXII.

LITERARY WORK.

1850–1873.

CHAPTER XXIII.

ILLNESS AND DEATH.

CHAPTER XXIV.

PERSONAL DETAILS—ILLUSTRATIONS OF CHARACTER.

APPENDIX.

CHAPTER I.

ON THE

PROFESSION OF ENGINEERING GENERALLY

B

INTEREST ATTACHING TO THE PROFESSION OF ENGINEERING—
ORIGIN OF THE TERM ENGINEER—EXAMPLES OF ITS EARLY USE—
ANCIENT ENGINEERING WORKS—PERSONS BY WHOM THEY WERE CON-
STRUCTED—THE ARCHITECT—THE ANCIENT PRIESTS' TITLE 'PONTIFEX'
—WORKS IN THE MIDDLE AGES—BRIDGES; THE 'FRÈRES PONTIERS'
—HYDRAULIC WORKS IN THE NORTH OF ITALY—APPRECIATION OF
SCIENCE—BELIDOR—WANT OF MEN TO EXECUTE SUCH WORKS—RISE
OF A NEW CLASS OF PRACTITIONERS CALLED CIVIL ENGINEERS—
ENGINEERING IN ENGLAND—EARLY WORKS—THE NEW RIVER—BRITISH
BRIDGES—INIGO JONES, LABELYE, EDWARDS—TRUE RISE OF ENGLISH
ENGINEERING WITH BRINDLEY AND SMEATON—FIRST USE IN ENGLAND
OF THE PRESENT NAME OF THE PROFESSION—SMEATON'S SUCCESSORS:
WATT, MYLNE, RENNIE, TELFORD—THE MODERN ERA OF RAILWAYS—
DEFINITION OF THE PROFESSION OF ENGINEERING, AND THE OCCU-
PATIONS COMPRISED THEREIN—IMPORTANCE OF THE PROFESSION AS
ESTIMATED BY THE MAGNITUDE AND VALUE OF THE WORKS EXECUTED.

CHAPTER I.

THE SUBJECT of this Memoir was a worthy representative of a class of men to whom we owe, in a large measure, the wealth and prosperity our country now enjoys.

The progressive improvements of the last hundred years, whether in our means of communication, in the spread of our knowledge, in the position of our science, in our arts and manufactures, in our provisions of war, or in our personal and domestic comforts and enjoyments, have been largely dependent on the work of the engineer. In some cases he has been almost the sole author of the progress made ; in scarcely any would such progress have been possible, unaided by the mechanical design and constructive art which it is his province to supply.

The profession of engineering has, indeed, now taken such a high position in the economy of modern life, and its members are called on to exercise such important functions in the community, that the nature of their occupation cannot but be a matter of general interest; and the life and work of an eminent engineer may, in the present day, be deemed, without presumption, as worthy of being put upon record as were the lives and works of heroes or statesmen in the olden time.

It will be an appropriate introduction to the Life of Sir William Fairbairn, to give some account generally of the profession to which he belonged.

The term *engineer*, as defining an occupation, is an

old one; but it was originally applied only to persons in the military profession, and does not appear to have been used by civilians until the middle of the last century. It is popularly supposed to be derived from the word *engine*, this impression being supported by the meanings given by Dr. Johnson, namely:—

1. One who manages engines; one who directs the artillery [*i.e.* the warlike engines] of an army.
2. A maker of engines.

In reality, however, the derivation lies much farther away. The root of the term is found in the Sanscrit *jan*, to be born, from which came the Greek form γεν, and the Latin *gen*, the latter being embodied in the old verb *genere*, with its compound *ingenere* (changed into *in-gignere*), to implant by birth, and in the later substantive *ingenium*, an innate or natural quality.

By some obscure process, this word came to be used, like the Greek μηχανή, to signify an instrument or machine (in the same manner as *ars* gave rise to the word artillery); and so it became transmuted into the old French *engin*, which has given rise to our *engine*, but which, in its own country, has become obsolete, being supplanted by the more modern word *machine*.

The term *engineer* comes more directly from another old French word in the form of a verb—*s'ingénier*. The meaning of this was ' chercher dans son génie, dans son esprit, quelque moyen pour réussir.'[1] All authorities, our own great lexicographer included, agree that this word is to be taken as the true origin; and thus we arrive at the interesting and certainly little known fact, that an engineer is, according to the strict derivation of the term, not necessarily a person who has to do with engines, but anyone who seeks in his mind, who sets his mental powers in action, in order to discover or devise

[1] Littré, *Dictionnaire de la Langue Française.*

some means of succeeding in a difficult task he may have to perform.

It would be impossible to give a nobler or more appropriate description than this, of the manner in which our greatest engineering works have been produced, or the nature of the qualifications by which the greatest men in the profession have acquired their renown.

The first form of the term applied to a person was the low Latin *ingeniator*; then came the Provençal *enginhaire*, or *enginhador*, and then the old French *engigneur*, which became modernised into *ingénieur*, and so we get *engineer*.

The following are examples of the early French use of the word:—

Twelfth Century.—' Il fait creuser souz terre, à pic et à martel à ses angigneors dont ot pris maint chastel.'

Thirteenth Century.—' Li engignieres fut moult sage.'

' Le Roy fit faire xviii. engins, dont Jocelin de Connant estoit mestre engigneur.'

Fifteenth Century.—' D'autre part il-y-avait dedans Mortaigne un maistre engigneur qui avisa et considera l'engin de ceux de Valenciennes et comment il grevait leur forteresse.'

' Un maître engigneur d'appertise (un homme qui fait les tours de force) avait attaché une corde, laquelle corde comprenait moult loin et par dessus la maison.'

Sixteenth Century.—' Ce que nos plus subtils ingénieux d'aujourd'hui appellent flancs-fichés.'

' La mécanique ou art des ingénieurs.'

In 1588 a curious work was published, in Italian and French, by a Capitano Agostino Ramelli, who styled himself ' Ingegniero del Christianissimo Rè di Francia e di Pollonia.' It is a description of various ingenious constructive devices for both military and civil use; and here, therefore, we have an early identification of the term engineer with precisely the kind of work that modern engineers are engaged in.

The Italians and Spanish, in adopting the term, have adhered more closely to the Latin form of the original in their *ingegnere* and *ingegnero*. The Germans adopt the French word.

The use of the term in England can be traced back to the thirteenth century. In the wardrobe account of King Edward I., A.D. 1300, occur the following passages :—

> To Master Reginald, engineer, for going by the King's order from Berwick-upon-Tweed to Newcastle-upon-Tyne, to the Sheriff of Northumberland, to procure and chuse timber for the making of machines for the castle of Berwick, for seventy-eight days' expenses in going and returning, and for hackneys for riding, &c., 2*l*. 8*s*. 0*d*. (Another article charges his pay at 6*d*. per diem.)

> Brother Thomas, of Bamburgh, and brother Robert de Ulm, master engineers, retained in the King's service for the Scottish wars, with Alan Bright, carpenter ; Robert at 9*d*. per diem, Alan at 4*d*.

> Gerard de Mayek, engineer, and Gaillard Abot, carpenter, employed by the King to make the pele of Dumfries at 6*d*. per diem each.[1]

In 1344, it would appear that 321 artificers and engineers were borne on the books of the Ordnance in time of peace.[2]

Coming down to Queen Elizabeth's time, we find the term used twice by Shakspeare. Writing about 1602, he makes Hamlet say :—

---

[1] Grose's *Military Antiquities*, vol. i, 1786.

[2] Major Duncan's *History of the Royal Artillery*, vol. i. 1872.

James's *Military Dictionary* gives 1650 as the earliest date when this title was used, but this is proved by the extracts in the text to be an error.

For this interesting information as to the origin and early use of the term engineer, the editor is indebted to the kind aid of Col. Pasley, R.E.

For 'tis the sport to have the engineer
Hoist with his own petard; and it shall go hard
But I will delve one yard below their mines,
And blow them at the moon.

A few years later, in 'Troilus and Cressida,' Thersites is made to say :—

Then there's Achilles, a rare enginer. If Troy be not taken till these two undermine it, the walls will stand till they fall of themselves.

These passages would seem to show that the word was a familiar one in Shakspeare's time.

The latter orthography is found in other places; Johnson quotes one, and in Cotgrave's 'French and English Dictionary,' 1611, the word *ingénieur* is translated ' enginer, engine-maker, fortifier.'

An engineer therefore was a person in military service, whose business it was not only to direct warlike engines or weapons (a duty transferred at a later period to the artillery officer), but to undertake the design and construction of fortifications, siege works, roads, bridges, buildings, machinery, and all other works for military service which required knowledge, experience, and skill, in the arts of construction.

Down to a recent period the title engineer was unknown in any application except its military one. It was not applied to the constructors of similar works in civil life. And yet the construction of such works generally has existed from time immemorial. One of the earliest fables of antiquity—the destruction of the Hydra by Hercules—is supposed to have referred to what we should now call the engineering work of draining the low lands of Argos, and damming up the sources of the inundations. And when we come to the more trustworthy records of history, we find that the most ancient civilised nations occupied themselves practically with works of an engineering character, and on a very large scale.

In Mesopotamia there must have been, thousands of years ago, men who possessed considerable mechanical knowledge and much constructive skill, and traces of their occupations still remain. The Phœnicians, too, constructed harbour and other engineering works with great ability.

The ancient works of Egypt are celebrated, not only for the colossal magnitude of the buildings, but also for the ingenious and useful character of the hydraulic arrangements. It is in Egypt that we find the invention of the arch, the first rudiments of which may be traced back, it is said, to the time of Amunoph the First, 1540 B.C. The original canal across the Isthmus of Suez was made under an Egyptian dynasty.

The Greeks, independently of their skill in building generally, must, from the extent of their coasts, have been well occupied in hydraulic constructions; but it is to their successors, the Romans, we may turn for the most remarkable examples of ancient engineering.

The immense extent of roads constructed by this nation, their durability, and the skill shown in surmounting the obstacles of marshes, lakes, and mountains, have excited astonishment and admiration. Twenty-nine great military roads centred in Rome, some of which were carried to the extreme points of the vast empire; and the whole of the roads were estimated as measuring 52,964 Roman miles.[1] Many of the more important of these were admirable specimens of construction, abounding in excellent detail. The bridges, built in great numbers, and many of great size, were remarkable for their solidity. Trajan's Bridge over the

[1] See a very full account of ancient engineering works in Cresy's *Encyclopædia of Civil Engineering*. 1856.

Danube, built about A.D. 120, was the most magnificent in Europe; it consisted of twenty arches, each 180 feet span.

In hydraulic constructions the Romans also excelled. The works for supplying water to cities were often of great magnitude, and laid out with much skill. For Rome alone many conduits were used, one of which, the Aqua Claudia, was nearly fifty miles long. The quantity of water brought into the city was very large, and in addition to the great and numerous public fountains, the houses had water laid on.

Aqueducts of Roman construction still exist in many parts of Europe; among these, the Pont du Gard, near Nismes, is one of the most celebrated. It is 560 feet long and 160 feet high, and is supposed to have been executed by Agrippa, who was governor of Nismes in the time of Augustus, and was declared *curator perpetuus aquarum*. The aqueduct of Segovia, in Spain, is 2,220 feet long, and was built by Trajan. That of Lisbon has thirty-five arches, and is 263 feet high.

Canal works were common in ancient Italy. The Etruscans had cut many for drainage purposes, and one in the Pontine Marshes was executed by the Romans 162 B.C. Pliny mentions several 'useful and magnificent' works of the kind constructed by Trajan.

The drainage of Lake Albano, 400 B.C., and that of Lake Fucino, A.D. 52, were great works, showing high skill and enterprise.

The town drainage of Rome, by the Cloaca Maxima, was also an engineering achievement that deserves mention.

From the nature of these works we may be fully convinced that they were designed by men well acquainted theoretically with the principles of natural philosophy current in their era; and, as a matter of practice, how excellently they were done is testified by the manner in which they have stood the ravages of time. We may indeed predict that there are few engineering works of our day which will, at the end of thousands of years, make as favourable an appearance as those of the ancients do now.

We have not much information as to who were the actual designers of such works; probably, however, the architect, who has in all ages been a well-defined practitioner, took on himself the responsibility of building constructions generally. Brunelleschi, who built the great dome of Florence, and Michael Angelo, who designed St. Peter's at Rome, acted as architects, but really did also the work of engineers.

There is a curious reminiscence of a very ancient office, somewhat of an engineering character, in the title of the Pope of Rome, namely, 'Pontifex,' or the Bridge Builder. It applied to an order of priests said to have been founded by Numa, the second king of Rome, and it was transferred to the Pope probably on the very foundation of his chair. What the origin of this title was has been a matter of dispute even among the Romans themselves; but the general opinion is that it related to bridges in some way, and Plutarch expressly says that the Pontiffs were commissioned to keep the bridges in repair, as one of the most indispensable parts of their holy office.

After the fall of the Roman Empire, we still find occasional examples of fine constructive works, as, for example, the great aqueduct of Spoleto, which was built by Theodoric King of the Goths A.D. 741. It has ten large Gothic arches, each seventy feet span, and is 328 feet high above the valley it crosses. It remains to this day in good condition, and still supplies water to the town.

About the twelfth century attention became strongly directed, in France, to the improvement of the internal communications of the country, and an association was formed under the name of the ' Frères Pontiers ' (Brethren of the Bridge), with the object of building bridges wherever rivers were dangerous or difficult to ford. This society, really a society of civil engineers, extended its branches over all parts of Northern Europe, and executed great numbers of important works, some of which are still in existence, as, for example, the Old Bridge at Lyons, and the celebrated one over the Rhone lower down, at St. Esprit, which was nearly half a mile long. The first stone London Bridge was also erected about the same date by the same body. The Ponte Vecchio at Florence, having three segmental arches of ninety-five feet span, was built in 1345, and the first stone bridge in Paris dates 1412. The Rialto at Venice, with a single arch ninety-seven feet span, was built by Michael Angelo in 1578.

The construction of works connected with water, or as they are termed hydraulic works, has always formed an important branch of engineering.

The establishment of the city of Venice, on artificial foundations, and the great embankments and canal communications of the Low Countries, all executed at early periods, showed great skill in such works; and we know that in the ninth and tenth centuries canals and river works for facilitating inland navigation were in course of construction. Charlemagne, for example, commenced a canal uniting the Rhine with the Danube.

The Italian Republics in the twelfth century, when they revived the arts and sciences, took measures to regulate and open the navigation by rivers long neglected, and many important works of this kind were executed in

Northern Italy, particularly on the course of the Po and the Mincio.

About the fifteenth century much was done by irrigation canals in the neighbourhood of Milan, in which Leonardo da Vinci—eminent for his constructive as well as his artistic talent—took a considerable share. The important system of *locks* was invented by two brothers Domenico of Viterbo, in 1481, and was introduced by Leonardo in the Milanese canals.

About the commencement of the seventeenth century the great rivers of the north of Italy appear to have relapsed into a bad state, and the consequences were felt in disastrous and extensive inundations. The inhabitants of the districts became alarmed, the attention of the government was roused, and the most learned scientific men of the day were consulted as to how the evils might be remedied. To this impulse we owe a series of valuable theoretical and experimental studies which have formed the basis of modern hydraulic science and practice, and the authors of which may be esteemed the fathers of hydraulic engineering. A great mass of Italian literature was devoted to the subject, but a concise summary of the most useful information was put on record in a more accessible shape by the publication in France, in 1737 and 1753, of the four quarto volumes of Belidor's 'Architecture Hydraulique,' a magnificent work deservedly esteemed, and which may be considered the earliest work on modern engineering.

The knowledge thus acquired spread rapidly throughout Europe, and gave a great impulse to hydraulic operations. But now arose a want of competent men to execute them. The architects, who had formerly undertaken constructive works generally, found these new studies somewhat foreign to their own business, and were moreover already well occupied in their more legitimate employment. Hence a new class of practitioners became necessary, who should devote their attention to hydraulic constructions, with all their necessary mechanical arrangements; and with these soon became associated the erection of buildings of a massive and unartistic character. Thus the new class of men undertook to design not only river and hydraulic works, but roads, bridges, docks, harbours, mills and machinery, and so on.

Such a class required a new name; and this was easily found. It was noticed that the kind of work undertaken by these practitioners was exactly analogous to that allotted to the ' engineers ' of the military service, and the new profession adopted the same title, prefixing, however, the word ' civil,' to indicate that they were civilians, and so to distinguish them from their military brethren.

Hence the origin of the present term 'civil engineer ;' its true meaning being a person who devotes himself to occupations of the kind originally practised by military engineers, but who belongs to the civil and not to the military community.

It is unnecessary to follow the spread of civil engineering throughout Europe farther than to notice the formation in France, early in the last century, of two official government corps of engineers of civil status, the ' Ingénieurs des Ponts et Chaussées,' and the ' Ingénieurs des Mines.' The members of these corps have been employed throughout the Empire in government or private civil engineering works, and have gained themselves high reputation, not only for their practical services, but for their scientific labours in the advancement of their profession.

It will be interesting now to say a few words on the progress of civil engineering in our own country.[1]

The earliest English engineering works of importance were the great systems of drainage and reclamation carried out on the east coast. The embankments of Romney Marsh and of the River Thames are so ancient that no authentic records exist as to their construction ; but the great drainage of the fen districts in Lincolnshire was executed about the middle of the seventeenth century by Cornelius Vermuyden, a Dutchman, and his countrymen were employed on similar works in other districts.

The first great engineering work done by an Englishman was the construction, in 1609–13, of the New River, to supply London with water from the springs of Hertfordshire. Hugh, afterwards Sir Hugh Myddelton, to whom this noble work is due, was brought up as a goldsmith and merchant ; and it is not easy to understand how he acquired the practical and scientific knowledge necessary to design and construct a work of this kind ; for it does not appear that he had any technical help worth notice, and the Italian hydraulic investigations were not then begun. He never called himself 'engineer,' for that title had not yet been applied to civilians ; but he has nevertheless been rightly styled the father of the English profession. After the completion of the New River, he carried out another great and useful work in the embankment of Brading Haven, in the Isle of Wight.

Bridge-building appears subsequently to this to have had some attention. In the middle of the seventeenth century we find the celebrated architect, Inigo Jones,

---

[1] The author has to acknowledge having obtained many data, in this and the following Chapter, from Mr. Smiles's excellent works, the *Lives of the Engineers* and *Industrial Biography*.

occupied in this class of work ; and in 1739 a Swiss engineer, Labelye, designed the second bridge over the Thames —Westminster Bridge—using therein new methods of foundation showing considerable ingenuity. Shortly afterwards a clever, self-taught Welshman, named Edwards, acquired considerable fame in the same line.

It was, however, about the middle of the eighteenth century before engineering in England may have been said to begin in earnest, by the employment of James Brindley to construct a large system of canals in Lancashire. Brindley was by trade a wheelwright and millwright, and, having naturally a mechanical turn of mind, he had acquired great skill in millwork and mechanical construction generally. The Duke of Bridgewater, having obtained in 1759 an Act empowering him to make a canal to convey his coals from Worsley to Manchester, about ten miles, and having heard of Brindley's ingenuity, resolved to employ him. In a few years the canal was completed, and Brindley afterwards executed many more, in that district as well as in other parts of the country, altogether about 360 miles in length, and involving engineering works of considerable magnitude and variety. He died in 1772.

Brindley has been usually held in great honour as an engineer; but it must be recollected that his works appear of higher merit because of the extremely backward state of engineering knowledge and practice in this country at that time. Hydraulic constructions, including the formation of canals and all appertaining works, were really in an advanced state on the continent before Brindley's day, and there was probably little done by him that had not been anticipated there. But he was an uneducated man, and even if the hydraulic information published by the Italians and French had penetrated to this country (which is very doubtful), it could hardly have been intelligible to him. Hence, he deserves credit for having, by his own unaided and unlettered practical intelligence and skill, accomplished so much in the face of what were no doubt great difficulties.

Another eminent man, who lived about the same time, John Smeaton, was in a very different position; as, to practical talents not inferior to Brindley's, he added the advantages of a good education and considerable scientific knowledge. He was, like Brindley, occupied at first with mechanical pursuits. He was apprenticed to a mathematical instrument maker, and afterwards went into that business on his own account. But he was fond of science, and he made several communications to the Royal Society, who, in 1753, elected him a Fellow, and in 1759 awarded him their gold medal. In 1756, the Eddystone lighthouse having been destroyed by fire, Smeaton was applied to, on the recommendation of the President of the Royal Society, to rebuild it. He had just before made a careful study of the great engineering works of Holland and Belgium, during a tour in those countries, and he felt confidence in undertaking the task. The new lighthouse was completed in 1759, and its construction, ably described by himself, has commanded universal admiration.

Smeaton was afterwards engaged, down to his death in 1792, in many other engineering works—river and canal navigations, drainage and reclamation of lands, harbours, roads, bridges, water supplies, pumping-engines, and machinery. His reports, which have been collected and published, are admirable models of what such documents should be. He did not execute any works of the gigantic character which has more lately so impressed the popular mind ; but considering his accurate and extensive scientific knowledge, his good education and position in society, his great practical skill and experience, his literary ability, his logical and sound judgment, and the zealous and conscientious care and attention he bestowed on whatever he undertook, he is admitted by all competent judges to hold the very highest rank as an engineer.

It is probable, too, that he was the first civil practitioner, at least in England, who formally adopted that title, and used the compound term 'civil engineer.' A report he made dated July 11, 1761, on a canal in Staffordshire is entitled, 'Report by John Smeaton, Engineer, concerning the Practicability &c. of a navigable Canal . . . . as projected by Mr. James Brindley, Engineer.' He awards the same title to his coadjutor, but there is no evidence that Brindley himself had previously used the term. The prefix 'civil' was sometimes added by Smeaton on state occasions, but he usually styled himself simply 'engineer.'

The profession being thus fairly launched and named, and an impulse given to the demands upon it by the improvements in the communications and trade of the country, many practitioners followed, among whom are several honoured names.

James Watt was a contemporary of Smeaton, but his part in engineering will be treated of more fully in the next chapter.

Robert Mylne, another contemporary, who, after the manner of the ancients, combined the professions of architect and civil engineer, built the third bridge over the Thames, at Blackfriars, in 1770.

John Rennie (1761-1821) designed Waterloo Bridge, Southwark iron Bridge, and new London Bridge, as well as the London Docks, the Plymouth Breakwater, and many other large and important engineering works of various kinds.

Thomas Telford is celebrated for the construction of

C

the beautiful Menai Suspension Bridge, the great Holyhead and Highland Roads, the Ellesmere and Caledonian
Canals, and many other works of importance.   He died
in 1834, which brings us to the time of the Stephensons
and Brunels, and the commencement of the era of railways, since which the progress of engineering has been
so well known that it is unnecessary here to follow further
the general history of the profession.

It may be desirable now to define with some precision
what engineering means, and what kind of occupations
are comprised in the profession or employment of a civil
engineer.

The exact definition of engineering has always been a
matter of some difficulty.

The meaning already drawn from the original derivation of the word, that an engineer is one ' qui cherche
dans son génie quelque moyen pour réussir,' though
applicable enough, is too comprehensive for a strict definition, as it would apply to many occupations which are
not engineering.

Similarly, another definition which has been offered,
namely, that engineering is ' the application of scientific
principles to the art of construction,' is too large.   Few
things involve more science in their design than a chro-
nometer or a microscope ; yet the makers of these are
not called engineers.

A very old Engineering Society, founded by Smeaton,
has adopted two mottoes.   One is Greek—

τέχνῃ κρατοῦμεν ὧν φύσει νικόμεθα.
We conquer by Art the difficulties offered by Nature.

which is certainly highly characteristic of the operations
of the engineer.   The other is Latin—

Omnia in numero, pondere, et mensura.

which gives the idea, also correct as far as it goes, that one of the principal functions of the engineer is the practical application of the *science of quantity* in the estimation of forces, resistances, velocities, and magnitudes. The more modern Institution of Civil Engineers define their profession as

The art of directing the great sources of power in nature for the use and convenience of man.

which would seem at first sight to apply more especially to the mechanical branch, but which is doubtless intended to comprise works of construction generally, in which the great powers of nature come into play.

Civil engineering may now be understood legitimately to comprise the art of constructing any large works, for civil purposes, in the design of which the mechanical sciences are applied.

Thus the practitioners in this art may have to do with many classes of works ; for example :—

1. Works for facilitating and improving internal communication; as roads, railways, inland navigation by canals and rivers, bridges, and the electric telegraph.

2. Works connected with the seacoast, and for facilitating communication between the sea and the land ; such as harbours, docks, piers, breakwaters, sea walls, lighthouses, &c. &c.

3. Works for the reclamation, irrigation, or drainage of land; the improvement of rivers as arterial drains ; the prevention or regulation of floods &c.

4. Municipal works ; such as the drainage, the water supply, the lighting, and the street arrangements of towns.

5. Large and massive buildings generally (excluding their artistic features, which belong to the architect,) and all scientific and mechanical arrangements belonging thereto.

6. The operations of mining, so far as they involve the application of mechanical science.

7. The design and construction of the mechanical prime movers; as steam-engines, water-wheels and other hydraulic motors, windmills, and other sources of power.

8. The design and construction of machinery and mechanical appliances of all kinds, excluding the more minute specialities, such as clock and watchwork &c.

9. The design and manufacture generally of all large and important structures in iron.

This is a comprehensive catalogue of duties; and if we consider the quantity of work that has been done under these various heads, during the last century, and contemplate the effect that this work has had on trade, on commerce, on finance, on government, on every branch of industry, and indeed on every possible aspect of human interests, we cannot hesitate to admit that the profession of engineering has become truly a great power.

It would be interesting to know the amount of money which has been laid out during the last century in works constructed by engineers; but this it is not possible to ascertain. In Railways alone, the expenditure in Great Britain has been 620,000,000l. And if to this we could add the outlay on municipal, coast, harbour, dock, river, canal, road, mining, and telegraph works, as well as the enormous sums invested in steam vessels, ironworks, manufactories, mills, engines, and machinery in endless variety, we should obtain an almost fabulous amount expended, in one small country alone, under the direction of this one profession. So far as the importance of a class of men can be estimated by the money value of the work they have to do, there has been no parallel with the engineering profession since the foundation of the world.

CHAPTER II.

MECHANICAL ENGINEERING

MECHANICAL ENGINEERING A BRANCH OF CIVIL ENGINEERING, AND NOT DISTINCT FROM IT—EARLY HISTORY OF PRACTICAL MECHANICS — ARCHIMEDES —HERO — VITRUVIUS — WORKS ON MECHANICS — MECHANICAL ENGINEERING IN ENGLAND—PETER MORICE'S WATER MACHINERY—MILLWRIGHTS—BRINDLEY—SMEATON—THE IRON MANUFACTURE—WORKS IN SUSSEX—DUD DUDLEY ; DARBY, AND COIEBROOK DALE—THE IRON BRIDGE OVER THE SEVERN—PUDDLING—CORT'S IMPROVEMENTS—WELSH IRON WORKS—SCOTCH IRON WORKS—THE CARRON COMPANY—SMEATON—WATT AND THE STEAM ENGINE—CONNECTION WITH ROEBUCK AND BOULTON—SOHO WORKS—THE ROTATING ENGINE—ALBION MILLS—RENNIE—GREAT STIMULUS TO MANUFACTURING PROGRESS.—LATER IMPROVEMENTS IN THE MANUFACTURE OF IRON—THE HOT BLAST—CLEVELAND AND LANCASHIRE IRON DISTRICTS — STATISTICS — IMPROVEMENTS IN WORKSHOP PROCESSES, TOOLS, AND APPLIANCES—EARLY DIFFICULTIES, AND HOW THEY WERE SURMOUNTED—FOUNDING, FORGING, RIVETING, SHAPING — TURNING, AND IMPROVEMENT IN LATHES—MAUDSLAY — BORING ; WILKINSON—PLANING ; CLEMENT—SHAPING AND SLOTTING MACHINES —SCREWING AND SCREW THREADS—WHITWORTH'S IMPROVEMENTS—DEVELOPMENT OF AUTOMATIC TOOLS LARGELY DUE TO STRIKES AMONG THE WORKMEN—DECAY OF THE MILLWRIGHT CLASS —LARGE STRUCTURES IN IRON—IRON BRIDGES, CAST AND WROUGHT—IRON SHIPS—IRON ARMOUR PLATES AND FORTS—HEAVY GUNS—FAIRBAIRN AS A MECHANICAL ENGINEER.

CHAPTER II.

IN the list of occupations of the civil engineer, given at the end of the preceding chapter, the three last, referring to the design and manufacture of engines and machinery, and of structures in iron, constitute what is now considered a special branch of the profession,[1] called MECHA-NICAL ENGINEERING.

[1] There has been a disposition growing up lately to separate 'mechanical' from 'civil' engineers, appropriating the latter title only to those who practise in works of building and earthwork construction, as railways, roads, harbours, docks, river-improvements, and so on.

There is not a vestige of authority or warrant either in precedent, etymology, or common sense for such a limitation of the title. The term *civil engineer* merely means an engineer who is a civilian, as contrasted with a military engineer who belongs to the army. Hence an engineer who designs a steam-engine, a power-loom, or a threshing-machine, is (if not a soldier) as properly a 'civil' engineer as the designer of a railway or a harbour.

In the Royal Charter granted to the Institution of Civil Engineers, on its foundation in 1828, the 'Profession of a Civil Engineer' is declared to be :

'The art of directing the great sources of power in nature for the use and convenience of man ; . . . . as applied;—

'In the construction of roads, bridges, aqueducts, canals, river navigation, and docks ;

'In the construction of ports, harbours, moles, breakwaters, and light-houses ;

'In the art of navigation by artificial power ;

'*In the construction and adaptation of machinery;* and

'In the drainage of cities and towns.'

It is perfectly clear, therefore, that the founders of this Institution considered the mechanical branch as legitimately included in Civil Engineering.

The earlier 'Society of Civil Engineers,' founded by Smeaton, held a similar view ; as Watt, and other persons who devoted themselves to mechanical practice, were admitted without question.

Nothing could be more incorrect, or in worse taste, than to assume for the

This branch has now become of immense extent and
importance, and practitioners in it usually devote to it
their whole attention. The number of mechanical engineers is very large, many being men of high attainments; and the late Sir William Fairbairn was one
of the most esteemed of them. On this account it
becomes desirable to give some special notice of the peculiarities of this branch of the profession, with which, in
the following pages, we shall have more particularly
to do.

An acquaintance with the art of working in metals
has always been considered one of the signs of dawning
civilisation, and machinery of some kind for the simplest
wants of life, such as raising water, grinding corn, and so
on, must have been in use in the earliest ages. But a
few centuries before the Christian era we come upon a
great man who is undoubtedly entitled to be called the
father of mechanical engineers, namely, Archimedes of
Syracuse. He combined great theoretical knowledge of
geometry and other sciences with singular inventive and
constructive skill, and his mechanical contrivances have
acquired for him a lasting renown.

After his day, many mechanical constructions were in
use which derived their origin from his discoveries, as, for
example, the clepsydræ or water clocks of Egypt, which
are said to have first contained that now universal element
of machinery, the *toothed wheel.* Hero, about 250 B.C.,
wrote treatises describing various mechanical contrivances; and the erection, about the same time, of the
great Colossus of Rhodes, showed much power in metal
work.

The Romans largely used mechanical appliances.

building engineer any superiority over the mechanical one, either in the
importance of his work or in its scientific and intellectual character.

The celebrated Roman writer on architecture, Vitruvius (B.C. 50), enumerates earlier writers on machinery, and enters fully into the mechanical principles and arrange- ments applicable to constructive purposes. He mentions an officer called a *machinarius*, who had charge of machines, and who was, in fact, the mechanical engineer of the time.

We know also that in these ages mills worked by water power were in use for grinding corn, and these must have involved some complexity and ingenuity of design.

After the revival of learning in Europe the mathema- tical and mechanical sciences began to be more culti- vated, and practical mechanics became a favourite study with ingenious men. Many works are extant which show this; among them one by Agricola (Georg Land- mann), in Germany, who died in 1555; another by Jacques Besson, in France, 1573; and a third, better known, entitled 'Diversi ed artificiose Macchine,' by Capitano Agostino Ramelli, published in 1588.

The curious work 'Les raisons des forces mouvantes, avec diverses machines tant utiles que plaisantes, par Salomon de Caus, Ingénieur et Architecte du Roy,' originally published in 1615, is celebrated as containing tolerably clear notions about the nature and power of steam. The Marquis of Worcester's well-known 'Century of Inventions,' published in 1659, may also be mentioned; as well as the splendid work of Belidor of 1737-53, 'Architecture Hydraulique,' already alluded to, which contains copious descriptions of the hydraulic machine known in his day.

In England, before the eighteenth century, the most important articles of machinery, such as windmills, water mills, &c., were brought from the continent, principally from the Low Countries. The celebrated pumping apparatus fixed at London Bridge in 1582, for supplying London with water, was erected by Peter Morice, a Dutchman.

As, however, such contrivances became more used, a class of native artificers sprang up, who made it their business to attend to them. They were called *millwrights*. They designed and erected windmills and water mills for grinding corn, pumping apparatus, and all the various kinds of rough machinery in use in those days.

It is probable these men were the first who, as a civil class, devoted themselves specially and exclusively to engineering work. They were therefore the earliest civil engineers, and their successors have descended to the present day in an unbroken line as practitioners in the mechanical branch of civil engineering.

Mr. Fairbairn, who was educated strictly as a millwright, and was never ashamed of calling himself by that name, gives the following account of this class of men:[1]—

The term millwright has long been a household word, and at no distant period conveyed the idea of a man marked by everything that was ingenious and skilful.

The millwright of former days was to a great extent the sole representative of mechanical art, and was looked upon as the authority on all the applications of wind and water, under whatever conditions they were to be used, as a motive power for the purposes of manufacture. He was the engineer of the district in which he lived, a kind of Jack-of-all-trades, who could with equal facility work at the lathe, the anvil, or the carpenter's bench. In country districts, far removed from towns, he had to exercise all these professions, and he thus gained the character of an ingenious, roving, rollicking blade, able to turn

---

[1] *Mills and Millwork,* Preface.

his hand to anything, and like other wandering tribes in days of old, went about the country from mill to mill, with the old song of 'kettles to mend,' re-applied to the more important fractures of machinery.

Thus the millwright of the last century was an itinerant engineer and mechanic of high reputation. In the practice of his profession he had mainly to depend on his own resources. Generally, he was a fair arithmetician, knew something of geometry, levelling, and mensuration, and in some cases possessed a very competent knowledge of practical mathematics.[1]

He could calculate the velocities, strength, and power of machines; could draw in plan and section, and could construct buildings, conduits, or watercourses, in all the forms and under all the conditions required in his professional practice.

His attainments as a mechanic and his standing in the useful arts, were, however, apt to make him vain, and with a rude independence he would repudiate the idea of working with an inferior craftsman or even with another as skilful as himself, unless he was 'born and bred a millwright.'

Such was the character and condition of the men who designed and carried out most of the mechanical work of this country up to the middle and end of the last century.

. . . .

I have deemed it necessary to give this brief account of the habits and character of a body of men whose skill and spirit of perseverance have done so much for the advancement of applied science, and whose labours have had a large influence on the industrial progress of the country. I am perhaps better qualified for this task than most others, from having been associated with them from early life, so that an experience of some fifty years must be my excuse for having imposed this narrative upon the reader.

[1] Millwrights were, however, not always so well educated. The editor of this work recollects that when he was serving his apprenticeship in a manufacturing establishment, he saw an old millwright, in fixing some letters on a piece of machinery, place one of them upside down. The looker-on, with youthful zeal, ventured to correct the mistake, but was met with the contemptuous remark that 'a regular millwright' must surely understand his own trade !

It is significant that the first Englishman, after Hugh Myddelton, who distinguished himself in the more general practice, Brindley, was properly and originally one of this class. He was apprenticed to a wheelwright and millwright, and afterwards worked on his own account in the same trade. He erected corn mills, paper mills, silk mills, pottery flint mills, and engines generally. It was his success in these things that caused him to be first employed on canals, and his mechanical skill and experience stood him in good stead in many ways during their construction.

Smeaton, though not a millwright by trade, had great aptitude for mechanical construction, and was well versed in mechanical science. His paper on Wind and Water Mills, which gained him the gold medal of the Royal Society in 1759, was an admirable and useful essay, founded on many years' experiments, and is still referred to as of high authority. His published reports show that he was largely engaged on mechanical engineering, as they refer to the construction of steam-engines, waterworks, pumps, boring machines, corn and oil mills, forges, and other machinery of various kinds.

It was about Smeaton's time that mechanical engineering took an enormous step in advance by the improvements which were effected in the *manufacture of iron*; and in explanation of this great element of the question it is necessary to say something here of the history of the iron manufacture.

The two great properties of iron, fusibility and malleability, which enable it to be either cast into shape by melting or worked into shape by hammering (thus forming what are now called *cast* and *wrought* iron-work respectively) appear to have been known at an early period. In the thirteenth century nails, horseshoes, and other wrought articles were largely supplied from Sussex, and cast cannon were founded there in the sixteenth century. The manufacture in this district reached its height towards the close of the reign of Elizabeth, when the trade became so prosperous that England began to export iron in considerable quantities. It gradually fell off, however, by the failure of the wood fuel employed; one of the last extensive contracts executed there being the casting, about 1700, of the iron rails which enclose St. Paul's Cathedral.

In 1620 the first step of the modern iron manufacture was taken, in the invention by Dud Dudley of iron smelting by coal. The inventor set up works in the midland counties, where he made in this way both malleable iron and castings; and in the civil wars occurring in the middle of the century he not only supplied the king with iron war implements and stores, but followed the army and acted as a military engineer.

Whether it was from the inferior quality of Dudley's iron, from prejudice against it, or from difficulties in the working, his system does not seem to have made immediate way; for the iron manufacture declined rather than advanced until the beginning of the eighteenth century, when Abraham Darby, a mechanic and millwright of Bristol, introduced from Holland a new method of making iron castings, chiefly hollow ware for domestic use, by moulding them in fine dry sand. He established, in 1709, iron works at Colebrook Dale in Shropshire, and his casting trade there was successful. At first he used charcoal for fuel, but coal being plentiful in the neighbourhood, he adopted it by previously making it into coke, and at a later period—about 1760—the coal was used raw.

In 1766 another great improvement was made by producing malleable iron, with pit coal as fuel, in a reverberatory furnace, it having previously been produced on a 'refinery' hearth with charcoal. This was the invention of two foremen at Colebrook Dale, named Cranege, and was carried out by Richard Reynolds, the manager there at the time.

By the exertions and enterprise of three generations of Darbys the Colebrook Dale works had become greatly enlarged, and had widely extended their operations; they had formed establishments in London, Bristol, and Liverpool, and had erected workshops for the manufacture of machinery generally, many of the atmospheric, or Newcomen's steam-engines being made there, to be used in mines in various parts of the kingdom. The Darbys were the first to substitute, in 1767, iron for wooden rails in the tram roads along which coal and iron were conveyed from one part of the works to the other, thus initiating the modern system of iron railways.

The Colebrook Dale works have also the credit of having erected the first iron structure of any magnitude, namely, a cast-iron arch bridge of large span. Some proposals and attempts at using iron for bridges had been previously made, but the material was prohibited by the great cost and even impossibility of obtaining it in sufficiently large masses.

Abraham Darby the third, when he entered the business as a young man, saw the necessity of forming a communication between the steep banks of the river Severn, to accommodate the large population which had sprung up on both sides. Emboldened by his improvements in iron manufacture, he designed an iron arch of 100 feet span, which was cast at the works, and was opened for traffic in 1779. It still stands as firm as ever, and Mr. Robert Stephenson said of it: 'If we consider that the manipulation of cast iron was then completely in its infancy, a bridge of such dimensions was doubtless a bold as well as an original undertaking, and the efficiency of the details is worthy of the boldness of the conception.'

After the successful example of Colebrook Dale, other iron works became established in different parts of the country, particularly in Staffordshire, Wales, and Scotland.

In 1783 a man named Peter Onions, working in the Welsh district, made a valuable improvement in the manufacture of malleable iron, by combining with the reverberatory furnace (introduced by the Craneges some years before) the peculiar process called 'puddling,' which has since been the universal mode employed.

At the same date some very important improvements were introduced by Henry Cort. In the course of his business as a navy agent or contractor, he had occasion to see the inferiority of English malleable iron to that imported from Russia and Sweden; he entered on a series of experiments with a view to its improvement, and he took out two patents in 1783 and 1784. They related in the first place to the mode of producing the malleable iron from the pig, and, secondly, to the mode of giving it certain merchantable forms.

In regard to the first of these, he adopted the reverberatory puddling furnace of Cranege and Onions, and does not seem to have added to it any novel feature of striking originality ; but he so altered and improved the details of working as to produce a very much better quality of iron.

His other invention was more original. In the first place he took advantage of the *welding* power of malleable iron, when in a highly heated state, in order to form masses of larger size than had been previously made. He piled several pieces together, heated the whole in a furnace to a white heat, and then subjected the pile to the blows of a heavy hammer, whereby it became welded and consolidated into one integral mass, which could be forged into any shape desired, as to make anchors and so on. But having a view to the more general usefulness of malleable iron in the shape of long parallel bars, he proposed to make these by forming his piles of a long shape, and effecting the consolidation, not by hammering but by passing the piles through grooved rollers, so that, using successively grooves diminishing in size, the iron could be drawn into long bars of any dimensions required.

It was one of Cort's objects, that by the force of the hammering or the pressure of the roll-drawing, not only should the iron be welded and consolidated, but the dross, scoriæ, or 'slag' should be thoroughly squeezed out, and the iron generally made purer and of better quality.

The processes described by Cort have been followed by iron manufacturers, with but slight modifications, to the present time. After the lapse of nearly a century the modes of manufacturing bar from cast iron, and of puddling, piling, hammering, and rolling, are all nearly identical with the descriptions he gave.

Cort expended a fortune of upwards of 20,000l. in perfecting his inventions, but he was robbed of the fruit of his discoveries by the villainy of officials in a high department of government, and he was ultimately left to starve. Mr. Fairbairn, as we shall see in a future chapter, took up warmly the cause of some of his descendants, and by great exertions succeeded in getting something done for them.

In 1759 the Carron Ironworks were established by Dr. Roebuck and others, on an excellent site, surrounded with coal and ironstone, near Falkirk in Scotland. Soon afterwards their mechanical arrangements

were taken in hand by John Smeaton, who by many
ingenious alterations and improvements enabled the proprietors to manufacture cast-iron of a much better quality
than before. Smeaton took advantage of this by introducing the use of iron more largely into machinery
and mechanical constructions generally. Formerly, the
staple material of the millwright had been wood, iron
being only used in small pieces, chiefly for binding the
woodwork together. Smeaton saw the immense advantage it would be to make the parts more extensively of
iron, and he was now enabled by the improvements at
Carron to do this, applying the material to many new uses.

The first cast-iron axis for a water wheel was made
there in 1769, and iron cog-wheels and shafts of all
dimensions gradually followed, although the use of the
new material was yet uncertain, and failures were not
unfrequent. The well-known carronades, or light cast-
iron guns, so long used in the navy, took their name from
the Carron Works, where they were originally made.

We now arrive at the date of the great improvements
in the steam-engine effected by James Watt.

About 1710 Newcomen had invented the earliest
really efficient form of steam prime mover, then called a
fire-engine, and subsequently many of these had been
erected for the purpose of raising water in the mines of
Cornwall and elsewhere. Brindley, in the course of his
millwright's practice, had paid some attention to them,
and Smeaton had also much improved their construction,
and had, shortly after 1770, erected some that were
pronounced the best in existence. The cylinders of the
early engines were made of brass, which caused them to
be very expensive, but as the manufacture of cast-iron
improved, Smeaton substituted this metal with great
advantage.

D

Watt took out his patent for the separate condenser in 1769, but he saw, with a truly practical eye, that he could make no progress with his machines till he could ensure their proper manufacture. With this view, finding the Carron Works promising well, he associated himself with Dr. Roebuck, proposing to establish his manufactory there. But while Watt was contending with his first difficulties of construction, Dr. Roebuck became embarrassed, and in 1773 sold his share of the patent to Mr. Matthew Boulton, of Soho.

The works at this place had been built about 1765, for the general manufacture of various kinds of Birmingham hardware, and Watt was so well pleased with the manner in which their mechanical arrangements had been carried out, that he desired nothing better than to find a home there for his own inventions. Fortunately his wish was gratified, and the Boulton and Watt partnership ensured the fulfilment of his most sanguine plans. His first successful engine was made in 1774, and soon afterwards, the merits of the invention being at once recognised, it came into extensive application.

For some years, however, the new engines were adapted exclusively to rectilinear motion for pumping water, the great field for their employment being the mines of Cornwall. The important change which enabled them to produce rotary motion was not perfected till about 1784, and this is therefore the date when the great prime mover which has since worked such wonders may be said to have really come into existence.

One of the first made was for the Albion Mills, a large establishment erected for grinding corn on the south bank of the Thames, a little to the east of Black-friars Bridge. In the design and construction of the machinery for this mill Mr. Watt was assisted by a young man, afterwards known as one of the most eminent

English engineers, John Rennie. This youth had learnt mechanics under a clever millwright, Andrew Meikle, the inventor of the threshing-machine, and had acquired such a good reputation that Watt entrusted to him a large share of the work.

The mill was not only novel in its motive power, but the machinery was on a larger scale and of a more advanced character than anything of the kind before constructed. The use of cast-iron was carried farther than had been done by Smeaton, and with better results, as the experience at Soho had been greater. The parts were more accurately formed, and their strengths better determined.[1]

This first example of modern millwork was set to work in 1788. It proved a great success, and measures were in progress for the extension of the mill, when it was unfortunately burnt to the ground in March 1791.

After the ruins were cleared away Mr. Rennie bought a piece of the land, on which he set up a manufactory for engines and machinery; and it was here that Mr. Fairbairn had his interview with him described in the fifth chapter. The manufacturing business, on Mr. Rennie's death, passed into the hands of his sons, and is still carried on, on the original site of the Albion Mills, by his grandsons, George and John Rennie.

During the century that has elapsed since Watt began his career, mechanical engineering has been ever advancing with rapid and gigantic strides. Every new application of power has stimulated industry and commerce, and this has reacted in calling for extended exertions on the part of the mechanical engineer. It

---

[1] See Watt's own description in Dr. Robison's *Mechanics*; also Farey *On the Steam Engine*.

would be vain to attempt here to enumerate the wonderful
results achieved in this way ; but we may dwell for a
little on the advances made, since Watt's time, in the
production of iron, and in the processes for applying it
to the purposes of mechanical engineering.

The production of iron has immensely extended.
One cause of this has been the introduction, by James
Beaumont Neilson, in 1828, of the *hot blast*, which has
rendered available a class of minerals and substances
formerly useless. It has, in fact (as Mr. Fairbairn has
remarked), effected an entire revolution in the iron industry of Great Britain.

The iron-producing districts mentioned in a former
part of this chapter, namely, the midland counties, Wales,
and Scotland, have enormously developed, the latter being
greatly extended by the discovery, in 1801, by David
Mushet, of the 'Black Band' ironstone.

In addition to these, other districts have been made
available for iron production, the most important being the
great iron fields of Cleveland, in the north-east of England.
The ironworks established within the last few years in the
valleys of the rivers Tees and Wear have an extent and
magnitude quite surprising, considering the suddenness
with which the industry has sprung up in the neighbourhood.

Another large seat of iron manufacture, also very
recent, is on the opposite or north-western coast, at
Barrow-in-Furness, in Lancashire, where large works have
sprung up for the utilisation of a particular kind of ore,
the red hematite, found plentifully there.

In the neighbourhood of Leeds, at Low Moor and
elsewhere, large works have also been built, chiefly with
the object of making iron of particularly fine quality;
and in many other parts of the country where ore has

been found, works for its conversion have come into existence.

The most recent novelty has been the introduction of certain new processes for the production of the higher classes of the material in a way more direct than formerly. The best known of these is what is called the *Bessemer process*, by which a metal having the qualities of malleable iron is produced by fusion. The metal has been found to possess certain advantages which have acquired for it a large consumption, and the effect has been to stimulate its manufacture on a corresponding scale.

As an illustration of the increase of iron production, the following figures may be given, partly taken from Sir William Fairbairn's book :—

THE QUANTITY OF IRON ANNUALLY PRODUCED IN GREAT BRITAIN :—

		Tons.
In 1740 was		17,350
„ 1788	„	68,300
„ 1796	„	108,793
„ 1820	„	400,000
„ 1827	„	690,500
„ 1857	„	3,659,447
„ 1865	„	4,768,000
„ 1870	„	5,963,500
„ 1872	„	6,742,000

Since this last date it has declined, and is now probably about 6,000,000 tons.

We have now to speak of the various processes and appliances necessary for working up this material, and for bringing it into the shape and condition required to form machinery and iron structures. The improvements made in this respect during the last century have been most extensive and important.

When Watt began to carry his improvements into

practice he was terribly hampered and delayed by the difficulty he found in getting his work made with the necessary accuracy. 'The machine projected,' says Mr. Smiles, ' was so much in advance of the mechanical capability of the age, that it was with the greatest difficulty it could be executed. When labouring at his invention at Glasgow, he was baffled and thrown into despair by the clumsiness and incompetency of his workmen. Even after he had removed to Birmingham, and he had the assistance of Boulton's best workmen, Smeaton (no bad judge of the state of mechanics in his time) expressed the opinion when he saw the engine at work, that notwithstanding the excellence of the invention, it could never be brought into use because of the difficulty of getting its various parts manufactured with sufficient precision. Nearly everything had to be done by hand. The tools used were of a very imperfect kind. A few ill-constructed lathes, with some drills and boring machines of a rude sort, constituted the principal furniture of the workshop.'

Watt endeavoured to remedy the defect by keeping certain sets of workmen to special classes of work, and allowing them to do nothing else. Fathers were induced to bring up their sons at the same bench with themselves, and initiate them. in the dexterity which they had acquired by experience ; and at Soho it was not unusual for the same precise line of work to be followed by members of the same family for three generations.

In this way as great a degree of accuracy was arrived at as was practicable under the circumstances ; but, notwithstanding all this care, accurate fitting could not be secured so long as the manufacture was conducted mainly by hand, and hence arose gradual improvements in *tools*, chiefly with the view of making them act automatically. By this means not only was their capability greatly increased, but far greater precision was attained than could ever have been ensured by manual labour. The facilities thus afforded led to a constant progressive improvement in the character of the work done, at the same time constantly diminishing the dependence on mere manual skill.

The manufacturing processes by which works in iron are constructed may be classed under four great heads—founding, forging, riveting, and shaping ; the latter including operations of many kinds.

Founding, or the manufacture of articles in cast-iron, is still pretty much as it was left by Abraham Darby. An impression of the object is moulded in sand, and this is filled with molten iron. All since done has been confined to details for improved accuracy and facility in moulding, and the formation of larger and sounder castings by peculiar modes of preparing the mould.

In malleable iron the manufacture of articles by the operation of *forging* received a great impulse about 1840, through the invention, by James Nasmyth, of the steam hammer. The power of men in wielding hammers was always limited ; and although huge hammers moved by steam were in use for the purpose of iron production, their action was too rough to admit of the formation of accurate shapes, and hence the use of forgings in machinery was much restricted. Nasmyth's apparatus, while it enabled the most powerful blows to be given, provided for their regulation and application with the greatest nicety of adjustment, and this at once brought the stronger, tougher, and more trustworthy material into use, for cases of a magnitude and variety unknown before. The gigantic wrought-iron stem and stern posts of iron ships, the huge shafts and axles of engines, and the monster wrought-iron guns lately produced, owe their existence entirely to the steam hammer; and by means of dies, fashioned in a proper way, small articles of peculiar shape can be forged with facility and certainty. Other ingenious machines have been introduced for forging bolts, nuts, rivets, and other small articles of large consumption, much facilitating and cheapening their production.

Riveting is a very useful process by which iron ships, boilers, tanks, and the most ordinary kinds of iron bridges are formed from malleable iron plates of small thickness. Holes being punched or drilled in corresponding positions in the edges of two plates, these are placed over each other, red-hot rivets are passed through and clenched over, and thus a strong union is formed. This process is a very old one, but it has been much improved by Fairbairn's invention of the riveting-machine, of which a notice will be found in a subsequent chapter.

We may next consider the processes necessary to bring pieces of ironwork, either cast or wrought, into the true shapes they are intended for, with the view either of ensuring their perfect mechanical action, or causing them to fit firmly and closely together. In this shaping we may distinguish four kinds of operations; namely, *turning*, *boring*, *planing*, and *general shaping*. Each requires tools of a special nature, and all have received much attention.

Turning is the most important operation, on account of the great predominance of parts of machinery which are of a circular or a cylindrical shape, or otherwise symmetrical round an axis. The great tool for this purpose— the lathe—has been in use from time immemorial, and in every engineer's shop the lathe is largely employed. The principle of the lathe is still what it was thousands of years ago; the article to be turned being caused to revolve about an axis, while a cutter is applied to its exterior, and caused slowly to move or slide so as to produce the desired profile.

There has been, however, a great improvement introduced in the *slide rest*—a very simple but beautiful contrivance—by which the cutter, instead of being held and guided by the hand of the workman, is attached to a holding-frame or *rest*, which is made to move or *slide*, either by a handscrew, or automatically by the same power which turns the lathe. The effect of this is not only to save skilled labour, but to give much more accuracy to the work, as well as the power of producing with the greatest ease effects which, by mere hand motion, would be scarcely possible.

This invaluable addition to the lathe was invented by Henry Maudslay, one of the men to whom mechanical engineering is largely indebted for its modern advancement. Originally a smith, he afterwards went to the shops of Joseph Bramah (the inventor of the hydraulic press, the Bramah lock, the water-closet apparatus, and many other ingenious things), where, about 1794, he first introduced the improvement in question. In 1810, he founded the celebrated engineering establishment in Lambeth, still carried on by the firm of Maudslay, Sons and Field.

The lathe has received a vast variety of ingenious additions for the purpose of executing fine complicated ornamental turning; but as used for large purposes in engineering work, it remains in nearly its simplest form, with the addition of the slide rest, and some improvements by Joseph Clement to equalise its action. It has, however, been given gigantic dimensions and great power for work of large size, and the most delicate accuracy for small uses.

Boring is an operation analogous to turning, but, so to speak, reversed, as it is in this case an *interior* surface, instead of an exterior one, which has to be made true. The cylinder of a steam-engine is one of the best examples of this kind of work. It is made of cast-iron; but it is necessary that its interior surface should be made accurately cylindrical and perfectly true and smooth, so that the piston may slide easily up and down, at the same time fitting perfectly tight in all positions, to prevent waste of steam and loss of power. This accuracy must be given by the operation of boring.

It was in this particular that Watt found the greatest difficulty, for his machine required greater accuracy than it had been necessary to give to the old fire-engines. His early cylinders were made at the Carron Works, where Smeaton had put up a machine for boring cannon, but they were so untrue that they were next to useless. The pistons could not be kept steam-tight, notwithstanding the various expedients of stuffing with cork, putty, chewed paper, and greased old hat. Watt complained, in regard to one of eighteen inches diameter, that it was so far from circularity, that ' at the worst place the long diameter exceeded the short by three-eighths of an inch!'

The defect of the ordinary boring apparatus was that it was fixed from one end only of the cylinder, as if boring a gun (for which purpose the machine was indeed originally made), and hence was not sufficiently stable in position to guide the tool accurately in its heavy work of cutting the interior surface. The first efficient boring-machine was contrived, about 1775, by a founder and millwright at Chester, named John Wilkinson. He conceived the happy idea of putting a strong bar completely through the cylinder, and fixing it firmly at both ends on lathe centres. Hence when this bar, being provided with proper cutters, was caused to rotate by the ordinary lathe motion, great power could be brought on the cutters without endangering their steadiness of position in regard to the axis. The 'boring bar,' as it was termed, has since been the universal tool for such work, having been, like Maudslay's lathe, made automatic, and given other improvements in detail.

Planing differs from turning and boring, inasmuch as it requires the metal to be operated on in right lines instead of curves, so as to form plane surfaces perfectly flat and true. It is, in fact, analogous to the well-known operation of the same name in woodwork, where a tool carrying a cutter is driven along by the workman's arm, shaving down the surface of the wood till the requisite smoothness is obtained.

Down to a late period no operation at all analogous to the planing of wood was practised with iron; for although a good steel tool could be made to cut iron with the aid of a lathe, it was beyond the power of a man to make such a tool take a shaving off iron in a right line. The usual mode of getting plane surfaces was by what was called 'chipping and filing.' The iron was first brought to something like a level form by chipping little bits off it with a steel chisel, and it was afterwards worked down by large files till a smooth surface was gained. It need hardly be said that such a plan was very laborious and troublesome, and also very likely to be inaccurate.

At length, as tools improved, it seems to have occurred to machinists that it would be possible to construct a sliding frame strong enough to hold and guide a cutting tool in a rectilinear path, so as to make it cut a shaving off a piece of iron underneath; and then, by repeating these cuts, to form the plane surface required. The thing was done, and so arose the planing-machine, a tool of the greatest utility.

The invention of the planing-machine has been claimed for several eminent mechanics. It is probable that, as the apparatus required considerable contrivance to make it successful, it grew up under several hands, but it is certain that a large share of the credit is due to a man named Joseph Clement. He was, like Maudslay, a workman of Bramah's, who afterwards went into business for himself as a mechanical engineer on a small scale, and was greatly celebrated for his ingenuity and mechanical skill, particularly in regard to the construction of tools. He was the only person to be found who could make the extremely accurate work required for Mr. Babbage's Calculating Engine. He made a planing-machine before 1820, and afterwards established a larger machine which for many years was the only good thing of the kind in existence. He allowed it to be used on hire by other engineers, and it brought him a considerable income.

The planing-machine is now extensively used, and of such size as to plane very large surfaces. It is one of the most indispensable tools in a large engineering factory, and its value in promoting accuracy of work has been very great. It is made in two forms: either the article to be planed is fixed, and the tool traverses backwards and forwards over it; or the tool is fixed, and the article is made to move underneath it. It is very customary to make the tool reverse after the forward stroke, so as to present its cutting edge in the other direction, and cut also on the return stroke, by which time is saved. In either case an arrangement is added by which the line of the cuts is caused to advance automatically by a small distance at every cut, so as to cover at length the whole surface to be planed.

'The planing-machine being once established, its principle was soon carried out more generally in what are called *shaping* and *slotting* machines. These are smaller but not less useful instruments, in which a cutter moving in a reciprocating line like that of a planing-machine, but in a path of only a few inches long, can be made to cut away portions of a piece of ironwork in any direction. If the exterior of the article is offered to the tool, it is *shaped* by the metal being cut away; or, by bringing the cutter to bear upon a hole already formed by casting or drilling, the hole can be enlarged and given a square or oblong form, or transformed into what is called a *slot*, whence one of the names of the machine.

The article to be shaped or slotted is placed on a movable frame, and made to advance automatically, and by altering its position great varieties of shapes can be produced.

These shaping and slotting machines are used in large numbers in good shops, and contribute essentially to accuracy and good finish of engineering work.

There are many minor but very useful improvements in engineering tools which are worthy of mention.

The mode of making screws, for example, has been much improved. Screws are so largely used in ironwork for connecting the parts together, that their manufacture, in the shape of what are technically called bolts and nuts, is a large trade of itself. The old method of forming the threads, namely the male thread by movable steel cutting ' dies,' fixed in a ' stock ' or handle, and the female by cutting ' taps,' is still the general one, but the arrangements have been much perfected, and the process has been much facilitated by screwing machines taking the place of hand labour. As machinery advanced, much inconvenience was found from the varying sizes of the threads, screws of the same diameter differing so much in this particular that it was scarcely possible to match a male and female screw unless they were actually made together. It occurred to Henry Maudslay that standard sizes ought to be adopted throughout the trade, and the idea was afterwards fully carried out by Whitworth, his pupil. In the present day, to form an ordinary screw-thread of any other size than 'Whitworth's standard,' is little less than a crime in the eyes of educated mechanical engineers. For large exceptional screws, the lathe with slide rest is used, the automatic sliding motion allowing of such a progression being given to the tool as will form the required spiral in any given proportions, and with absolute perfection.

Sir Joseph Whitworth has also much promoted mechanical excellence in other respects; one for example in the mode of getting perfectly plane metallic surfaces; another in the establishment of a series of 'standard gauges,' for obtaining great accuracy and uniformity in the dimensions of moving parts in machinery.

The construction of automatic machine tools has been much stimulated and improved by the 'strikes' and combinations of workmen that have taken place from time to time. These have caused so much inconvenience to the trade, that efforts have naturally been made to lessen the amount of manual skill requisite, and to reduce the human labour to a kind which may be performed by less practised hands. Hence every strike has been followed by improved tool machinery; already, not only has skilled labour been largely superseded, but the quality of the work has been immensely improved, and the price generally reduced also.

Mr. Whitworth gives an example of this in regard to the planing-machine. The original price for making a surface of iron true by the old process of chipping and filing was twelve shillings a square foot, whereas now it is done very much better by the planing-machine at a cost for labour of less than a penny.

The improvements in tools changed the mode of doing mechanical work, by rendering necessary large and carefully laid out manufactories. The old millwrights had little need of large or expensive premises or plant. A small workshop and a few simple tools were all they required; but under the improved conditions brought about by Watt's inventions, these no longer sufficed; it was necessary to have more systematic arrangements, and tools of complicated and often expensive character, and these necessities brought about the establishment of large manufactories, which gradually supplanted the old millwright's trade.

In these manufactories the designing and direction of the work passed away from the hands of the workman into those of the master and his office assistants. This led also to a division of labour; men of general knowledge were only exceptionally required as foremen or out-door superintendents: and the artificers became, in process of time, little more than attendants on the machines.

One important result of the improvements in the iron manufacture has been the use of this material for structures of much greater magnitude than formerly.

Iron bridges have been the most prominent objects of this kind. The example set at Colebrook Dale in 1779 was followed in other places by Telford and other engineers, and the cast-iron bridge culminated in the erection by Mr. Rennie, in 1819, of the magnificent Southwark Bridge over the Thames, which contains 6,000 tons of iron.

When malleable iron had come into use, of a quality that could be depended on, it was adopted in the first instance for bridges on the suspension principle, of which the elegant structure erected by Telford over the Menai Straits, in 1826, is the best-known example.

The introduction of railways soon after this date involved the necessity for bridges in large numbers, of a more substantial kind, and sometimes of large dimensions; and malleable iron being a material very suitable for their construction, from the facility with which it could be fashioned and put together, a great demand for iron bridges set in. No very large structure, however, of this kind existed until the erection of the great Tubular Bridges over the river Conway and the Menai Strait, in regard to which, as will be seen hereafter, Mr. Fairbairn took an active and important part. The Menai Bridge is 1,511 feet long, and contains 11,468 tons of malleable iron.

Other examples of large structures in iron are found in modern iron ships. These have lately assumed great magnitude; the great war frigates of our modern navy often containing many thousands of tons of metal. The celebrated 'Great Eastern,' designed by Mr. Brunel in 1858, weighs nearly 20,000 tons.

The iron armour-plates used on the war frigates are huge masses of malleable iron, the provisions for manufacturing which are of gigantic character; and the use of this material for defensive purposes has been carried further by the construction of massive iron forts of great strength and solidity.

The modern rifled wrought-iron guns, of many tons in weight, are not only very heavy forgings, but are fine specimens of accuracy in workmanship, that could only have been brought about by admirable perfection in the tools and mechanical arrangements employed in their manufacture.

From the foregoing description the reader will be able
to form an idea of the nature and extent of the profession
of which Sir William Fairbairn was one of the most distinguished members.

Having undergone a thoroughly practical apprenticeship with working millwrights and mechanics, he commenced business in 1817 by setting up a manufactory at
Manchester; and from this date to his death, in 1874,
he was in active and constant practice as a mechanical
engineer.

During this long period he was engaged in the design
and practical construction of engineering works in great
variety, and on a large scale. Steam-engines, water-
wheels, millwork and machinery of all kinds, steam navigation, the iron and steel manufacture, iron defences, iron
bridges, and other large structures in iron, locomotives,
and in fact almost every kind of subject embraced in the
mechanical branch of the profession occupied his attention, and almost everything that he touched received
some improvement at his hands.

But if he had done nothing more than what occupied
him in his business capacity, he would not have acquired the name he has left behind him. He was not
only an able designer and skilful manufacturer, but he
devoted much time to original investigation and to the
promulgation of mechanical knowledge. He was not,
strictly speaking, an eminent theorist, for his education had been too plain and practical to allow of his
acquiring high theoretical attainments; but he had a
scientific mind, a great love of experimental enquiry, an
indefatigable perseverance in tracing out mechanical
truths, and a gift of expressing clearly the results he had
obtained.

These qualifications prompted him to contribute

E

largely to the spread of knowledge on professional subjects. He wrote many complete works, which became very popular ; he sent many able but less known papers to scientific bodies ; he was continually appealed to on intricate or difficult questions; and he was largely sought after to give public lectures or addresses on subjects bearing on mechanical science.

His ability and public spirit were acknowledged by the award to him of honours of the highest character. He was made a Fellow of the Royal Society, and received their gold medal ; he was chosen President for one of the meetings of the British Association ; he received honorary degrees from two British Universities ; he had the great distinction of being elected one of the few foreign members of the Institute of France ; and passing over many other marks of respect of a minor kind, he had, as a crowning honour, the dignity of a Baronetcy graciously conferred on him by Queen Victoria.

A long life, so spent and so rewarded, cannot fail to be of public interest, and the story of this life it is the object of the following pages to tell.

CHAPTER III.

FROM BIRTH TO THE END OF RESIDENCE AT KELSO

AGE, TO 14.

1789—1803

CHAPTER III.

WILLIAM FAIRBAIRN was born in the town of Kelso, in Roxburghshire, on February 19, 1789.

His father, Andrew Fairbairn, was descended, on the male side, from a humble but respectable class of small Lairds, or, as they were called 'Portioners,' who farmed their own land, as was the custom in Scotland in those days.

On the female side the pedigree may have been of a higher character, for Andrew's mother was said by him to have claimed descent from the ancient Border family of Douglas. This lady's maiden name was Anderson; she was a tall, handsome, commanding woman, and lived to a great age.

William writes thus of his father :—

My father was never brought up to any business, and simply learned to read when very young at Smailholme. At the early age of twelve, my father's parents considered it time that he should be doing something for himself. His brother William, then only fifteen, was teaching a school at Holy Island; and my father was accordingly hired out to a neighbour as an assistant on the farm. In this humble situation he learned to be an expert ploughman, and one of the first agricultural operatives in that part of the country. The commencement of my father's career as a practical agriculturist was at the time when the new systems of draining, deep ploughing, and rotation crops were making some noise in the country. It was a new era in the history of agriculture, and one that has produced, and is yet producing, very extraordinary results. With these new pro-

cesses my father became perfectly familiar, and the knowledge
subsequently served him in the development of those resources
which exhibited themselves some years afterwards in Rossshire.

He afterwards went to reside near a seaport in England,
where, during the American war, he was pressed on board a
frigate, from which he was drafted into a ship of the line, and
served under Lord Howe at the destruction of the Spanish fleet
off Gibraltar. At the close of the war, the fleet was ordered
round to Spithead, where he was when the 'Royal George' sank
(August 29, 1782), and assisted in saving the survivors. On
receiving his discharge he returned to Scotland, and married
shortly afterwards.

William's mother was a Miss Henderson, the daughter
of a tradesman in Jedburgh, and the direct descendant of
an old Border family of the name of Oliver, for many
years respectable stock-farmers in a pastoral district at
the northern foot of the Cheviots.

At four years of age William was sent to a small day
school, not so much for the purpose of learning as to
keep him out of mischief. As, however, his chief recollections at this time refer to the frequency and severity
of the punishments he received, it would not appear that
even this object was successfully attained. The first real
steps in education he describes as follows :—

From Mr. Ker's seminary I was in due time transferred to
the parish school, kept by Mr. White, a man of considerable
talent, and a good English scholar. Mr. White had a large
school, with an usher, Mr. Phail, a young man of some learning,
but irritable in his temper, and with knuckles harder than flint,
which he applied with a peculiar jerk to the cranium ; he was
by nature unfit for a teacher. His superior, Mr. White, was
quite the reverse : with a fine open benevolent countenance, he
enjoyed the reputation of being an agreeable companion and a
man of great goodness of heart. He was one of those men of
whom there are many in Scotland, who love their profession ; he
was full of enthusiasm, a strict disciplinarian, and took great
delight in exhibiting his pupils not only in the various

branches of learning, but more particularly in their powers of declaiming selections from our best poets, such as Dryden's Alexander's Feast, the orations of Cicero, Paul before Agrippa, &c. All these used to be favourite exercises, and great preparations were made for the annual examinations, which took place every autumn before the ministers and the influential people of the town.

I learned to read, in Scott and Barrow's collections, pieces selected from some of our best poets and prose writers, amongst whom may be enumerated Addison, Fielding, Swift, De Foe, Hume, Goldsmith, Robertson, Johnson, &c. If to these be added a course of arithmetic as far as Practice and the Rule of Three, they will constitute the whole of my stock of knowledge up to my tenth year.

He was early fond of athletic exercises. He records that when very young he succeeded, after many fruitless attempts, in climbing a high boulder-stone with polished sides and a conical top ; but, falling off, he cut a gash in his forehead, the mark of which remained all his life.

While at school he kept up his skill by running races and so on, and he adds :—

I also learned to improve my climbing propensities by performing with a number of others certain feats of ascent to the top of the mouldering turrets of the old Abbey at Kelso, which, next to Melrose, still remains as one of the finest specimens of the Norman Gothic in Scotland.

With every tower, arch, and cranny I was familiar, and the great feat used to be which of us could reach the bells over the western window in the shortest time, starting altogether by different routes from the kirkyard. At that time the ruins were open to any intruder, and in too many cases they were the receptacle of stray cattle, ' cuddies,' donkeys, and all the filth of that part of the town.

He gives an animated description of the family circumstances in his early youth :—

During the time I was at Mr. White's school, my father lived in Kelso, at the foot of the Woodmarket, in the same

house with Mrs. William Curl, the aunt of the late Sir Walter
Scott. My father was on terms of intimacy with the Scotts of
Sandy Knowe. His father was the gardener there, as well as
for another family at Meliston, and, although inferior in station
to the family at Sandy Knowe, he was, nevertheless, highly respected by every member of it, and more particularly by Mrs.
Curl and Miss Scott. Both families lived at Smailholme Tower,
and my father, although a few years older than Sir Walter, was
well acquainted with him, and, as a boy, used often to carry
him when unable to walk from the dislocation of the hip-bone,
which made him a cripple for life. All these circumstances of
early association promoted a degree of intimacy with the family
which was kept up with Mrs. Curl and Miss Scott till their
deaths.

My mother, although exceedingly active, never enjoyed
good health. She had a very limited income on which to
maintain and bring up her family ; and the efforts she was
called upon to make in her domestic duties, and her desire to
assist in the education and maintenance of five small children,
by extraordinary exertions in spinning upon the long and small
wheel, exhausted her strength and frequently incapacitated her
for the performance of the ordinary duties of the family. I
remember that those extraordinary efforts were a constant cause
of anxiety to my father, whose strong attachment for his wife
caused him to remonstrate on the folly and impropriety of her
conduct.

His attempts were, however, fruitless, as absence from home
during six days in the week furnished abundant opportunities
for keeping the spinning-wheel constantly in motion and increasing the evils of which my father complained. By these
exertions it must, however, be borne in mind that the whole of
my father's clothes and those of all the children, till I was fourteen years of age, were spun and manufactured by my mother.
She bought the wool and the flax, spun it into yarn, reeled it
into hanks, and gave it out to the weaver to be manufactured.
When the woollen cloth came home it was carefully measured,
and sent to the fulling-mill to be dressed and finished ; and
when the linen web was finished she bleached it herself; and
many were the times I was set to watch and water the web. For

nearly twenty years, from 1785 to 1804, I believe the whole, or nearly' the whole of the woollen clothes, shirting, sheets, and blankets, were spun and manufactured by my mother. In addition to these industrial resources, which always formed a prominent feature in my mother's character, there were her knowledge and skill in the useful arts. She was thoroughly acquainted with dyeing and bleaching ; when my father resided in the Highlands of Scotland, she made his coats, waistcoats, and breeches, as well as all the jackets and trousers for her sons. She was also an adept at dress-making, and used not only to make for herself and daughters, but frequently cut out for the neighbours, and she encouraged the same system of economy in other families as she practised in her own.

My father, on the other hand, possessed a strong and muscular frame, an excellent constitution, and could undergo any amount of fatigue. He was a hard worker, a great reader, and a man of unblemished integrity of character. No exertion was too much for him ; and the respect in which he was held by all the more wealthy and intelligent classes was a great source of pride and gratification to my mother. To each other they entertained the most tender affection, and excepting only the words which occasionally passed between them on the subject of the long wooden wheel, they were a happy couple. In politics my father was a Liberal, or what was considered in those days a staunch Whig, with a tendency to Jacobinism ; but he was never violent, as my mother, who was more Conservative, exercised considerable influence over him, and retained him within the bounds of moderation.

. In their religious tenets they were both of the Church of Scotland, from which they never deviated, and from which my mother in particular derived great consolation. She was pious and discreet, much more so than my father, who I always thought was tinged with scepticism.

The writer of the autobiography proceeds with his story, which comprises many interesting incidents :—

I must, however, now return to that part of the narrative where I had been entered at the parish school, and where I had attained some little proficiency in reading, writing, and arith-

metic. As near as I can recollect I was about three years in
that establishment, and during that time I remember Mrs.
Curl's nephew, Mr. Walter Scott, who was then an advocate at
Edinburgh, spending some months of two summers at Kelso.
I believe he was then collecting materials (or, as his aunt used
to say, 'foolishly spending his time amongst all the auld wives
of the country,') for his ' Minstrelsy of the Scottish Border.' It
was at this time I frequently saw Mr. Scott, who used to hear
me read to his aunt, and rewarded me, when I read distinctly,
with some little mark of his attention. From the intimacy of
those days I cannot recall any indication of those great powers
of imagery which afterwards became the delight of every reader
in Europe.

During the long winter evenings, when my father was from
home, which, as already stated, was five nights out of the seven,
Mrs. Curl used to bring down her wheel and join my mother at
a camp with the ' pirns,' or my mother went up to her, as best
suited their convenience. They were both good spinners, and
used to engage in a friendly competition as to the quantities
each could turn off in a given time. My mother was generally
the winner, as she spun with the double rock and both hands,
whilst Mrs. Curl never attempted more than the single ' pirn.'
Eighty years ago spinning was common in all the farm-houses
of Scotland during the winter months; at Mervinslaw, where my
mother was brought up, all the lasses were engaged at the wheel,
and, in order to encourage the rivalry and lighten the task, the
Border songs were chanted in no unmeasured time, and with a
pathos and good feeling that not unfrequently touched the heart.
The same rivalry was carried on between the two friends during
the winter months of the residence of the family at Kelso.

In the autumn of 1799 the pleasing monotony of this quiet life
was materially changed by new prospects which were held out to
my father in Rossshire, when he was offered the charge of a farm
of 300 acres. The farm was to be the joint property of himself
and his brother, Mr. Peter Fairbairn, for many years a resident
in that country and secretary to Lord Seaforth, of Castle Brahan.
The farm was leased from his lordship, on the express condition
that one half of the stock, and one half of the proceeds, should
belong to my father. It was situated at Moy on the banks of

the river Conan, about five miles from Dingwall, and although possessing a few fertile spots, the greater portion was overgrown with whins and brushwood, and covered with stone and rocks, some of them of great magnitude.

The stocking of the farm was a heavy business, as my uncle had a large family, with a limited income, and a very scanty capital. My father had none; but he was to find skill and industry in the management; and having purchased a good assortment of carts and ploughs, and all the necessary implements, as used in the best farms in the south, our little establishment at Kelso was broken up, very much to the regret of Mrs. Curl and my mother. To effect the transport my father bought an old horse, and having bent some canvas over one of the carts, he left Kelso in October with a delicate wife and a family of five children, the youngest only six weeks old, on a journey of upwards of two hundred miles through a wild country, at a most inclement season of the year. It will not be necessary to recount the difficulties we had to encounter, with a broken down and restive horse, under rain and sleet, at that inclement season, over the Grampians. Suffice it to observe, that my mother was so ill as to be lifted in and out of the cart every night and morning.

At length we arrived at our destination, but unfortunately the house intended for our residence on the farm was not finished, and we had reluctantly to take up our quarters in a temporary hovel very inferior to the comfortable abode we had enjoyed for so many years at Kelso. Early in the spring the house was completed, and my father set vigorously to work on a series of improvements, which, in less than two years, completely changed the face of the farm.

I have already observed that the whole surface of the farm was nearly covered with whins and rocks, and to remove these my father adopted an ingenious method. Having cut down the brushwood and piled it upon the large blocks of whinstone, the fuel was ignited, and, the stones becoming heated to almost a red heat, the ashes were cleared away, and a small stream of water being applied from a bottle, the rapid condensation, or rather contraction, caused a fracture of the rock in any required direction.

This to the surrounding and wondering neighbours was an extraordinary performance, which some of them did not hesitate to attribute to an agency much more powerful and dangerous than the little bottle which effected such wonders.

Two years were employed in this way, and the farm began to exhibit, in place of whins and rocks, fine crops of turnips and barley ; and from the introduction of a good system of draining, which was practised by deep trenching, several fields were thus reclaimed that had never before felt the coulter of the plough.

The failure of the crops in 1800 and 1801 did great damage, and ruined most of the farmers, and amongst others it bore severely upon the owners of the Moy farm, which had incurred an expensive outlay without yielding any return. That was not, however, the greatest evil that the family had to endure, as my uncle, whose company as well as services had become indispensable to Lord Seaforth—who was deaf and dumb—had engaged to go out with his lordship as secretary on his appointment to the Governorship of Barbadoes in the West Indies. This appointment made a total change in the prospects of both families. My father was urged to continue his improvements on the farm until my eldest cousin became of age, and I was selected, as the eldest of my father's family, to go out to India, through the influence of his lordship, as a cadet.

This arrangement, had it been carried out, would have changed the whole course of William's life ; but it was frustrated by unforeseen difficulties, and he remained at the farm with his father.

The effect of the residence at Moy on William's education and prospects is described as follows ; and here we get the first indications of that taste for mechanics which moulded his future career :—

The residence of the family at Moy was entirely lost as regards the education of my brother Tom and myself. One of the conditions of the agreement with my uncle was that a tutor should be engaged for both families, and that we should have the benefit of a good education along with my cousins. For some reason or other, which I could never clearly understand, this was never accomplished ; and the whole two years spent at Moy proved a serious loss to myself, as well as the other branches of the family. Attempts were made by both my father and mother to rectify the error, but the laborious engagements to which my father was subjected in carrying forward the improvements, and the assiduous duties of my mother in keeping us all right and tight at home, were as much as they could accomplish, and, with the exception of an occasional lesson, and the reading on Sundays, I may with safety affirm, that this time was for the most part unprofitably spent and produced no good or lasting impressions.

It will readily be seen that a boy of eleven years, with all the activity and bustle of youth, if not engaged in some useful pursuit, is likely to do mischief. Fortunately my inclination took a different turn. After the first year's residence at Moy, my younger brother, Peter, then a child of fifteen months old, required a great deal of nursing, and as that duty devolved upon my eldest sister and myself, I managed, in order to relieve myself of the trouble of carrying him on my back, to make a little waggon with four wheels, and by attaching a piece of old rope, used to drag him in all directions, sometimes to a considerable distance from the farm. The construction of the waggon was, however, a formidable undertaking, as I had no tools but a knife, a gimblet, and an old saw. With these implements, a piece of thin board, and a few small nails, I managed to make a respectable waggon, which, though frequently out of repair, was nevertheless much better than could be expected. The greatest difficulty was the wheels, which I surmounted by cutting sections from the stem of a small alder tree, and with a red-hot iron burnt the holes in the centre to receive the axle.

The success which attended this construction led to others of greater importance, which I continued to practise, and which my father encouraged during the whole time we were in the Highlands. In the formation of boats and ships I became an expert artificer, and was at once a ' Jack-of-all-trades,' having to build, rig, and sail my own vessels. From ship-building, I proceeded to construct wind and water-mills, and attained such proficiency that I had sometimes five or six mills in operation at once. They were all made with the knife. The water-spout was composed of the bark of a tree, and the mill-stones were represented by round discs of the same material. It is not for me to offer an opinion as to the influence these exercises had upon my future fortunes, I may leave others to form their own judgment.

Shortly after the departure of the uncle for the West Indies, it appears that family differences arose as to the management of the farm, and Andrew, who could not brook what he considered improper interference, relinquished his post at Moy, and engaged himself as steward to Mackenzie of Allangrange, where he removed with his family.

William's prospects of education then brightened, as he was sent to a school at Mullochy, a mile and a half away ; he says :—

The Mullochy school was conducted by a Mr. Donald Fraser, a good classic and severe disciplinarian. Under this gentleman's tuition I made great progress in reading, writing, and accounts, but learned neither Latin or Greek, confining my studies, according to my father's orders, to a plain English education. The want of a good grammatical course, and a slight knowledge of the classics, has always been to me a serious loss. I have repeatedly found the want of it, and to the present day I am unable to determine whether I write or speak correctly. Mr. Fraser was a gentleman well qualified to impart this knowledge, but it was not only considered as not essential, but as standing in the way of the more practical and useful branches of study, to which it was necessary I should apply. The classics were therefore at once abandoned for arithmetic, book-keeping, and a smattering of mensuration, which, with the exception of three months with my uncle at Galashiels, constituted the whole extent of education I ever received.

Whilst noticing the Mullochy school, I may mention that it consisted of about forty boys and twenty girls, a considerable number of them coming barefooted, and without bonnets or caps, from a considerable distance. The boys were all dressed in tartan kilts, and the winter always entailed severe trials upon the wearers. What with poor feeding and thin clothing, the greatest sufferings from cold were endured, often at the expense of the health, and sometimes endangering the lives, of the children. I have before observed that Mr. Fraser was a severe disciplinarian, and in order to enforce the system he had adopted for the regulation of the school, he called a muster roll every Thursday at three o'clock, and having ascertained the defaulters in attendance, negligence, &c., for the week, the whole list was cleared off by the usual application of the 'tawse' which never failed to effect a demonstration on that part of the person which may be described as being the most sensitive, and the least liable to injury. I must, however, do Mr. Fraser the justice to say, that my brother and myself (being differently dressed and wearing the Saxon costume) in some degree escaped the severity of this application, from the difficulty and trouble incurred in the unbuttoning and removal of the tight trowse. This did not, however, enable us entirely to escape, and a transfer was occasionally made from those parts to the palm of the hand, which never failed to ensure pain and preserve a glowing heat for a considerable time afterwards. These were some of the drawbacks upon the system which at that time was pursued throughout Scotland, but in other respects, it must be admitted that Mr. Fraser was an excellent teacher, and made several scholars who afterwards distinguished themselves.

Andrew Fairbairn remained only two years in his steward's place.

My father was never satisfied with the Highlands, as the whole of his time had been spent in laborious improvements, which enriched others, but presented to himself and family no result. Thoroughly disgusted with the people and the country, he accepted an offer made to him by Sir William Ingleby to remove to Yorkshire and take the management of his farm at Ingleby Manor, near Knaresborough. This arrangement made a total change in the condition and prospects of his family, and

having sold off everything in the shape of furniture, our
necessaries were packed up, and in three days we embarked at
Cromarty.

After a tedious voyage we landed at Leith on the King's
birthday, June 4, 1803, and what caused me to recollect the
date were the rejoicings which we witnessed at Edinburgh on
the evening of the same day. A few days more replaced us at
Kelso, where we found on enquiry that Mrs. Curl had left the
old house at the foot of the Woodmarket, and we were therefore
content to take up our residence in a small cottage in another
part of the town. Having settled the family, my father lost no
time in preparing for his departure for the scene of his future
labours in Yorkshire.

Previously, however, to leaving Kelso, William, his eldest
brother at Galashiels, proposed to take me for a few months, in
order to improve my arithmetic, and give me a short course of
book-keeping and land-surveying. These offers were gladly
accepted by my father, and I forthwith started on foot for my
new destination. My uncle had been at the head of the parish
school for nearly thirty years. He was a good English scholar,
an excellent land-surveyor, and a person of considerable attainments as a practical mathematician. Like other members of
his family, he was self-taught, and he had exercised the vocation
of a schoolmaster from fourteen years of age till the day of his
death, which was occasioned by a severe cold caught during his
surveys in the autumn of 1809. To my uncle I was indebted
for some knowledge in land-surveying, but he was a severe task-
master. I think too much so, as he exacted from his pupils
lessons which to me were exceeding disagreeable, such as verses
from the Psalms of David, which he insisted should be committed to memory every Sunday. I laboured incessantly at the
119th Psalm, until I got thoroughly disgusted with the whole
book ; and such was my antipathy to the task that, to the present day, I never look into it without thinking of the unprofitable labour to which I was at that time subjected. At
Galashiels I, however, made some progress, but the time was so
short—only three months—that I was only beginning to understand what I was about when I was removed.

William being now a tall lad of fourteen, it was considered desirable he should render some assistance towards the support of his younger brothers and sisters; and, in August 1803, he was taken away from school, and sent back to Kelso. He goes on :—

In a few days, through the influence of some of the neighbours, I got employment at the New Bridge, which was then building under the direction of the late Mr. Rennie, and a more chaste and beautiful structure, with the exception, probably, of the Waterloo and new London Bridges, does not exist. I was only a few days in this employment, to which I took a great dislike, when I met with an accident which nearly crippled me for life. Those who noticed the methods in use at that time for carrying the materials for buildings would observe that the smaller stones were, carried on handbarrows by two men, one before and another behind. On this occasion I was the leader, and during the process of carrying the stone, one much beyond my strength, with a coarse, unfeeling fellow behind, I sank under the load, and the stone fell over upon my right leg, making a fearful gash, which effectually barred my claims for the honourable distinction of a mason's clerkship. Nearly three months' confinement was the result of this accident; and a hard struggle we had for it, as the money my father was enabled to send from Yorkshire was a mere trifle. My earnings were only three shillings per week—and to increase the difficulties, my father's money was badly paid, which caused him to throw up his appointment, and return again to Kelso. All these hardships were endured with resignation by my mother. What added to the misery, and increased the troubles under which she laboured, was the loss of my youngest sister, Eliza, a beautiful child of two years of age. This was the heaviest blow my poor mother had yet received. She appeared to sink under her affliction, and I well remember the intensity of her grief when she saw her eldest boy, almost a confirmed cripple, take the place of his father in the position of chief mourner. My sister's funeral, doctor's bills, and the limited remittances received from Yorkshire, entailed a great deal of suffering upon the family, and before the following November, when my father

F

returned, we had expended the last shilling and were almost in a state of destitution. His return was most welcome to my distressed mother, whose health had suffered from the anxieties attendant upon the loss of her child and the exhausted state of the funds upon which she depended for support.

CHAPTER IV.

FIRST EMPLOYMENT AND APPRENTICESHIP

AGE 14-21

1803—1810

APPOINTMENT OF ANDREW AT PERCY MAIN COLLIERY, NORTHUM-
BERLAND—WILLIAM JOINS HIM—PROSPERITY AMONG THE PITMEN
AND SAILORS ; ITS CONSEQUENCES —BOXING MATCHES ; WILLIAM'S
FIRST VICTORY—BOUND APPRENTICE TO A MILLWRIGHT—ENDEAVOURS
TO IMPROVE HIS MIND—PROGRAMME OF STUDY—FIRST LOVE ATTACH-
MENT ; ITS INFLUENCE ON HIS LITERARY ABILITIES—FREDERICK AND
FELICIA—MATHEMATICS, HISTORY, AND POETRY—MECHANICAL PUR-
SUITS—DESIGN FOR A CLOCK-ORRERY; ITS FAILURE—MUSIC AND
MUSICAL INSTRUMENTS—THE STORY OF A FIDDLE—HOME-BREWED
MUSIC—TAKES CHARGE OF THE STEAM-ENGINE AND PUMPS OF THE
COLLIERY—SEVERE·AND TRYING NATURE OF THE DUTIES—SUBSCRIP-
TION TO THE KEG—ITS CONSEQUENCES—COMPLETION OF HIS TERM OF
APPRENTICESHIP—GEORGE STEPHENSON.

CHAPTER IV.

THE unhappy state of things so pathetically described at the end of the last chapter did not last long ; for Andrew Fairbairn was a man of energy and strong will, and having now a growing family, he determined to exert himself to the utmost to put them in better circumstances.

Soon after his return he succeeded in getting another appointment at Percy Main Colliery, near North Shields, as steward of a farm belonging to the coal-owners. The pay put him in comparative comfort, and he retained the appointment for upwards of seven years.

The family remained for some time at Kelso, but William followed his father as soon as he was able. He says :—

As soon as the bargain was fixed, my father again started for his new destination, and early in the following February, 1 804, my leg being healed, I was packed off by the carrier to join my father at the colliery, and here commences a new and probably the most important part of my history.

Percy Main Colliery is situated within a distance of two miles of North Shields, which at that time and during the whole of the late war was one of the most flourishing seaports in the kingdom. These were days of prosperity for both coal and ship-owners. Bounties and wages were high. The colliers were demanding from 18l. to 20l. binding money, and the able-bodied seamen were in receipt of eleven to twelve guineas per voyage (to London and back), and some of them, if they had the good fortune to escape the press-gang, made as many as ten

voyages in the year.   Wages were high and men were scarce;
but I doubt much whether periods of extreme prosperity are not
on the whole injurious.   This occasion was marked by the
greatest excesses, and, although the Methodists exercised a
salutary influence over a considerable number of the pitmen, yet
the sailors were fairly adrift, without rudder or compass, on a sea
of reckless dissipation.   The great majority of the colliers were
almost beside themselves; and from that day to this I never
witnessed the same extent of demoralisation as I did at that
time.   Pitched battles, brawling, drinking, and cock-fighting,
seemed to be the order of the day, and there was no excitement,
however coarse, but what was seized upon by the majority of the
recipients of the 18l. bounty.   Amongst the 'pit lads,' boxing
was considered a manly exercise and a favourite amusement, and
I believe I counted up no less than seventeen battles which I
reluctantly had to fight before I was able to attain a position
calculated to ensure respect.   Naturally I was averse to these
encounters, but I had no alternative, as, immediately on my
arrival from Kelso, I was placed in a position where I had to
lead coals in a one-horse cart from behind the screen to the pitmen's houses, and what with my Scotch accent and different
manner, I became the mark of every species of annoyance, which
I frequently returned with interest, but not before I was soundly
drubbed by some selected pugilist much stronger and older
than myself.

These attacks were very discouraging, and I was several
times on the point of abandoning the work altogether rather
than undergo the buffeting to which I was almost every day a
martyr, when an occurrence took place which effectually turned
the scale on my adversaries.   This was an attack made upon me
by the son of one of the 'sinkers,' and his companion, a young
engine-wright, who for several months had watched every opportunity for carrying on the persecution.   One afternoon, when I
was at work as usual behind the screen, a volume of water was
squirted down behind my neck, and immediately after the
attack the perpetrator took to his heels.   I lost no time in the
pursuit, and picking up a brick, I let fly at him with all my
force, and cut him in the heel to the bone.   His companion
came to his assistance, and, after using the most abusive

epithets, he retired, supporting his helpless assistant. The occurrence of the brick relieved me from further attacks, but it did not rest there, as the associate of the wounded lad, a noted boxer, was determined I should pay the penalty for my temerity. Accordingly, some time afterwards, I was challenged to fight him under circumstances which I repeatedly declined, but one of the men perceiving the insults to which I was subjected, took my part, and the kindly feelings of the stranger operated so powerfully upon me as to renew my courage, and the battle began. For the first five minutes I had the worst of it, and the heavy blows I received on the stomach not only exhausted my breath, but caused me to feel sick, and I was ready to drop, when one of the lookers-on called on us to stop, which gave me time to breathe till the contest again commenced. In this round I was driven to desperation. I laid out right and left at his face and nearly blinded him, in fact, I threw my head first, and then my whole body upon him with such force, that it brought us both to the ground, and I was declared the victor. That was the last of my battles.

During this time it would appear that William only acted as helper in some way to his father; but he was shortly put into a better and more definite position by entering regularly on his course of education as a mechanical engineer. On March 24, 1804, he was, at the instance of the owners of the colliery, bound apprentice to a Mr. John Robinson, described in the indenture as ' of Percy Main, in the county of Northumberland, millwright.' The indenture was for seven years, and he was to receive wages beginning with five shillings per week, and increasing to twelve shillings.

Mr. Fairbairn continues :—

Mr. Robinson, who held the appointment of engine-wright, and had the charge of all the machinery and engines, was the person appointed to give me instruction. Mr. Robinson had been nominated to the office by the late Mr. Buddle, one of the most eminent coal-viewers in the North of England, the friend and supporter of Sir Humphrey Davy, and a gentleman highly distinguished in his profession. To Mr. Buddle we are indebted for many improvements in the art of mining, both as respects the nature of the working and the principle of ventilation, to which he directed his attention with considerable success. Mr. Robinson was considered a good colliery engineer, with a rough, passionate temper, but in other respects an easy, good-hearted man. As was the fashion in those days he indulged in what was considered amongst a certain class an ornament of speech, profane swearing, and this was carried to such an excess amongst the leading men of the colliery, that an order was scarcely once given, or a sentence uttered, unless accompanied by an oath. At the present day such language would not be tolerated in any society, even in that of bargemen or navvies.

I had entered upon my fifteenth year, when I commenced the business of an engineer. I had good wages, which, with extra work in making wooden wedges and blocking out seg-ments of solid oak for walling the sides and drawing off the water of a new pit, which was sinking at Howden Pans, gave me an opportunity of making some money which was of great use to the family. I sometimes doubled the amount of my wage, and rendered great assistance to my parents, who were still struggling against a very limited income, and the increasing expenses of my younger brothers and sisters whose school fees had to be paid.

For three years I continued to work in this manner, and, during the winter evenings, when I did not work overtime, I entered upon a course of study, which I have since, under the blessing of Divine Providence, turned to moderately good account. My limited knowledge, and the very few opportunities which, up to that period, had presented themselves for improve-ment, operated forcibly upon my mind. I became dissatisfied with the persons I had to associate with at the shop, and feeling my own ignorance, I became fired with ambition to remedy the evil, and cut out for myself a new path of life. I shortly came to the conclusion that no difficulties should frighten, nor the severest labour discourage me in the attainment of the object I had in view. Armed with this resolution, I set to work in the first year of my apprenticeship, and, having written out a programme, I commenced the winter course in the double capacity of both scholar and schoolmaster, and arranged my study as follows :—

Monday Evenings for Arithmetic, Mensuration, &c.
Tuesday   „   Reading History and Poetry.
Wednesday „   Recreation, Reading Novels and Romances.
Thursday   „   Mathematics.
Friday   „   Euclid, Trigonometry.
Saturday   „   Recreation and Sundries.
Sunday   „   Church, Milton, and Recreation.

These were the exercises of the week, which I kept up with wonderful constancy and with few interruptions, considering the temptations and attempts at ridicule which occasionally I had to combat from some of my shopmates, an annoyance of little moment, as I very soon altered their tone and turned the tables upon them, probably as much for their benefit as my own. What, however, led to my perseverance was the line of conduct I had laid down for my guidance and improvement, and the kindness of my father, who bought me a ticket in the North Shields subscription library.

Here the writer gives an account of an attachment he formed to a young girl who attended the same place of worship. As this had no result influencing his future life, it would be unnecessary to notice it here, were it not that it led him to practise literary composition by a somewhat odd process which he thus describes :—

It led me into a course of letter-writing which improved my style, and gave me greater facilities of expression. The truth is, I could not have written on any subject if it had not been for this circumstance, and my attempt at essays, in the shape of the papers which I had read with avidity in the ' Spectator,' may be traced to my admiration of this divinity.

In the enthusiasm of my first attachment it was my good fortune to fall upon a correspondence between two lovers, Frederick and Felicia, in the ' Town and Country Magazine' for the year 1782, Nos. 3 and 4. This correspondence was of some length and was carried from number to number in a series of letters. Frederick was the principal writer, and although greatly above me in station, yet his sentiments harmonised so exactly with mine, that I sat down at Frederick's desk and wrote to my Felicia with emotions as strong as any Frederick in existence. Frederick by his writing was evidently a gentleman, and in order to prepare myself for so much goodness as I had conjured up in Mary, I commenced the correspondence by first reading the letter in the magazine, and then shut the book for the reply, and to write the letter that Frederick was supposed to have written. I then referred to the book, and how bitter was my disappointment at finding my expressions unconnected and immeasurably inferior to those of the writer. Sometimes I could trace a few stray expressions which I thought superior to his, but, as a whole, I was miserably deficient. In this way did I make love, and in this way I inadvertently rendered one of the strongest passions of our nature subservient to the means of improvement.

He did not, however, let this agreeable occupation trench upon his other studies. He goes on :—

For three successive winters I contrived to go through a complete system of mensuration, and as much algebra as enabled me to solve an equation ; and a course of trigonometry, navigation, heights and distances, &c. This was exclusive of my reading, which was always attractive, and gave me the greatest pleasure. I had an excellent library at Shields, which I went to twice a week, and here I read Gibbon's ' Decline and Fall of the Roman Empire,' Hume's ' History of England,' Robertson's ' History of Scotland,' ' America,' ' Charles the Fifth,' and many other works of a similar character, which I read with the utmost attention. I also read some of our best poets, amongst which were Milton's ' Paradise Lost,' Shakespeare, Cowper, Goldsmith, Burns, and Kirke White. With this course of study I spent long evenings, sometimes sitting up late ; but, having to be at the shop at six in the morning, I did not usually prolong my studies much beyond eleven or twelve o'clock.

During these pursuits I must in truth admit that my mind was more upon my studies than my business. I made pretty good way in the mere operative part, but, with the exception of arithmetic and mathematics, I made little or no progress in the principles of the profession; on the contrary, I took a dislike to the work and the parties by whom I was surrounded.

The possession of tools and the art of using them renewed my taste for mechanical pursuits. I tried my skill at different combinations, and like most inventors whose minds are more intent upon making new discoveries than acquiring the knowledge of what has been done by others, I frequently found myself forestalled in the very discovery which I had persuaded myself was original. For many months I laboured incessantly in devising a piece of machinery that should act as a time-piece and at the same time as an orrery, representing the sun as a centre, with the earth and moon and the whole planetary system revolving round it. This piece of machinery was to be worked by a weight and a pendulum, and was not only to give the diurnal motions of the heavenly bodies, but to indicate the time of their revolutions in their respective orbits round the sun. All this was to be done in accordance with one measure of time, which the instrument, if it ever could have been com-pleted, was to record. I looked upon this piece of mechanism as a perfectly original conception, and nothing prevented me from making the attempt to carry it into execution but the want of means, and the difficulties which surrounded me in the complexity and numerous motions necessary to make it a useful working machine. The consideration of this subject was not, however, lost, as I derived great advantage in the exercise which it gave to the thoughts. It taught me the advantage of concentration, and of arranging my ideas, and of bringing the whole powers of the mind with energy to bear upon one subject. It further directed my attention to a course of reading on mechanical philosophy and astronomy, from which I derived considerable advantage.

Finding the means at my disposal much too scanty to enable me to make a beginning with my new orrery, I turned my attention to music, and bought an old Hamburg fiddle, for which I gave half-a-crown. This was a cheap bargain, even for such a miserable instrument, and what with new bracing of catgut and a music-book, I spent nearly a week's wages, a sum which I could ill afford, to become a distinguished musician. I however fresh rigged the violin, and, with a glue-pot, carefully closed all the openings which were showing themselves between the back and the sides of the instrument. Having completed the repairs, I commenced operations ; and certainly there never was a learner who produced less melody or a greater number of discords. The effect was astounding, and after tormenting the whole house with discordant sounds for two months, the very author of the mischief tumbled to pieces in my hands, to the great relief of every member of the family.

I was not, however, to be frustrated in my attempts to become a musician, and the old fiddle proving useless, I set to work with inflexible determination and made a new one. This operation cost me five weeks' hard labour, chiefly at nights ; and having made the necessary tools out of old hand-saw files, I completed the violin, which, to my astonishment, emitted tones as loud and sonorous as an organ. The transfer of the strings and bridge of the old instrument to that of the new one was to my mind a day of secret rejoicing, which confirmed me still more in my determination to persevere in acquiring the neces- sary knowledge and skill to play. For the attainment of these objects I once more commenced my studies, and proceeded to acquire a knowledge of the notes and to finger them, in which I found little or no difficulty ; yet I never could attain a good bow-hand, which I afterwards found was one of the essentials for becoming a good musician. Repeated discomfitures at last con- vinced me that nature never intended me for a fiddler ; and, impressed with this opinion, I consulted an old man who played at weddings and other merry-makings, as to what I should do. He advised me to become his pupil, and to bring my violin with me on the following night, when he had no doubt he could after a few lessons make me an accomplished performer. Follow- ing this advice, I repaired to his house, and after two or three lessons he offered twenty shillings for my violin, and advised me to abandon all thoughts of ever rising in the profession. After some consideration I declined the offer ; and having paid him for my instruction, I departed, under the conviction that in case the instrument was worth twenty shillings to a person who con- sidered himself an artist, it must be of the same, if not more, value to myself. Impressed with this conviction, the violin became my constant travelling-companion for a number of years. I could play half-a-dozen Scotch airs, which served as an occasional amusement, not so much for the delicacy of execution as for the sonorous energy with which they were executed. For several years after my marriage, my skill was put to the test for the benefit of the rising generation; and although duly appreciated by the children, the fiddle was never taken from the shelf without creating alarm in the mind of their mother, who was in fear that some one might hear it. A dancing-master, who was giving lessons in the country, borrowed the fiddle, and, to the great relief of the family, it was never returned. Some years after this I was present at the starting of the cotton-mill for Messrs. Gros, Deval & Co., of Wesserling, in Alsace, where we had executed the water-wheel and millwork (the first wheel on the suspension principle in France). After a satisfactory start, a great dinner was given by Mr. Gros on the occasion to the neighbouring gentry. During dinner I had been explaining to Mr. Gros, who spoke a little English, the nature of home-brewed ale, which he had tasted and much admired in England. In the evening we had music, and perceiving me admire his performance on the violin, he enquired if I could play, to which I answered in the affirmative, when his instrument was in a moment in my hands, and I had no alternative but one of my best tunes, the 'Keel Row,' which the company listened to with amazement, until my career was arrested by Mr. Gros calling out at the pitch of his voice, ' Top, top, monsieur, by gad, dat be *home-brewed music.*'

The construction of the violin brings me to that part of my story which eventually led to a new epoch in my history, and that was my removal from the workshop to take charge of the pumps and steam-engine of Percy Main Colliery, which required to be kept constantly at work in order to clear the mine of water. This department was much more to my taste than the mere operative part of the work. I was more independent, and so long as I kept the engine and pumps in order, I was entirely my own master. Besides, I had ever a mortal antipathy to be rung in and out by bells; force work was to me the most irksome duty I had to perform. Now I was free; and having attained a responsible trust, I made up my mind to discharge it with the greatest fidelity.

The duties were at times exceedingly severe and trying to the constitution, particularly in winter; and from the nature of the water, which contained much salt and sand, the wear and tear upon the pumps were very great. I, however, devised every possible means to keep the pumps in good repair; but much depended upon the quality of the leather used for the buckets and clacks, as in some cases I have known a bucket wear to pieces in half-an-hour, whilst others would last for a couple of days. The depth of the pit was 150 fathoms, with four sets of pumps; and what with broken pump-rods and other casualties, I have frequently been suspended by a rope during the winter nights, with the water pouring upon me, for seven to eight hours at a stretch, until every limb was numbed with cold. This often repeated, and being roused out of bed at all hours, and having to descend the shaft (which was a cold downcast draught) with a flannel shirt and trousers, a leather hat, and buckskin to protect the head and neck from the water, which descended like a shower-bath, the whole duty on these occasions was one of great severity, in fact, so severe as seriously to injure the health of one, and destroy the life of another, of my fellow-assistants. These trials, and many others of nearly equal severity, I have, with the blessing of God and a strong constitution, overcome, for which I have ever felt most grateful.

The great and important advantage of this new office was, however, the number of days and hours of leisure which I had at command. To fill up these hours usefully, I applied myself assiduously to reading. I frequented the library at Shields every other night, and being a favourite with the librarian's daughter, a young quakeress, I was enabled to procure a perusal of nearly all the new publications before they were sent into circulation. Thus with a book in my pocket, I could stroll into the fields; and having erected a tall flag-staff over the sheers of the pit, I extended my excursions for two or three miles in every direction, so as not to lose sight of the signal-staff; this I found of great convenience, as the moment anything was wrong, up went the flag, and I hurried home.

During these intervals of leisure, I had several local adventures, which, although productive of no results, nevertheless exhibited the moral condition of a certain class of workmen. It used to be a custom in the shop where I was employed to club together once or twice a week, and to subscribe for what was denominated the *keg*. This keg was a nine gallon barrel of ale, which on particular days was brought by an unfrequented and circuitous route from the Howden Pans Brewery, about a mile and a half distant. It generally arrived about two o'clock in the afternoon, and was placed upon the bench with one of the apprentices to ' watch hawks,' and to give notice by a loud whistle when any appearance of danger was likely to threaten the community. The result of these indulgences was a beastly state of intoxication, in which the elder men had to be led home after dark by myself and other apprentices, who enjoyed the amusement of landing them in a wet ditch before they were delivered up to their wives. This practice, during the five years I was at Percy Main, was pursued with a perseverance which ended in making most of the young men confirmed drunkards, and ruined the reputation and health of those whose duty it was to set a better example. I was afterwards often thankful at having escaped the contagion of those irregularities, which at a more matured period told with tenfold force, and hastened the ruin of some of my contemporaries.

William remained in this situation till he was of age, and had completed his seven years' apprenticeship, the indenture being duly and honourably cancelled by Mr. Robinson on March 26, 1811.

During this time he made the acquaintance of George Stephenson, who had then charge of an engine at Willington Ballast Hill, only a mile or two from Percy Main Colliery. The two young men, who were nearly of the same age, and were both earnest in their love for mechanics, here formed a friendship which lasted through life. It is on record [1] that in the summer evenings Fair-

---

[1] Smiles, *Lives of the Engineers*, vol. iii. p. 41.

bairn was accustomed to go over to see his friend, and would frequently attend to the Ballast Hill engine for a few hours, in order to enable Stephenson to take a two or three hours' turn at heaving ballast out of the collier vessels, by which he earned a small addition to his regular wages. George Stephenson had recently married, and established a humble but comfortable home in a cottage at Willington Quay, where his friend was a frequent visitor.

Mr. Fairbairn, in after life, often alluded with pride and satisfaction to his early intimacy and close friendship with the great founder of the railway system.

CHAPTER V.

REMOVAL TO LONDON—EMPLOYMENT THERE

AGE 21-24.

1810—1813

CHAPTER V.

MR. FAIRBAIRN continues his story :—

I had now reached my twenty-second year, and having finished my apprenticeship, I left reluctantly the scene of my trials and many friendships, and went in search of other employment. Some of the other young men did the same ; two of them went to sea as ship's carpenters, and another married and turned out a confirmed drunkard, and a prize-fighter. As regards myself, I went to Newcastle, where I got employment as a millwright, at the erection of a saw-mill in the Close. Here I worked for a few weeks, where I made the acquaintance of a young man named David Hogg, from Tweedmouth. Hogg was about my own age, a very powerful man, and good-looking. He was a good workman, and had more experience in that description of work than myself. At the saw-mill we had 20s. per week, but a gentleman from Sunderland, of the name of Norval, who wanted hands to go to Bedlington, engaged us at 24s. per week, and we accordingly left Newcastle and went to Bedlington, where I spent the summer very agreeably.

Here I first met my future wife, who then lived with Mrs. Barker, an elderly lady, to whom she was much attached, and from whose house she was married five years afterwards. I was then in the vigour of youth, I had a good wage, few cares, and was alive to every impression. In a word, all nature smiled around me. I was happy, and in love with the world and all mankind. With these feelings I was more inclined to gaieties than study, and although I kept up my reading by subscribing to a circulating library at Morpeth, I must admit I did not read with the same assiduity as I did at Percy Main. The summer evenings were generally spent in short excursions into the country; I became the leader in a Discussion Society, and patronised the players. The manager, Mr. Brady, was very poor, which caused me to exert myself to procure him a house, and occasionally to assist behind the scenes. Another way of assisting Brady was to induce Mr. William Waddle, the poet of Plessey,[1] to recite some of his pieces. The poet liked his drink, and on the nights of representation we seldom failed to give him as much as would steady his nerves and enable him to go through his part with *éclat*. Unfortunately Willie did not always suit the action to the word; but that was of little consequence, as his friends were always ready, by way of encouragement, to come down with a shower of plaudits, calculated to please the performer, but not always successful in concealing the defects of the performance.

The whole summer was passed over in this manner, and what with these amusements, and occasional visits to Mrs. Barker's, I spent one of the most agreeable half-years of my life. Mrs. Fairbairn's maiden name was Dorothy Mar, the youngest daughter of Mr. John Mar, a respectable burgess of Morpeth, who had for many years occupied a farm on the Wansbeck, which went by the name of Mar's Banks. To these banks I used to resort as a sort of pilgrimage, to contemplate the spot which had formerly been the residence and playground of the object of my affections. In this and many other things I entertained wild and romantic notions, and my reveries on these occasions were such as to form ideal plans, build castles in the air, and picture to myself a paradise, in which my imagination realised all the forms of domestic happiness and many enjoyments which I promised myself in our little house. It was to have a neat parlour, every corner filled with books, and I painted my smiling wife, with a couple of pledges of our mutual love, as prominent objects in the foreground, to give force and colouring to the picture.

How exceedingly vain and proud I was of my future habitation and its inmates—which, considered merely as a dream, was not without its influence upon my future fortunes. The impression that I must have such a retreat, with such a wife, never forsook me; and I never lost sight of these charming objects, first

[1] Waddle had published a small volume of Poems, in imitation of Burns, so much in vogue at that time.

traced in imagination on the banks of the Wansbeck, and after-wards realised by perseverance elsewhere.

It is stated by one of the ancient sages that ' there is nothing new under the sun,' and with equal propriety I may observe that there is nothing permanent, as the month of November, which generally deprives nature of its gayest attire, also changed the aspect of my affairs. The works at Bedlington were finished, and, as was frequently the case in the North, I was thrown out of employment with a very distant hope of obtaining another situation during the winter. Business was flat, and work scarce, and no other prospect appearing but a dreary winter before me, I carried into execution a long-projected plan of leaving that part of the country to try my fortunes in some other district, where the chances and facilities for advancement were greater than appeared to exist at New-castle. Impressed with this resolution, I took leave of Miss Mar, after an interchange of promises of unalterable affection, and with half-a-dozen new shirts, a new suit of clothes, a watch, and four pounds in my pocket, I embarked on board a collier, on December 11, 1811, at North Shields, for the metropolis. This may be considered as another epoch in my history.

The war with France, and our great naval victories, had drained the coasting trade of its able-bodied seamen to such an extent that the collier ships from Shields and Sunderland were left almost destitute of men. The result of this reduction proved seriously injurious to the service, as every winter during the war increased the number of wrecks, and many lives were lost for want of hands to work the ships. In the ship in which I had taken a passage (with my old friend and companion Hogg, who agreed to accompany me), there were only three old men, with the captain, the mate, and three boys; altogether they num-bered eight hands, whereas, in the midst of winter, twelve was the complement. Under these circumstances, we were no sooner at sea than I had to render assistance throughout the voyage, and to work like any of the sailors to keep the ship afloat. Hogg should have done the same, but he was prostrated with sea-sickness, and never showed face above deck but once during the twelve days which elapsed before we reached the Nore. It would be endless to recount the difficulties we had to encounter in a ship sunk to a few inches from the deck, badly manned, with a strong gale from the north-east which lasted for nearly a week. The vessel rolled like a tub, with the sea sweeping the decks in every direction, and for nearly eight days we were constantly drenched with water. One night, when at anchor in the Swin,[1] and riding out the gale till daylight, the ship dragged her anchors, and we had the greatest difficulty to bring her up and prevent her drifting on the breakers which were close upon our stern. We, however, succeeded, through the exertions of the mate, the captain being unfortunately in that state which rendered his services of little value. Two days more and we reached the Nore, and I shall never forget the sensations I felt when I passed close to the North Fleet, in all the pomp and splendour of an armament which had proved invincible, the only drawback to its beauty being the sight of one of the seamen undergoing the punishment of being flogged.

In working up the river to Gravesend, Woolwich, and Black-wall Reach, where we anchored, I was deeply interested in everything I saw, and here my reading became useful, as I had made myself acquainted with Gravesend, Tilbury Fort, the Woolwich Docks, and all the places of historical interest on the Thames ; for to a foreigner, or even to a native who has never before visited the capital, by far the most imposing approach is by the river.

We arrived at Blackwall early in the afternoon, and towards dusk the captain, who was anxious to save a tide, made preparations for walking up to Wapping ; and conceiving there would be no objection, I asked permission to accompany him, to which, after some hesitation, he consented. We accordingly started through Blackwall, and along the road to the West India Docks, but I soon found, as we went along, that the captain had been making free with the bottle before he started, and instead of making his way through Limehouse, we sauntered through the upper streets of Shadwell in the direction of Stepney Church or Whitechapel. It was in vain that I remonstrated with him, and told him I was sure we were leaving the river ; he persisted

---

[1] Merchantmen at that time had to take the inner and more dangerous channel between the sands, on account of the number of privateers hovering about the coast and the outer channel.

that I knew nothing about it ; until, at last, I made enquiries, and found to my mortification that we were wandering in a totally wrong direction. Laying hold of my companion, I dragged him along, till we at length reached our destination, two hours too late for delivering the papers. The captain, however, ordered supper, and after supper followed large potations of spirits and water, until the evening wore late, when the captain, after repeated applications, at last consented to return to Blackwall. We accordingly sallied forth, but were again brought to anchor in a pot-house up a narrow lane, where there was a tremendous noise of screaming, singing, and dancing. I refused to enter this den, and left him with the intention of making my way to the ship. It was now twelve o'clock, and finding no chance of reaching Blackwall, I enquired of the watchman where I could obtain a lodging for the night. He walked with me to a house in a narrow street, where I got a bed, and was soon in a profound sleep, which continued till morning. At break of day I was suddenly awakened by a loud noise in the street, and having hastily dressed, I found that some persons had been murdered in a house the next door, or next but one—I forget which—to where I had slept. After paying the landlord I went into the street, but the crowd was so great that I could not reach the door. I found I was in a street called New Gravel Lane, and that a whole family of the name of Williamson (who also kept a public-house), including the servant girl, had been murdered during the night. These acts of violence, and a similar murder which had taken place a fortnight before on a family of the name of Mar, in Ratcliffe Highway, gave me a most unfavourable impression of London ; I even began to doubt my own safety, and having made the best of my way back again to the ship, I entered on board with feelings of thankfulness for my escape.

On my arrival at Blackwall I found the captain had not made his appearance, and the ship, which should have moved up to the Pool by the morning tide, was left at anchor, the mate declining to take the responsibility during the absence of his superior. At two, the skipper made his appearance, having, as I afterwards found, been charged before the Police magistrate with disorderly conduct during the night. Thus occurred my first entrance into London, which we reached in safety on the following day.

After settling for the passage, and bidding adieu to the captain (without much regret), Hogg and I took a lodging in a garret in Duke's Court, St. Martin's Lane, until we could obtain employment. We counted our money, and found that Hogg had 3*l*. and some odd shillings left, and I had 2*l*. 7*s*. 6*d*., together about 6*l*., to provide for our lodging and maintenance till we could obtain work. Hogg had some friends ; a brother, Mr. Wm. Hogg, and a sister, Mrs. Brown, living in Burr Street, where St. Catherine's Dock now stands. I had no friends but a cousin of my mother's, who was married to Mr. Stewart, a joiner and builder, and lived in St. Martin's Lane. To them I applied for advice, and they recommended the lodging in Duke's Court, of which we took immediate possession.

In London we found things totally different from what we had been accustomed to in the country. Provisions and fuel were exceedingly dear, a keen frost had set in, and, living close to the tiles, we found our quarters exceedingly cold and dis- agreeable. We further discovered that unless we used the most rigid economy there was no chance of our money lasting above a fortnight or three weeks. We had to purchase everything, even to a bundle of chips for lighting the fire, and the girl whose duty it was to wait upon us, finding it not likely to be a profitable employment, left us to our own resources, and forced us to perform the various duties of housemaid, and others of an equally onerous description. The landlord, who was a tailor, appeared to encourage the slut ; but we subsequently revenged ourselves in a way he little expected.

Having fixed our residence, we started the next morning in search of work, and the first person we applied to was the late Mr. Rennie, at Blackfriars Bridge.[1] Mr. Rennie at that time had just commenced the building of the Waterloo Bridge, and so highly was he spoken of, both as an engineer and a mill- wright, that amongst the workmen he went by the name of the

---

[1] *i. e.* At his manufactory near Blackfriars. See *ante*, p. 35. The present Messrs. Rennie tell me that the tradition of this application has remained in their establishment, and that the room was identified in which the inter- view took place.—ED.

'almighty Rennie.' I was most anxious to see the great engineer, and accordingly we went there direct. It was arranged that I should be the spokesman, and having enquired for Mr. Rennie, we were admitted to the office, where we found him seated at a desk, with a small model in his hands. After we had stated the object of our visit, he enquired where we came from, what description of work we had been accustomed to, and the reason of our leaving Newcastle at that inclement season of the year. To these enquiries we replied that we had no alternative, there was nothing doing at Newcastle, and we had come to try our fortune in London. After a strict examination he desired us to go to Walker (the foreman), and he would give us work. With light hearts, and grateful acknowledgments, we proceeded in search of Mr. Walker, who informed us that we might commence on the following Monday ; but, he said, ' You will have to see the Millwrights' Society (a body who monopolised the right of determining who should be employed in that and other shops in London) before you can start work.'

Mr. Walker desired us to call at the club-house, and we should receive all the necessary information for our admission. We accordingly waited upon the secretary, who informed us that a general meeting of the members would be held on the first Tuesday of the following month, when our claims would be taken into consideration, but not before. This was a damper to our hopes, as the last monthly meeting had taken place only two days before, and the question now was, how we were to live on 5l. for that length of time ? There was, however, no alternative.

Having ascertained the terms of admission, and other facts connected with this most important body, we returned to Duke's Court, and starved ourselves for a month, and what with the cold garret, empty stomachs, and sharp appetites, we spent one of the most uncomfortable months of our existence. It is true we made up for our six meagre days by a capital dinner on Sundays, as I always had an invitation at St. Martin's Lane. Hogg went to his brother's, whilst I was creating the greatest alarm in the mind of Mrs. Stewart as to my powers of digestion, which she was afraid would suffer by what, good woman, she considered a dangerous habit. I entertained no fears of this sort.

Our scanty meals were not worse than the cold which we suffered at the top of the house. We slept two in a bed—one of Goldsmith's—'A bed by night, a chest of drawers by day;' and this was fortunate for our comfort, as we never could have escaped being frost-bitten but for the natural warmth which we imparted to each other. Fuel was so dear that we collected papers from every bill-holder that we passed in the streets, in order to save the expense of the matches we had to buy for lighting the fire. We carried on this practice for some time, till one day, rummaging under a back-stair that led to the roof, and where we kept our coals, I run my hand against some pieces of wood, which we found to be an old bedstead; and to square accounts with the tailor and his daughter, we set to work and slit up every bit of it except the beech posts, which we could not accomplish with the knife. When half of the curtain-frame was demolished we got alarmed, and the following ten days kept us in misery for fear the landlord might want his bed, and find it cut up. To prevent discovery, however, we purchased a bundle of lighters, which we took care to exhibit every morning in passing through the shop, and we were fortunate in making our escape before the bed was wanted.

At the end of the month the two men presented themselves again before the junta of the Millwrights' Society; but from some informality in their qualifications (in regard to the nature of which the autobiography is obscure, and appears somewhat inconsistent,) their claims were rejected, and they were refused permission to work for Mr. Rennie.

The narrative continues :—

Having made sure of obtaining employment, we had given up our lodgings in Duke's Court, and had deposited our clothes with Mrs. Stewart in St. Martin's Lane; we were therefore free from incumbrance; and having called on Mrs. Brown, where we slept on the carpet, we started before daylight next day for the country, and taking the north road, travelled as far as Hertford, through rain and sleet, and over roads nearly impassable. We reached Hertford wet to the skin, without food, and with only thirteen pence in our pockets.

At this town we were directed to a master millwright who wanted hands ; but we found that he had only a prospect of obtaining a new mill to build as soon as the days were a little longer. I told him how we had been treated in London, that our funds were exhausted, and that we should be glad of even two or three days' work. He appeared interested in our story, said we were two nice young men, and offered us half-a-crown to help us on our way. At this kind offer my pride took alarm, and though we were without money, and almost fainting for want of food, very much to the annoyance of Hogg, who pressed hard in whispers for me to take it, I peremptorily refused the half-crown, and whilst passing through the churchyard, Hogg seated himself on a wet tombstone, burst into tears, and obstinately refused to move an inch further. I used every endeavour to pacify him, but the only reply was a cutting remonstrance at my having refused to accept the money. I sat down beside him, and the weather having in some degree cleared up, the sun burst from under a dark cloud, and seizing the occasion, I remarked that we were perfectly safe, as the beams of the setting sun thus bursting upon us were a sure omen of our ultimate success. We moved on at a slow pace towards the outskirts of the town, and had not proceeded far, when arriving at a wheelwright's shop I stopped to enquire if he knew of any place where we could obtain employment. The master entered freely into conversation, and after some further enquiries he recommended us to make the best of our way to Cheshunt, about ten miles off, where a person from Chelmsford was building a windmill, and was, he believed, in want of hands.

With renewed hopes we moved on at a rapid pace, almost ankle-deep in melted snow, till we reached Cheshunt, nearly exhausted with hunger and fatigue. We took up our quarters at a little public-house, and on the faith of more encouragement for the morning, I had promised my friend that he should have an excellent supper, whether it was paid for or not. Accordingly, as soon as we were seated, the landlady, a good-tempered middle-aged woman, laid before us the remains of a cold leg of mutton, a large loaf, and a quart of ale. Nearly the whole disappeared to the bare bone before she returned from some domestic duties she had to attend to in another part

of the house ; when, casting her eyes on the table, she ex-
claimed, in a good-natured tone, 'Bless your hearts, but you
must have been hungry.' We smiled in the affirmative, on
which she handed out the cheese, with which we finished our
repast, and then retired to rest. Early next morning we presented ourselves at the mill, and to our great joy procured
employment for a fortnight. During that time we remained
inmates with our kind friend, the landlady of the Black Bull.

Our engagement being temporary, we received our wages
at the expiration of the time, and with nearly three pounds in
our pockets, were again on the road. We parted reluctantly
from our kind friend at the Black Bull, and directing our
steps towards London, we had time to consult as to our next
movements, when, after some deliberation, we concluded to try
London once more, and if unsuccessful there, to proceed forwards to Portsmouth, where we proposed to embark on board
some ship, and work our passage to America. Our second entry
into the metropolis was, however, more fortunate than the first ;
as my friend David met an old shopmate and schoolfellow from
Coldstream, who ridiculed our ignorance of the trade and the
ways of the town. He told us he had been only eighteen ·
months in London, had only served three years to the business,
had good employment at seven shillings a day, and made from
nine to ten days in the week. Moreover, he was secretary to
the Independent Millwrights' Society, — 'a society,' as he
stated, 'founded on liberal principles, and greatly superior to
the vagabonds at Little Eastcheap.'

From this man, whose name was Dewer, we learned that
there were three Societies in London, viz., the old Society, the
one at which we had been rejected ; next, the new Society, and
lastly, the Independent Society, who were less stringent in
their rules than the other two. All of them, however, took
cognizance of the hours of labour, which at that time were from
light to dark in winter, and from six to six in summer, with
two hours for refreshment. They also regulated the rate of
wages, and no man was allowed to work for less than seven
shillings a day, and as soon as he entered the Society he was
bound by the rules to maintain the rights and privileges of the
trade in their full integrity. This system of dictation and ex-

clusiveness was kept up in London for the whole of the last and part of the present century by a body of men, most of whom had never served any time to their business, and whose moral character was far from exemplary. The natural result of such a combination was to create disgust in the minds of their employers, and to raise a powerful opposition amongst a class equally meritorious as workmen, and infinitely superior in moral worth. From their excesses, and from the unwarrantable demands. made by the Societies on the employers and the employed, the clubs in London may date the decline of their power, and the almost ultimate extinction of the name of mill-wright as a distinct profession. Previously to that time it was held in great respect in almost every part of the United Kingdom. The members were generally men of talent, and ranked amongst them the celebrated names of Brindley, Smeaton, and Rennie.

To return, Dewer moved our admission as members of the Independent Society. This was accordingly done, and two days afterwards we were enrolled as members. Having been thus legalised, we shortly afterwards got employment at a Patent Ropery belonging to a Mr. Grundy at Shad-well, where both Hogg and I continued till the completion of the works, about eighteen months after we commenced. At the close of Mr. Grundy's work, I went for a few weeks to Wandsworth, and then to Mr. Penn, of Greenwich, where I con-tinued till the spring of 1813, when business became slack, and I left the great metropolis in search of information and employment in another quarter.

I cannot pass over two years of the most important period of my life without referring to the pleasures and advantages which I derived from my residence in London. During the greater portion of the time I had constant employment, and an income which varied from two to three pounds a week. I lived moderately, renewed my.reading and studies, and subscribed to a library in Ratcliffe Highway, where I had a moderately good choice of books. I further got acquainted with some friends at the West End, attended the theatres once or twice a week, visited the Westminster Forum, and heard Major Cartwright and Gale Jones declaim. In a word *my hat covered my family,* and I had never before been so happy or so independent.

During the whole of my residence in London I seldom missed dining on the Sundays with my relatives in St. Martin's Lane.   They had a small shop in front, and a workshop behind. The first floor was the family residence, and a clergyman of the name of Hall occupied the chambers above.   Mr. Hall was a regular Sunday guest at Mrs. Stewart's table, as well as myself; he was a great projector, had taken out a patent for making hemp from beanstalks, and was a writer in ' Tilloch's Philosophical Magazine,' and in several other periodicals of the day. He was a native of Perth, eccentric in his manners, somewhat loose in his religious principles, but a powerful reasoner, and intimately acquainted with most of the literary and scientific men of the day.   Through Mr. Hall I was introduced to the Society of Arts, to Mr. Tilloch, and to several distinguished persons, and the advantages which I derived from this connection were greater than I could have expected, considering the position in which I was placed as a common workman.

CHAPTER VI.

FURTHER EMPLOYMENT

MARRIAGE AND SETTLEMENT IN MANCHESTER

AGE 24–28

1813—1817

CHAPTER VI.

Mr. Fairbairn continues :—

For some time before the termination of my engagement at the Patent Ropery, I had frequent conversations with Mr. Hall on agriculture and spade husbandry. He had written an essay on this latter subject, describing its superior advantages; and it had occurred to him that a machine might be made which, if worked by steam, would answer all the purposes of digging by hand. To this scheme I saw many objections; but, like all men of a sanguine disposition and a speculative turn of mind, he overruled them; and after many persuasions I was at last induced to make a model of the machine; it being left to me to devise the means and arrange the parts according to my own judgment. It was finally agreed that we should bear equal shares in the expense of the model. He was to write a paper in our joint names for the Society of Arts, and in case it should prove successful we were to take out a patent, and make our fortunes. Such were the inducements held out to me by my speculative friend. The model was accordingly made, and along with it a miniature field of sand, wherein it was to dig. This model showed some ingenuity in its structure, and rolled along upon a movable tramway, with three spades worked by cranks on one side, which enabled the machine to move on the unbroken portion of the field, while it left the portion dug up perfectly open to the action of the atmosphere as it left the spades. The machine was exhibited before the Duke of Norfolk, then President of the Society of Arts, but it met with considerable opposition from some of the council; both Mr. Hall and I defended it, but unsuccessfully, as the argument was against us, and objections were raised which on mature consideration I found it difficult to combat.

H

The objections raised against the principle, as well as the practical application of the machine, confirmed my previous doubts ; but not so with Mr. Hall, who maintained a contrary opinion, and insisted on exhibiting the model to the Board of Agriculture, whose practical experience would enable them to discover its merits, and recommend its application. I was, however, sufficiently convinced of its inutility, and declined any further interference. It was subsequently sent to the Board of Agriculture, and for anything I know to the contrary, may be still found amongst the relics of that institution.

The construction of this machine, and the want of employment, made a serious inroad upon my funds. I had saved upwards of 20*l*., but it all went in the purchase of materials and labour ; and on application to Mr. Hall for his share of the expenses, I found he was in no better condition than myself ; and therefore I made an agreement with a pork-butcher in Tottenham Court Road to make him for 33*l*. a machine for chopping meat for sausages.

This machine was constructed with a fly-wheel and a double crank and connecting rods on each side, which worked a cross head, containing a dozen knives crossing each other at right angles, enabling them thus to mince or divide the meat on a revolving block. The machine did its work admirably, and I had reason to be proud of it, as it was the first order I had on my own account.[1]

The pork butcher paid me handsomely for the machine, and finding no chance of obtaining any more work in London for some time, I resolved to make a tour in the south of England, and with 7*l*. in my pocket I took an outside place, on the evening of April 13, 1813, for Bath. It was a keen frost

---

[1] I should here mention that the chopping-machine was only part of the apparatus ; there was also an iron cylinder which turned upon centres like the trunnions of a gun, filled with the minced meat, and having a conical end with a tube, on which the tripe was drawn ready for filling. At the other end was a piston worked by a rack and pinion, which pressing upon the meat in the cylinder discharged the sausages from the tube, well filled, in lengths from six to eight feet. The pumping process completed the operation, excepting only tying them into lengths, which was afterwards done by girls, the sausages being hung up in the shape of chains with round links.

when the coach started from the Golden Cross, and we had scarcely crossed Hounslow Heath when a fall of snow came on, and being thinly clad, without a great-coat, I suffered dreadfully from cold during the night. We, however, reached Bath at seven the next morning, when a good washing and a warm breakfast completely restored me.

At Bath I found myself quite at home, as I had read the whole of Smollett's works and Fielding's ' Tom Jones.' I remembered the Pump Room, and the famous Master of the Ceremonies of a former period, Beau Nash, and entered into all the reminiscences of those days, and made myself familiar with all the haunts of the town. I went to the theatre to hear Incledon sing in the opera of the ' Lord of the Manor,' and on the following morning, Sunday, I entered a sedan-chair, and directed two Welshmen to carry me to the Pump Room. I would not have incurred this unnecessary expense, but I had two reasons for doing so ; namely, to ascertain the motion of a sedan, and to make myself sure of admission to the rooms. As regards the latter, it was superfluous, and so far as respects the former I should have been much better on my feet.

In the afternoon I went to Frome on a pilgrimage to the shrine of Molly, immortalised in ' Tom Jones,' who with a thigh-bone from a new-made grave exerted her powers with such effect amongst the rustics of Somersetshire. These visits occupied a period of three days; and on the Monday following I commenced work at Bathgate, where I remained six weeks, and then moved on—always on foot—to Bradford and Trowbridge. Then making a rapid detour to the south I returned by the nearest route to Bristol. Here I remained a few days to look at the town, and then moving onwards I visited South Wales, spent a few days at Newport and Cardiff, and having inspected the cathedral at Llandaff, I sailed on the following day in a small sloop bound for Dublin, where I arrived after a voyage of four days.

My entrance into Dublin was anything but propitious, as after paying the passage money I found my funds reduced to the small sum of three-halfpence. It was early in the morning when we arrived, and having wandered about the city for a whole day, I was at last compelled through hunger to exhaust the remains of my purse in the purchase of a roll and a few raisins, on which I breakfasted and dined during a promenade along Ormond's Quay. As the evening closed in I went in search of lodgings, and after some trouble I took up my quarters in a small house in a back street near St. Patrick's Cathedral. The following day was a holyday, and finding the people all in motion in the direction of the Phœnix Park, I joined the crowd, and after an hour's walk found myself in the presence of the Duke of Richmond, then Lord Lieutenant, at a grand review of all the troops in Dublin and the surrounding country. After the evolutions, great numbers adjourned to the tents, where I witnessed all the fun and amusements of an Irish fair, and what with whisky, rags, and rigmarole, the remainder of the day, and if I mistake not the greater part of the night, were spent in a medley of singing, dancing, fighting, and drinking. I could not, however, afford to be present during the whole of the revelry, and having no inclination to join in the mêlée which was fast approaching, I returned to my quarters at Pat Kearney's, where I supped on potatoes and cold beef, and went to bed.

Next morning I went in search of employment, and after several applications I at last succeeded in making an engagement with Mr. Robinson, of the Phœnix Foundry, to make a new set of patterns for some nail machinery, which he was then introducing into Dublin. These machines had been tried in Birmingham, and were found to answer for some purposes, but the nails proved defective in ductility, and were liable to break when the points were ' clinked,' or bent round upon the board. In other respects they were found, after being carefully annealed, to succeed much better, particularly for sprigs and flooring nails. The construction of these machines occupied the whole of the summer, and gave me an opportunity of becoming acquainted with Irish character.

At the lodgings which I occupied at a cottage behind the barracks, I became acquainted with a young man of the name of Meagher. He was a native of Kilkenny, had received a liberal education, and with his assistance I endeavoured to improve myself by reading some of the best authors and discussing the style as well as the subject-matter of the writers. Meagher was an excellent grammarian and an able declaimer; he had words at command, and I was often lost in admiration at the facility with which he could embody his ideas in the choicest language, and convey them to the minds of his hearers in the most pleasing and agreeable form. He was never at a loss, and from what I could learn of his history he had been educated for the bar, but the poverty of his family had deprived him of the means of completing his studies, and he was ultimately compelled to leave college and take the humble situation of an usher.

In the month of October I finished the nail machines, and after taking an affectionate leave of my friend and fellow-lodger, whom I never afterwards heard of, I embarked on board one of the packets for Liverpool. The passage from Dublin to Liverpool occupied two days, which we considered a good passage, as there had been instances when the packets were a week on the voyage. The same distance is now accomplished in ten or eleven hours.

In Liverpool I remained only two days to look at the town, and then proceeded by coach to Manchester, where I conceived a much wider field was open for the exercise of my profession. In this conception I was not mistaken, for I soon got employment with Mr. Adam Parkinson, with whom I remained for above two years. I was in my twenty-fourth year when I entered Manchester, and being employed at a short distance in the country, I resumed my studies, chiefly in History, Natural Philosophy, the first books of Euclid, and Algebra. In the three first I made some progress, but the last I found difficult, and ultimately I had to give it up.

Shortly after my arrival in Manchester I caught the scarlet fever, which laid me up for the whole of the winter. It was during the great frost of 1813-14, and it was the end of February before I was able to leave the house and take short walks, which at first did not exceed fifty yards : they gradually extended as I gathered strength, until I was able to walk out every day, when I rapidly recovered.

During my illness I was frequently visited by Mr. James Houtson, the foreman of the works, whose kindness of heart and hospitality made him everywhere loved and respected. To

Mr. Houtson and his family I was indebted for many acts of kindness; I spent many happy hours in his house, and retained till the day of his death a liberal share in his friendship.

Part of Mr. Houtson's house was occupied by his brother, Mr. John Houtson, whose unfortunate history was full of events of considerable interest. He was a native of Lawder, in Rox-burghshire. He left his native place when young, and settled in Manchester, first as an assistant in a mercantile house, and subsequently as a master for himself. In Scotland he had exercised the profession of a schoolmaster, whereby he had acquired a taste for reading; and having a good address, his society was agreeable, and much sought after by his friends and acquaintance. He had a taste for poetry and for literary pur-suits, and was in acquirements above his position in life.

His career as a merchant was abruptly terminated. As already mentioned, he commenced business as a spinner and manufacturer, but with borrowed money, which not being equal to his demands, he took to the bill system, on which he subsisted for a few years, but at last became bank-rupt. After winding up his affairs and paying ten or twelve shillings in the pound, he engaged to go out with some gentle-men to the island of Fernando Po, to found a colony there, and to restore his fortune by trading in ivory and gold-dust along the African coast. For a few years he was employed in this trade, but the colony turned out a failure; and having made the acquaintance of Belzoni, the celebrated traveller, he joined the expedition into the interior, where one after another the party fell victims to disease. He was the last man to close the eyes of Belzoni, and after great suffering reached the coast with life, but with a broken constitution. He brought a ring and the dying wishes of the great traveller to his wife, and took his passage to Ava, where he died a few days after his arrival.

His letters, some of which I read, describing the expedition, were valuable as illustrative of some of the most trying scenes and stirring incidents of the expedition; and one or two of them, giving an account of Belzoni's death, were published in the papers of the day. But they have never been collected in a separate form.

At Mr. Houtson's house used to assemble a party of kindred

spirits, and on Sunday, and sometimes on Saturday evening, I used to make one of the party. These meetings were partly of an instructive and partly of a convivial character. The first part of the evening was generally appropriated to literary discussions, but after supper they often ended in singing, or some other genial amusement. Amongst the number who met on these occasions was the late Dr. Hardie, an eminent physician, and another of the party was 'Mr. Leo Schuster, who afterwards became a well-known successful merchant.

I remained two years with Mr. Parkinson, and during that time I not only kept up my correspondence with Miss Mar, but I began to entertain thoughts of a settlement, and of making her my wife. Arrangements were made for the union as soon as a little money could be raised for the purpose of furnishing a small house.

With this view, I made a determination to work hard and spend little. This I steadfastly adhered to, and in less than twelve months I had deposited in the hands of my intended wife and banker upwards of 20*l.* On her side the same economy and industry were observed; and by the time I had finished some work in the country, of which I had the charge, I was master of nearly 30*l.*, the largest sum I had ever possessed.

My bachelor days in Manchester were fruitful of many benefits. I had some leisure for study, and made some progress in the first three books of Euclid. I also renewed my attempts on the violin, but in stringing it after an interval of more than twelve months, I found it had been seriously injured on the voyage from Dublin, and I had no alternative but to restore its broken tones by a new belly of the same material and construction as before. Having repaired the instrument, I still found it in good voice, but the power to give it expression was as bad as ever, and after some months' rubbing and scraping I was forced to content myself with the old tunes.

Another amusement in which I took great interest when residing in the country was watching the sports and peculiar habits of the labouring classes of the districts round Manchester. At that period they were fond of field-sports, such as trail hunts, following the hounds on foot, and other athletic exercises. Drinking and dancing in holyday times frequently led to quarrels and dangerous fights; but these evils have more lately been suppressed, and now the population of Lancashire may be said to be the best disposed, the most active and laborious people in the United Kingdom.

I was now able to direct my attention to the fulfilment of my engagement with Miss Mar. We were married at Bedlington on June 16, 1816, and after a few days' residence at Morpeth and Newcastle, we took our places on the coach for Manchester, where we arrived in a few days. The important event of a marriage, and the altered conditions and circumstances which it involves, are such as to open a new epoch in every man's history. It did so in mine; and the responsibilities which it involved operated as a powerful stimulus to carry into effect what I had long before contemplated, namely, an ardent desire to emancipate myself from daily labour, and to acquire that independence of position which I was most anxious to attain. My young wife was less ambitious, and she appeared content to labour with me in a quiet unostentatious manner; and I am persuaded her affection would have been more than equal to carry her through the numerous difficulties by which we were surrounded. With an income of only thirty shillings a week, I felt great reluctance to submit her to constant drudgery, and we began by taking lodgings at Macclesfield, where I was employed by the late Mr. T. C. Hewes. We spent several months in that town, and then removed to Manchester, where I took a small cottage of two rooms, and fitted it up in a style of neatness of which we were both of us justly proud. The first articles of furniture which came into the house were three oil paintings and three mahogany knife-cases, which I bought at a sale. These purchases appeared no better in the eyes of Mrs. Fairbairn than the bargain of the green spectacles made by Moses in the ' Vicar of Wakefield.' They were articles not for immediate use, but they looked handsome, the first on the walls, and the latter on a neat mahogany table. Shortly afterwards the pictures became, and have continued to be, the most favoured articles in the house, and they decorate the walls of my dining-room at the present moment.

By the early spring I had finished the works at Macclesfield, and returned in time to be at hand during Mrs. Fairbairn's confinement, which took place on March 30, 1817, when my daughter, afterwards Mrs. Bateman, was born. This event was one which nearly deprived Mrs. Fairbairn of life, and after remaining in the most critical state for ten or twelve days, she began to give indications of recovery from a state of the greatest exhaustion. In this state of affairs, the nurse, who had never left us from the commencement, accidentally set fire to the bed-curtains, which were instantly in a blaze, and both mother and child must have perished if I had not fortunately been in the house ready to render assistance. The screams of the nurse brought me in a moment to the rescue, when I found the bed in flames. It was the work of a moment to snatch both of them from the bed, and having laid them on the floor, I at last succeeded in extinguishing the flames by tearing off the burning curtains, after being severely scorched.

This unfortunate accident was a severe blow to us, and my wife's long and protracted illness, in addition to the expense incurred in furnishing the house, exhausted the whole of our funds. Many months passed before we surmounted the difficulties of this visitation. But my little daughter grew apace. Her mother, through the unwearied skill and attention of Mr. Ainsworth, an eminent surgeon, renewed her strength, and our little cottage was again in order. This was a year of trial, and it required more than ordinary care and economy to make both ends meet. We, however, kept out of debt, with the exception of 5l., which I borrowed from Mr. Chantry, of Macclesfield, during this long season of illness, and which was afterwards duly paid.

Manchester is divided from Salford by the river Irwell, over which there were at this time two good bridges, the one called the Old Bridge, and the other the New Bayley Bridge. Another wooden bridge, called Blackfriars, between these two, was so exceedingly inconvenient as to render a new one indispensable, and the authorities offered two premiums of 150l. and 100l. for the first and second best designs for a bridge calculated to meet a more extended traffic. I was then employed as a draughtsman by Mr. Hewes, and conceiving there could be no objection to my employing my leisure hours in preparing a design for this intended bridge, I set vigorously to work, and completed one of a single cast-iron arch before the time appointed for delivering the plans. Fearing, however, that Mr. Hewes might be similarly employed, I considered it my duty to show him the drawings, and to solicit his advice as to the expediency of giving them in. I repaired to his lodgings, and having communicated my intentions, he hastily replied that he could not advise me on such a subject without acting in a double capacity, as he was himself a candidate.

The affair of the bridge (which was ultimately built of stone) rendered my future residence with Mr. Hewes uncomfortable; and I consequently gave notice that I should resign my situation at the end of the following week. Disappointed in my hopes of rising in the profession so long as I continued as a workman, and having before me the prospect of an increasing family, I determined no longer to remain the servant of another, but by one bold effort to take an independent position in those departments of practical construction in which I conceived I had some chance of success. I had laboured for five years as a journeyman, and during that time I had acquired a considerable amount of practical knowledge, calculated to develop other resources than those to which my attention had hitherto been applied. I was never one of those who take notes, and keep a diary in which to record the construction of every machine, or to notice every event which occurred. I could never act the part of a copyist, and during the whole course of my professional career I never accomplished any improvement or any discovery of the least value if I attempted it by a slavish imitation of my predecessors. It would be presumptuous if by this declaration I attempted to assume a character for originality in my conceptions to which I may not be entitled; on the contrary, I must candidly admit that whatever improvements I have effected in practical science have originated in some useful hint which I have applied, when ruminating on the subject, for the purpose I wished to attain. Having once seized an idea, I never lost sight of it till the object in view was accomplished, or abandoned if proved on reflection to be unsound in principle. I believe this to be the case in almost every instance where great discoveries are made, and on a careful review of the workings of the mind it will be found that we are all indebted to impressions received from others for many of our most useful inventions. The examples of Franklin, Ferguson, and Watt were always before me, and though I laboured under great difficulties as regards education, and had little time at my disposal for study, nevertheless I so far imitated their example as to be able to go on cheerfully and enthusiastically in my endeavours to be useful and my determination to excel.

CHAPTER VII.

COMMENCEMENT OF BUSINESS IN MANCHESTER SUCCESSFUL ESTABLISHMENT OF MANUFACTURING WORKS

AGE 28–34

1817—1823

DETERMINATION TO SET UP FOR HIMSELF IN BUSINESS—FIRST
ORDER UNDERTAKEN—PARTNERSHIP WITH LILLIE—PATENT CLAIM—
DIFFICULTIES AND DISCOURAGEMENTS—SMALL ORDERS—THE IRISHMAN
AS A MOTIVE POWER—MR. MURRAY—ORDER TO REARRANGE HIS MILL
MACHINERY—THE POVERTY OF THE LAND—NATURE OF THE ALTERA-
TIONS—DEFECTS OBSERVED AND IMPROVEMENTS INTRODUCED—THEIR
IMPORTANCE AND SUCCESS—REPAIRS ON SUNDAYS ABOLISHED—NEW
MILL FOR M'CONNEL AND KENNEDY—REMINISCENCES OF MURDOCH,
OF SOHO—RISING FAME OF THE NEW FIRM OF FAIRBAIRN AND LILLIE
—INCREASE OF THE MANUFACTURING ESTABLISHMENT—CONSTANT
OCCUPATION.

CHAPTER VII.

Mr. Fairbairn now describes his successful start in business as a manufacturing engineer :—

My retirement from the service of Mr. Hewes took place in November 1817, at a time when business was slack, and when I could ill afford to be idle even for a single day. Having, however, made up my mind to make an attempt at something better than a weekly wage, I went over to Messrs. Otho Hulme and Sons, at Clayton, near Manchester, for whom I had erected some printing machinery whilst I was with Mr. Parkinson, to consult Mr. J. Hulme, the active partner, what was best to be done. At that time there appeared no chance of obtaining orders for millwork, but he made me the offer to construct an iron conservatory which he proposed erecting in the garden. I gladly accepted the offer, and having prepared the drawings, which were approved, I looked round for some clever, active person as a partner to join me in the undertaking. This partner I found in an old shopmate, Mr. James Lillie, to whom I communicated my intentions, and asked him to join me. After some hesitation, he consented; and we commenced a few days afterwards as coadjutors for the construction of the hothouse; and thus arose a connection which lasted for fifteen years.

In a few weeks the patterns were made, and we had just commenced casting, when the whole of our operations were stopped by a letter from Birmingham giving notice of the infringement of a patent which the writer said belonged to himself. This interdict and the threats which were held out closed our connection with Mr. Hulme, and I was again thrown upon the world without resources and without money. Mr. Lillie, who was no better off in this respect than I myself, after some fruitless attempts to get work, expressed a wish to retire, and advised me to abandon what he conceived could not be accomplished.   I however had made up my mind to persevere, and notwithstanding a fortnight's suffering from insufficient food, I urged him to be firm, as I had made up my mind never again to work as a journeyman.   This determination, and an offer to allow him to withdraw if he did not like the connection, decided the question, and he renewed his promise either to succeed, or remain with me to the last.   This determination increased our energy and gave us fresh vigour.   We redoubled our exertions, issued printed cards announcing our intentions, and made a complete tour amongst the manufacturers of Manchester and the neighbourhood.   Amongst others, I called on Messrs. Adam and George Murray, the extensive cotton-spinners, and taking with me the designs of the bridge, I showed them to Mr. Murray, and requested to know if we could be of service to him in the erection of any millwork he might require.   Mr. Murray received me kindly, and after looking at the drawings, desired I would call on the following day, and bring my partner with me.

In the interval since the stoppage of our work at Mr. Hulme's, we had, however, got small orders for the erection of a callender in Cannon Street, and a calico-polishing machine in Shakespeare Street.   These were small jobs, but sufficient to enable us to make a lathe ; and having hired a miserable shed for about twelve shillings a week, we erected the lathe, and with the assistance of James Murphy, a muscular Irishman, we contrived to turn and finish the whole of our work in a very creditable manner.   At that time, 1817, even Manchester did not boast of many lathes or tools, except small ones in the machine shops ; ours was of considerable dimensions, and capable of turning shafts of from 3 to 6 inches diameter.   For two years afterwards this lathe did the whole of our turning work.

According to appointment, we waited on Mr. Murray, and having stated to him the objects we had in view, he took us through the mill, and asked if we could renew, with horizontal cross-shafts, the whole of his millwork that turned the mule spinning.   We gladly agreed ; but before any contract was made, he stipulated that the work must be well done, and said that he would visit our shop on the following day, and judge for himself as to the means we had at command for the attainment of that object.

This proposition was anything but encouraging, as both of us were aware of the ' poverty of the land,' and the risk we should incur by such an exhibition. There was, however, no alternative ; come he would, and immediately on our return we set to work to put the ' house in order ' for his reception. On the following day he came punctually to the time, and after looking round he observed that there was no approach but through an entry about four feet wide, and that having only one tool we should never be able to execute a work of such magnitude. We earnestly assured him to the contrary; and having made an agreement with him, we commenced, with glad hearts and willing minds, what we considered our first and best order as men of business. One of the conditions was to execute the alterations without stopping the machinery, or only such portion as we might require for the time being. This we accomplished satisfactorily, and having worked from five in the morning till nine at night, we completed the order within the specified time, and in such a manner as to satisfy Mr. Murray and his friends.

The alterations effected in Mr. Murray's factory opened a new field for our exertions. Up to that time neither Mr. Lillie nor I were much acquainted with cotton-mills ; our previous employment had been chiefly confined to corn-mills, printing-works, and bleaching-works; and the operations of spinning being nearly new, we had everything to learn in that extensive department of our national industry. The alterations in Mr. Murray's mill gave us a great deal of insight into the business ; and as my department lay in the designs and erection of the work as sent out by Mr. Lillie from the shop, I had an opportunity of examining with care and attention the whole of the main-gearing, and the machinery of transmission to the remotest parts of the factory.

In my examination of Mr. Murray's mill, and others to which I had access, I thought I discovered great defects in the principle as well as in the construction of the millwork. All the cotton mills that I had seen were driven with large square shafts and wooden drums, some of them 4 feet in diameter. The main shafts seldom exceeded 40 revolutions per minute ;

I

and although the machinery varied in velocity from 100 up to 3,000 revolutions, the speeds were mostly got up by a series of straps and counter drums, which not only crowded the rooms, but seriously obstructed the light where most required, in the more delicate and refined operations of the different machines. This defect I mentioned to Mr. Lillie, and proposed that we should change the system by the introduction of lighter shafts at double or treble the velocity, and by using smaller drums to drive the machinery at the same speed. I instanced an argu-ment which I had had with a spinner, who contended that the straps would slip on small drums ; but I showed that the front wheels of a carriage, though much smaller than those behind, went over the same ground, and that the quick shafts and smaller drums would not only by their increased velocity do the same, but would do it with a great saving of power. Thoroughly convinced of this, we set to work ; and from that time we may date the revolution which followed, and our own prosperity as the leading millwrights of the district.

Another defect observed was in the construction of the shafts, and in the mode of fixing the couplings, which were con-stantly giving way, so that a week seldom passed without a break-down. For the first six years we could never calculate on the Sunday as a day of rest ; we were almost constantly em-ployed in repairs ; and when trade was good the loss of a single hour was an object when compared to the difference of cost in a Sunday's repair. Working on Sundays, and on the previous and following nights, had a most injurious effect on the morals and condition of that class to which I belonged. It debarred them from that association with their families, and that im-provement in the domestic circle to which this day of all others is most appropriate, particularly for the working man. The introduction of a new system of quick speeds and light shafts, accompanied with a greater degree of accuracy in the workman-ship, led to a change which gradually abolished work on Sundays.

The completion of Mr. Murray's order gave a new impetus to our business. Our exertions had not been lost upon him, for he immediately recommended us to the attention of Mr. John Kennedy, partner in the firm of Messrs. M'Connel and Ken-nedy, then the largest spinners in the kingdom. They were on the point of building a new mill, and owing to Mr. Murray's recommendation we found no difficulty in making arrangements with Mr. Kennedy.

I waited upon that gentleman, and followed his instructions with the utmost attention. I laid down all his plans for the new mill to a scale, calculated the proportions and strength of the parts, fixed the position and arrangement of the different machines, and introduced, under that gentleman's direction, a new system of double speeds, which, I believe, was an original invention of his own, for giving an increased quantity of twist to the finer description of mule yarn. The mule, as is well known, was the invention of Crompton; and it owes a great deal to Mr. Kennedy's improvements, particularly in those constructions exclusively adapted to the finer numbers. I shall have occasionally to speak of this gentleman in the course of the following narrative, and I feel greatly indebted to him for his early and continued friendship during his long and useful life.

The erection of M'Connel and Kennedy's new mill was a great step in advance; we had now become engineers and millwrights of some consequence, and the complete and satisfactory execution of the millwork established our characters as young men who were likely not only to do well, but also to introduce improvements in the construction of machinery, millwork, and the general mechanism of other branches of industry. Mr. Kennedy was fully aware of the advantages of these improvements, and he not only gave them full encouragement, but recommended us to all his friends. The results of these recommendations were a press of orders which poured in upon us from all sides, and an amount of work much greater than we could execute. Our means were but small; and although we had removed from the shed into an old building in Mather Street, immediately after the completion of Mr. Murray's work, we were nevertheless without a steam-engine, or any other power, except Murphy and three more assistants who turned the lathes, having added to the number since our removal from High Street. With the two first lathes, and a new and a larger one which we erected temporarily at Mr. Kennedy's mill for turning the large shafts, we completed the whole of the millwork in a satisfactory manner, both as regarded solidity and appearance.

It was during the progress of this work (in 1818) that I became acquainted with Mr. Murdoch, of Soho, a gentleman well known to science and to the public as the inventor of the D valve, the improver of the Cornish pumping-engine, and the author of illumination by carburetted hydrogen gas. Mr. Murdoch was at this time upwards of seventy years of age, tall and well-proportioned, with a most benevolent and intelligent expression of countenance. He was the oldest mechanical engineer of his day, and, exclusive of his discoveries in practical engineering, he contrived a variety of curious machines for compressing peat moss, when finely ground and pulverised, into the most beautiful medals, armlets, bracelets, and necklaces, which, under immense pressure, being stamped and brilliantly polished, had all the character and appearance of the finest marble. Mr. Murdoch was the right arm of the illustrious Watt, and greatly assisted him in his improvements of the steam-engine by ingenious contrivances for casting, boring, turning, and fitting the various parts. The steam-engine is, therefore, in no small degree indebted to the ingenuity and persevering exertions of Murdoch; as also to another eminent contemporary mechanical engineer, the late Matthew Murray, of Leeds, who was the first to set an example to Boulton and Watt themselves in that superior finish of the steam-engine which has now become general.

Mr. Murdoch, on the occasion referred to, came down to Manchester to start Mr. Kennedy's 54-horse-power engine, and during his week's residence there I had frequent opportunities of noticing the great intelligence which he evinced on almost every subject connected with his professional avocations. He was, like his friend Mr. Kennedy, full of anecdotes, and could relate all the old Scotch saws and sayings which used to be the delight and amusement of the people of those days. It was then the fashion to tell a good tale, and none could do it better than Mr. Murdoch and Mr. Kennedy.

The services which we had rendered, and the improvements which were introduced, caused us to be much talked of as good millwrights and ingenious young men. Our business increased, and a large cellar under a factory was added to the shop. I was designer, draughtsman, and book-keeper; and in order to meet all the requirements of the concern, and keep Mr. Lillie's department in the shop constantly going, I had to rise with the sun in the summer, and some hours before it in the winter, in order to make the entries and post the books before breakfast. For the remainder of the day I had either to draw out the work, or to ride fifteen or sixteen miles on a hired hack to consult with proprietors, take dimensions, and arrange the principle and plan on which the work was to be constructed. For many years I continued these exertions; and, like every other act of persevering industry, the result was a great economy, by saving the expense of clerks, draughtsmen, and all those supernumeraries which can only exist and can only be maintained in a large concern.

Four or five years passed in this manner; and, though we were always short of money, and had to work from hand to mouth, we were nevertheless in a prosperous way of business. Our tools were increasing in number; new patterns were made; and at the end of five years we found ourselves worth (in material, stock, and tools), a sum of 5,000*l.* It is true there was no ready money, but, having occasional assistance from Heywood's Bank, we ventured on the purchase of a 16-horse-power second-hand Boulton and Watt's steam engine, bought a small plot of land on chief rent, and erected a more convenient and commodious workshop. This was a bold undertaking, without a farthing of capital; but we had good friends and considerate customers; and we found no difficulty in obtaining money on account for work in hand and in progress of delivery. With this assistance, and the same continued activity, we struggled through; and in less than two years we found ourselves in possession of the new shop and steam-engine, without any considerable diminution in our funds.

It will be perceived that a constant and unremitting attention to business precluded all chance of continuing my studies, either by reading or other pursuits. My time was too much engaged to admit of a single hour of leisure; and the only consolation which I derived was the reflection that I had previously stored my mind with some useful knowledge, which I was now turning to good account.

CHAPTER VIII.

WATER-WHEELS AT CATRINE BANK
CONNECTION WITH ESCHER
JOURNEY TO THE CONTINENT AND WORK THERE

AGE 34-41

1824—1830

CHAPTER VIII.

THE Autobiography continues :—

Six years passed in this manner, each succeeding year adding to the general stock, when in 1824 we had a visit from Mr. Buchanan, of Catrine Bank, in Ayrshire, the partner of Kirkman Finlay, the then member for Glasgow. The object of his visit was to establish an entirely new arrangement of the water-power of the Catrine Cotton Works; and here again Mr. Kennedy was our friend and adviser. I had been recommended to Mr. Buchanan as a person well able to devise, plan, and execute the work; and after several meetings and conversations, I was engaged to visit Ayrshire and spend a fortnight at Catrine Bank.

This was an important undertaking. The mills were extensive, and the water-wheels and steam-engines then at work were estimated at between 200 and 300 horse-power.

The Catrine Cotton Works are situated on the banks of the river Ayr, about fifteen miles from the town of that name. The mills were built by the late Mr. Alexander, of Balochmyle, and were worked by him, I believe not very successfully. About 1795 they came into the hands of Messrs. James Finlay and Co., Kirkman Finlay being the leading partner of the firm, and Mr. Buchanan took charge of the new works at Catrine.

The machinery of the mills was driven by four water-wheels, erected by Mr. Lowe, of Nottingham. His work, heavy and clumsy as it was, had in a certain way answered the purpose, and as cotton-mills were then in their infancy he was the only person qualified from experience to undertake the construction of the gearing. Mr. Lowe was therefore in demand in every part of the kingdom where a cotton-factory had to be built.

The water-wheels at Catrine were ill-constructed, deficient in power, and constantly breaking down or getting out of repair. This was a grievous drawback at a time when trade was good, and to remedy the evil Mr. Buchanan erected two 40-horse-power steam-engines, which for some years kept the works going, but at a considerable sacrifice arising from repeated failures in the water-wheels. The evil at last became so great, that Mr. Buchanan and his partners in Glasgow came to the determination to pull them out, and remodel the whole of their motive power on an improved and more efficient principle. It was in this condition of the works that I was requested to make a journey to Scotland, and arrange matters with Mr. Buchanan for the changes and alterations contemplated.

In conformity with these views, I was soon on the road to Scotland, and having reached Catrine Bank the day after my departure from Manchester I was most kindly and hospitably received, and the next morning commenced a thorough and complete survey of the whole establishment. It was not long before I discovered the evils under which the concern had laboured, and I did not hesitate to recommend a concentration of the whole of the motive power, and that instead of dividing a fall of forty-seven feet into two, the two falls should be united on two powerful wheels, each fifty feet in diameter, and 120, collectively 240, horse-power. This was computed to be equal to the entire resistance of the machinery in all the mills, and by a proper form of bucket, and a judicious application of the water, they were considered amply sufficient to turn the whole of the then existing machinery without the aid of steam. In order, however, to provide for future contingencies and extension of the works, it was considered advisable to make provisions in the watercourses, tail run, and main gearing, for two more wheels of the same power and dimensions as those intended to be made, and thus to provide increased water-power in case of an increase of the machinery. Another inducement to these enlarged views was the existence of an extensive reservoir, which some years before had been constructed on the high grounds near Muirkirk, to regulate the quantity of water in the Ayr, and afford supplies in dry seasons.

Having arranged the preliminaries, I set to work; and in the course of a week I had the whole laid down to a scale, and in less than a month from that date the order was given, and the work was in progress at Manchester.

The construction of the Catrine wheels, apart from the profits arising from the transaction as a matter of business, was one of the most interesting and most gratifying circumstances I ever experienced in the whole of my professional career. My plans were approved, the prices proposed were accepted, and the works were completed in a manner highly satisfactory, not only to Mr. Buchanan and myself, but to every other person of the firm. The two first waterwheels were started in June 1827; they have never lost a day since that time, and they remain, even at the present day, probably the most perfect hydraulic machines of the kind in Europe. Mr. Buchanan was a true citizen of the world; noted for simplicity, benevolence, and goodness of heart. He was the poor man's friend, the good Samaritan, the father of his people. To these qualifications he united an excellent flow of spirits, an inexhaustible fund of anecdotes, and a dry broad humour that enlightened every countenance, and often kept the table in a roar. He was moreover well educated, a great reader, and possessed of an extraordinary budget of miscellaneous and useful information.

Simultaneously with the construction of the Catrine waterwheels, we had other works of importance to attend to; and as an instance I may here give an account of a journey which I made in the autumn of the year 1824 to Switzerland, for the purpose of erecting and remodelling another mill, and erecting two water-wheels for Mr. G. Escher, of Zurich. That gentleman visited Manchester for the first time in 1814, and again in 1824 when I first made his acquaintance. In early life he studied architecture in Italy, and for some time he served in the Austrian Artillery under the Archduke Charles, who commanded along with the Russian General Suwarrow, the combined armies against the French under Massena. At the commencement of the present century he built a small cotton-mill on one of the bastions of the fortifications of Zurich, and during the revolutionary wars it was alternately in the hands of the French, the Austrians, and the Russians. When the town was bombarded the mill escaped injury, with the exception of a single shot, which did little or no damage. On one occasion, it was, however, on the point of being reduced to ashes by a battery erected an the other side of the Limmat, for the purpose of dislodging a strong force of Russians who were in possession of that part of the town, when Mr. Escher, to save the only mill in Switzerland, presented himself at head-quarters, and obtained a promise from the French general that the mill should be respected, which promise was faithfully kept, notwithstanding a tremendous cannonading which took place on other parts of the bastion only a few yards distant. The following day found the French in possession of the town, and the Austrian and Russian armies in a new position in the valley of the Limmat, some miles distant.

Such were the early attempts at cotton-spinning in Switzerland, and such were the troubles my friend had to contend with in a country which for many years was the seat of war. The celebrated physiognomist, Lavater, lost his life on the occasion referred to above, either in his endeavours to interfere in a desperate conflict between some French and Russian soldiers, or, according to some accounts, by an accidental shot when walking in his own garden.

The constant alarm and exposure to destruction seriously affected the peaceful operations of Mr. Escher's mill; and it was not till some time after the retreat from Moscow, and the battle of Leipsic, that Mr. Escher could calculate on security, either for life or property. The whole of the manufactures on the frontiers were in a similarly precarious condition : and I believe one large establishment in Alsace was for some weeks occupied as a barrack, and nearly the whole of the machinery seriously injured. The abdication of Napoleon in 1814 liberated and enlarged the views of the spinners and manufacturers of the Continent. Mr. Escher and many others visited for the first time the far-famed mart of industry, Manchester, and arrangements were then made for extending those branches of industry in every department where it had located itself on the line of the Rhenish frontier. My firm had the good fortune to be selected for that purpose, and the first of our business connections took place with Mr. Escher on the occasion of his visit to Manchester in 1824.

Mr. Escher, now that the peace of Europe was finally settled, contemplated an extension of his cotton-mills, and in order to prepare his son, Mr. Albert Escher, then seventeen years of age, to be his successor, he brought him to Manchester to perfect his education on the English system as a spinner and manufacturer. In addition to a knowledge of cotton and yarn, I undertook to allow him free admission to our works, and to give him such instruction in practical mechanics as my limited time would allow. I further agreed to return with Mr. Escher to Zurich to inspect his establishment on the Limmat, and devise means for increasing his water-power, and for driving a new mill which he had erected the previous year immediately adjoining the old one, which had survived the conflicts of contending armies, and which was then in active and successful operation.

The industry of all nations was then bursting into new life, and the prospects of a good understanding and a long peace amongst nations gave renewed energy to the industrial resources of every country in Europe. Switzerland was rising into notice, and both France and Germany, in resting from the labours and expense of raising armies, and from all the distressing and conflicting elements of war, were settling down into a state of repose extremely favourable to the cultivation of the useful arts and the development of manufactures. These results were just beginning to show themselves, when in 1824 I first visited the Continent, and having made excursions to most of the manufacturing establishments in Alsace and the department of the Vosges, I had an opportunity of witnessing a spirit of enterprise and a prosperity to which these countries had for many years been strangers. It was highly gratifying to my fellow-traveller and friend, Mr. Escher, as well as to myself, to be received with the greatest good-will and hospitality by every manufacturer in France. The name of Fairbairn and Lillie was known to them before my arrival, and they were glad to avail themselves of my experience as a mechanical engineer and a person intimately connected with the manufactures, and to receive such instructions and suggestions as I was able to furnish.

The result was several extensive orders for water-wheels, mill-gearing, &c., on our new principle of construction. As this journey was fraught with interest, and affords the most pleasing recollections, I may recall a few of the incidents and early impressions of my first journey to France.

In travelling through France, at that time the cheapest and

most expeditious plan for more than one person was to buy a carriage and post. The regulations were good, charges moderate, and horses always ready when you arrived at the end of the stage. Mr. Escher, having his son with him, had posted with his own carriage from Zurich to Calais, where we found it on our arrival at the hotel, on our landing from the packet on the 8th of August.

Our journey lay through St. Omer to Lille, where we remained for a day, and called on some of the leading manufacturers of the place. Here, again, everything was new to me; the fortifications, drawbridges, ramparts, and esplanades, and the peculiar dress of the military, were all new and attractive. I am a great lover of old towns, such as can only be seen in France; full of historical recollections of the numerous contests in which that singular people have been engaged.

The following day brought us to Paris, and we entered this brightest of cities shortly after sunrise.

On reaching the capital I found much of it known to me from my previous reading. The Tuileries, the Louvre, the Palais Royal, the Champ de Mars, the Champs Elysées, and many other places, were familiar; and I soon found my way on foot through almost every part of the city. The old parts of the town, beyond the Pont Neuf, were particularly inviting, as I found I could identify some of the lodgings of the poor students, and of some of my own countrymen who used to be located here during the days of the Cavaliers, and the Scotch College, then the principal seat of education for the better classes in that country. There is something of the sublime and venerable creeps over the stranger as he saunters through the narrow streets of this part of Paris; the very filth smells of antiquity; and even to this day I never revisit the gay city without strolling amidst the narrow streets and tall houses of the Paris of former days.

A week's sojourn in Paris enabled me, through the kind assistance of my friend, to see everything worthy of note; and the Monday succeeding our arrival found us again on the road, via Troyes, Vesoul, and Belfort, to Switzerland. We travelled night and day, but made a short detour in order to visit some manufacturing works in the neighbourhood. We also visited some ironworks to look at a new horizontal water-wheel, since so well known as the Turbine. Here I was introduced to Mr. Fourneyron, the inventor, who was then only known as an ingenious mechanic, but whose persevering labours have procured for his invention a lasting name in the annals of science. The following morning found us at breakfast at the Three Kings Hotel, Basle, where I first saw the Rhine.

From Basle we took the German side of the Rhine, crossed Massena's military wooden bridge, and passed through the battered walls of Rheinfeld; we hurried on through the little town of Brugg, at the confluence of the Aar and the Limmat, and next evening we reached Mr. Escher's delightful country residence on the banks of the Lake of Zurich.

Three weeks were spent in this delightful country, partly in devising the necessary alterations and improvements for the cotton-works, and partly in short excursions on the Lakes Wallenstadt, Lucerne, and Zurich. At the mill there was a great deal to do, and for ten days I was constantly employed in surveys of the river, and in making arrangements of the machinery, millwork, &c., for driving the new, and renovating the old, mill. This latter was driven by two old wheels, which in certain seasons, when the snows were melting on the Alps, and in winter, when the water was low, were scarcely able to drive the machinery. We had now two mills to drive by the same water, and in order to double the power and render it uniform as well as efficient at all seasons, it was necessary to improve the principle and enlarge the capacity of the wheels to an extent suitable to that portion of the river to which Mr. Escher was entitled. I had further to consider how to obviate the difficulty under which they laboured at the extremes of high and low water, and so to modify the conditions as to furnish a given amount of power at all times when required for the mills. To accomplish these desiderata I had to cause the water-wheels to rise and fall with the river, and always to retain the immersion of the floats and the maximum depth in the stream. This was done by suspending each wheel on powerful cast-iron levers, the fulcrums of which revolved round the pinion of the main shaft which worked into the segments of the water-wheel. Nothing could answer better than this arrangement. The wheels were fully equal to their work. They rose and fell with the water in the river, and from that time to this they have supplied a steady, cheap, and regular power to the mills.

The completion of our business arrangements enabled Mr. Escher to devote a portion of his time to excursions; and, besides those on the lakes, we ascended the Righi from the head of Lake Zug, and reached the summit some hours before sunrise. At break of day we were out on the top of the mountain, which I afterwards ascertained to be about the level of the snowline, or that part where vegetation ceases. I had observed, on the ascent from the valley below, which was overspread with magnificent trees in full foliage, that these progressively gave way to varied forms of vegetation corresponding with the altitude, until at last we entered a forest of tall pines, which in their turn diminished in size until they tapered off to the size of a walking-stick; a little further up these again gave way to the lichens and such other plants as derive a scanty subsistence at the very edge of perpetual snow. It was a sublime and magnificent sight to witness the first glance of the morning sun over the pinnacles of the mighty Alps. The immense glaciers lay encircled in the arms of these lofty mountains; and from the silence which reigned all around they appeared to repose in the sleep of death, whilst the projecting towers of granite, like the turrets of some vast cathedral, rose high in the air.

This was a panorama of Nature's own construction, and nothing could equal the grandeur of the scene. Turning round and glancing over the immense precipice of conglomerate (or pudding-stone) which seemed to overhang the lake at a height of 4,000 feet, there was nothing to be seen but a sea of clouds, like flakes of wool, rolling to and fro. In a few minutes the whole of this fairy scene disappeared, the mist was suddenly dispersed, and again turning round there was a scene of beauty and animation revealed beyond my powers to describe. Down at our feet lay the mirror-like Lakes of Zug and Lucerne, beyond which were seen the wide and expansive valleys dividing the Alps from the Jura, which, like an immense rampart, shuts out the tamer landscape of *La belle France*. The whole was a picture of surpassing beauty.

The journey to Switzerland was productive of great advantages to our little establishment, as numerous orders for water-wheels followed in succession those of Mr. Escher; and in the three succeeding years we erected several new water-wheels in the Vosges, Alsace, and other parts of France. In fact, we continued to receive orders from all parts of the Continent till the principle became generally known, and the French were able to construct the improved wheels for themselves. Irrespective of these benefits, I had formed a bond of union and friendship with Mr. Escher which from that time to the present has suffered no diminution. His eldest son, Mr. Albert Escher, having received mechanical instruction at the works in Canal Street, immediately on his return to Zurich commenced a large machine establishment, which, till the day of his death, June 1844, stood high in the estimation of the Swiss, Italian, and German public. For a considerable number of years I transacted business with Mr. Escher's new establishment in the manufacture of iron steamboats and engines, of which four still ply on the Lake of Constance, and others on the Lakes Wallenstadt, Lucerne, and Geneva.

The construction of the large water-wheels at Catrine and Deanston, and the introduction of similar structures with our new system of millwork on the Continent, gave a name and reputation to the firm of Fairbairn and Lillie, which it retained for more than a dozen years, till we separated in 1832. Up to the time when we received Mr. Buchanan's order we had conducted our business in the old building in Mather Street. The construction of such large hydraulic machines as the Catrine water-wheels, fifty feet in diameter, required more tools and space. We had, therefore, to hire a yard in order to meet the exigencies of the case, and to furnish the necessary facilities for conducting a more extended business. This business continued to increase both at home and abroad, and a few years enabled us to realise a handsome competency, and made us what we considered rich men. In 1830 our stock-book showed a balance of nearly 40,000l. in our favour, and left us sufficient capital to enable us to build a foundry, and increase our works in other departments to the extent of giving employment to upwards of 300 hands.

K

In 1830 Mr. Fairbairn formally enrolled himself among his professional brethren by joining the Institution of Civil Engineers, a society then newly incorporated, but which has since taken gigantic dimensions, and has become one of the most important scientific bodies in the world.

The following is a copy of the certificate of Mr. Fairbairn's election :—

No. 231.

Admitted April 20, 1830.

Institution of Civil Engineers, Buckingham Street, Adelphi.

William Fairbairn, of Manchester, now practising as a mechanical engineer, being desirous of admission into the Institution of Civil Engineers, we, the undersigned, from our personal knowledge, propose and recommend him as a proper person to become a member thereof.

Witness our hands, this 30th day of March, 1830.

J. WALKER.

ROBERT STEVENSON.

JOHN FAREY.

The Council of the Institution of Civil Engineers, meeting on the 30th day of March, 1830, present the above-mentioned candidate to be balloted for as a corresponding member.

Signed,

THOMAS TELFORD, *Chairman.*

CHAPTER IX.

STEAM LOCOMOTION ON CANALS—IRON BOATS—
VOYAGE OF THE 'LORD DUNDAS'—TROUBLES
IN BUSINESS—DISSOLUTION OF PARTNERSHIP

AGE 41–43

1830—1832

CHAPTER IX.

ABOUT this time Mr. Fairbairn was engaged in a work of considerable importance, which, by the circumstances which grew out of it, had an important influence on his future career. It was the investigation of the properties of iron boats, and the possibility of applying steam-power for traction on canals. The story is told for the most part in his own words :—

In the early part of the year 1830, Mr. Houston, of Johnstone, the chairman and principal proprietor of the Ardrossan canal, availing himself of the use of a light gig-boat, such as is used in regatta or in rowing matches, made an attempt to increase the speed of the packet-boat between Glasgow, Paisley, and Johnstone. To this boat he attached two of the track-horses, and, urging them forward at their utmost speed, he found, to his surprise, that instead of a heavy surge rolling along the canal before the boat, the gig rode smoothly over the surface, and the horses actually worked with greater ease upon the collar at the high velocity than they appeared to do at a lower speed. This was so contrary to all received theories, that doubts were entertained as to the accuracy of the results. Mr. Houston was not, however, a scientific person, and in order to test the accuracy of the experimental trials made with the gig-boat, I was requested by the Forth and Clyde Canal Company to visit Glasgow, and to conduct a series of experiments on a light twin-boat built by Mr. Graham for that purpose.

Mr. Houston's experimental trip with the gig, and my own experiments with the twin-boat, appeared to bring out a new law in the resistance of fluids, which encouraged the idea of attaining quick speeds on canals. At that time this was a subject of vital importance to everyone connected with canal interests. The Liverpool and Manchester Railway had just been opened with unexpected and extraordinary success. A new principle of traction had come into operation; the flight of the swiftest bird and the fleetness of the race-horse were surpassed by the iron bones and muscles of the locomotive; the tales of the ' Arabian Nights' were realised; and no wonder that such apparent magic should create fear and consternation in the minds of proprietors and shareholders of canal stock. A speed of four and a half miles per hour for passengers, and of two and a half for goods, were all that canals could then boast of, and a new project which held out hopes of increased velocity was seized upon with avidity. Hence every encouragement was given to the new theory, as exhibited by the experiments on the Forth and Clyde and the Ardrossan Canals. The Forth and Clyde proprietary, who had great interests at stake, confirmed the report which I gave in, viz., that after having duly ascertained the resistance to a floating body passing through the water of a canal at from five to fourteen miles an hour, it was found that such resistance might be overcome by a light iron boat, with a steam-engine on the locomotive principle.

In this report I was guarded not to raise hopes that might not be realised; but I considered the experiments of such importance as to recommend further trials, and accordingly on that recommendation I was ordered to proceed with the construction of a new vessel, and all the necessary machinery requisite to propel her at the required velocity of from nine to ten miles an hour.

The experiments referred to were made two years before the separation which took place between Mr. Lillie and myself, and although he did not oppose, he nevertheless did not cordially join with me in the undertaking. The experiments were published in 1831, at the request of the governor and council of the Forth and Clyde Canal; and although the book was imperfectly got up, and was my first publication, it was nevertheless well received by the profession; and at a meeting of the Institution of Civil Engineers, of which I was a member, I received the thanks of the society from the president, Mr.

Telford, in a manner highly complimentary. As a comparatively young engineer, this was more than I had reason to expect ; but it had the effect of a stimulus in the right direction, and in all my subsequent engineering projects I had the privilege of consulting that great and eminent man, Mr. Telford, who from the commencement of our acquaintance always received me with marked kindness.

The book above mentioned deserves some further notice, on account of its being the author's first essay in engineering literature. It consists of ninety-three octavo pages, with five lithographed plates, and the title is as follows :—

Remarks on Canal Navigation, illustrative of the advantages of the use of steam as a moving power on canals. With an appendix containing a series of experiments, tables, &c., on which a number of proposed improvements are founded. Also plans and descriptions of certain classes of steamboats, intended for the navigation of canals, and the adjoining branches of the sea. By William Fairbairn, Engineer. London, Longmans and Co., 1831.

As to the literary style of this first attempt, we cannot do better than quote the opinion of the celebrated Dr. Henry, who, writing to Mr. Fairbairn shortly after the publication of the book, says :—

I have read with great pleasure your ' Remarks on Canal Navigation.' They are written (as such books should be) in a plain, perspicuous, and unpretending manner—no small merit in this age of quackery.

The author describes at some length the discussions which had taken place between himself and some of the Scotch canal proprietors, with the view of improving the communication on their lines, and the experiments made in consequence, with boats of different kinds. The results were so encouraging as to induce the Forth and Clyde

Company to order Mr. Fairbairn to construct a light passage boat, worked by steam-power, to ply between Glasgow and Edinburgh. The remarks he makes on this commission are interesting as showing a trait of character usually not over-prominent in young engineers of an enterprising turn of mind—namely, a sense of the importance of practical utility and commercial advantage in engineering designs. Mr. Fairbairn says:—

The business I had now in hand was to ascertain how, and at what cost, the object which I recommended the Forth and Clyde Canal Committee to pursue, could be attained. It was not an abstract question of practicability, but how far a very high rate of velocity could be *advantageously obtained*; at what cost, and what might be the comparative difference of expense between the proposed new principle and the present mode of trackage.

In pursuance of this commission he proceeded to design and build the 'Lord Dundas,' of which he gives, in the book, drawings and detailed dimensions.

She was 68 feet long, 11 feet 6 inches breadth of beam, and 4 feet 6 inches deep, drawing sixteen inches of water. She was built of iron plates, about one-sixteenth of an inch thick, strengthened with light angle iron and T iron ribs, and she was fitted with cabins fore and aft.

The engine was on the locomotive pattern, having two cylinders, one on each side, and was equal to about 10-horse power. It worked a single paddle-wheel 9 feet diameter and 3 feet 10 inches wide, placed a little aft of midships, and intended to make fifty or sixty revolutions per minute. The wheel worked in a trough extending fore and aft, to allow of the flow of the water to and from the paddles. From this feature the boat was called a 'twin' boat, although the name hardly applied, as the general construction of the body was single.

The whole weight of the boat, including the engine, paddle-wheel, &c., was 7 tons 16 cwt.

Mr. Fairbairn says of this boat :—

This little vessel was constructed exclusively for lightness, and in order to give her bows and sides the required tenacity and stiffness, light angle irons were introduced as ribs, and the whole firmly riveted together. When the boat was finished, I was forcibly struck with her lightness, solidity, and strength.

She was ready in 1831, and Mr. Fairbairn continues his narrative :—

I waited with anxiety our first experiment ; and having launched the vessel and fixed the machinery, we proceeded down the river Irwell some miles below Manchester for the purpose of making our first trial.

During the time required for building the boat I had frequent opportunities of considering the nature of the engagements into which I had entered with the Forth and Clyde Canal Company. It was true I had made no promise to accomplish by steam what had been done by horses, but I considered it worthy of trial, and engaged to build the boat and machinery, and to undertake the superintendence of the experiments. So far the undertaking was clear on both sides ; but subsequent considerations, and greatly matured reflections, modified my expectations, and notwithstanding that the lightness of the vessel and the power of the engines promised success, yet my doubts and misgivings continued to increase, and I approached the day of trial in a state of nervous excitement of no enviable description. It was clear, as I used to reason with myself long before the boat was finished, that I had given no pledge to the company. But the public as well as the proprietary would expect the realisation of their wishes ; and if I did not succeed, I must fail, and a failure was, of all things, to my mind, the most obnoxious and disagreeable. In this way I tormented myself, and passed many a sleepless night in order to devise the means of ensuring success. At last the dreaded day arrived ; and a party of friends from Glasgow, Liverpool, and Manchester embarked for the purpose of testing the qualities of the new boat.

The spot selected for the trial was a narrow, straight reach of about a mile in length; which distance being carefully measured, we commenced the run with and against the current, and the maximum velocity was found to average about eight miles an hour, and that with a considerable surge in front of the boat. The whole day was spent in the experiments, and a faithful record was kept of the time in which the distance was run both ways.

Mr. Graham, of Glasgow, who took great interest in the experiments, maintained that as a first essay it was very successful. I thought differently, but kept quiet, as with all the power we could raise we did not materially increase the speed, but raised the surge before and behind the boat to a much greater height than before with horses; and thus, by sinking the vessel in a trough between the crests of the preceding and following waves, we appeared to hang on the water with a persistence which no power emanating from the boat itself could overcome.

This effect was to me far from satisfactory; as I thought in this early stage of the experiments I could perceive, what was afterwards realised, that the propulsion of a vessel having the propelling power within itself is entirely different from the force employed in the shape of traction from a towing-path. In the latter case the vessel is free from the load of machinery which in the former case sinks her to a greatly increased depth. With horse traction the vessel rises upon the surface of the water with comparative ease, and with diminishing resistance overrides the wave; but when hampered by a steam-engine the vessel, from its increased weight, floats at a greatly increased depth, and accumulates rather than diminishes the intensity of the surge.

The 'Lord Dundas' had a second trial on the river cut from Warrington to Runcorn, and a third from Runcorn to Liverpool in the open tideway. In the narrow canal our speed was reduced to something under six miles. In the open water of the Mersey, however, the engines had good play, and we drove along at the rate of ten miles an hour. In the trial from Runcorn to Liverpool I had the pleasure of the company of Mr. George Rennie, to whom I was greatly indebted for many useful and friendly suggestions. He took great interest in the experiments, and made many enquiries as to the results, which he considered, under the circumstances, highly satisfactory. In the passage from Runcorn to Liverpool Mr. Rennie got alarmed at the fragile nature of the vessel; and when he was informed that it was our intention to navigate her from Liverpool to the Clyde, he expressed great fears of our safety, and advised us strongly not to venture to sea unless well provided with cork jackets.

I had, however, great faith in the stability of the vessel, and early on the following morning she sailed for the Isle of Man, with instructions to wait for me there, where I should arrive by the regular steamer the following day. As this voyage turned out more perilous than I expected, and as some interesting phenomena were exhibited in the navigation by the attraction of the iron in the ship's hull upon the compass, it may be useful to describe the circumstances under which they occurred.

The boat sailed from Liverpool at five o'clock one morning in June 1831. At seven she made the floating light, and before two the land which the captain called the west side of the Isle of Man was in sight. For some time they kept steaming towards the shore, but the commander could not reconcile his course and the chart, nor yet the appearance of the land, and on nearing the shore they found, instead of the Isle of Man, they were close upon the coast of Cumberland. This very wide discrepancy between the course apparently steered, and the position of the little vessel, completely upset the calculations of the skipper. He maintained that he was correct in his course; but before he had time to settle the difference he had to ''bout ship,' and run for Morecambe Bay, in order to avoid a stiff breeze which commenced blowing from the west. Here they took shelter for the night; and it was the afternoon of the next day before they were able to weigh anchor and sail for the place of rendezvous, Douglas, in the Isle of Man. It was here that I had to meet them, and for that purpose I sailed for that port the afternoon of the day they left Liverpool. When I reached Douglas I found, to my surprise and great disappointment, that such a vessel as I described had never been seen; and alarmed at this non-arrival, I took the first vessel for the Clyde, conceiving they must have gone on.

On arriving at Greenock there was still no account of the vessel; and there being six persons on board, Mr. Elliot (my superintendent), an engineer, a stoker, the captain and two sailors, I felt all the misery and responsibility of having been, in some degree, if not entirely, the cause of a serious loss of life. Labouring under these painful feelings, I went down to the Comries, and in a little boat searched all the islands, and made enquiries in every direction, but without effect.

Feeling great uneasiness and alarm, I became dreadfully nervous, and after spending a great portion of the day in a fruitless search, I returned to Greenock, and took the first vessel I could find for the Isle of Man. On my second arrival at Douglas I made instant enquiries about the vessel, and to my great relief I found that one answering the description had reached Ramsey, and was then at anchor in the bay. This information was welcomed with a thankful heart, and there never was a journey undertaken with more heartfelt satisfaction than mine on an old horse from Douglas to Ramsey. On reaching the summit of the last hill which overlooks the bay of that town, the first sight that met my eyes was the ' Lord Dundas,' like a speck on the waters, riding quietly at anchor on a sea as smooth as glass.

Hurrying down the hill, I made enquiries for Mr. Elliot and the captain, but no person could give me any information. At last a sailor informed me that I should find them at a public-house in the neighbourhood. On enquiry I learnt they had been there, but were all gone to a country fair about five miles inland, where they were enjoying themselves, without once thinking of the misery I had endured on their account for the last three days. At first I felt annoyed at their behaviour, but after a little reflection I was but too glad to find them in the land of the living, and waited their return with perfect good-will, and a determination to give them a cordial reception.

On the return of the party from the fair, I soon ascertained the cause of the mistake which had occurred in making the coast of Cumberland instead of the Isle of Man; and in order to prevent a recurrence of any further errors, I had the compass examined on the following morning before sailing.

Mr. Fairbairn then describes how he tested the boat's compass, with the aid of a second one fixed on shore, and determined the effect of the iron in causing the erroneous deviation. This is a very common process now, when iron is the most usual material of ship construction; but it must be recollected that at that time an iron boat was quite a new thing, and the prompt discovery of the error, the experimental determination of its exact amount, and the immediate application of an efficient remedy and correction, showed great ability on the part of the young engineer.

He continues :—

To remedy this error there was no difficulty, as the natural suggestion was to place a piece of iron in the opposite direction of the ship's attraction, until the needle on board was brought in a line parallel to that on shore. With this rough-and-ready correction we proceeded on our voyage with perfect certainty and without any further mishap.

It was the early part of the forenoon that we sailed from Ramsey, and the little vessel, which at the stern was only a few inches from the water, steamed away at a great rate, and reached Port Patrick in the afternoon. We did not call at that port, as we were desirous of reaching the Clyde, if possible, before midnight. But two naval officers came off in a boat to examine the craft, which, they informed us, had been watched by the telescope for two hours previous; and their astonishment was great as to the nature of the little vessel and the adventurous navigators on board. After a careful examination of the vessel and her machinery, with which they expressed themselves highly pleased, they landed again, amid the cheers of some hundreds of persons assembled on the pier to witness the performances of so small and lively a craft. Before reaching the Mull of Galloway, and all the way from that point to the entrance of Loch Ryan, we encountered a considerable swell, but the little light and pliable steamer danced upon it like a canoe, and if it had not been for a strong wind from the west which came on to blow after sunset, we should have made the Comrie Isles, at the mouth of the Clyde, that night. As it was, the sea was beginning to wash over our frail bark, and on reaching the northern point of the Galloway coast we deemed it expedient to run to Stranraer for the night, and make the Clyde on the following morning. We did not reach Stranraer till after midnight, but we roused the landlady and her maid, and kept them frying herrings till two in the morning.

Early the next morning we got up the steam and started for Glasgow, where we arrived in the afternoon. The boat was afterwards tried on the long reach of the Forth and Clyde Canal, but the experiments confirmed the results previously obtained on the Mersey, and showed that high speed never could be obtained upon canals, where the vessel had to carry her own machinery and be propelled from the water. This was undeniable; and although we had abundance of power to propel the vessel at nine and ten miles an hour in open water, we never, in our most successful experiments, attained more than seven and a half miles an hour on the canal, with a high swell in front, and a corresponding one following behind.

At a low velocity of five to five and a half miles an hour the 'Lord Dundas' steamed beautifully, and at that rate she carried passengers from Port Dundas, Glasgow, to Port Eglintoun, Edinburgh, for upwards of two years.

The experiments made with the 'Lord Dundas' were sufficient to convince the most sanguine of the canal proprietary that nothing could be effected in the shape of high velocities on canals to compete with the new locomotives, then in the process of development on the Liverpool and Manchester Railway.

Strongly impressed with the conviction that we—the canal interest—had no chance whatever with our able competitors, I advised the governor and council of the Forth and Clyde Company to abandon the attempt of carrying the passenger traffic by light steamboats, and to confine their operations to a class of steamers that would act as tug-boats, taking the barges in fleets, and thus to expedite the delivery of goods at both ends of the navigation. I further advised the construction of iron vessels adapted to canal and sea navigation, which by increased rapidity of transit would meet the demands of an increased traffic in parcels and light goods. These suggestions were acted upon, and I had the satisfaction to be the first to open this new system of transport on canals, and at the same time to direct attention more prominently to the construction of iron ships in general.

At a later period of Mr. Fairbairn's life he was asked by the eminent French savant, the Baron Charles Dupin, to give him an account of his early labours in regard to the construction of iron vessels; and as his letter gives a much more complete account of his experiments than is conveyed in the Autobiography, an extract from it may be inserted here :—

London, May 25, 1853.

My dear Baron Dupin,—It was my intention to have replied direct to your queries respecting the first introduction of iron as a material for ship-building; but as it may be some weeks before I can make my promised visit, and as you may require the information before that time, I beg leave to state that iron boats navigating canals have been made in Scotland and Staffordshire for upwards of fifty years ; but the application of this material for the building of large vessels did not take place until the years 1830 and 1831.

The discovery of accelerated velocities by light boats on canals occurred in the spring of 1830, and the new theory of *riding* the wave, or the undulating motion produced in the fluid by the haulage of a light vessel along its surface, was first accomplished by Mr. William Houston, of Johnstone, on the Ardrossan Canal, between the towns of Paisley and Glasgow. This discovery—which took place at the opening of the Liverpool and Manchester Railway—was received with more than common interest by the canal proprietary of the United Kingdom, and during the heat and fervour of the moment it was looked upon as the only competition to the threatened destruction of their property by railways. To save that property, and investigate by experimental research the laws on which this new theory of the resistance of fluids was founded, I undertook, at the request of the governor and council of the Forth and Clyde Company, the enquiry which led to new constructions and new results, and was published in the following year under the sanction of the council and other Canal companies.

The objects I had in view of the prosecution of these experiments were threefold.

First, to ascertain the resistance offered to light vessels when drawn through narrow channels of water at velocities varying from 4 to 14 or 15 miles an hour.

Secondly, to determine by what description of vessel this could best be attained; and,

Lastly, to ascertain whether or not steam could be used as motive power for accomplishing those objects.

As respects the first, it was proved that the resistances from 3 to 5 miles an hour increased nearly as the squares of the velocities; from 5 to 8 miles the resistance was considerably more than the squares; and from 8 to 14 miles—when the vessel rose upon the surface and *skimmed* upon the water—the force of resistance was so greatly diminished as to reduce the obstruction to the vessel's progress considerably under that ratio. But you will find these facts more clearly demonstrated from the following summary of results as taken from the fourth series of experiments on July 12, 1830.

Results of Experiments, made with a Twin Boat $5\frac{1}{11}$ Tons Weight, on the Monkland Canal.

No. of Trips in both Directions	Time min. sec.	Rate Miles per Hour	Force of Traction in lbs.	Horses Power	Remarks
1 and 2	12 24	4·83	82·0	1·000	No swell.
3 ,, 4	9 38	6·23	205·3	3·410	Swell a little increased.
5 ,, 6	8 16	7·28	378·5	7·342	A swell in front at the stem.
7 ,, 8	5 10	11·63	433·4	13·490 ⎫	No surge in these experiments,
9	4 48	12·50	439·3	14·643 ⎬	the velocity of the boat greater than that of the wave.
10	4 36	13·04	390	13·936 ⎭	

In the last experiment, No. 10, the boat was lightened of its cargo, and reduced to 57 cwt.

From the averages arranged in the above table, it will be observed that the rates of velocity are to the forces as 4·8, 6·2, 7·2, and 11·6 to 82, 205, 378, 433, &c., which are less than the squares of the velocities, at the rate of 11½ and 12½ miles per hour, when the surge is overcome, and when the boat is moved forward, unaccompanied by the heavy swell that is invariably present at a speed varying from 5 to 8½ miles per hour.

Having ascertained the resistances and the extent to which the velocities could be carried by animal power (which it will be observed never exceeded 14 miles an hour), the next consideration was the introduction of steam and the construction of a vessel uniting the double qualification of strength and lightness. Now this could not be accomplished by wood, as a light timber-built vessel would never carry a steam-engine of sufficient power to propel the vessel at 12 to 14 miles an hour, and the only resource was therefore iron.

A vessel of this kind—the ' Lord Dundas '—was accordingly built at my suggestion ; and although it did not realise the objects for which it was originally constructed, namely, the attainment of high velocities, it nevertheless paved the way to a new system of marine construction which has since become general amongst the nations of Europe and America.

In the construction of the ' Lord Dundas,' which was intrusted to my care, several important ideas presented themselves. First, the superior strength of iron as compared with wood ; the distribution of the material in these constructions ; and the superior strength and lightness which a judicious application of this material afforded. All these circumstances were present to my mind in the construction of the ' Lord Dundas,' and by the introduction of T and angle ¬ iron as frames and ribs, I found that the required rigidity and strength was attained at a comparatively small expenditure of material.

In the construction of iron ships I may mention that our knowledge at the commencement was very imperfect ; and I had to watch with the utmost care and attention the position and disposition of the material, in order to effect economy in its use, and that with as near an approach as possible to the maximum of strength.

In this respect I laboured under great difficulties ; and having no data on which we could rely for guidance in these constructions, I felt the want of information, and at a very early period (1834) determined to institute a series of experiments on the strength of malleable iron of different forms and conditions, in order to effect an improved system of construction, both as regards the strength and a judicious application of the material.

These experiments were read before the Royal Society, and published in the Transactions of that body, of which I think you have a copy.

I have the honour to be,

My dear Baron Dupin,

Your faithful obedient Servant,

WM. FAIRBAIRN.

Hitherto the business in which Mr. Fairbairn was engaged had been entirely prosperous and pleasant, but about this time some troubles began to arise, which resulted in an important change.

It appears that a few years previously three gentlemen had associated themselves together for the purpose of establishing large dye-works in the neighbourhood of Manchester. An Italian merchant living in that town found the capital; a Swiss engineer, who had made himself known by great ingenuity and prolific production in mechanical inventions, was to design the machinery; and another Swiss gentleman, a practical chemist and dyer, was to superintend the practical processes. The parties do not seem to have begun in perfect harmony; for the chemist declared that all he wanted was a few cisterns, tubs, kettles, and wash-wheels; but such a primitive plan did not please the mechanical inventor. He proposed great savings by extensive self-acting machinery; and as his counsels prevailed, an estate of nearly 100 acres was bought near Egerton, and weirs, dams, and water-courses were laid out, and new buildings constructed, filled with machinery on an entirely new principle, designed to accomplish every motion and every process by mechanical power, instead of in the ordinary way, by hand.

In this way upwards of 40,000*l.* had been spent without any immediate prospect of the manufactory being completed, when the capitalist took alarm, and refused to find any more money. The works were stopped, and the whole property was offered for sale at a price greatly below what it had cost.

Mr. Fairbairn writes :—

Mr. ——, failing to effect a sale, again applied to me, requesting I would endeavour to find him a customer. I consulted with Mr. Lillie, and applied to a firm whose mills and property were situated a little further down the river. We were on intimate terms with the members of this firm, for whom we had erected a water-wheel, and done other work at their mills. They had very little spare capital, but they urged me to buy the estate, at a fixed price, and said they would join Mr. Lillie and me in converting the buildings into a cotton-mill. The whole property was bought in our joint names for 13,000*l.*, each paying one-fourth of the purchase-money. The completion of the contract was the signal for active operations. We set vigorously to work, and in less than twelve months one side of the principal building was removed, and the mill made double the width. The weir and overflows were also completed, as also a new water-wheel 62 feet in diameter and 130 horse-power; and the mill-work and part of the machinery were erected and at work in less than fifteen months.

The drains caused on the capital of the firm of Fairbairn and Lillie for this work were so great as to cripple their legitimate business as millwrights to a serious extent; for after the mill was set to work all the money made was expended in enlargements or other capital investments returning no interest to the proprietors.

Four or five years went on in this way—all outlay and no income—when a source of serious trouble arose, namely, a commencement of misunderstanding and mistrust between the two partners. Mr. Fairbairn in his diary enters at some length into the causes and circumstances of the disagreement, but it is needless to reproduce the particulars here.   It will suffice to quote his concluding observations :—

All these circumstances convinced me of the necessity of a speedy dissolution of partnership, and from 1830 to 1832 I urged upon Mr. Lillie the necessity of a change.   At the beginning he refused to listen to such a proposal, remarking that there was no reason for such a step, that he was willing to take his fair share of the business, and that he thought me unreasonable in wishing to break up a connection which had for many years been so successful.   Perhaps there was some reason in these observations ; but after a careful consideration of the circumstances I felt convinced that we could no longer go on together with safety or comfort.   I offered either to take the concern entirely into my own hands, and pay his share as it stood in the books ; or for him to retain it, as we might ultimately decide.   Finding further persuasives unavailable, and a separation determined on, it was ultimately arranged that I should take the works on payment of a sum of money equivalent to his share as it stood in the books.   This was accomplished in 1832, by my handing over my share in the Egerton Cotton-mills ; and on paying a sum of money down, the works in Canal Street became mine as sole proprietor.   At the same time a dissolution took place with the Egerton firm, who agreed to pay the capital which stood in both our names over to Mr. Lillie, also a retiring partner, by instalments.

This change of circumstances, throwing Mr. Fairbairn entirely on his own resources, was a serious one, and cost him much anxious thought to determine on.   But he was confident in the soundness of his judgment, and strong in his self-reliance, and the event showed he was right.

Mr. Lillie decided to enter into business on his own account, and took new premises within a few hundred yards of the old ones.   It seems that an impression had been circulated that he had been harshly treated, and forced out of the business against his will, and in consequence he received much sympathy and support in his opposition to the old establishment. Mr. Fairbairn, however, stood up manfully, and the more his difficulties increased the greater was his determination to overcome them. He says :—

I felt alone, but with renewed energies; and I hoped in a short time, by an indomitable spirit and unflinching industry, to conquer every difficulty. I had come to the determination to strike out a new path for myself; and in spite of the breaking up of the different departments, by the loss of the foremen, who nearly all went over to Mr. Lillie, I nerved myself for an active opposition from whatever quarter it might arise. I entertained the utmost confidence in my own powers; and knowing that Mr. Lillie was neither more active nor more industrious than myself, I came to the conclusion that I had nothing to fear, and that ultimate success was sure to follow. Armed with these resolutions, I set vigorously to work, and never relaxed till I had taken a position entirely independent of any competitor.

In all our subsequent transactions I must, however, do this gentleman the justice to say that I found him as an opponent the same honourable, kind-hearted man that I had found him as a partner.

CHAPTER X.

IRON SHIPBUILDING — RIVER BANN — EXPERI-
MENTS ON IRON — THE RIVETING MACHINE

AGE 43–50

1832 — 1839

IRON SHIP-BUILDING—THE 'MANCHESTER' CANAL STEAMER—
OTHER IRON VESSELS—ESTABLISHMENT OF A SHIP-BUILDING YARD
AT MILLWALL—COMPETITION—DIFFICULTIES AND ANXIETY—PERSE-
VERANCE AND ENERGY—EVENING MEETINGS FOR DISCUSSION—PRO-
POSED ESTABLISHMENT OF 'THE WORKSHOP' PERIODICAL—HODGKINSON
—WOODCROFT — NASMYTH—LITERARY AND SCIENTIFIC AMBITION—
SOHAM MERE DRAINAGE—REPORT ON THE RIVER BANN—MR JOHN
FREDERICK BATEMAN—RECOMMENDATIONS ADOPTED—CONSTRUCTION OF
RESERVOIRS—RIVER DON—EXPERIMENTS AND INVESTIGATION ON HOT
AND COLD BLAST CAST-IRON IN CONJUNCTION WITH MR. EATON HODG-
KINSON, FOR THE BRITISH ASSOCIATION—PAPER FOR THE MANCHESTER
LITERARY AND PHILOSOPHICAL SOCIETY—THE RIVETING MACHINE—
MR. ROBERT SMITH—PATENT TAKEN OUT.

CHAPTER X.

WHEN Mr. Fairbairn entered on the sole charge of his business he appears to have turned his attention to a new branch of engineering manufacture. He reverts in his diary to the investigation he had made a year or two before, on the application of steam-power to canals, and he goes on to say :—

The experiments and constructions above described were the precursors of that great department of our national industry, *Iron Shipbuilding*, from which this country has derived so much benefit, and to which mankind are indebted for that rapidity of ocean communication which distinguishes the steamers of the present time

Although nothing could be done for the attainment of high speeds on canals, it was perfectly possible to open a useful steamboat communication between Glasgow and the towns on the eastern coast through the Forth and Clyde Canal. For this purpose I constructed an iron steamer, called the ' Manchester,' on the same principle as the ' Lord Dundas,' with the paddles at the stern ; and having launched her on the Irwell, and fitted her with high-pressure engines of 40-horse power, she was tried on the Mersey with the greatest success, and had such speed that she steamed round the fastest boats then at Liverpool. She made the passage from Liverpool in a comparatively short time, and having been stationed on the canal, she carried on a regular and considerable traffic for a number of years between Port Dundas and the towns along the Firth of Forth up to Dundee.

The success which attended the ' Manchester,' her great strength, buoyancy, and lightness, and her qualities as a sea-

boat, pointed out the advantages to be derived from the use of
iron, and induced the building of other iron vessels of greater
burden.   During the two succeeding years not fewer than eight
vessels were built in sections at Manchester, taken to pieces,
and reconstructed at the ports.

The system, however, of building ships of 100 to 250 tons
burden in an inland town, taking them to pieces, and having to
rebuild them at some convenient seaport, was in itself a process
that could not be long maintained, and the only alternative
left was either to abandon iron shipbuilding altogether as a
business, or establish an entirely new concern for that purpose
in Liverpool or London.   The former town offered many advantages ; but after mature consideration, London being the
seat of government, and a railway communication having been
determined on, I arrived at the conclusion that the metropolis
held out more encouraging prospects for the formation and extension of this new business than Liverpool.   Having foreseen
from what had already been done that iron shipbuilding must
of necessity increase, I came to the determination to establish
works in London, and for this purpose I bought a plot of land
at Millwall, Poplar, and with one of my own pupils, Mr. Andrew
Murray,[1] who was given a small share in the business, entered
on the premises early in the year 1835,   The following year we
had orders for twelve iron vessels for navigating the Ganges,
for the East India Company, and four others for different parts
of Europe.

About this time the subject began to attract much public
attention.   Others embarked in the trade, and we had to contend with a formidable opposition which was started against us
by several shipbuilders on the Thames.   This competition we
had to fight against for many years; but we were well supported by the Government and the East India Company, and
by increased orders from abroad.   We made many blunders as
to prices &c. in a business which we had yet to learn, and the
rapid increase of the demand for iron vessels, and the consequent necessary outlay and extension of the works in
buildings, tools, &c. trenched so hard upon our limited capital

[1] This gentleman was subsequently chief engineer at H.M. Dock Yards,
Woolwich and Portsmouth.

as to hamper us for a long time. Unfortunately, also, I could not attend personally to the London establishment, as by doing so that in Manchester, of much greater importance, and which in fact created the other, would have been neglected. My young friend Murray, who was without experience, and had everything to learn, could not do much, and although he exerted himself to the utmost, it could hardly be expected that so young a man could exercise all the judgment and precaution of a person whose training had attained greater maturity.

In this situation I felt all the responsibility of both concerns. I was hurried backwards and forwards between Manchester and London for more than five years, without a moment's repose, and with a degree of mental strain and anxiety that would have broken down a constitution of less rigidity than my own. Nature had, however, supplied me with an elasticity of spirits which enabled me to throw off for a time the mortifications and anxieties attendant upon arduous undertakings; and having the power and determination to forget, in a change of scene or conversation, the cares and troubles of the moment, I found the greatest relief from such relaxations. Many were the times that, seeing no relief at hand, I have, from this buoyancy of disposition alone, returned with redoubled energy to the charge, mastered every difficulty, and given a new colouring and new features to the prospects before me. Thus constituted, I never for an instant gave way to despair. I was often disappointed; sometimes miserable, but never discomfited; and I attribute to this peculiar quality of temperament that constant desire to rise, and that never-tiring exertion, which carried me through troubles and difficulties apparently insurmountable.

In relating this part of my history I should be wanting in gratitude if I did not allude to the exertions of an excellent young man, Mr. John Elliot, now no more, who acted for several years in the capacity of foreman of the millwrights at Manchester, who assisted at the trials of the 'Lord Dundas,' and who ultimately was offered a small share in the works at Millwall.

During my residence at Medlock Bank, Manchester, I frequently received visitors in the evenings; among these were Mr. Elliot above mentioned, (whom I found exceedingly intelligent), Mr. Eaton Hodgkinson, Mr. Bennett Woodcroft, the scientific adviser of the Commissioners of Patents, and Mr. James Nasmyth, engineer, and inventor of the steam-hammer. The evenings were most agreeably spent—chiefly in philosophical and scientific discussions. Amongst other projects which at that time we had in contemplation, was the establishment of a quarterly publication, to be entitled 'The Workshop,' and intended chiefly for the working classes. The subjects to be treated of were the industrial and mechanical arts; mathematics as applied to them; biographical sketches of eminent men; and such other subjects as would interest, stimulate, and improve the class it was intended to benefit. It was further intended to give accounts of all the improvements, suggestions, and discoveries in the manipulations of the workshop—the origin and management of tools, the division of labour, and the rise and progress of inventions of every description within the reach of the editors and their contributors. Last but not least, a portion of the work was to be set apart for essays on domestic culture, moral improvement, and such other matters as would raise the character of the workman, correct dissipated habits, encourage economy, ensure self-respect, and render his domestic hearth attractive, instructive, and happy. All these objects the projectors of 'The Workshop' had in view; and I went so far as to write the introduction and prospectus, and some other papers.

As will readily be supposed, these papers, and the project altogether, were of a most sanguine description. We had some practice in our peculiar walks of life. My friend Hodgkinson was an able mathematician; Woodcroft was an original inventor; Nasmyth imaginative; Elliot cautious and persevering; and I myself with a slight mixture of the whole; so that there would have been a singular compound—a literary 'hotch-potch,' not perhaps very refined, but which might have been acceptable to those it was intended for.

Unfortunately the intentions of the projectors were never carried into effect. We were all of us well employed, and could not devote much time to such a pursuit. The arrangement and classification of the subjects, as far as they went, were satisfactory, but we never got beyond that point; and the whole affair at last died away.

I was incessantly engaged in conducting my two large establishments in London and Manchester, where I had collectively upwards of 2,000 hands employed. With such a business I could not have done much for 'The Workshop' if that publication had gone on. I could not, however, suppress the desire I always had of giving to the world such information as I had collected in the varied forms and pursuits of my profession. I confess that nature had endowed me with a strong desire to distinguish myself as a man of science. I was pleased to see myself in print, and the only fear I entertained was the imperfections of style, and the great difficulty I had to encounter in expressing my ideas in a clear and perspicuous manner. This was a difficulty I laboured hard to overcome, and I have up to the present moment no clear perception whether I am right or wrong in any composition in which I have been engaged.

The imperfection which I have just admitted, and which, like Meg Merrilies to Dirk Hatterick, has always been a 'rock a-head,' has not, however, deterred me from attempting, every now and then, to launch my uncouth barque amongst a host of critics on the sea of literature; for almost every year from 1834 to the present time I have had some communications, or scientific enquiry, ready for the press.

Although Mr. Fairbairn's chief practice lay in the mechanical branch of the profession, he did not confine his attention exclusively to that subject; for we find him, at this period, undertaking several engineering matters of a more general nature.

In 1832 he was desired to examine the drainage of a fen district called Soham Mere, near Ely, in Cambridgeshire. He found the existing arrangements imperfect, and he reported, on March 23 in that year, explaining the facts, and making recommendations for the improvement of the drainage operations.

In 1835 he was engaged by the millowners on the River Bann, in County Down, Ireland, to examine the

locality, and to report on the best means of improving
the water-power. Numerous linen factories had been
established on the river, but they were much hampered
by the irregularity of the stream. In dry seasons there
was not water enough to work the wheels, while during
rains the floods were so great as to drown the machinery,
and often do much mischief.

Mr. Fairbairn undertook the commission, associating
with him in the work a young engineer, Mr. John
Frederic Bateman, who had commenced business in
Manchester shortly before, and with whom he had formed
a friendship. Mr. Bateman afterwards married his
daughter, and attained to high eminence in the profession.
They examined the district together, and in January
1836 Mr. Fairbairn made a report, which, from its importance to the industrial interests of the district, he was
requested to get printed for general circulation. The
title was :—

'Reservoirs on the River Bann, in the County of Down,
Ireland, for more effectually supplying the Mills with Water.'
Manchester, printed by Robert Robinson, St. Anne's Place.
1836.

It was prefaced by an address 'To the Noblemen and
Gentlemen of the County of Down, and particularly those
interested in the improvements of the River Bann districts, and connected with the proposed Reservoirs for
supplying the Mills with Water,' in which the author
urged the benefits that would arise from the improvement
of the industrial resources of the country. In the report
itself he showed that the measures for the cure of
the evils complained of should consist of the formation,
on the course of the stream, of large reservoirs, which
would catch and impound the excess of water in time of
floods, allowing it to be distributed down the stream in

dry seasons, in aid of the natural scanty flow at those times. He pointed out three sites where such reservoirs could be made, and gave an estimate of the probable cost of their construction. He further examined, economically, the alternative plan of providing steam-power, and showed that the reservoirs would, in the end, be cheaper by the large sum of 7,000*l.* a year.

The report went fully into the scientific calculations of rainfall, evaporation, water-power, &c., bearing on the question, and was illustrated by a large map showing the works proposed, and signed jointly by Mr. Fairbairn and Mr. Bateman.

The recommendations of the report were adopted by the mill proprietors; funds were raised, and the works were afterwards successfully carried out, the detailed designs and construction being entrusted, at Mr. Fairbairn's wish, entirely to Mr. Bateman.[1]

About the same time Mr. Fairbairn made an enquiry of a very similar character in regard to the River Don, in Aberdeenshire, Scotland. He reported to the mill proprietors in November 1835, also recommending the construction of reservoirs on the stream. But this proposal does not appear to have borne any fruit.

In 1835 Mr. Fairbairn took part in an investigation of great scientific and mechanical importance, and with which his name has ever since been honourably associated; —namely, the determination on a large scale, and with great accuracy, of the strength and other mechanical properties of cast-iron. The previous knowledge on the subject was limited, and great uncertainty existed as to the effect which had been produced by the introduction, a

---

[1] Full descriptions of the works, communicated by Mr. Bateman to the Institution of Civil Engineers, will be found in their Proceedings for 1841, page 168 ; and for 1848, page 251.

few years before, of the new process of manufacture by the hot blast. Some iron-masters, in one part of the country, had come to the conclusion that the new process greatly deteriorated the quality of the iron produced; while others from other neighbourhoods maintained, on the contrary, that no deterioration resulted from the process, which was admitted by all to diminish the cost of production.

These widely differing opinions, both expressed by persons largely connected with the manufacture of cast-iron, were brought to the notice of the British Association for the Advancement of Science, at their meeting at Dublin, in September 1835, and the Committee resolved to submit the whole question to the joint investigation of Mr. Eaton Hodgkinson and Mr. Fairbairn. Mr. Hodgkinson had previously been engaged in making experiments at Mr. Fairbairn's works, and he afterwards acquired great eminence for his scientific investigations on the strength of materials. The resolution was as follows :—

That Messrs. Hodgkinson and Fairbairn be requested to undertake a series of experiments on the difference of strength and other mechanical properties of iron obtained by the hot and cold blast, under similar circumstances as to the nature of the coal employed, and from the same manufactory ; and that a sum not exceeding 30l. be placed at their disposal for that purpose.

The preparations for the enquiry, the collection of samples, &c., occupied more time than had been anticipated; and at the Bristol meeting, in 1836, the matter was re-considered, and an additional sum of 60l. was granted for expenses.

It appears that during the course of the investigation Mr. Fairbairn had the opportunity of making many trials of the properties of cast-iron generally, independently of the special instructions from the Association; and, not wishing that the results thus obtained should be lost, he gave an account of them in a preliminary paper which he read, on March 7, 1837, before the Literary and Philosophical Society of Manchester, and which was afterwards published (1842) in vol. vii. of their Transactions. It is entitled

‘An experimental Enquiry into the Strength and other Properties of Cast-iron, from various parts of the United Kingdom.’ By Mr. William Fairbairn.

It contains accounts of experiments on thirty-nine samples of cast-iron, twenty-two being of English, fourteen of Welsh, and three of Scotch manufacture. They were tried for what is called *transverse strength*. A bar, one inch square, was cast from each kind of iron, and placed horizontally on supports 4ft. 6in. apart. A weight was then hung on the middle point of the bar, and was gradually increased till the bar broke, the deflection and elasticity of the bar being carefully noted at the different stages of loading. The results were all carefully tabulated, and useful remarks were added on the practical qualities of the various kinds of iron.

At the Liverpool meeting of the British Association in September 1837, reports were submitted having more formal reference to the enquiry ordered by that body. It appears that when the two investigators began to work, they found that it would be more convenient to divide their labours. It was proposed to test the strength of the various kinds of iron in three ways, namely—1. By tension, or tearing the metals asunder in the direction of their length. 2. By compression, or crushing. And 3. By transverse strain. Mr. Hodgkinson undertook the two former of these, and Mr. Fairbairn the third, and each experimenter reported to the Association separately on

M

his branch of the subject, the two reports being printed in the Report of the Association for that year, vol. vi.

Mr. Fairbairn's report is entitled :—

' On the Strength and other Properties of Cast-iron obtained from the Hot and Cold Blast.' By W. Fairbairn, Esq.

It gives elaborate accounts of numerous experiments, conducted generally in the same way as described in his earlier paper, but directed more especially to the comparison of the two kinds of iron, the result being that on the average of the whole but little difference existed between them.

In addition, however, to the main question submitted for investigation, Mr. Fairbairn voluntarily undertook two collateral branches of enquiry; first as to whether, when the loading was long continued, any appreciable weakening of the metal took place; and, secondly, to what extent the strength of the iron was affected by variations of temperature. On the first point he summed up his results with the following pithy sentence :—

It is now upwards of fifteen months since the bars were charged, and if we are to judge from the hardihood displayed in their resistance to the load, there is every probability of the experiments outliving the experimenter.

The results of the temperature experiments were too complicated to admit of brief summary.

The Association, at this meeting, resolved that the experiments should be further prosecuted, and should be extended to wrought-iron, granting another 100l. for expenses; and the names of Professor Willis and two other gentlemen were added to the committee; but we do not find that Mr. Fairbairn published, or attached his name to, any further report on the subject to the Association.

About this time Mr. Fairbairn introduced an invention which has been of the greatest utility in engineering manufacture—namely, the riveting machine.　He gives the following account of its origin :—

I have before alluded to a circumstance which occurred at this time, namely, the stoppage of a part of the works at Manchester by a strike of the boiler-makers.　For some time previously we had been busily engaged in the construction of boilers, and nothing could have been more injurious than the stoppage of the works at such a time.　I remonstrated with the men, but without effect; and perceiving no chance of coming to terms in any reasonable time, I determined to do without them, and effect by machinery what we had heretofore been in the habit of executing by manual labour.

In arranging this Mr. Fairbairn took into his counsels his assistant-engineer, Mr. Robert Smith.　Two plans were proposed, one to act on the rivet by a lever (on the principle of the ordinary punching machine), the other to compress it by a screw.　Mr. Smith was in favour of the latter plan, and wished to make drawings of a new machine on that principle; but Mr. Fairbairn says :—

I replied that the screw would be too slow; and before any further steps were taken, I insisted on making a trial with the punching-machines which were in daily use.

This was done on the following day, and Mr. Smith produced as fine a specimen of riveted work as I have seen either before or since.　This was the origin and history of the riveting machine, which so much improves the quality and reduces the price of labour in this important branch of mechanical construction.

Previous to the experiment made with the punching machine, which was accomplished by the simple introduction of two steel dies corresponding with the ends of the rivet, it was argued that compressed rivets would never be tight, that they would become loose and spoil the work; and many other objections were brought against the project by persons interested in the maintenance of the old process.　To these, and also to the threats that were

held out by the workmen, I turned a deaf ear; and after the
first trial I was fully convinced that the principle was sound,
and that we had nothing to fear from one or the other. Having
convinced myself of the practicability of this new invention, a
patent was taken out for it; and as Mr. Smith was the person
first to accomplish the task, it was taken out in his name, but
at my expense, and he was given an interest in it.

The patent, in the name of Robert Smith, is dated
February 16, 1837 (No. 7,302), and entitled 'Certain Improvements in the means of connecting Metallic Plates
for the Construction of Boilers and other purposes.' It
gives a full description and drawings of the riveting machine, and it claims ' the manner of connecting metallic
plates for the construction of boilers and other purposes,
by riveting them together by compression obtained by
the aid of machinery.'

Mr. Fairbairn continues his account:—

The new machine effected a complete revolution in boiler-
making and riveting, and has substituted the rapid and noise-
less work of compression for the eternal din of the hammer;
besides making the work infinitely superior in quality and
strength.

The introduction of the riveting machine gave great facilities for the despatch of business. It fixed, with two men and
a boy, as many rivets in one hour as could be done with three
men and a boy in a day of twelve hours on the old plan; and
such was the expedition and superior quality of the work, that
in less than twelve months the machine-made boilers were preferred to those made by hand, in every part of the country where
they were known. This success was not attained without opposition; and, as happens in all similar cases, I had not only to
contend against modifications and improvements, but I had to
combat prejudice and opposition from quarters where it was
least expected. The patent, however, expired some years since,
and the machine is now in general use; and I have reason to
be satisfied that it has not only answered the purpose intended,
but has been of use to the public in the development of a new
and important principle in the constructive arts.

CHAPTER XI.

JOURNEY TO CONSTANTINOPLE AND WORK FOR THE TURKISH GOVERNMENT

AGE 50–54

1839—1843

CHAPTER XI.

In the year 1838, Mahmoud, Sultan of Turkey, sent some intelligent and trustworthy officers to England for the purpose of making enquiries with a view to certain technical reforms which he desired to carry out. He wished to place several of the government works and manufactories, especially the arsenal and the dockyard, on a better footing, and to introduce such mechanical improvements into them as would enable them to meet the requirements of the service with greater promptitude and despatch. The commissioners reported the high state of perfection in which they found the mechanical and useful arts in England, and the benefits which would be likely to follow if some of those arts were introduced into Turkey.

It appears that the commissioners visited Mr. Fairbairn's works, both in Manchester and in London, and he may tell the result in his own words :—

A few months after the commission had given in their report, I received through the Ottoman ambassador then in London the commands of the Sultan that I should repair to Constantinople for the purpose of surveying and reporting upon the different establishments then in operation.

With the numerous engagements I had in hand in London and Manchester, and the mercantile difficulties which were pressing upon me, I found it next to impossible to absent myself for so long a time as the work would require; and I was about to give up the journey at once, when I was again summoned to London with fresh offers from the ambassador, and a renewed request that I would comply with the wish of the Sultan. This new application, and an understanding which I came to with Mr. Smith at Manchester, and Mr. Murray in London, that they would, to the best of their ability, manage the business at both places, induced me to undertake the journey; and I set out [in 1839] with the necessary credentials, taking with me my eldest son, for Marseilles, where we embarked in a French steamer for Constantinople.

On our arrival at the Turkish capital, we found an Armenian officer, Ohanes Dadian, and a dragoman, waiting our arrival, with an intimation that the Sultan would give us an audience at the palace on the following Wednesday. Unfortunately, that audience never took place, as his majesty died the very morning of the appointment. In consequence, my inspections and surveys of the public works were suspended for some days, and during that time I had an opportunity of delivering my introductory letters to the British ambassador, Lord Ponsonby, at his residence up the Bosphorus at Therapia. His lordship received me with great courtesy, and invited my son and myself to remain with him till after the funeral.

During the interval I made several excursions into the country which surrounds the Ottoman capital; and as there were no roads excepting tracks for camels and horses, we had to perform our journey on horseback. What struck me very forcibly in these excursions was the immense area of good land lying waste in almost every direction in which we travelled. Some spots were under cultivation, and I noticed that the land was excellent. I remarked, however, that it was covered with what I at first thought were boulders, all of the same dimensions, but which, on inspection, I found to be tortoises engaged in devouring grubs and worms which infest the soil.

On our return to Stamboul—the Turkish quarter of Constantinople—I received orders from the Grand Vizier to proceed with my surveys and reports. In the performance of these duties, I found the Imperial dockyards, small-arms manufactory, cannon foundries, powder mills, and roperies, in a very primitive state. Some additions and new machinery had been introduced a year or two before my arrival, but they were far from perfect, and the native workmen appeared to me to be at a loss how to work and manage machinery of such a complicated character.

The object of my visit was, however, to report on the different works as I found them, and to advise the authorities what was necessary to be done, in order to place them in a more perfect and efficient state.

In the course of five or six weeks I had inspected and reported on all the government works, and recommended what I considered essential to their efficiency and improvement. Much was required in this way in the dockyards and roperies. In the former I found that a powerful steam-engine and a new set of pumps were required to empty the docks when repairs were wanted, instead of having to wait three or four days for the slow action of mules and horses, the only motive power then in use for driving the imperfect machinery. In the roperies the spinning, stranding, and laying of cables were entirely done by hand. Since that time good and improved machinery have been introduced in both establishments, greatly to the benefit of the government.

At the powder-mills, under the superintendence of Boghos Dadian, I found things in a more forward state, with new machinery for grinding charcoal, saltpetre, &c., imported from England. The sheds for the grinding and dangerous processes were placed at distances of about 100 yards from each other, and the machinery was driven by compressed air conveyed through pipes to the different sites. This was an expensive plan, and I recommended the same system that has since been introduced into the powder-works of our own government at Waltham Abbey.

In the small-arms manufactory I found much new machinery from Messrs. Rennie, and Maudslay and Field, which had been introduced only some fifteen or eighteen months before. But with all this new plant, little or nothing was doing in the shape of manufacture, through the apathy of the Turks and their aversion to new things.

My attention was next directed to the cannon foundries; and here I found the works in the same state as when they were erected two centuries ago. They consisted of large circular buildings of great strength; brick domes lighted from the top, and massive wood cranes and sheaves, and ropes almost as thick as small cables. These cranes were for raising and lowering the moulds in the casting-pit, and I was informed that it required many weeks to prepare the moulds ready for casting. As an example of the dilatory manner in which the works were conducted, a day was appointed when a large gun, which had been in the mould for a considerable number of weeks, had to be cast, and I was advised by the Seraskier to be present at the casting, and to see the superintendent, in order that there might be no mistake. In our visit to this dignitary, along with the dragoman, we found him seated on an ottoman with his attendants, in the full enjoyment of his coffee and pipe. Having intimated our desire to be present at the casting—as directed by the Seraskier Hallil Pasha—on the Monday, he took out a Turkish almanack, and unfolded it from a small bobbin, which he carefully consulted. After pondering for some time, he at last said that it could not be done, as the appointed day was unlucky, and the casting could not take place. Although all was then ready, it had to wait till some more fortunate day in the following week, before which I had sailed for Malta.

During my short residence in Constantinople, I had opportunities of witnessing more of the Turkish habits and customs than most other visitors. Being engaged on the part of the government, I had access to the different government departments, and the officials by whom they were conducted. Among the most active was the Seraskier Hallil Pasha, who was at the head of the war-department. With this functionary I had the honour of dining; and every person at the table, which was very low, had two servants in attendance; one with a glass goblet of clear water, and the other with a napkin. These were in requisition after every course; and the repast, after a tureen or goblet of sherbet, wound up with pipes and coffee.

There was a party of twelve at dinner, composed of officers and effendis, connected with the war and ordnance departments. There were also present my Armenian friend, Ohanes Dadian, and the dragoman, whose presence was necessary in order to interpret the conversation which ensued at dinner and during the time pipes and coffee were introduced. This conversation was chiefly made up of queries as to the improved state of practical science in England, and the introduction of railways, which appeared to them inexplicable, if not entirely beyond their comprehension. They could not realise the idea of travelling at the rate of forty miles an hour, and doubted the correctness of the descriptions that had reached them. I could not object to this reserve, as railways had not extended beyond England and Belgium, and the results came so unexpectedly upon the public as to astonish those who had never seen a railway train.

My frequent intercourse with the ministers and officers of the different departments gave me opportunities of studying the habits and customs of the Turks in their daily intercourse, and the way in which they conducted their business. Constantinople proper, or Stamboul, is, like all other Oriental cities, divided into sections, where the different trades are carried on. The wares are exhibited in shops under brick arches lighted from the top, and well protected from the summer's sun and the winter's rain and snow.

These covered markets are laid out in departmental order. In one quarter will be found gold and silversmiths; in another, linen and woollen drapers; in a third, bookbinders, stationers, and workers in toys and other light ornamental articles. But what struck me as the greatest novelty was the way in which the work of manufacture was done. For example, in the trade of joiners, cabinet makers, turners, &c., a great part of the work appears to be done on benches in front of the shops, on which the operator or workman sits, with his tools and work before him. In turning—whether for furniture or tobacco pipes, which appears to be the most extensive trade in the capital—the lathe consists of two head-stocks, between which the article to be turned is placed, and by a line of catgut attached to a wood spring above and a treddle below, a reciprocating motion is produced, which being acted upon by the foot of a powerful operator, the shavings fly in all directions at every alternate stroke. It was surprising to me to witness the process, and in most cases I noticed the work was done sitting, and the tool was held and guided by the large toe and the hand. In fact, I was so much interested with this mode of working that I got permission from one of the workmen to try my own hand at it; but in taking off my stocking, I gathered such a crowd about me from the contiguous benches, as caused me to desist after a fruitless attempt to imitate the operation.

The visit to Constantinople was an important event for me, as it eventually led to large orders which I executed for the government after my return. Immense quantities of iron ore deposits were found at Samakoff, on the shores of the Black Sea, and furnaces, forges, and rolling-mills were sent out for the purpose of smelting, forging, and rolling it into bar and plate iron: but I never could learn with what success. I apprehend the enterprise was ultimately abandoned for want of fuel, as they chiefly depended on some beds of lignite for the reduction of the ore. I also sent out a large woollen mill and machinery for the manufacture of clothing for the army, and driven by a large and powerful water-wheel on the principle of suspension. There were also silk and cotton model mills, a corn mill, an iron house for the Seraskier Hallil Pasha, and a large workshop and tools.

In 1843 the Turkish Government sent a second mission to England, in furtherance of the designs of the Sultan for introducing useful arts and manufactures. The Turkish officer already mentioned—Mr. Ohanes Dadian—was the head of this mission, and he was aided in his object by his Excellency Ali Effendi, the Ambassador to the Court of England, and the Consul-General, Mr. Edward Zohrab. Mr. Dadian spent some months in England, during which time he was in frequent communication with Mr. Fairbairn on the subject of the Turkish works : and Mr. Fairbairn seems to have formed a high opinion of his ability and character.

Among other objects of his mission was one already alluded to in Mr. Fairbairn's notes, namely, to investigate the best means of utilising certain iron ores which existed in the Turkish dominions in large quantities, and of a very pure quality.

Many scientific and practical men expert in the iron

manufacture were consulted on the subject—Mr. Fairbairn among the number—and many experiments and trials were made at Mr. Dadian's suggestion. Mr. Fairbairn was led to combine with this enquiry others upon certain English ores of similar kinds, and the results are given in a paper that was laid before the Institution of Civil Engineers on April 30, 1844, and is printed in the volume of their Minutes for that year. It is entitled

'Experimental Researches into the properties of the Iron Ores of Samakoff in Turkey, and of the Hæmatite Ores of Cumberland, with a view to determine the best means for reducing them into the cast and malleable states. And on the relative Strength and other Properties of Cast-iron from the Turkish and other Hæmatite Ores.' By William Fairbairn, Mem. Inst. C.E.

In this paper the author, after stating that the art of reducing the richer class of iron ores had not kept pace with the advancement made in regard to the commoner and poorer varieties, gives an account of the experiments and enquiries undertaken by himself in conjunction with Mr. Clay, a metallurgical chemist, and others, upon the class of iron in question, and describes the processes which it was considered most advisable to follow in the manufacture. He also adds a classified table of the comparative strengths and other qualities of fifty-two different kinds of iron, including those mentioned in the paper.

This communication was rewarded by the Institution with a silver Telford medal.

Mr. Fairbairn gave some further account of his Turkish work at a meeting of the Institution of Civil Engineers, March 21, 1843.[1] The following are extracts from the published Proceedings :—

Almost all the houses and many of the public buildings in Turkey, being constructed of timber, destructive fires were

[1] Min. Proc. Inst. C.E. 1843, page 125.

frequent. In many parts of the country the common building materials were expensive, iron had therefore been resorted to for construction, and Mr. Fairbairn had already sent over an iron house for a corn mill, fifty feet long, twenty-five feet wide, of three storeys in height, and with an iron roof. It was finished in 1840, and erected at Constantinople in the following year.

The success of this attempt led to a second order, which was for an extensive woollen factory, to be composed entirely of cast-iron plates, the interior being framed throughout of brick arches, upon cast-iron columns and bearers, with an iron roof. The machinery was to be driven by a fall of water twenty-five feet in height, of the computed average power of 180 horses.

Several ingenious devices were introduced for preventing any objectionable effects from the high conducting power of the metal. The piers between the windows were hollow, so as to admit a current of air through during the hot season, and the iron roofs were so arranged as to have beneath them a coating of plaster, to serve as a non-conducting substance.

The two principal rooms were, one 272 feet long, 40 feet wide, and 20 feet high; and the other 280 feet long, 20 feet wide, and 20 feet high; with a great number of other rooms for the several processes in the manufacture of coarse woollen cloths, for the counting-houses, apartments, &c. &c. The area of the enclosed surface, including the courtyard and buildings, was nearly three acres; the floor surface in the whole of the rooms was 71,100 square feet.

This building was erected near the town of Izmet in Turkey.

The following interesting letter, written a few years later by the Turkish officer who had been instrumental in employing Mr. Fairbairn, will show the estimation in which he was held by the Turkish authorities. It is given just as written by the author, in English :—

Malta, March 14, 1847.

William Fairbairn, Esq.

Dear Sir,—I have had the pleasure of writing you some time ago that I should have the honour of seeing you in England soon, and have an honourable conversation with you, which I intend to do in a few months, if God pleases, after having travelled over Italy, France, and some other countries in Europe.

Before I see you, allow me to inform you, and at the same time explain to you what I meant by an honourable conversation, that His Imperial Highness, Sultan Abdul-Megid has been good enough to give you a decoration set in diamonds along with a *Ferman*, in which he is kind enough to write you to be the chief fabricator of the machineries required to be cast and fitted up in England for the use of His Imperial Majesty's Factories, and that it is given to you as a reward for your old services to him in making a great number of machineries for the Government; so the Ferman is the document belonging to the grand decoration, indicating the right of you deserving such a mark of honour to be presented to you by His Majesty, which I shall take with me to London, and then write you the day you are to come there and meet at the Turkish Ambassy, so as the Turkish Ambassador may present you the decoration with the valuable document, from the part of His Imperial Highness the Sultan, in my presence, and explain you the good and kind heart of His Imperial Majesty, which is sure to induce him to reward all the faithful persons who serve so well to His Government as you, my dear friend.

I hope you will not forget me to be your intimate friend, and you will think me always as one who has the interest of your welfare at heart, consequently I expect, hope, and I am also sure, that as you have had the same good feeling towards me, so you will also have it hereafter, and pay the greatest attention to my interest and honour, by executing carefully the small number of orders I shall have soon to give you, respecting some more machineries and other articles.

Please to remember me to Mrs. Fairbairn, and tell her that I hope I shall see her in perfect good health, when I come to England, and I shall also see your children and embrace them, as I long to have the pleasure of seeing them all.

I write with pleasure to inform you also that, though we have had a dispute with Mr. —— some time past, consequently he was out of our service, yet as I was coming away from home to Europe, I did not wish to leave him in sorrow behind me, out of employment in a foreign country, therefore I have sent for him, and forgiving him his trespasses, as the Christianity demands from us to do so to one another, got him into the new Iron Works at Zetia Bourni, where is going to be a school built by the Government for the instruction of the young men of our country in different branches of mathematics and chymistry, &c. so Mr. ——— will be the professor of the mathematics in this new school at the Iron Works.

I remain your most faithful friend,

OHANES DADIAN.

CHAPTER XII.

MISCELLANEOUS MATTERS

AGE 51-60

1840—1849

CHAPTER XII.

THE autobiography, which has formed the substance of the nine preceding chapters, extends no further, in any connected shape, than about 1840, when Mr. Fairbairn had completed his fiftieth year. Some notes remain, referring to matters of a later date; but they are fragmentary and incomplete, and can only be made use of as subsidiary explanations.

But although, in regard to that portion of his life and work which remains to be chronicled, we lose the benefit of his own interesting and vivid narration, we are fortunately not left altogether without guidance. Mr. Fairbairn was very fond of writing; nothing gave him greater pleasure than to put his ideas on paper; and hence, in regard to the later occupations of his life, there exists a mass of information from his hand, either published or in manuscript, which has served not only to facilitate the task of the biographer, but to render the accounts given authoritative and trustworthy.

In the present chapter it is proposed, in the first place, to give a brief notice of several miscellaneous matters, scientific and professional, which occupied Mr. Fairbairn's attention between his fiftieth and sixtieth years; and, secondly, to chronicle some few private and domestic events of interest that happened during the same period.

In 1840 Mr. Fairbairn was consulted regarding the best means to be adopted for draining the lake of Haarlem ; and he appears to have devised an ingenious mechanical arrangement to facilitate the process ; but no record of any report on the subject can be found.

In the same year he became one of the managing council of a society formed in Manchester under the presidency of the Right Hon. Lord Francis Egerton, called the *Manchester Geological Society* ; and although not properly speaking a geologist, he contributed a paper to their meetings which was read on October 29, 1840, and was published the following year in vol. i. of their Transactions.

The paper was entitled ' On the Economy of raising Water from Coal Mines on the Cornish Principle.' It gave an account of the improvements made in the steam-engines for draining the mines of Cornwall, and the great economy of fuel resulting therefrom ; and it advocated the introduction of similar improvements in the colliery districts. It was illustrated by drawings of the engine, and by copies of diagrams of the steam-pressure indicator.

Mr. Fairbairn continued to prosecute his experiments on the strength of cast-iron ; and in November, 1840, he read, before the Literary and Philosophical Society of Manchester, a second paper, entitled

' An experimental Enquiry into the Strength and other Properties of Anthracite Cast-iron, being a continuation of a series of experiments on British irons from various parts of the United Kingdom.'

This paper was published in the same volume as the former one, and it gave an account of the extension of the trials to a new kind of iron that had been introduced into the market, named anthracite iron from its being prepared with anthracite coal.

The following letter from Mr. Fairbairn's fellow-worker in these important iron experiments will be interesting as showing the zealous and earnest part Mr. Fairbairn took in the investigations. The parts omitted refer to private matters.

Manchester, December 11, 1840.

My dear Sir,—Very many thanks for your kind letter of this morning. . . . The sentiments your liberality has inspired are deeply engraven upon my heart.

It is perhaps not less than a dozen years since I first availed myself of your (and your then partner's) kind offer to afford me the means of making experiments at your works. In that interval more experiments, of a really useful character, have been made there, either by yourself or me, than have been made at any one place in Europe in the time ; and when one considers that the expense has been wholly borne by yourself . . . your public spirit deserves the highest praise. This praise has been expressed to me a hundred times, and every man of science seems willing to join in it.

.   .   .   .   .

I had not expected that we should have parted so soon. We have both run for some years an interesting race for reputation in practical science, mutually indebted to each other ; and though your name is now not bounded by Europe, it might have been (perhaps) no worse for either of us if it had been our lot *jointly* to investigate the steam-engine.

I should have gone to-day, but as the extra copies of the paper on Pillars arrived at the same time with your letters of introduction, I thought they might be an auxiliary if taken with me, and I would stay till Monday and dispose of some of them. I have sent five for your use besides those which are addressed, and if you would like more I will send you any number.

Remember me with every sentiment of respect to Mrs.

Fairbairn and your amiable daughter. Thank them for the kindness they have long shown to me, and believe me,

Ever yours,

Wm. Fairbairn, Esq.   EATON HODGKINSON.

Another letter, written by the same gentleman a little later, is in the same strain :—

March 19, 1842.

My dear Sir,—I have received the medals safe, which through your liberality in the encouragement of enquiries into practical science, I have had the honour to obtain. It will afford me very great pleasure to visit your hospitable lady and yourself on Monday at six. Mrs. H. is, thank God, somewhat better to-day, and if ever I saw a gleam of pleasure marked strongly upon her countenance, it was when she saw the medals which you have enabled me to obtain.

With every feeling of affection and gratitude, believe me, my dear Sir (both on her part and my own) most truly yours,

Wm. Fairbairn, Esq.   EATON HODGKINSON.

In 1841 Mr. Fairbairn was applied to, at the suggestion of the government, to give advice as to the best means of preventing accidents to workpeople in factories by their getting entangled in the machinery. It was considered advisable that mill-owners should be compelled to box or fence off all dangerous moving parts ; but that the opinion of skilled persons should be taken as to how far this could be done without interfering with the convenience of working. Mr. Fairbairn gave the required information at some length in a report to Mr. Heathcote, the local factory inspector, dated April 8, 1841, and he encouraged the enforcement of the protection, if kept within reasonable bounds.

In 1842 he took out a patent (July 7, No. 9,409) for ' certain improvements in the construction of metal ships, boats, and other vessels, and in the preparation of metal plates to be used therein.'

The object of this invention was to avoid the weakening of wrought-iron plates due to the ordinary process of riveting. To prepare for this process it is necessary to punch holes in the edges of the plates to be riveted, by which of course the metal is considerably cut away, and much loss of strength ensues. To remedy this, Mr. Fairbairn proposed to roll the plates somewhat thicker on the edges, so that the holes being made in the thickened parts, the extra strength would compensate for the area removed by the holes.

This invention was partially carried into practice. An iron steamboat of some magnitude was built for the Admiralty on the system, and it was also used to some extent for locomotive boilers. But it has been found that the extra trouble and expense of getting plates specially rolled with the thickened edges are objected to, and hence the plan has not come into general application.

In 1842 and the following year Mr. Fairbairn undertook some elaborate investigations on a subject that had often excited the attention of practical engineers, but on which very crude and indistinct notions appear to have generally prevailed, namely, the *prevention of smoke* from steam-engine boilers. At the meeting of the British Association at York, in September 1844, he presented a report ' On the Consumption of Fuel and the Prevention of Smoke,' which was published in the volume of Transactions for that year.

It begins by stating—

There is perhaps no subject so difficult, and none so full of perplexities, as that of the management of a furnace and the prevention of smoke. I have approached this enquiry with considerable diffidence, and, after repeated attempts at definite conclusions, have more than once been forced to abandon the investigation as inconclusive and unsatisfactory.

After alluding to the nature of the difficulties, the author adds :—

I shall endeavour to show, from a series of accurately-conducted experiments, that the prevention of smoke, and the perfect combustion of fuel, are synonymous, and completely within the reach of all those who choose to adopt measures calculated for the suppression of the one and the improvement of the other.

He divides his essay under four heads of enquiry :—

The analysis or constituents of coal and other fuels.
The relative proportions of the furnace and forms of boilers.
The temperature of the furnace and surrounding flues.
The economy of fuel, concentration of heat, and prevention of smoke.

All which are fully treated in the paper.

In the same year (1844) Mr. Fairbairn was called on, in the course of his professional business, to investigate a subject which occupied him for a long time afterwards, namely, the *use of iron in the construction of large buildings.*

The first occasion for this study was an application from Liverpool, where, for some years, an enormous loss of property had been sustained by fires in large warehouses. From 1795 to the end of 1842 this loss had amounted to two millions and a quarter sterling; and the damage by one fire alone, in September 1841, was estimated at 380,000*l.* In fact, Liverpool had acquired an unenviable notoriety for the frequency and extent of the fires ; the character of the town had become stamped as insecure for the storage of merchandise, and the rates of insurance had been raised to such a pitch as to prove a most serious charge and embarrassment to the commerce of the port.

This led to an urgent demand for ameliorations in the construction of the warehouses, particularly by the free use of iron in place of timber. But as such an application of this material was to a certain extent novel, it was felt to be desirable that the opinion and advice of a thoroughly competent engineer should be obtained; and at the end of March 1844 Messrs. S. and J. Holme, large builders and contractors of Liverpool, applied to Mr. Fairbairn to visit that town, and make a report on the matter, as they were about to erect a new warehouse of great magnitude, covering nearly an acre of ground. 'The subject,' said Messrs. Holme, 'is most important to the commerce of the town, as well as to many persons individually, and as we shall not like to take any steps in regard to the large pile, we shall esteem it a favour if you will name the earliest day in your power to visit Liverpool.'

Mr. Fairbairn paid the visit asked for, and made his report on June 3. He pointed out that fire-proof modes of construction had for some time been introduced for mills and factories, described their peculiarities, particularly in regard to the strength of the iron columns, girders, &c., and recommended the application of the same principles to the case of warehouses, concluding with the following remark :—

In my own mind there is not the shadow of a doubt as to the security of such a structure, and I do not hesitate to assert that a well-built and properly-arranged fire-proof warehouse can not only be constructed, but may be made to entail upon the commercial and manufacturing communities of this country an important and lasting benefit.

This Report was thought so valuable to the Liverpool interests, that it was published, with introductory remarks by Messrs. Holme, for general circulation, and was reprinted in the 'Edinburgh New Philosophical Journal,' vol. xxxviii., 1845.

A few months later Mr. Fairbairn's attention was again directed to the construction of large buildings by a dreadful accident that occurred at Oldham. On October 31 a large cotton-mill in that town fell in with a tremendous crash, burying a number of work-people beneath the ruins, and destroying property to a very large amount. At the coroner's inquest the jury expressed a wish that the circumstances should be enquired into by Mr. Fairbairn, in association with a Mr. D. Bellhouse. This was done, and a joint Report, dated November 6, was presented at the adjourned inquest by the two gentlemen, who also gave *vivâ voce* explanations. They ascribed the accident to the weakness of some of the iron beams, which it appeared had been constructed without due regard to the mechanical principles determining their strength. The jury, in returning a verdict of accidental death, added ' their unanimous opinion that the causes of the accident were fully pointed out in the able report of Mr. Fairbairn and Mr. Bellhouse.'[1]

At this time a Commission or Committee was sitting on Fire-proof Buildings, the Commissioners being Sir Henry de la Beche, the eminent geologist, and Mr. Thos. Cubitt, the well-known builder, of Pimlico. These gentlemen, hearing of Mr. Fairbairn's investigation of the Oldham accident, requested him to give evidence before them, which he did; but no report or publication of the proceedings of the body can be found.

A year or two afterwards he followed up the subject by a paper ' On some Defects in the Principle and Construction of Fire-proof Buildings,' read before the Institution of Civil Engineers, April 20, 1847, and published in vol. vi. of their Minutes of Proceedings. It was

[1] *Manchester Guardian*, November 9, 1844.

founded on an examination of another cotton-mill in Manchester that had fallen shortly before ; and the paper pointed out that in this case, as at Oldham, the iron beams were far too weak for the load they had to sustain.

Some years later he published a book on this subject, which will be noticed in a subsequent place.

In 1847 Mr. Fairbairn was applied to by the authorities of the city of Basle to design a bridge for crossing the Rhine at that place. He accordingly made drawings and estimates of a bridge on the hollow girder principle. It was to be in several spans each 100 feet long, and was to cost 34,000*l*.

It does not appear, however, that anything further resulted from this offer.

In the second chapter of this work allusion has been made to the large use of iron bridges consequent on the great extension of railways that took place soon after 1840. Some of these structures proved faulty on trial, and some serious accidents occurred from their giving way. The conditions were to some extent new, on account of the vibrations and concussions to which the bridges were exposed by the passage over them of heavy trains, often at high speed ; and doubts were felt as to the state of engineering knowledge in regard to their design. This attracted the attention of government ; and in August 1847 a Royal Commission was appointed 'for the purpose of enquiring into the conditions to be observed by engineers in the application of iron in structures exposed to violent concussion and vibration.' The Commission consisted of Lord Wrottesley, Professor Robert Willis, Captain Henry James, R.E., Messrs. George Rennie, William (afterwards Sir William) Cubitt, and Eaton Hodgkinson, and Captain Douglas Galton, R.E., was the Secretary.

The Commission collected much information and examined many witnesses, among whom Mr. Fairbairn, from his large practice in ironwork, was one of the most prominent. He gave evidence in November 1847, describing iron structures he had designed, stating his experience in regard to the properties of iron, and the mode of using it, and explaining his views as to the forms of iron beams, the mode of testing them, the influence of vibration, &c. &c. In a subsequent communication he gave useful suggestions for experiments, and furnished full particulars of the investigations he had made for the Britannia and Conway Tubular Bridges. The Commissioners made their report in July 1849, in a Blue Book which is well known, and often quoted when the properties of iron are in question.

In January 1849 Mr. Fairbairn read before the Institution of Civil Engineers a paper 'On Water-wheels with Ventilated Buckets,' which was afterwards published in vol. viii. of their Minutes of Proceedings. It contained an account of an invention originally introduced by him many years before, and which has been always admitted to be of great value.

In the course of manufacture of waterwheels for Catrine Bank and elsewhere, at an early period of his mechanical practice, Mr. Fairbairn had the opportunity of carefully studying their action and of making many improvements, the most important of which was an arrangement for what was called the 'ventilation of the bucket.' It had been found that difficulty had existed in getting the water to enter the buckets freely, particularly when the opening was contracted, as was often necessary. This difficulty arose from the fact that the air in the bucket could not get away to make room for the water. Mr. Fairbairn saw that

from this simple defect many large water-wheels lost
an important proportion of their power; and he took
steps to remedy the evil.   His mode of doing so was
simply to construct a small passage opening upwards
out of the bucket, by which, when the water entered, the
air could rise and get away, and so leave the whole content free for the reception of the water.   The following
section of the buckets (taken from the published paper)
will illustrate at a glance the nature of this simple and
elegant contrivance.   The arrows show the course of the
escaping air.

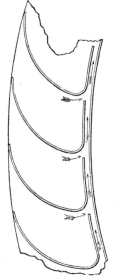

VENTILATED BUCKETS FOR WATER-WHEELS.

It should be added that the same improvement which
ensures the quick admission of the water also facilitates
its quick discharge (an object also of much importance)
by allowing the air to enter again into the bucket.

The first wheel constructed on this principle was at
Handforth, in Cheshire, in 1828.   No patent was taken
out for the invention; but the contrivance so much

improved the action of the wheels as to acquire great notoriety, and to bring large orders to the firm. The arrangement was subsequently improved and extended to various classes of water-wheels, and full descriptions are given in the paper.

———————

The following matters, of more personal interest, may be noticed in this place for the purpose of preserving the chronological arrangement of events in Mr. Fairbairn's life.

He occasionally took pupils into his manufactory, which, from the care and knowledge with which it was laid out and worked, formed an excellent school for mechanical engineering. One of the young men so taken, the son of the celebrated founder of Mechanics' Institutions, Dr. Birkbeck, was also a frequent visitor at Mr. Fairbairn's house. The following extracts from the father's letters may be interesting :—

38, Finsbury Square, April 13, 1840.

Dear Sir,—On my visit to Millwall, I had a very satisfactory conversation with your partner, Mr. Murray; and your kind and liberal communication from Manchester has quite confirmed my favourable impressions.

I have decided, quite with my son's concurrence, that he should proceed to Manchester and enter your establishment there. I really hope that he will render himself worthy of the opportunity which he will enjoy of acquiring sound and varied practical information. He will, I think and hope, be greatly interested in the construction of the beautiful and splendid pieces of mechanism which must continually be in progress in your establishment; one of the most extraordinary, I understand, in the most wonderful school for mechanical invention in the world, the town and neighbourhood of Manchester.

If I mistake not, judging from the kind and rational remarks which you have made on the duties of young men des-

tined for a liberal profession, my son will be very likely to
enter with great cordiality into your views.

I wish it was in my power to accept your invitation to visit
Manchester; this is a pleasure, however, which must be deferred
until the weather is a little more settled, and until, by the
practice of taking exercise, not very convenient to me in winter,
I may acquire strength and activity enough to cope with the
demands which Manchester would make upon my curiosity and
my exertion.

About thirteen years ago, on my return from a hasty journey
into Yorkshire, Westmoreland, and Lancashire, I spent one day
in Manchester. My friend Sir Benjamin Heywood kindly disposed of the principal part of my day, in which of course the
Mechanics' Institution was not forgotten. If I once more return I shall be at your disposal in regard to this interesting
object, and many others since brought into operation.

With great respect, I remain, my dear Sir,
Very faithfully yours,

Wm. Fairbairn, Esq.   GEORGE BIRKBECK.

38, Finsbury Square, January 18, 1841.

My dear Sir,—We all rejoice in the effects of my son
George's residence under your superintendence. His feelings
are better regulated in consequence of the influence of occupation, under kind and friendly control, and he has acquired a
taste for industrious pursuits, which I am persuaded will benefit
him through life. He speaks in the highest terms of yourself
and Mrs. Fairbairn, and the rest of the family. I had formed,
I confess, great expectations from this engagement, and it is
no small gratification to me to feel that I have not in any
respect been deceived or mistaken.

Dr. Birkbeck died in December of this year.

In September 1841 Mr. Fairbairn's daughter Anne was
married to his young friend Mr. J. F. Bateman, an alliance
which gave him great pleasure. He was much attached
to her, and from that time he often spent the leisure
which he snatched from business with Mr. and Mrs. Bate-

man and their family, sometimes also accompanying them on tours and excursions either on the Continent or in the picturesque districts of Great Britain.

The business connection of Mr. Bateman with his father-in-law in some important works in Ireland has already been mentioned. After that their communications on engineering matters were very frequent; and Mr. Bateman's previous engineering education and scientific tastes enabled him to be of considerable service to Mr. Fairbairn. Indeed for many years there was scarcely any engineering scheme or scientific investigation undertaken in which Mr. Bateman's assistance was not called in, until the time when Mr. Fairbairn's own sons grew up, and were able to render him efficient help in his business transactions.

In January 1846 Mr. Fairbairn's father died at the great age of eighty-six. The following letter, written to his wife on receiving the news, is characteristic :—

Millwall, January 17, 1844.

My dearest Dorothy,—I have this moment arrived from Paris and received the announcement of my poor father's demise. It came upon me unexpectedly, and although he had reached a good old age, yet I feel the stroke most severely, and can scarcely reconcile myself to the change. The last link which bound us to the last generation is now snapped asunder, and the many events of my childhood, with the endearing attentions of my good parents, rise up before me as fresh as on the days of their occurrence. Poor old man ! I used to listen to him with great attention, and always admired his sound judgment, and above all his unflinching integrity, which was never absent under whatever circumstances he was placed. I shall always cherish his virtues and look back with pleasure to the happy days I spent under his roof.

I feel my heart fill now they are gone, and although a father myself, I experience the weakness of a child at the bereavement I have sustained. I have been up for the last two nights, but

I must move again by this evening's train to Leeds, and from thence join my brother at Newcastle, in order to perform the last sad duties to my excellent and affectionate parent.

Your very affectionate,

W. FAIRBAIRN.

The following letter from an eminent but unfortunate artist will be read with interest, and shows the character Mr. Fairbairn had acquired for kindness of heart. It is no breach of propriety now to allude to the circumstances of the writer, for they have been but too clearly told in his published life.

14 Burwood Place, London, December 22, 1844.

My dear Mr. Fairbairn,—You once gave me hopes of an order.

Shall I make a proposition? Frank goes up for examination and his degree in a week or ten days, at furthest.

His fees are 15l., and his college bill 40l. 14s. 11d.= 56l. 14s. 11d.

I have brought him through all his terms but this last, and if this last be not paid up, he is ruined and will not have his degree.

I will paint you a small picture for that amount, or for any portion you will advance me at once. You were kind to Frank, and may feel an interest in getting him through.

I never broke my word about a picture in my life. Close at once and you shall have an ornament for your house.

I hope you and Mrs. Fairbairn and boys and all are well.

Mrs. and Miss Haydon's kind respects.

Yours truly,

B. R. HAYDON.

Mr. Fairbairn endorsed the letter : 'Answered February 15, with an order for a picture, value to be 30l.'

Poor Haydon did not break his word. One day, about the middle of June 1845, he called at the house, in London, of one of Mr. Fairbairn's relatives, and left

O

an unfinished sketch in the hall, giving a hasty message for its care. On the 22nd of the same month he shot himself in his painting-room.

The picture, the subject of which is 'Christ before Pilate,' is still in the possession of Lady Fairbairn.

The pride Mr. Fairbairn took in his long friendship with George Stephenson has already been noticed. The following letter is curious, when it is recollected that at this time the two men's ages were fifty-eight and sixty-six respectively :—

Tapton House, January 5, 1847.

My dear Sir,—I have only this day received yours of January 1.

It will give me great pleasure to accept your kind invitation to Manchester when you return from Ireland. Should I find it convenient to do so, I will inform you in due time. In the meantime let me wish you and Mrs. Fairbairn many returns of the season.

Now for the challenge to wrestle. Had you not known that I had given up that species of sport, you durst not have made the expressions in your letter you have done. Although you are a much taller and stronger looking man than myself, I am quite sure that I could have smiled in your face when you were laying on your back! I know your wife would not like to see me do this, therefore let me have no more boasting, or you might get the worst of it.

Notwithstanding your challenge,

I remain yours faithfully,
GEO. STEPHENSON.

CHAPTER XIII.

THE CONWAY AND BRITANNIA TUBULAR BRIDGES

1845–1849

CHAPTER XIII.

DURING the period comprised in the previous chapter Mr. Fairbairn was engaged, for four years, on a work of such importance and novelty as to merit special description. This was the great series of experimental investigations necessary to determine the details and proportions of the colossal wrought-iron tubular bridges erected on the Chester and Holyhead Railway.

After the close of his connection with this work, in 1849, Mr. Fairbairn published a book, the title of which is as follows :—

'An Account of the Construction of the Britannia and Conway Tubular Bridges; with a complete history of their progress, from the conception of the original idea to the conclusion of the elaborate experiments which determined the exact form and mode of construction ultimately adopted.' By William Fairbairn, C.E., Memb. Inst. Civil Engineers, Vice-President of the Literary and Philosophical Society, Manchester, &c. London : Weale ; Longman & Co. 1849.

As this work expressed Mr. Fairbairn's matured views on this subject, it will naturally form the most appropriate basis for the brief notice to be given in this chapter, Reference may be made to the work itself for further details.

The following extracts give an account of the origin and early history of the proceedings :—

In the construction of the Chester and Holyhead Railway two formidable obstacles had to be overcome. The deep and rapid tidal streams at the Conway and Menai Straits had to be crossed by bridges which must necessarily be of extraordinary span, and of great strength. No centerings or other substructures, such as are usually resorted to for putting such massive structures together, could be erected.

Under such circumstances the most obvious resource of the engineer was a suspension bridge, but the failure of more than one attempt had proved the impossibility of running railway trains over bridges of that class with safety. Some new expedient of engineering was therefore required, and an engineer bold and skilful enough to conceive such an expedient and to apply it. That engineer was found in Mr. Robert Stephenson, and that expedient is the one, the history of which it is the object of the following pages to relate.

. . . .

Having to encounter extraordinary difficulties of execution, and being compelled by the Admiralty [who opposed the erection of any structure which should offer a hindrance to the free passage of vessels under it] to abandon the ordinary resources of the engineer, Mr. Stephenson conceived the original idea of a huge tubular bridge, to be constructed of riveted plates and supported by chains, and of such dimensions as to allow of the passage of locomotive engines and railway trains through the interior of it.

It was with reference to this expedient, after all others had been found inapplicable, that I was consulted by him, and that my opinion was requested, first as to the practicability of the scheme, and secondly as to the means necessary for carrying it out. This consultation took place early in April 1845, and, as far as could be gathered from Mr. Stephenson at the time, his idea then was that the tube should be either of a circular or an egg-shaped sectional form.

. . . .

At this period there were no drawings illustrative of the original idea of the bridge, nor had any calculations been made as to the strength, form, or proportions of the tube. It was ultimately arranged that the subject should be investigated experimentally, to determine, not only the value of Mr. Stephenson's original conception, but that of any other tubular form of bridge which might present itself in the prosecution of my researches. The matter was placed unreservedly in my hands; the entire conduct of the investigation was entrusted to me; and, as an experimenter, I was to be left free to exercise my own discretion in the investigation of whatever forms or conditions of the structure might appear to me best calculated to secure a safe passage across the Straits. This freedom of action was obviously necessary to the success of my experiments. I cannot but feel myself to have been honoured by that confidence in my judgment which it implied.

The whole series of experiments (detailed in the Appendix) was conducted at my works, Millwall, Poplar.

.   .   .   .

By July 21 a considerable number of experiments had been made; nearly the whole of the cylindrical tubes had been tested, and preparations were then in progress for the rectangular and elliptical forms. The difficulties experienced in retaining the cylindrical tubes in shape, when submitted severe strains, naturally suggested the rectangular form. Many new models of this kind were prepared and experimented on before the end of July, and others, with different thicknesses of the top and bottom plates, or flanches, before August 6.

On this day he wrote a letter to Mr. Stephenson, which clearly pointed to the principle thenceforward adopted in regard to the beam—namely, that of treating it as a hollow girder. The letter says:—

From these investigations we derive several important facts one of which I may mention, namely, the difficulty of bringing the upper, as well as the lower, side of the bridge into the tensile strain. For this object several changes were effected, and attempts made to distribute the forces equally, or in certain proportions throughout the parts, but without effect, the results being in every experiment that of a *hollow beam* or *girder*, resisting, in the usual way, by the compression of the upper and extension of the lower sides. In almost every instance we have found the resistance opposed to compression the weakest; the upper side generally giving way from the severity of the strain in that direction.

These facts are important so far as they have given rise to a new series of experiments calculated to stiffen or render more rigid the upper part of the tube, as well as to equalise the strain, which in our present construction is evidently too weak for the resisting forces of compression.

Mr. Fairbairn continues his narrative :—

It will be seen by this letter that the weakness of the tube had been recognised in its upper surface, which yielded to compression before the under side was upon the point of yielding to extension ; and that the course which the experiments henceforth took, of so strengthening the upper surface that it should not be on the point if yielding to compression until the under surface was about to yield by extension, had been already shaped out . . . I had ordered the *top of the tube* to be thickened. It now occurred to me that the top might be strengthened more effectually by other means than by thickening it, and I directed two additional tubes to be constructed, the one rectangular and the other elliptical, with hollow triangular cells or *fins* to prevent crushing.

These experiments led to the trial of the rectangular form of tube with a corrugated top, the superior strength of which decided me to adopt that cellular structure of the top of the tube which ultimately merged in a single row of rectangular cells. It is this cellular structure which gives to the bridges now standing across the Conway Straits their principal element of strength.

In a letter to Mr. Stephenson, dated September 20, 1845, Mr. Fairbairn, after describing the experiments with the tubes, adds :—

It is more than probable that the bridge, in its full size, may take something of the following sectional shape.

The parts *a a* being two longitudinal plates, divided by vertical plates so as to form squares, calculated to resist the crushing strain in the first instance ; and the lower parts *b b*, also longitudinal plates, well connected with riveted joints, and of considerable thickness to resist the tensile strain in the second.

Mr. Fairbairn remarks on this :—

The reader will not fail to observe how much this sketch resembles the tubes actually constructed for the Conway and Britannia Bridges.

MR. FAIRBAIRN'S FIRST SKETCH FOR THE TUBE
OF THE BRITANNIA BRIDGE.

Towards the end of August Mr. Fairbairn considered that the experiments had assumed a shape which seemed to require the assistance of a mathematician, in order to deduce, from the trials on a small scale, formulæ and modes of calculation applicable to a larger size.   For this purpose he invited the assistance of Mr. Eaton Hodgkinson, who, it will be recollected, had already been associated with Mr. Fairbairn in investigations on the strength of iron.   Mr. Stephenson concurred in the proposition, and Mr. Hodgkinson first visited Millwall on September 19.

The square cell tube, although so clearly indicated in the above letter, was not, however, at once tried; for Mr.

Fairbairn preferred to experiment on another modification of the same principle—namely, a rectangular tube having a corrugated top, resembling in section the eyes of a pair of spectacles. This was tried on October 14, and Mr. Fairbairn, writing the next day to Mr. Stephenson, says :—

Our experiments of yesterday were the best and most satisfactory we have yet made ; and, agreeable to expectation, the form, as per annexed sketch, gave not only the greatest strength, but what was of equal importance, there was a near approximation to an equality of the forces on the top and bottom sides. . . . . It is evident we are approaching the strongest form. . . I think we have sufficient data to guide you as to the security of such a structure.

Mr. Fairbairn adds :—

It is from this period that I date the disappearance of almost every difficulty respecting the construction and ultimate formation of the Britannia and Conway tubes. The powerful resistance offered to compression by the cellular form of the top, as exhibited in the last experiment, at once decided in my mind the form to be adopted in those for the large tubes ; and from that time forward I had no doubts as to the practicability and complete success of the undertaking.

Towards the end of the year it became necessary for Mr. Stephenson to make some report to the directors of the Chester and Holyhead Railway. They had up to this time shown a great deal of patience, and had watched with much interest the progress of the experiments at Millwall ; but as the next general meeting of the shareholders was approaching, the directors naturally desired to have some definite statements to produce.

It was accordingly arranged that Mr. Stephenson's own report to the directors should be accompanied by two separate ones, by Mr. Fairbairn and Mr. Hodgkinson respectively, each giving his own views relative to the experiments, as well as to the chances of ultimate success in the construction of the bridges.

Mr. Stephenson's Report was dated February 9, 1846, and the three documents are given entire in Mr. Fairbairn's book. A few extracts will serve to illustrate Mr. Fairbairn's position in the matter. Mr. Stephenson says :—

> I will lay before you the results of the experimental investigation, which, with your sanction, I commenced some months ago in reference to the construction of the bridge over the Menai Straits.
>
> In conducting this experimental investigation I saw the importance of avoiding the influence of any preconceived views of my own, or at least to check them, by calling in the aid of other parties thoroughly conversant with such researches. For this purpose I have availed myself of the assistance of Mr. Fairbairn and Mr. Hodgkinson; the former so well known for his thorough practical knowledge in such matters; and the latter distinguished as the first scientific authority on the strength of iron beams.

He then gives a *resumé* of the experiments made to that time, which had, he said, served to determine finally two essential points—namely, the form of the tube, which should be rectangular, and the distribution of the material, which should be such as to throw the greatest thickness into the upper side. The important question remaining to be determined was the absolute ultimate strength of a tube of any given dimensions, which required further experimental elucidation.

There had been an idea, in the first instance, of using, for the erection of the tubes, large suspension chains on each side, and Mr. Stephenson had contemplated retaining these permanently in their position as an auxiliary support for the tubes. Mr. Fairbairn had expressed the opinion that these were unnecessary, and Mr. Stephenson remarks on the subject as follows :—

You will observe in Mr. Fairbairn's remarks that he contemplates the feasibility of stripping the tube entirely of all the chains that may be required in the erection of the bridge ; whereas, on the other hand, Mr. Hodgkinson thinks the chains will be an essential, or at all events a useful auxiliary, to give the tube the requisite strength and rigidity. This, however, will be determined by the proposed additional experiments, and does not interfere with the construction of the masonry, which is designed so as to admit of the tube, with or without the chains.

The application of chains as an auxiliary has occupied much of my attention, and I am satisfied that the ordinary mode of applying them to suspension bridges is wholly inadmissible in the present instance ; if therefore it be hereafter found necessary or desirable to employ them in conjunction with the tube, another mode of applying them must be devised, as it is absolutely essential to attach them in such manner as to preclude the possibility of the smallest oscillation. In the accomplishment of this I see no difficulty whatever, and the designs have been arranged accordingly, in order to avoid any further delay.

It will be noticed that Mr. Fairbairn was the only one of the three reporters who gave a positive and decided opinion against the use of chains ; Mr. Hodgkinson decidedly recommending them, and Mr. Stephenson appearing, by his expressions, rather favourable to them than otherwise. Now, as ultimately the chains were abandoned, not only for permanent, but even for temporary use, the event testified strongly to Mr. Fairbairn's sagacity and soundness of judgment in a matter so confessedly novel and obscure.

Mr. Fairbairn's Report gave a succinct account of the experiments which had been conducted—namely, 9 on cylindrical tubes, 5 on elliptical, and 10 on rectangular tubes. These tubes varied from about 17 to 30 feet long, and from 7 to 24 inches in transverse dimensions, and the trials clearly proved the superiority of the rectangular form and the cellular top. Mr. Fairbairn expressed great confidence as to the ultimate success of the undertaking and the self-supporting power of the tube.

After the presentation of these reports, the experiments were continued, with the view of determining more accurately the dimensions and strength of the structure; but before much more was done Mr. Hodgkinson, in March 1846, requested that his share of the work should be performed separately and under his own control; and as Mr. Stephenson acceded to this, Mr. Hodgkinson had no further connection with Mr. Fairbairn's proceedings.

In April Mr. Fairbairn communicated to Mr. Stephenson an account of further experiments, which had enabled a rough preliminary estimate to be made out of the dimensions of the real tube. Mr. Fairbairn also began to give some attention to the details of construction, proposing certain modes of connecting the plates by riveting, which he considered would be advantageous.

It was further determined to construct a large model tube, in every respect accurately proportioned to one-sixth of the dimensions of the real structure; this, Mr. Fairbairn remarked to Mr. Stephenson, would complete everything necessary for their practical guidance.

About April 1846, the design of the bridges was commenced in earnest, the drawings were put in hand, and measures were considered and discussed for obtaining the material and arranging the manufacture. The distribution of the metal, the sizes of the plates, and the methods to be pursued for putting them together, became matters of considerable importance, and much time and thought were devoted to them.

Mr. Fairbairn's duties now became more onerous. It was no longer the making and testing of small models that he had to do. He was required to render efficient aid in the designs and manufacture of the largest and most important iron constructions that had ever been known, thousands of tons in weight, and involving great novelty, both in principle and detail. Hence it became desirable that his position and occupation in regard to the work should be acknowledged and clearly defined; and, with Mr. Stephenson's concurrence, this was done at a board meeting of the directors of the Chester and Holyhead Railway on May 13, 1846. The following is an extract from the official minutes :—

Resolved :—1. That Mr. Fairbairn be appointed to super-intend the construction and erection of the Conway and Britannia Bridges, in conjunction with Mr. Stephenson.

2. That Mr. Fairbairn have, with Mr. Stephenson, the ap-pointment of such persons as are necessary, subject to the powers of their dismissal by the directors.

3. That Mr. Fairbairn furnish a list of the persons he re-quires, with the salaries that he proposes for all foremen or others above the class of workmen.

4. That advances of money be made on Mr. Fairbairn's requisition and certificates, which, with the accounts or vouchers, are to be furnished monthly.

The works connected with the first bridge it was intended to erect, that at Conway, may be said then to have fairly commenced, and we find Mr. Fairbairn hard at work in regard to various practical matters connected with the construction—visiting ironworks, arranging workshops and tools, preparing for letting the contracts, and so on. The large model tube was pushed on, and was completed, ready for experiment, in June. It was 75 feet long, 4 feet 6 inches high, and 2 feet 8 inches wide. It was tested to destruction, by hanging weights on it till it gave way, the object being to find out the weak places, and to ascertain how it would fail. After each trial the injured and defective parts were cut out and the tube was restored to its original form, with plates of altered strength, as indicated by the nature and appearance of the fracture, and as circumstances might require. This was done seven different times, until proportions were arrived at which appeared to be satisfactory, as giving all the strength of which such a tube was capable. By the middle of July a decision had been come to as to the proportions and distribution of material to be adopted in the real tubes.

About this time we find Mr. Fairbairn considering and proposing plans for the erection and fixing of the bridges, and earnestly urging on Mr. Stephenson the abandonment of the proposed suspension chains. In August he was at the Menai Straits attending to the arrangements there.

Mr. Stephenson was away on the Continent till the end of September, and on his return the contract drawings and specifications, which had been prepared by Mr. Fairbairn in conjunction with Mr. Edwin Clark (Mr. Stephenson's chief assistant on the bridge), were ready.

The contracts took some time to settle, but they were not of such a nature as to shut out alterations and improvements in the forms or proportions of the tubes, as new information was obtained. The experiments and investigations still went on, and the forms of the cells and other points of detail underwent careful discussion.

At the end of the year 1846 Mr. Fairbairn, after visiting several manufactories, reported progress in the preparations for the construction of the tubes.

When the contracts were first considered, it was proposed that Mr. Fairbairn's firm should take an important share in the manufacture. Mr. Stephenson, writing to Mr. Fairbairn on October 25, said :—

I am sincerely glad that your son and Ditchburn [another maker] have succeeded in arranging with the Company. We must put the whole of the Britannia into their hands, as I am sure the others are unequal to the thing. We must visit both their establishments when I come down to Manchester.

In reference to this, Mr. Fairbairn says afterwards :—

A joint contract, which had been entered into by my son, as representative of the firm of Messrs. Fairbairn and Sons, Millwall, with Messrs. Ditchburn and Mare, of Blackwall, for constructing the greater part of the tubes for the Britannia Bridge, was looked upon with suspicion by the board. Although interested as a partner, I had not personally interfered in the matter, and I was even unacquainted with the terms of agreement between the two firms; but when the feelings which were entertained by the directors were made known to me, and as it appeared difficult for me, in consequence of the partnership, to maintain a perfectly independent position, I urged a transfer of the whole contract into the hands of Messrs. Ditchburn and Mare. This transfer was afterwards satisfactorily arranged by my son and Mr. Mare, and approved of by the Company.

The detailed dimensions of some parts of the tubes continued to be under consideration, as more light was thrown on the nature of the forces and resistances, until about the spring of 1847, when the whole may be said to have been finally arranged.

All this time Mr. Fairbairn was occupied in various matters connected with the work, and, among others, with the mode of erecting it. On March 24, 1847, he wrote to Mr. Stephenson :—

I have now completed, or nearly completed, the whole of

the drawings for the framework, girders, &c., for lifting the tubes. The arrangement of the hydraulic apparatus, chains, &c., is also complete; and as soon as we have copied the drawings &c., the whole shall be laid before you. I am now well satisfied as to the security of the ends of the tubes, where the chains [for lifting them] are to be attached, as also the large girders, and all the roller platforms, which are now secure and in a most satisfactory position.

The actual manufacture of the tubes also engaged his attention, although the superintendence of this was not strictly within his province. On June 8 Mr. Stephenson wrote to him :—

I am much gratified at your resolution to devote a considerable portion of your time to looking the tube builders up, and getting a good job made of the whole affair. . . . . What would be most valuable is a regular periodical visit, so that the progress may be narrowly watched, and advantage taken of every new continuation [contrivance] as it occurs. Of these there will be many, which must suggest improvements in our arrangements.

Mr. Fairbairn answered, June 9 :—

I have made up my mind to devote my best energies to the construction and due completion of the tubes, and I will watch narrowly and regularly the progress of each construction, that the work be well done, and free from blemish in every respect.

As the time approached for making arrangements for the erection, Mr. Fairbairn wrote, August 16, to Mr. Stephenson :—

Will you write me whether it is your wish that I should take charge of the floating and raising of the tubes? I have no objection to do it, and to take the management of the whole thing, subject to your approval, and to be responsible for the result.

Mr. Stephenson answered, August 23 :—

P

I was surprised at your letter this morning, asking if I wished you to take charge of the floating and lifting. I consider you as acting with me in every department of the proceedings, and I shall regret if anything has been done which has conveyed to you the idea that I was not desirous of having the full benefit of your assistance in every particular.

On January 7, 1848, Mr. Stephenson wrote :—

I am glad to hear from your note, received this morning, that all is progressing satisfactorily, though not with that despatch which could be desired. Your presence will do much, and I hope you will give as large a portion of your time as you can possibly spare.

It had been decided that, in order to ascertain the strength of the structure by actual trial, the first tube completed, that at Conway, should, before putting it in its place, be tested by supporting it on its ends and loading it with a considerable weight. This test was made at the end of January, and on February 2 Mr. Fairbairn wrote to the effect that the anticipations derived from the experiments on the model had been fully borne out by the trials of the real tube. A few weeks later the tube was hoisted into its place, and the trains passed through it in April 1848, Mr. Fairbairn continuing to give his aid in the matter until the solution of the great problem was practically completed.

Shortly after this time, some misunderstandings having unfortunately arisen as to the precise nominal position Mr. Fairbairn occupied (there could be none as to the value of the services he had rendered) in regard to the bridges, he did not feel it consistent with his self-respect that he should continue his connection with them, and on May 22, 1848, he wrote to the directors resigning the appointment he had formally received from them two years before.

He then put in hand the book mentioned at the beginning of the present chapter, with the object of giving an authentic record of the proceedings he had been a party to, in reference to these bridges, and thereby establishing his claims to what he considered an important share in the merit of their construction. In the preparation of this work (the largest literary effort that had yet proceeded from his pen) he had the assistance of many friends, among others the late Rev. H. Moseley, Canon of Bristol, and Mr. Tate, of Battersea, the latter gentleman furnishing the many mathematical calculations which the book contained.

Many other men eminent in science also actively interested themselves in Mr. Fairbairn's work on these bridges, among whom may be mentioned Sir David Brewster, Mr. George Rennie, Mr. James Nasmyth, Dr. Andrew Ure, Mr. C. Babbage, and Professor James D. Forbes.

Mr. Babbage wrote thus in answer to an invitation from Mr. Fairbairn :—

My dear Sir,—I very much regret the impossibility of my accepting your very agreeable invitation for next week. I have been compelled to leave London on account of my health, and am endeavouring, by the aid of sea air and quietness, to recruit it. This will detain me in the West of England as long as circumstances permit. It is now several years since I have visited your part of England, and I know how rapidly it advances. I am, therefore, very anxious to take the earliest opportunity of renewing my acquaintance with it, and of studying those great mechanical advances in which you have taken so large a part.

I am, my dear Sir, yours faithfully,

C. BABBAGE.

Ashley Combe, Portlock, Somersetshire,
September 3, 1848.

Another letter, from one of the cleverest practical

mechanics of the age, contains also some interesting passages :—

Patricroft, December 15, 1849.

My dear Sir,—Feeling such a lively interest as I shall always do in all that relates to your well-earned fame, and having, from the first, through your great kindness, noted the development of this masterpiece of your genius, I did not fail to purchase a copy of your work when it first came out, and have perused it again and again with the deepest interest. I assure you I feel most proud in being thought worthy of receiving a copy of your work direct from the author, and shall store it up along with a few other much valued treasures, and so let my locomotive copy free to run about telling the truth in many a quarter where the truth ought to be known, and where it can be justly appreciated.

The Earl of Ellesmere has taken a most lively interest in this affair, and, after carefully perusing your work, I think it would have done your heart good to have heard the way in which he gave forth his verdict, one afternoon, before some rather influential folks. Long may you live to enjoy the fame (and, I trust, the profit) which shall attend your triumphant introduction of a new era in engineering, which is destined to do mankind most mighty service!

With kindest regards to Mrs. Fairbairn, in which Mrs. Nasmyth desires to unite,

Believe me, I am yours most faithfully,

JAMES NASMYTH.

During the course of Mr. Fairbairn's experiments it seems to have occurred to him that the principle which was being developed might be made of extended application for bridges generally, particularly on railways; and as its application involved points of novelty, he, with Mr. Stephenson's concurrence, took out a patent for the improvement. It is dated October 8, 1846, and bears the official number 11,401. The title is for 'Improvements in the construction of iron beams for the erection

of bridges and other structures.' It states the nature of
the improvement to consist—

In the novel application and use of plates of metal, united
by means of rivets and angle iron, for such or similar purposes,
and forming by such combination a hollow iron beam or girder.

The drawings show several varieties of wrought-
iron girders, all embodying the hollow or ' box ' construction with a cellular top, combining peculiar stiffness and
lightness with great facility of construction.

Mr. Fairbairn states in regard to this patent:—

The patent for wrought-iron girder bridges was a joint affair
between Mr. R. Stephenson and myself. It was in my name as
the inventor, but he paid half the expense, and was entitled to
one half the profits, but it ultimately became a dead letter, and
was abandoned by Mr. Stephenson.

Under the circumstances the question was, shall I continue
to build the bridges. I chose to do so, and I believe I did
right, as the principle was quite new, and no one understood
the construction so well. I therefore gave designs, and received
orders for more than one hundred bridges in the course of a
very few years. Up to the present time, 1870, I have built
and designed, with the assistance of the Fairbairn Engineering
Company, nearly one thousand bridges, some of them of large
spans varying from 40 to 300 feet.

CHAPTER XIV.

BRIDGE OVER THE RHINE AT COLOGNE

1849—1852

CHAPTER XIV.

FOLLOWING closely on the great Welsh bridges, and arising out of Mr. Fairbairn's connection with them, was another design of a similar character which, though it was not carried into execution by him, made his name favourably known on the Continent, and brought him into contact with some very eminent men. This was a plan submitted by him in 1849-50 for a large bridge across the Rhine at Cologne.

Mr. Fairbairn gives the following account of the circumstances that led to this commission : [1]—

During the progress of the construction of the Britannia and Conway Tubular Bridges, and shortly after the completion of the latter, in October 1849, I was invited by his Excellency the Prussian Minister, Chevalier Bunsen, to visit Berlin and the Rhenish Provinces, for the purpose of conferring with the authorities on the expediency of erecting a tubular bridge for carrying the railway and general traffic across the Rhine at Cologne.

Some time previous to that visit a chain suspension bridge from the designs of the government engineer had received the sanction of the government, and preparations were being made to carry it into effect.

The flexibility of a bridge of this character would render it unsuited to the support of railway traffic, and to remedy this serious defect it was intended to split the trains into sections, and after raising them by machinery to the required level of the bridge,

[1] *The Application of Cast and Wrought Iron to Building Purposes,* 1857-8, p. 261.

to drag them piecemeal by means of horses from one side of the river to the other. A more complicated and unsatisfactory plan, and one better calculated to create delay and inconvenience, could hardly have been devised.

Although this plan had received the Royal assent, it was, at his Majesty's request, postponed until the government could make themselves acquainted with the system about to be adopted in the great railway bridges in England.

The Chevalier Bunsen visited Manchester in September 1849, and entered into communication with Mr. Fairbairn, and the following letter was written soon afterwards :—

Manchester, October 7, 1849.

Dear Sir,—The completion of the drawings convinces me of the superior efficiency of the tubular girder bridge to meet all the requirements of railway and general traffic across the Rhine at Cologne. I am further convinced, now that the scheme is more fully developed, that the bridge will be constructed for less money, and prove more durable than any other description of bridge calculated to attain the conveniences contemplated in this design.

Having attained this conviction, and your Excellency having done me the honour to request that I would visit Cologne, and submit the whole project to the proper authorities in that city, I would respectfully suggest how far it would be advisable for me to proceed direct to Berlin, and fortified with your kind recommendations, to lay the whole of the designs before his Majesty and the Prussian government, after which I would return to Cologne.

I offer this suggestion from having heard that a difference of opinion exists between the government and the authorities [of the city] as to the propriety of making the proposed bridge *double acting*, for the united purpose of railway and general traffic. The Corporation of Cologne, as I understand, require a bridge only for carriages and foot-passengers, whereas upon the plan I propose both objects can be obtained without incurring much, if any, additional cost. I think these are the views of your Excellency and the government, and I shall deem it a great honour to be the engineer to carry these objects into effect.

I am sure your Excellency will pardon me, if in this, as in all other transactions, I speak freely and openly. On the construction of this great work, should it be executed, it is not my intention to become the contractor; the government or the authorities of Cologne shall make their own selection as to those who shall do the work, but I shall give all the designs and working drawings, superintend, and take the responsibility of the execution and security of the work, and that upon some scale of remuneration which may hereafter be agreed upon.

I have the honour to be your Excellency's
faithful obedient servant,
WM. FAIRBAIRN.

His Excellency the CHEVALIER BUNSEN, &c. &c.

This proposal was agreed to, and Mr. Fairbairn left for Berlin towards the end of October. He had been given letters of introduction by the Chevalier Bunsen, and was met on his arrival by the Baron Alexander von Humboldt, who, although occupying no official position in the Prussian government, was residing at Potsdam, in immediate communication with the King, and was honoured with his Majesty's friendship and confidence

The following letter to the Prussian Consul in England will show Mr. Fairbairn's first impressions on arriving in Berlin :—

Berlin, October 29, 1849.

My dear Sir,—You will be somewhat surprised to hear of my being in Berlin, but I was hurried off from Manchester without the possibility of consulting with you before my departure.

A recent visit of the Ambassador Chevalier Bunsen to Manchester, whom I had the honour to meet at the Bishop's, suggested the propriety of this visit, for submitting to the authorities here and at Cologne, a project for the construction of a bridge upon a new principle across the Rhine at the latter city. It was my intention to have written you direct from that place, but I found so many conflicting opinions, that I was under the necessity of extending my journey here to deliver letters to the different ministers, with which I was entrusted by the Ambassador.

I was in hopes, after consulting with the different authorities, by whom I have been most kindly received, that I should be enabled to write you definitely upon this subject; but I find so many difficulties to encounter with the different interests as almost oblige me to leave the matter as we found it. Some gentlemen will, however, be sent over from this country to investigate the properties of this new description of bridge, and I should be delighted, should the business go on, to see it entirely in your hands. I hope to be in London in the course of a week or ten days, when I shall do myself the pleasure of calling on you immediately on my return. In the meantime a note will find me at the Hôtel de Belle Vue, Bruxelles, on my way home.

Yours faithfully,

WM. FAIRBAIRN.

B. HEBELER, Esq.

The king being absent, Mr. Fairbairn went to Dresden, from whence he wrote to the Baron von Humboldt as follows :—

Dresden, October 30, 1849.

My dear Sir,—I send you a rough draft of a letter I have addressed to the Minister of Commerce. It contains my views respecting the construction of the bridge across the Rhine; and the minister having taken great interest in my new principle of construction, and I think being fully aware of its importance, he proposes accompanying me on Thursday to Potsdam, in order through your kindness to present me to his Majesty. I shall bring the model of the bridge with me, and I hope through your considerate attention to impress his Majesty with the importance of having the work executed on a permanent and solid principle of construction. My chief object is to offer to the Prussian government and the Prussian public a bridge that shall be permanent and secure, and on a plan that has been eminently successful. I do not deny that it will be exceedingly grateful to my feelings to become the instrument of its introduction. I shall wait the commands of his Majesty, which you will probably communicate to me, at the Hôtel de Russie.

I have to apologise for this intrusion upon your valuable time.

And have the honour to be, dear Sir,
Your devoted humble servant,
Wm. Fairbairn.

The Baron von Humboldt, &c. &c.

The Baron answered:

Je reçois, Monsieur, votre intéressante lettre, datée de Dresde du 30 Octobre, si tard, que je suis incertain si ma réponse vous arrive à temps. Le Roi, auquel j'ai pu dire combien vous êtes pressé de partir avec votre aimable famille, désire vous recevoir à dîner demain, Jeudi 1ᵉʳ Novembre à 3 h. à Sans Souci, conjointement avec le Ministre de Commerce.

Agréez, je vous prie, l'expression de ma haute considération. Mes respects à Lady Fairbairn.

Le Baron de Humboldt.

A Potsdam, Mercredi soir,
[Oct. 31] 1849.

The following is a translated extract of a letter written by Humboldt to Chevalier Bunsen the day after Mr. Fairbairn's reception by the King:—

Potsdam, November 2, 1849.

Most honoured Friend,—The haste with which the excellent Mr. Fairbairn, the creator of the gigantic structure, will leave us, after coming back from Dresden, obliges me to thank you only with a few lines for your letter of October 12. I cannot be grateful enough to you for having made us acquainted with a man possessing so much knowledge, so highly esteemed by all, so amiable and so modest.

The designs for suspension bridges, which Mr. Fairbairn deems very dangerous, were already decided upon for the Rhine and Vistula; but the presence of this celebrated man, which we owe to you, has made such a deep impression upon the Minister of Commerce, M. von der Heydt, that he begins to be undecided about his designs for suspension bridges. He has occupied himself very much and very kindly with Mr. Fairbairn by means of interpreters, and has accompanied him to Potsdam, when the latter was invited to the King's table, and showed, till half-past six in the evening, the model, as well as all the drawings for tubular bridges.

When Mr. Fairbairn arrived I made haste immediately for Berlin, to offer my services to him and to his family, as well as to the most amiable Mr. Horner, son of the astronomer, the companion of Krusenstern. The King was then hunting for many days in the Harz. I advised, therefore, Mr. Fairbairn, who wanted to leave already the next day, to come here again from Dresden for a few days only. I knew for certain that, according to your wish, so warmly expressed, the King would receive Mr. Fairbairn immediately after his arrival in Sans Souci, and the departure of the Queen for Vienna.

The King was enchanted by the demeanour of the great man, and Mr. Fairbairn did not like less the frank and hearty demeanour of the King. The King was very much pleased too, to see Mr. Horner, having made the acquaintance of his father at Königsberg on his return from Russia to Zurich, and having got his likeness in a painting of Krusenstern's travels, which he ordered as pendant to a painting of the Chimborazo journey.

The family, which I expect in an hour for viewing the palaces, will start this evening for Ostend.

As the King himself has no personal influence in the matter, and the minister being dragged along by the councillors, it is yet unknown to me whether the propositions will be definitely adopted or not. For my part I do all that is in my power to show clearly the boundless resistance of the cellular system, &c.

The next day Mr. Fairbairn left Berlin, after writing a warm letter of thanks to Baron Humboldt for the cordial reception he had been honoured with at the Prussian court. The following letter to an old and intimate friend, Dr. Robinson of Armagh, gives his impression of the Berlin journey :—

London, November 14, 1849.

My dear Sir,—We have just returned from a tour in Prussia, which you will recollect was in contemplation when we had the pleasure of your company in Manchester. Mrs. Fairbairn and my son George have been with me first to Cologne and Coblentz, and subsequently to Berlin. In my visits to these cities I went fortified with introductions from the Chevalier Bunsen, not only in furtherance of the objects of my journey—the bridge across the Rhine—but to most of the ministers and leading members of the Prussian government, amongst others to the distinguished traveller and philosopher Humboldt. From all these gentlemen I received the most marked attention, but above all from the Baron Humboldt, who, at the great age of eighty, came all the way from Potsdam to Berlin to pay his respects to Mrs. Fairbairn and myself. It was my duty to have gone to him, and I am sure it was a great deal more than I could possibly deserve or expect for him to come to me. But be this as it may, I am certainly indebted to his Excellency for the gracious reception I received from his Majesty a few days afterwards, and to whose table I was invited to dinner.

I dare not inform Dr. Robinson of the sayings and doings which took place on that occasion. It would savour too much of a weakness which I fear I have in common with many others. I must endeavour to suppress this rising vanity, and reserve what I have to say for a private *tête-à-tête* with Mrs. and Miss Robinson. I must, however, inform you that I was seated with feelings of pride and gratification beside a greater man than the King, and enjoyed the benefit of a conversation similar to that I had the pleasure to listen to on the occasion of a recent visit of a highly-valued friend of kindred mind and pursuits. I cannot express to you how much I valued the society of this amiable and distinguished man. At eighty years of age he possesses the mental energies of a man of forty, and retains what appears to me to be the desideratum of advancing years, a mind susceptible of impressions, with a power of discernment and retention which can only be looked for in the maturity of life. Such, however, is the mind of Humboldt, perfectly alive to every improvement and every development in the advancement of his favourite studies.

By the different ministers I was kindly received, and (by the help of a model) explained to them the principle of the construction which I ventured to recommend for the bridge across the Rhine at Cologne. I did not, however, make much progress until Humboldt made himself master of the subject, when the difficulties quickly disappeared, and the authorities at once saw the advantage of a perfectly rigid bridge supporting a continuous line of railway, instead of the flexible chain-bridge which had partly been decided upon, and the transport of the carriages by horses one by one from one side of the river to the other. I have urged upon the government the necessity of avoiding this expensive and complex process, and of having the power not only to have a continuous uninterrupted traffic from one extremity of the Prussian dominions to the other, but I have further recommended a double bridge, one side for the railway and the other for general traffic, as exhibited in the following rough sectional sketch which you will clearly understand.

The bridge in this case would be composed of three principal girders, with galleries outside for foot passengers, and the river being 1,288 feet wide, it would be composed of four spans of 320 feet width. This plan I am convinced would not only meet the requirements of the railway, but that of general traffic, and procure ample accommodation for the public and citizens of Cologne. I must apologise for thus troubling you with matters that more immediately concern myself. The interest you have all along taken in the development of this new principle of construction must, however, plead my excuse. Believe me to be, my dear Sir, with kind remembrance to Mrs. and Miss Robinson,

Yours faithfully,

WM. FAIRBAIRN.

The following official acknowledgment of Mr. Fairbairn's proposals followed in a few weeks, after the government had had time to consider their general nature:—

9, Carlton Terrace, November 29, 1840.

Sir,—Although you will have received verbally the expression of the high satisfaction which the inspection of your model, and the examination of the drawings and plans, illustrating the principle of the cellular or tubular construction, with particular applications to the projected bridge over the Rhine at Cologne, has given not only to the committee charged with examining the same, and to the Ministers of Trade, of the Home Department and Engineering, and of Finance, to whose departments this subject particularly refers, but to his Majesty in person ; I have been ordered to express to you officially the high sense of the value of that construction and of those plans and proposals which his Majesty's government entertains.

Although the plan for a suspension bridge (which, of course, could only have served for the ordinary passage) had already been approved of, the government are so convinced of the superior advantages of your system, calculated as well for the railway passage as the ordinary passage of carriages, horses, and foot passengers, that they have ordered two of their most experienced engineers to avail themselves of your kind offer to show to them the constructions already terminated or in progress in England, according to the plan of tubular bridges, and to lay before the government without delay a professional report, preparatory to his Majesty's government's final decision, of which in due time I shall have the honour of informing you. I remain, Sir, with high consideration,

Your obedient servant,

BUNSEN.

WILLIAM FAIRBAIRN, Esq., Manchester.

The commissioners arrived in England soon after this date, and their proceedings, so far as Mr. Fairbairn was concerned, are related in the following letter which he wrote to Baron Humboldt :—

Manchester, December 3, 1849.

My dear Sir,—The Chevalier Bunsen, our mutual and excellent friend, has communicated to me the flattering terms in which you have written to him on the occasion of my late visit to Berlin. For these kind expressions I am most grateful, and notwithstanding they are so far beyond my deserts, I nevertheless receive them with no small degree of satisfaction ; not in

Q

the vain hope of approaching the distinguished eminence of the donor, but with a sincere desire, by future exertions and honourable conduct, to merit their application. It will indeed be one of the most fortunate events of my life to have the good opinion, and I hope along with it the friendship of an intellect so highly cultivated and so universally honoured as that of the Baron Humboldt.

The deep interest you have from the first taken in the project I have in contemplation, not only for the extension of the useful arts, but for the benefit of Prussia, induces me to hazard your displeasure by making you acquainted with the progress I have n ade with the gentlemen of the commission appointed to enquire into the nature of the construction I have had the honour to propose for acceptance in Prussia. That commission consists of (three names illegible). The first is a gentleman of talent and discernment, and I think will take a fair and candid view of the subject; the second is highly respectable, but having originated the project of the chain-bridge across the Rhine, it cannot be expected that his mind will be free from bias which naturally inclines in the direction of his own design. The other gentleman is equally committed to the flexible structure, as the author of the chain-bridge across the Vistula, and unless the superior strength, rigidity, and safety of the tubular system which I have exhibited to them has brought conviction to his mind, I should look in vain for support in that direction.

I must, however, do the whole of these gentlemen the justice to state that they collectively expressed themselves satisfied with what they witnessed at the gigantic operations now going forward in the floating and raising the large tubes at the Menai Straits. They further acknowledged their surprise at the immense strength and solidity of the Conway tube when standing in the middle of it during the passage of the trains. Altogether I hope their journey has not been unprofitable either as regards the interests of practical science or the introduction of those improvements into Prussia and other parts of the Continent of Europe.

On the return of the Commission to Berlin it is more than probable you will become acquainted with the result of their labours, and I have no doubt they will report in full as to what should be done in the case, not only of the bridges at Cologne and the Vistula, but of all other bridges of similar import and character. As to the nature of the Report I am unable to form an opinion, but whatever it may be, it must come from the sound judgment of Mr. —— ; and I have no doubt, from the opinions laid before him and the experimental tests made in his presence, that he will speak favourably of this new principle of construction, and recommend it for adoption both at Cologne and the Vistula.

The Minister of Commerce and Public Works, M. Van der Heydt, will undoubtedly be guided by the Report he receives from this gentleman, and to enlarge the objects of the Commission I shall write to his Excellency in a few days, with a statement of the different bridges these gentlemen have seen, and the places visited by them. To your Excellency I will simply state that I met the gentlemen in London, and accompanied them to Lincoln, and from thence to Gainsbro', where they were shown the tubular bridge of two spans 160 feet each, and the model of which I had the honour to exhibit at Potsdam and Berlin. At this bridge they had an opportunity of witnessing three different railway trains run in succession over it at full speed ; and at Liverpool they examined two bridges of the same kind each 154 feet span. From Liverpool we proceeded, *viâ* Chester, to Conway and the Menai Straits in North Wales, where they had ample means for forming a judgment as to the efficiency of the immense structures, partly finished and partly in progress, and with which your Excellency has done me the honour to make yourself fully acquainted. At the Conway Bridge, which is finished, the gentlemen stood in the middle of one of the tubes (400 feet span) when the train ran through it at nearly thirty miles an hour, and I believe with no more vibration or yielding than is found in a stone tunnel or on the solid ground. All these experiments were made and exhibited before the eyes of the deputation, and having completed their survey, they proceeded direct for Scotland, called here again on Thursday, and are now in London, after having visited the Great Western and Devon Railways, Plymouth Dockyards, &c.

I have much reason to apologise for the trouble I am inflicting upon you in the perusal of so long a letter, and should

not have ventured to do so but that I deem it a duty to make
you acquainted with everything that has transpired since I last
had the pleasure of seeing you at Potsdam.

I retain a lively recollection of the great satisfaction I experienced on the occasion of making your acquaintance, and the
pleasure which the meeting gave to Mrs. Fairbairn, Mr. Horner,
and my son : they collectively and individually unite in kind
enquiries, and that you may yet be long spared, with increasing
health and honours, is the earnest wish of

Your Excellency's obliged and humble Servant,

WM. FAIRBAIRN.

His Excellency the BARON VON HUMBOLDT.

The Baron answered this letter, as the answer is
alluded to in a correspondence, about a month later, between Mr. Fairbairn and General (afterwards Sir Edward)
Sabine, President of the Royal Society ; but unfortunately
it has not been preserved.

Towards the end of February Mr. Fairbairn, becoming
impatient, again wrote Baron Humboldt a letter, which
he enclosed to the Ambassador with the following :—

Manchester, February 23, 1850.

My dear Chevalier Bunsen,—It would appear ungracious
and unbecoming on my part if I attempted to forward my communication, relative to the propositions I had the honour to
make at Berlin, without your sanction and approval. Next to
yourself, there is none I so much reverence and highly esteem
as the good and talented philosopher to whom the accompanying letter is addressed. It is your Excellency to whom I am
indebted for the kind and flattering introduction which first
ushered me into the presence of his Majesty Frederick William,
and also into that of your friend, and I hope mine also, the
Baron Humboldt.

I can assure you the good opinion and friendship of such
men is to me of more value than the building of a thousand
bridges. Still I have a profession, and must be useful in it,
and I feel impressed with the conviction that I owe to myself

and our distinguished friend, to use my best efforts, and leave nothing undone, to substantiate your good opinion and kind recommendation I have received. To do so effectually I must build the bridge across the Rhine, and that in a manner which I make no doubt will redound to the honour of all concerned. It is from this feeling that I venture so often to trouble your Excellency, and again to thrust myself upon the notice of our friends at Berlin. I hope I am not doing so inopportunely, but finding some energetic competitors on the spot, and me at a distance, is one of the reasons which induce me to commit the enclosed to your care. If you think such a letter is proper and will be well received, you will do me the honour to transmit it to its destination. On the contrary, should you think it premature and likely to do harm, pray return it, and oblige

Your Excellency's faithful and very obedient Servant,

WM. FAIRBAIRN.

P.S.—We are going to have a public meeting on Tuesday, on the Great Exposition of 1851. I remarked you in the 'Times' on Friday, and will send you a paper showing what we are about. Do you think it will be possible for me to have an interview with H.R.H. Prince Albert next time I am in town? I should like him to see the drawings of Westminster Bridge and the model, in which I think he will take much interest. His R.H. fully understands the subject.

The following is the reply, which it will be seen begins to convey some doubts as to the acceptance of Mr. Fairbairn's plans :—

9, Carlton Terrace, March 20, 1850.

My dear Mr. Fairbairn,—Allow me to introduce to you by these lines M. Kreuter, Engineer to H.M. the Emperor of Austria, a highly distinguished gentleman, whom that Government had charged in 1848 with the plan of a railway from Semlin to the Adriatic, a plan which he has published with all details, and which is highly approved. He wishes now to study your tubular bridge system, and in general your new constructions on railways. I therefore take the liberty of addressing him to you. He has also been lately at Berlin.

Your two letters arrived safely. The letter to Humboldt was sent immediately. I delayed writing, because the newspapers communicated the resolution of government to lay before the Chamber next summer or in November their proposals respecting the two bridges on the Rhine and Vistula, but had first to receive the proposals and objections of the Municipality of Cologne. Soon afterwards I received a despatch from government, announcing they would *soon* send me a programme about those bridges, or at least that over the Rhine. I am in daily expectation of receiving it, and then alone shall I feel able to judge how far they are dealing justly with you or not, and what guarantees are demanded and given as to projects presented. A gentleman of the War-Engineering Office of Berlin, who was here for some other business, told me the Cologne people had declared they would *never* consent to a bridge being made 15 feet in height, which would obstruct the view of Cologne from Deutz! I suppose this all turns about the selection of the place for the bridge. I expect that not much will be done before the great German business is settled. As soon as I hear something I shall let you know.

Ever yours sincerely,

BUNSEN.

The next intimation of the state of matters is contained in a letter from Mr. Fairbairn to Mrs. Edgeworth (a relation of Maria Edgeworth), whose acquaintance he had made shortly before :—

Manchester, April 16, 1850.

Dear Mrs. Edgeworth,—I have purposely delayed my reply to your kind and interesting letter until I had ascertained my movements relative to a journey which I am about to undertake to Sweden and Russia. I have now fixed the time, and shall probably leave this country about the middle of the ensuing month.

I entertain a lively recollection of my hurried but interesting visit to Edgeworth Town, and I am sure I ought to apologise for the unceremonious manner in which, a total stranger, I came upon you. But having the railway to Mullingar, and my friend Hemans as a companion, I could not resist the temptation of becoming acquainted with a family I had long respected and had heard so much about.

These tubular bridges are a never-ending theme of discussion ; in the scientific world they seem to engage the attention of those who are very competent to judge of their merits. . .

My late journey to Prussia is likely to turn out a fruitless one, as I have just received a letter from the Minister of Public Works, thanking me for the information I have given them, but the government have come to the conclusion to put up the bridge across the Rhine to competition, and a programme has been issued stating that they will not require the bridge to carry the railway, as they have concluded to split the trains into a number of pieces, and send them across the bridge, *bit by bit*, by men or horses. This is the decision of government, having before their eyes a solid bridge which I offered to construct for less money ; that it should open a continuous railway communication from one extreme of the kingdom to the other ; that it should not obstruct the currents or the navigation of the stream, and that it should carry railway trains with double engines at all speeds, and give all the facilities required for general traffic ; also splendid galleries for pedestrians outside the girders. All this I offered, and this was approved by his Majesty and declared to be correct by Humboldt ; and yet, in the face of the whole, this wise government is going to build a bridge whose rickety and palsied frame will shudder at the sight of a locomotive.

I have written my friend Humboldt about it.

.   .   .   .

The letter to Humboldt expressed, at much length and in somewhat strong terms, Mr. Fairbairn's remonstrance against the proposed measure. The Baron's answer was as follows, and it is impossible not to admire the skilful way in which he conveyed to Mr. Fairbairn, under cover of the most courteous and even flattering expressions, information which he knew would be distasteful to him.

Mon cher Monsieur,—Je suis bien coupable d'avoir tardé si longtemps à vous écrire, à vous exprimer l'hommage de ma vive reconnaissance de tout ce que deux de vos lettres, et surtout celle dont vous venez de m'honorer, en date du 15 Avril, renferment d'aimable pour moi. Soyez bien persuadé que les impressions que vous avez laissées dans les régions que j'habite, sont restées les mêmes que pendant votre trop court séjour parmi nous. Mon trop long silence n'a tenu ni au vif intérêt qu'inspirent nos intérêts Germaniques, que j'embrasse avec la même ardeur que notre digne ami M. le Chevalier Bunsen, ni à un changement d'opinion à votre égard. Je suis resté silencieux comme j'ai l'habitude de le faire dans ma position auprès du Souverain aussi longtemps qu'il m'était resté l'espoir de vous être utile, mon cher Monsieur. J'aime mieux agir qu'écrire sur des choses non terminées. Le Roi, qui a conservé une haute opinion de votre talent, de la dignité de votre caractère, de la courageuse sagacité avec laquelle vous avez lutté avec les élémens, n'a pas été dans la situation d'exercer une influence directe et active dans une affaire toute matérielle et technique. La nature de notre gouvernement constitutionnel laisse la liberté d'action et la responsabilité au ministre du commerce et des travaux publics. Deux jours après avoir reçu votre première lettre et des renseignements utiles que m'avait donnés M. le Chevalier Bunsen, je me suis rendu au ministre. La personne que vous avez vue à la tête de la commission a été admise à la conversation. On a discuté les frais, les difficultés de donner passage aux bateaux mâtés, la tendance de renoncer au passage des 'wagons' au moyen d'une locomotive, preférant (comme ébranlant moins) le passage au moyen des chevaux. . . . . Le parti de ne pas se résoudre définitivement avant d'avoir porté le problème devant le public m'était déjà positivement annoncé. Vous savez combien les discussions verbales ramènent toujours les mêmes motifs sans faire changer les résolutions prises d'avance! La déclaration du concours publique a été maintenue et vous avez vu à quelles contestations les conditions proposés ont déjà donné lieu dans les journaux. Le ministre a commencé à entrer en lutte avec la Gazette de Cologne. Tout cela m'a paru peu concluant, toute comparaison de frais très vague, lorsque les localités diffèrent tant de votre admirable et

monumental ouvrage du grand Tubular Bridge! Un événement
tristement instructif a eu lieu depuis en France. J'espère qu'il
fera faire des sérieuses réflexions sur ce changement mysterieux,
mais suffisamment constaté dans la forme et juxtaposition des
molecules comme effet du mouvement ondulatoire. Les opinions
ont aussi leur mouvement d'oscillation et le temps amène
quelquefois des chances favorables. Puissiez vous jouir, mon
cher Monsieur, dans l'heureuse indépendance que vous devez à
votre beau talent, de ce calme intérieur et de cette sérénité que
donne la confiance des propres forces et l'aspect du bien que
vous regardez autour de vous. Je vous prie d'agréer vous-même,
Monsieur, votre fils, et mon aimable compatriote Germano-Suisse,
l'expression renouvelée de mon dévouement affectueux.

Mon respectueux hommage à Madame Fairbairn, votre
digne épouse.

Votre t. h. et très obéissant S.

A. v. HUMBOLDT,

A Potsdam, le 30 Avril, 1850.

A month before the date of this letter, namely, on
March 30, 1850, the government issued a notification
inviting engineers, either Prussian or foreign, to send in
designs for the bridge in competition. The conditions
were that it was to be built in a line with the Cathedral,
that it was to provide for the ordinary road traffic, and
also for the railway so far as to allow loaded carriages
and waggons to pass over without locomotives. The designs were to be sent in by August 1 in the same year,
and the two best designs were to be rewarded with
prizes.[1]

Sixty-one designs were sent in, and the prizes were
awarded, one to a Prussian engineer, Mr. Schwedler, for
a suspension bridge; the other to Captain W. Moorsom,
the well-known English engineer, for a lattice bridge on
the American plan.

[1] *Zeitschrift für Bauwesen*, September 1, 1851, p. 138.

The judges, however, came to the resolution that none of the plans, not even the rewarded ones, were so satisfactory as to warrant their recommending them for adoption, and so the question still remained open.

The government then determined to send over a second time to England for the purpose of examining further into the nature and the merits of the iron bridges that had been erected for the railways in this country. The commissioner this time was General Radowitz, a distinguished military engineer.

This measure emboldened Mr. Fairbairn to persevere in his project, and he accordingly proceeded to prepare his plans and estimates with more completeness, and they were despatched to Berlin in March 1851, as appears by the following letter :—

9, Carlton Terrace, March 11, 1851.

My dear Mr. Fairbairn,—To-day your beautiful drawings and memoir are in the hands of General Radowitz. They came just in time for the King's messenger. The General will report on the same to the King directly.

I assure you that I deeply feel the kind confidence you have shown me and my illustrious friend on this occasion, and I hope it will not be without final good effect in Prussia. I am sorry to find that you have been confined to your room, and hope soon to wish you joy in person here for your perfect recovery.

Believe me, dear Mr. Fairbairn,
Yours faithfully,
BUNSEN.

Mr. Fairbairn also wrote directly to Baron Humboldt at the same time, recommending the new plans to his further consideration.

The plans submitted by Mr. Fairbairn have been published by him.[1] They consisted of two different designs.

---

[1] In the work above cited.

One was in four spans, the two middle ones 326 feet each from centre to centre of the piers, and the two end ones 244 feet. There were to be three parallel lines of wrought-iron box-girders, on the plan patented by Mr. Fairbairn, providing between them for railway and carriage roads, and having external footpaths on each side. The cost of this structure was estimated to be about 400,000*l*.

The other design was for two spans only, of 570 feet each, and for these Mr. Fairbairn proposed two lines of hollow rectangular tubular girders, similar to those of the Britannia Bridge, but larger. Each tube would admit one line of railway within it, and there was to be a carriage way between them, and footpaths on the sides. The cost of this was estimated at 470,000*l*.

The result of the further consideration of the matter in Berlin was, that the Government abandoned their own scheme of a suspension bridge, with an interruption of the railway traffic, and adopted Mr. Fairbairn's suggestion so far as it comprised a strong and rigid structure over which the trains could cross in their complete state. This measure of establishing a free railway connection between the north and south banks of the river was really the great point of his recommendation.

But the Government, while adopting his ideas as to the general nature of the bridge, demurred to his proposed mode of construction, that of large tubes formed of solid wrought-iron. They probably attached more weight than he did to æsthetical considerations of design, and in such a situation they feared that a bridge of the same description as that of the Britannia and Conway tubes would be objectionable in appearance.

Whether, under these circumstances, they ever entered into communication with Mr. Fairbairn (as it would have been not only courteous but just for them to do) with a

view to inducing him to modify the construction, does not
appear. But, however this may be, the Government decided that the bridge should be constructed on the lattice
or open-work principle, which had been shortly before
adopted for a large bridge carrying one of the Prussian
railways over the Vistula.[1]

Mr. Fairbairn, being informed of this, wrote to Humboldt, on August 23, 1852, a letter from which the following is an extract :—

> From the condescending manner in which I was received by
> his Majesty, and the unwearied attention you personally be-
> stowed on the objects of my journey, I was taught to believe
> that at no very distant period I should again have the pleasure
> of meeting you, and that the projected bridge across the Rhine
> at Cologne, in which you took so deep an interest, would sooner
> or later have been carried into effect. I believe this is now
> likely to be accomplished, not upon the principle I recom-
> mended, but some other construction, which doubtless the
> authorities believe superior to those I had the honour to lay
> before them. One important consideration was, however, ob-
> tained by our united exertions, and that was to condemn an
> imperfect and abortive construction, and to direct the public
> mind to the importance of having a structure that was not only
> capable of supporting the railway, but all the other objects con-
> templated in the requirements of the public traffic. These
> objects have now been attained; at least I am so informed;
> and that the drawbridges, as well as the hoisting and lowering
> of the carriages from one level to another, are to be dispensed
> with. This, you will recollect, is what we contended for; and I
> consider it fortunate for the country that his Majesty suspended
> the perpetration of a project that would never have realised the
> expectations of the Government or the wants of the public.

Mr. Fairbairn then goes on to criticise the proposed
plan of construction, and to vindicate the superiority of
his own, after which he adds :—

---

[1] *Zeitschrift für Bauwesen*, 1857, p. 309.

Altogether, I trust the investigation of this subject has not been without its use; and although I have received official notice that the authorities decline adopting the system I have recommended, I nevertheless still hope to find their constructions founded upon the same principles I have had the honour to advocate, and which I make no doubt will be for the benefit as well as the security of the public.

No further reference seems to have been made to Mr. Fairbairn, but the plans, according to the new conditions, were elaborated by two Prussian engineers, Messrs. Wallbaum and Lohse, and after several changes, resolved themselves into the form of the present bridge, which was commenced in 1855, and finished some years later. It crosses the river, in a line with the axis of the cathedral, in four spans, each 313 feet wide in the clear, and consists of two pairs of girders, side by side, one pair carrying a double line of railway, and the other the road traffic. The girders are formed of open lattice-work, instead of plates, as Mr. Fairbairn had proposed; but in other respects there has not been much material departure from Mr. Fairbairn's designs.

CHAPTER XV

SCIENTIFIC HONOURS

AGE 61–64

1850—1853

CULMINATING POINT IN MR. FAIRBAIRN'S LIFE—EFFECT OF CONTRO-
VERSIES—THE ROYAL SOCIETY OF LONDON—MR. GEORGE RENNIE—
CERTIFICATE—ELECTION AS F.R.S.—THE NATIONAL INSTITUTE OF
FRANCE—ITS FOUNDATION AND CONSTITUTION—THE FRENCH ACADEMY
AND JOHNSON—VACANCY—MR. FAIRBAIRN PROPOSED AS A CANDIDATE
—COMMISSION OF THE ACADEMY OF SCIENCES—CORRESPONDENCE WITH
ARAGO, DUPIN, MORIN, PONCELET—WATER-WHEELS—ELECTION—THE
ATHENÆUM CLUB—ITS OBJECTS AND MODE OF ELECTION—RULE II.—
MR. FAIRBAIRN ELECTED WITHOUT BALLOT—MINOR HONOURS.

CHAPTER XV.

THE publication of Mr. Fairbairn's work on the great bridges formed a culminating point in his life; and the controversies which took place on the subject, although they caused him much annoyance at the time, were not without advantage to him, inasmuch as they brought his name more prominently before the world, and called more general attention, not only to the part he had taken in the works in question, but to his distinguished position generally as a mechanical engineer.

The appreciation of his merits was manifested immediately by some honours being paid him of very high character.

The first of these was his admission into the Royal Society of London. This society elects fifteen members every year, who are selected carefully by the council, out of a large number of candidates, on account of eminent scientific merit; and consequently the fellowship of the society is a high distinction.

The proposal appears to have originated with the late Mr. George Rennie, who, writing to Mr. Fairbairn on December 4, 1849, said:—

Few men would have a better chance, as your name and reputation are too well known to the world at large to permit of any doubt of your success. I will desire the assistant secretary to send you a printed form to be filled up, and to be sent

R

round to your friends for signature, in which I will assist, although I am precluded from signing it myself.

The form, or *certificate*, as it is called, was ultimately filled up as follows :—[1]

William Fairbairn, Engineer, Manchester, author of numerous papers which have been from time to time published in the Transactions of the British Association for the Advancement of Science, in the Memoirs of the Literary and Philosophical Society of Manchester, and the Transactions of Institution of Civil Engineers. These papers embrace an enquiry into the comparative strength of hot and cold blast iron, an extended investigation of the strength and other properties of all the irons of Great Britain, and of the Samakoff Turkish iron ; an Essay on the Combustion of Fuel, on the most Economical Method of Raising Water from Mines, &c. The author also of a work descriptive of the Conway and Britannia Tubular Bridges, and containing also an experimental research to determine the law which governs the strengths, &c., of Wrought-Iron Tubular Bridges and Girders ;—being desirous of admission into the Royal Society of London, we, the undersigned, propose and recommend him as deserving that honour, and as likely to become a useful and valuable member.—Dated this 31st day of January, 1850.

It was signed by the following names, among which many will be recognised as of great scientific eminence :—

Henry Holland, Henry Moseley, John Rennie, J. Walker, W. Cubitt, Joshua Field, James Booth, F. Beaufort, W. C. Mylne, G. R. Porter, Robert Willis, John Barrow, Charles Babbage, Andrew Ure, William Brockedon.

The council included Mr. Fairbairn's name in the selected list of candidates ; and he was elected into the Society, June 6, 1850.

[1] Inserted by permission of the Society.

Within a year after Mr. Fairbairn's election into the Royal Society another honour was paid him, which was still more distinguished, on account of the very few of his countrymen on whom it has been bestowed—that of admission into the National Institute of France. As the nature and constitution of this body are not generally known in this country, a few explanatory words may be in place here.

The Institute of France was founded by the Republic on the 5 Fructidor (August 22), 1795, its declared object being :—

1°. A perfectionner les sciences et les arts par des recherches non interrompues, par la publication des découvertes, par la correspondance avec les sociétés savantes et étrangères. 2°. A suivre, conformément aux lois et arrêtés du Directoire executif, les travaux scientifiques et littéraires qui auront pour objet l'utilité générale et la gloire de la Republique.

It was confirmed by Bonaparte some years later ; and again by Louis XVIII. in 1816, and by Louis Philippe in 1832.

The body termed 'l'Institut de France' comprises five 'Académies,' the constitution of which is as follows :—

1. L'ACADÉMIE FRANÇAISE.

This consists of forty members chosen from the most eminent literary and public men of the kingdom.[1]

---

[1] This body is older than the Institute generally, having been ' employed in settling the French language and editing the celebrated dictionary ' before Johnson's time. Garrick's complimentary epigram on Johnson's Dictionary says, alluding to them :—

> And Johnson, well arm'd like a hero of yore,
> Has beat forty French, and will beat forty more!

2. L'Académie des Inscriptions et Belles Lettres.

This consists of men eminent in antiquarian and polite literature, and the members are :—

Académiciens	40
Académiciens libres	10
Associés étrangers	8
Correspondants, French	20
„ Foreigners	30

3. L'Académie des Sciences.

This is divided into eleven sections, and the numbers of members of different grades are :—

Académiciens.

Geometry	6
Mechanics	6
Astronomy	6
Geography and Navigation	3
General Physics	6
Chemistry	6
Mineralogy	6
Botany	6
Rural Economy	6
Anatomy and Zoology	6
Medicine and Surgery	6
	63
Académiciens libres	10
Associés étrangers	8

Correspondants.

Geometry	6
Mechanics	6
Astronomy	16
Geography and Navigation	8
General Physics	9
Chemistry	9
Mineralogy	8
Botany	10
Rural Economy	10
Anatomy and Zoology	10
Medicine and Surgery	8
	100

4. L'ACADÉMIE DES BEAUX ARTS.

This also is divided into sections, with numbers as follow :—

Académiciens.

Painting	14
Sculpture	8
Architecture	8
Engraving	4
Musical Composition	6
	40
Académiciens libres	10
Associés étrangers	10
Correspondants	40
Correspondants honoraires	3

5. L'ACADÉMIE DES SCIENCES MORALES ET POLITIQUES.

The subdivisions in this Academy are :—

Académiciens.

Philosophie	6
Morale	6
Législation, Droit public, et Jurisprudence	6
Economie politique, et statistique	6
Histoire générale et philosophique	6
	30
Académiciens libres	7
Associés étrangers	5

Correspondants.

Philosophie	7
Morale	7
Législation	7
Economie politique	10
Histoire	7
	38

TOTAL OF THE INSTITUTE,

Académiciens	213
Académiciens libres	35
Associés étrangers	31
Correspondants	228
Correspondants honoraires	3
	510

When a vacancy occurs by the death of any acade-
mician, a list of at least three names is drawn up and
presented to the Institute by the Academy in which the
vacancy arises, and the choice between them is made by
the general body. The corresponding members in each
Academy are elected by that Academy, on the presentation of a list by the section in which the vacancy occurs.

In the middle of the year 1851, a vacancy occurred
among the corresponding members of the Mechanical
Section of the Academy of Sciences by the death of Sir
Mark Isambard Brunel. Mr. Fairbairn had previously
made the acquaintance of some influential members of
the Institute, among whom were Generals Poncelet and
Morin, Baron Dupin, and M. Arago; and on the encouragement of these and other friends, he decided to
offer himself as a candidate. He went to Paris in September, and shortly afterwards sent over full particulars
of his claims, accompanied with the following letter to
General Poncelet :—

Manchester: October 1, 1851.

Dear General Poncelet,—The interest you have taken in
wishing me to become a candidate for admission as a corresponding member of the Institute of France, induces me to lay
before you a brief statement of facts in connection with my
past and present history. I would not have ventured to aspire
to the dignity but for the encouragement I received from yourself and M. Arago; nor is it my intention even now to present
myself before the members of the Academy unless well supported
by friends who may consider me worthy of such a distinction.
I have no doubt there will be found many claimants of higher
standing and much greater learning than myself, entitled to
such an honour, but I should deem myself ungrateful, after the
encouragement I have received, if I did not lay before the
Academy a list of my qualifications, with copies of such as I
have in my possession, which I now forward for acceptance by
that distinguished body.

I have further drawn up for your guidance a short account of my early history, and a brief statement of my endeavours to be useful in my professional capacity, and the advancement of practical science. In these attempts I have laboured under an imperfect education, and many other disadvantages, which nothing but an indomitable perseverance could overcome. How far I have been successful I must leave my works to determine; and all I have now to offer is (in case of my election) the same determined spirit to be useful to the Institute of France, as I humbly trust I have been to the Institutions I have been connected with in this country.

Yours faithfully and obliged,

WM. FAIRBAIRN.

The Academy named a commission of three members to investigate Mr. Fairbairn's claims; and, the result of this being satisfactory, an official letter was addressed to him as follows:—

Paris, le 13 Novembre, 1851.

Mon cher Monsieur,—Il y a eu ce moment une vacance de Membre Correspondant de la Section de Mécanique à l'Académie des Sciences à Paris.

Les grands et beaux travaux que vous avez dirigés et executés vous mettent au nombre des personnes sur lesquelles doit se porter la pensée de l'Institut. Je vous prie donc de me faire savoir si votre intention est de vous porter comme candidat en titre de Membre Correspondant de l'Académie des Sciences (Section de Mécanique), et dans le cas de l'affirmative, de m'envoyer une note des principaux travaux sur lesquels s'appuierait votre candidature.

Recevez, Monsieur, l'expression de la haute considération de votre dévoué serviteur,

Le Colonel d'Artillerie, Membre de l'Institut, Administrateur du Conservatoire des Arts et Metiérs,

A. MORIN.

Monsieur WM. FAIRBAIRN.

This letter was answered in due course, but the stirring political events of the end of the year so interrupted the even course of routine business that nothing was done towards the elections for some months. Many vacancies had occurred, and the French members had to be elected before the claims of the Corresponding members could be entertained. Mr. Fairbairn, however, continued to receive strong expressions of support from his distinguished friends, as is shown in the following interesting letter from one of the greatest mechanics of the age :—

Paris, le 4 Fevrier, 1852.

Mon cher et très estimé Collègue,—Mon long silence n'aurait aucune excuse légitime, sans les événements politiques qui sont venus nous surprendre. D'une autre part, lors de vos premières communications et de l'envoi de vos nombreux titres aux suffrages de l'Institut, la plupart de mes collègues de la section de mécanique étaient absente de Paris, et il a fallu attendre leur retour pour les mettre au courant de notre projet d'élection, sans trop en brusquer le dénouement et leur faire penser que notre parti était pris et arrêté à l'avance. Aujourd'hui, malgré les événements, les choses sont beaucoup plus avancées, et j'ai tout bien de croire que votre nom sera porté en tête de la liste des candidats de la section de mécanique.

A l'égard de vos titres et des divers travaux de votre laborieuse carrière, ils seront, vous pouvez en être sur, appréciés à leur juste valeur. Pour moi, je les trouve, en tous points, dignes des suffrages de l'Académie des Sciences, soit au point de vue pratique, soit à celui de l'invention et des recherches expérimentales entreprises en vue d'éclairer la science de construction. Vos immenses travaux comme ingénieur et constructeur, votre ingénieuse machine à river, et la manière dont vous avez su, l'un des premiers, assouplir la tôle et en propager l'emploi dans l'industrie manufacturière, et les grandes constructions nautiques, sont dignes de la plus haute estime. Enfin je suis tout à fait de l'avis du Dr. Ure quant aux éloges qu'il donne à votre système d'établissement des arbres de commande dans les filatures, &c.

.   .   .   .

Votre bel ouvrage sur les ponts tubulaires ne laisse rien à désirer à cet égard [vos droits comme inventeur et perfectionneur]; j'en dirai autant de votre machine à river, et de vos con-structions de roues hydrauliques, où chacun appréciera les belles dispositions adoptées; neanmoins pour les hommes tels que moi allés peu au courant du progrès que les constructions de ce genre ont reçu en Angleterre, il serait utile de connaître la filière historique des idées. Au sujet de vos grandes et belles roues à augets courbes ventilés à système de suspension, je trouve des renseignements précieux dans le mémoire que M. Ferey a bien voulu me remettre de votre part, et dont je vous adresse mes bien sincères remerciments. Vos systèmes de construction sont sans contredit supérieurs à ceux qui avaient, jusque-là, été employés, et je les crois très propres à rendre les services auxquels il sont destinés; cependant je ne pense que l'évacua-tion de l'air en dehors les augets soit le seul obstacle opposé à l'introduction de l'eau dans les augets, et que par conséquent le moyen de ventilation si simple que vous employez soit le dernier mot de la question. D'après des études très anciennes que j'ai faites de cette question, le rapport des vitesses de la roue et de la veine d'eau, les angles des augets et de cette veine avec la circonférence extérieure de la roue doivent exercer aussi une très grande influence, et c'est dans cette vue que j'ai imaginé des dispositions nouvelles, pour les roues en dessus et de côté, qui diffèrent beaucoup de tout ce que l'on avait imaginé jusqu'à présent, outre que j'ai eu aussi en vue une accélération de vitesse.

. . . .

GÉNÉRAL PONCELET.

M. Poncelet added a lucid description of his im-provements in water-wheels, illustrating it with sketches. These improvements have now long been known, and have become highly appreciated among engineers, for their elegant scientific merit and their practical utility; but the description is too technical for insertion here.

A little later, another great mechanic wrote :—

Paris, le 14 Mars, 1852.

Mon cher Fairbairn,—J'ai tardé bien longtemps à vous écrire au sujet de l'affaire qui vous intéresse ici, parce que je voulais pouvoir vous en donner quelques nouvelles certaines. Après des pourparlers assez longs, et difficiles, nous sommes parvenus, MM. Dupin, Poncelet et moi, à faire décider par la section de mécanique que vous seriez présenté pour être nommé membre correspondant de l'Institut avec MM. Babbage, Hodgkinson et Willis ; mais que la section declarerait que dans l'état actuel des besoins de la science elle demande que vous soyez choisi. M. Dupin se charge de faire le rapport.

Votre bien affectionné,
M. Morin.

The final proceedings are detailed in the following letters, which are given verbatim, as they were written in English by the great man whose signature they bear.

Paris, May 6, 1852.

Dear Sir,—Monday last I had the honour and pleasure to read my report, in the name of Mechanics' Section of the Institute of France, to propose the candidates for the place of correspondent, vacant by the death of Sir M. I. Brunel.

I have been happy enough to obtain that your name should be the first of all candidates.

I can say you that I have been quite enthusiastic with the study of your numerous and so meritorious works and inventions ; the picture of them did strike the whole Academy with admiration.

I hope next week to be able to write again to you a letter announcing your election as our worthy Correspondent, and nobody will be more happy for that result than I shall be.

I am, Sir,
Your most devoted servant,
Baron Charles Dupin.

Paris, May 11, 1852.

Dear Sir,—I rejoice very much in giving to you notice that you have been elected to-day *Correspondant* of the National Institute of France, and your majority has been enormous, thirty-seven against four.

I am, dear sir,
Your most devoted *colleague* and friend,
Baron Charles Dupin.

The official announcement of the election was as follows ;—

Institut de France, Académie des Sciences, Paris, le 11 Mai, 1852.

Le Secrétaire perpetuel de l'Académie pour les Sciences Mathematiques.

Monsieur,—J'ai l'honneur de vous adresser l'extrait ci-joint du Procès-verbal de la séance du Mardi 11 Mai, dans laquelle l'Académie vient de vous nommer l'un de ses Correspondants pour la Section de Mécanique, en remplacement de feu Mr. Brunel.

En vous offrant ce titre comme un témoignage de son estime, l'Académie vous invite, Monsieur, à lui faire part du fruit de vos recherches dans les sciences dont elle s'occupe.

Veuillez, Monsieur, agréer l'assurance de ma considération la plus distinguée.

F. ARAGO.

Enclosure.

L'Académie procède par la voie du scrutin à l'élection d'un Correspondant, appelé à remplir la place devenue vacante par suite du décès de Mr. Brunel.

Le résultat du scrutin donne la majorité absolue des suffrages à Mr. Fairbairn à Manchester.

En conséquence M. le Président le proclame élu correspondant.[1]

Pour extrait conforme,

F. ARAGO.

[1] It may be interesting to add a list of the Englishmen who were members of the Institute about the time of Mr. Fairbairn's election :—

Académie des Inscriptions.

Horace Hayman Wilson, Oxford, Associé Étranger.
William Martin Leake, London, Correspondant.
Thos. Gaisford, Oxford,   „
Thos. Wright, London,   „
H. Rawlinson, Bagdad,   „
B. H. Hodgson, Bengal,   „

Académie des Sciences.

Robert Brown, Associé Étranger.	Capt. Scoresby, Correspondant.
Michael Faraday, „ „	Admiral Beaufort, „

In 1853 came a third distinction, one highly appreciated by those who know its nature, namely, his election without ballot, into the Athenæum Club.

This institution was founded in 1824, with an object independent of all political or party views, namely, 'for the association of individuals known for their scientific or literary attainments, artists of eminence in any class of the fine arts, and noblemen and gentlemen distinguished as liberal patrons of science, literature, or the arts.' The number of members is 1,200 ; and although admission into the club has not been exclusively confined to persons who come within the avowed classification, it is

David Brewster, Associé Étranger
W. R. Hamilton, Correspondant.
H. Moseley,   „
W. Fairbairn,   „
Sir John Herschel,   „
General Brisbane,   „
G. D. Airy,   „
Capt. Smyth,   „
J. R. Hind,   „
Dr. Buckland, Correspondant.
Sir R. Murchison,   „
Sir H. de la Beche,   „
— Wallich,   „

Sir Edward Parry, Correspondant
Sir John Franklin,   „
Sir James Clark Ross, „
Prof. Barlow,   „
Prof. Forbes, Edinburgh, Correspondant.
Prof. Wheatstone, Correspondant.
Prof. Graham,   „
Prof. Conybeare,   „
— Bracy Clark, Correspondant.
— Lindley,   „
Richard Owen,   „
Sir B. Brodie,   „

Académie des Beaux Arts.

Chas. Cockerell, Associé Étranger.
T. L. Donaldson, Correspondant.
Howard Vyse,   „

Académie des Sciences Morales et Politiques.

Lord Brougham, Associé Étranger.
H. Hallam,   „   „
J. R. MacCulloch, „   „
Sir W. Hamilton, Edinburgh, Correspondant.
Dr. Whateley, Dublin, Correspondant.
John Austin, London, Correspondant.

William Jacob, London, Correspondant.
Nassau Senior, London, Correspondant.
C. Babbage, London, Correspondant.
— Tooke, London, Correspondant.
T. B. Macaulay,   „

understood that the club is distinguished from all others by the predominance of members of scientific, literary, and artistic pursuits and tastes.

The ordinary mode of admission into the club is by the usual process of a ballot among the members generally; and so great is the demand for admission that there are at present above 1,500 candidates on the books waiting their turn for election, and a name has to stand about fifteen years on the list before it is called on.

The club has, however, a feature peculiar to itself, namely, the existence of a rule which requires the managing committee to keep up its special character by introducing into it, without being subject to the general ballot, nine members annually, chosen for their eminence in the objects for which the institution was founded. The following is the rule in question :—

It being essential to the maintenance of the Athenæum, in conformity with the principles upon which it was originally founded, that the annual introduction of a certain number of persons of distinguished eminence in science, literature, or the arts, or for public services, should be secured, a limited number of persons of such qualifications shall be elected by the committee. The number so elected shall not exceed nine in each year. The elections shall take place during the months of January, February, March, and April. The committee shall be specially summoned for the purpose, at least one week before the intended election ; no election shall take place unless nine at least of the committee be actually present, and the whole of those present be unanimous in their election. Not more than one-third of the total number of persons to be thus admitted within the year shall be elected at any one meeting.

The club intrust this privilege to the committee, in the entire confidence that they will only elect persons who shall have attained to distinguished eminence in science, literature, or the arts, or for public services. The names of members so elected are to be immediately hung up in the public rooms.

In December, 1852, Mr. Fairbairn's name was entered in the candidates' book, being proposed by Mr. George Rennie, and seconded by Sir Roderick Murchison. On February 1, 1853, he was elected by the committee under the rule above cited. Among those similarly introduced in the same year were Thomas Carlyle, Baron Marochetti, and Sir Francis Grant, now P.R.A.

The following honours were paid him at subsequent periods of his life, on account of his scientific merits.

In November, 1855, he was elected member of the Académie Nationale Agricole, Manufacturière et Commerciale, Paris ;—

In December, 1856, a Corresponding Associate of the Royal Academy of Sciences, Turin ;—

In November, 1860, an Honorary Member of the Prussian 'Verein für Beförderung des Gewerbfleisses,' Berlin ;—

In July, 1861, an Honorary Member of the Royal United Service Institution, London ;—

In November, 1861, a Corresponding Member of the Literary and Philosophical Society of Liverpool ;—

In the same month, an Honorary Associate of the Institution of Naval Architects, London ;—

In February, 1862, an Honorary Member of the Yorkshire Philosophical Society ;—

In June, 1862, an Honorary Associate of the Society of Arts, Geneva ;—and

In October, 1867, an Honorary Member of the Society of Engineers, London.

CHAPTER XVI.

STEAM BOILERS AND MATTERS CONNECTED THEREWITH

1844–1874

STEAM-BOILERS—MR. FAIRBAIRN ENGAGED LARGELY IN THEIR CONSTRUCTION—IMPROVEMENT IN THEIR DESIGN—THE TWO-FLUED, OR LANCASHIRE BOILER—BOILER EXPLOSIONS—THEIR FREQUENCY IN THE MANUFACTURING DISTRICTS—MR. FAIRBAIRN'S FREQUENT EVIDENCE AT CORONERS' INQUESTS—LECTURES AT LEEDS AND OTHER TOWNS—PAPER AT THE BRITISH ASSOCIATION—FOUNDATION OF THE ASSOCIATION FOR THE PREVENTION OF BOILER EXPLOSIONS—FIRST IDEAS—FIRST STEPS FOR THE FORMATION OF THE SOCIETY—FAIRBAIRN AND WHITWORTH—NOTICES BY THE PRESS—PRELIMINARY MEETINGS—FORMAL ESTABLISHMENT—MR. FAIRBAIRN BECOMES PRESIDENT—PRESENT STATE OF THE ASSOCIATION— THEORETICAL INVESTIGATIONS UNDERTAKEN BY MR. FAIRBAIRN—PAPER TO THE ROYAL SOCIETY—THE RESISTANCE OF TUBES TO COLLAPSE—THE STRENGTH OF GLASS—THE PROPERTIES OF STEAM—LETTER FROM REGNAULT—LEGISLATIVE INTERFERENCE IN REGARD TO STEAM BOILERS —MR. FAIRBAIRN'S OPINIONS THEREON—COMMITTEES OF THE BRITISH ASSOCIATION AND OF THE HOUSE OF COMMONS—SIR WILLIAM'S LATE IMPROVEMENTS IN BOILERS—COMMUNICATION WITH THE ASSOCIATION NEAR THE CLOSE OF HIS LIFE—TRIBUTE BY THEM TO HIS MEMORY.

CHAPTER XVI.

A SUBJECT that much interested Mr. Fairbairn during the best part of his life, and one on which he did most valuable service, was that of steam-boilers.

In his large practice as a manufacturer of steam-engines, he could not fail to see the extreme importance of that element of the machine from which its power was derived. He had his attention directed to the frequent occurrence of disastrous explosions; and hence he was led to study carefully the mechanical principles involved in the construction and arrangement of boilers. He noticed many defects, and introduced several important improvements. He further made it his business to promulgate knowledge by writings and lectures on the structure and management of boilers; and last, though not least, he founded a public association for the object of promoting safety in their use for manufacturing purposes generally.

Mr. Fairbairn began to make steam-engines soon after 1832, and the construction of the boilers for them formed an extensive manufacture in itself. In 1837 he applied to them his new invention of the riveting machine, as described in Chapter X.; and a few years later, viz., in 1844, he introduced a valuable change in boiler design.

He was always an advocate for high-pressure steam, on account of its economical advantage; but its use was limited by a fear of danger in the vessel wherein it was generated. The kind of boiler which had been found by experience to be best adapted for this purpose was that known as the Cornish or Trevithick's boiler.[1] This was of cylindrical form, having a tube running through it in which the fire was placed, in the manner shown in the first of the following figures.

This had the disadvantage that the tube must necessarily be of large size, so as to admit sufficient fire, and it was on that account exposed to a severe external crushing strain, which its form was not well calculated to bear. It had also the evil that the water over the top of the tube was only of small depth, and that if by accident the water level happened to get low, the top of the tube, being exposed to the most intense action of the fire, was liable to become overheated, which would lead to danger of explosion. The steam space was also contracted by the necessary height of the water line.

Mr. Fairbairn's improvement consisted in using *two* internal fire-tubes, of smaller size, instead of one large one. These tubes were subject to a much diminished external strain, while at the same time they allowed of an increase of the fire-grate and heating surface; and, what was of more importance, a much greater depth of water could be maintained over them, and the level could, if necessary, be lowered so as to enlarge the steam room. The second figure shows the improved arrangement.

The idea, though extremely simple, was admirably practical and useful; and the invention was patented by Wm. Fairbairn and John Hetherington (an engineer who had aided him in it), on April 30, 1844 (No. 10,166).

---

[1] See Pole on the Cornish Engine, Arts. 124 to 150.

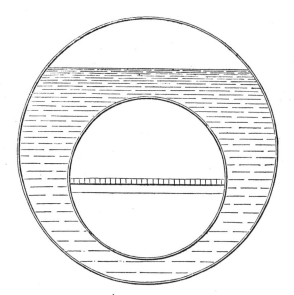

TREVITHICK'S, OR THE CORNISH BOILER.

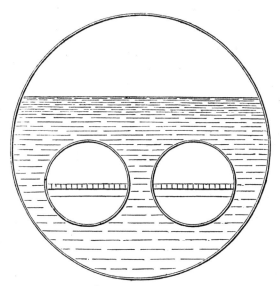

FAIRBAIRN'S, OR THE LANCASHIRE BOILER.

This form of boiler found great favour. It was soon widely adopted, and is now by far the most usual construction for high-pressure boilers in the manufacturing districts. Indeed, so common is it there that it is often called the 'Lancashire Boiler' in contradistinction to the 'Cornish' one, which prevails in the south-western counties.

Independently, however, of his practice in the construction of boilers, Mr. Fairbairn had his attention called to them in another way, as it had been his lot to see many lamentable cases where either inattention to the proper principles of construction, or careless management, had caused disastrous explosions and fearful destruction of life and property.

The great extension of manufacturing industry in the Lancashire and Yorkshire towns had led to the employment of steam-power to a vast extent; steam-engines were required in great numbers, and their manufacture was often undertaken by persons not well instructed in scientific principles, and at prices which did not admit of all possible care being taken in regard to the proportions or the practical workmanship.

Moreover, these engines were not unfrequently worked under careless management, being put into the charge of incompetent or ignorant men, unable to see where danger arose, or unscrupulous as to overtaxing the powers of the apparatus. Hence, boiler explosions became but too common in these districts; and when they did occur, from the magnitude of the buildings and the great number of people employed, the consequences were usually very severe.

The worst feature of the case was that the causes of these explosions were often very difficult to trace out. The destruction was so complete that tangible evidence was in a great measure destroyed; and, it usually happened that the persons who would have been best able to throw light on the causes were killed. The proprietors or managers, not wishing to criminate themselves, were loth to admit that there had been anything amiss in construction or attention, and hence all sorts of fanciful theories were conjured up, such as electric action, chemical decomposition of the steam, and mysterious agencies of many kinds, to account for what was merely a natural sequence from simple mechanical conditions.

At the inquests held on such occasions the juries were often puzzled by these various theories, and it became a common custom for coroners or magistrates to call in an independent and impartial engineer to aid in the investigations, and to endeavour to throw light on the causes of the accidents.

Mr. Fairbairn, from his great experience and high reputation, was much in request on these occasions, a few of which may be named.

In November 1845 he attended at Bolton, to examine into the circumstances of a disastrous explosion, by which fourteen lives were lost. He gave evidence at the inquest, pointing out defects in the boiler arrangements, and the jury returned a verdict of manslaughter against one of the partners, with a recommendation that Mr. Fairbairn's report 'should be forwarded to the Secretary of State for the Home Department, with a view of bringing the subject of steam-boilers before the legislature.'

In December 1850 he was called in by the magistrates of Halifax, to investigate a serious explosion that had taken place there, and which he succeeded in tracing to the weakness of a certain part of the boiler.

In November 1853 he attended at Blackburn, to give

evidence on the bursting of a boiler at a mill in that town, by which seven persons were killed, and which he traced clearly to the defective condition of the boiler. He declined to receive remuneration for his services, directing that the fee offered him should be applied for the benefit of the families of the sufferers.

Many similar accidents were investigated by him, among which was the unfortunate explosion of a locomotive during its testing at the Atlas Locomotive Works of Messrs. Sharp, Roberts & Co., Manchester, in July 1858, by which nine persons were killed.

It was felt that it would be very useful both to the manufacturers and users of steam machinery if Mr. Fairbairn would make some publication of the knowledge he had gained on this subject, and at the beginning of 1851 he received the following letter :—

Leeds, January 11, 1851.

My dear Sir,—It has occurred to the Committee of the Yorkshire Union of Mechanics' Institutes that you might confer an important boon on the manufacturing classes of Yorkshire if you could deliver a lecture on 'Steam-Engine Boilers, the causes of explosion, and the means of prevention,' or something to that effect.

You have bestowed so much attention on the boiler explosion at Halifax, that we hope the preparation of the lecture would not be attended with much trouble.

That, and other similar calamities, would cause your lecture to be received with great interest. Our idea is that it should be a lecture expressly adapted to *practical* men, both to masters and engine tenters. We should ask the favour, if your numerous engagements would permit, of your delivering the lecture first to the Leeds Mechanics' Institution; and should say that you would lay the public under additional obligation if you could afterwards repeat the lecture in the Mechanics' Institutions of the three other great manufacturing towns of Yorkshire, Bradford, Halifax, and Huddersfield.

We feel that this is a very bold request to make, and we could not have made it had we not known your public spirit, and also that you are already fully charged with all the facts on the subject.

The report of the lecture in the papers would make it useful through the whole of Yorkshire and far beyond.

You are aware that the Earl of Carlisle has set a noble example by delivering two lectures to our Mechanics' Institution; but you do not need an example, as you have always been friendly to the diffusion of science and the advancement of the operative classes.

Requesting your kind consideration of our proposal,

I am, dear sir, yours truly,

EDWARD BAINES,

President of the Yorkshire Union of Mechanics' Institutes,

Wm. Fairbairn, Esq.

He complied with this request, and on April 23rd and 24th he delivered two lectures before the Leeds Mechanics' Institution. In the first lecture, 'On the Construction of Boilers,' he discussed the forms, proportions, and material of such vessels, and the forces they were subject to; in the second, 'On Boiler Explosions,' he explained the various probable causes of such accidents (giving many examples in illustration), and described various precautionary measures with the object of guarding against them. The lectures were repeated in several manufacturing towns, and were printed by the committee in the form of a cheap tract, 'in the hope that much practical benefit might result from their publication in that manufacturing district.' They were afterwards re-published in 'Useful Information for Engineers,' and in several foreign scientific periodicals.

At the meeting of the British Association at Hull, in September 1853, Mr. Fairbairn communicated a paper, entitled 'Experimental Researches to determine the

Strength of Locomotive Boilers, and the causes which lead to explosion.' This was brought about by the bursting of a locomotive boiler belonging to the London and North-Western Railway at Manchester. Differences of opinion had arisen among engineers in regard to the causes of the failure of the boiler, and Mr. Fairbairn instituted a series of experiments for the purpose of settling the question. They were directed to the resistance of locomotive boilers generally, and in particular to the strength of the screwed stays by which the internal fire-box is secured to the outer shell. A locomotive boiler was subjected to hydraulic pressure, increased till the boiler gave way, and it was inferred that it would bear 300 to 350 lbs. pressure per square inch before bursting. A trial was also made to determine the rate at which the pressure would rise, supposing the fire kept up and the safety-valve closed, and it was found that in about half-an-hour a bursting force would be attained.

But, not satisfied with merely talking or writing about boiler explosions, the idea occurred to Mr. Fairbairn of doing something practical to prevent them, or at least to render them less frequent; and this idea led to the foundation by him of an 'Association for the Prevention of Steam Boiler Explosions,' which has been of incalculable benefit in the saving of life and property, and, in fact, has become, under his guidance, one of the most valuable mechanical institutions of the country. It is only due to him to give an account of the rise and progress of this excellent society.[1]

___

[1] The early particulars are chiefly taken from a report by Mr. Lavington Fletcher (the engineer to the society), made in August 1874, immediately after Sir Wm. Fairbairn's death.

His notion was that, as he was convinced all boiler explosions arose from ordinary mechanical causes easily avoidable, it would be possible, by careful and frequent inspection or examination, to discover when anything was likely to go wrong, and so to apply a remedy in time. And he conceived that, by the formation of a society, this inspection might be made systematic, and might combine other advantages with that of safety.

It was about 1851 that he first gave expression to this idea. In his evidence with regard to a boiler explosion at Stockport, about April of that year, he said :—

It seems to me that there should be some association, either under the local authorities or under Government, by which registers should be kept, not only with reference to the safety of the public, but also to show what duty engines and boilers perform. The best results have arisen from such regulations in Cornwall, and it has led there to the greatest possible economy.

Further, at the Blackburn case in 1853, he again called attention to the subject :—

I think the inspection would be better in the hands of the proprietors of steam-engines, if they would undertake it, than in those of the Government. If the proprietors undertook the work it would have to be done under *an Association of employers*, and I have no doubt it would be much more acceptable to manufacturers that they should have the control of their own engines and boilers than that the Government should interfere.

The following extract of a letter shows that he had about this time been discussing the subject with his friends :—

Manchester, July 29, 1854.

Dear Sir,—The recent lamentable boiler explosion has recalled to my mind the subject of a conversation we had some time since, when we accidentally met in a railway carriage.

I think you then expressed the opinion that much would be done to prevent these catastrophes if owners of steam-engines could agree to retain the services of a suitable inspector, who should periodically examine and report upon the condition of the boilers and engines.

I hope that the importance of the subject will lead you to lay your views in some practical form before the public, and thus add one more to the many services you have already conferred upon it.

I remain, dear sir,
Your obedient servant,
RICHARD JOHNSON.

WM. FAIRBAIRN, Esq.

Mr. Fairbairn replied, and promptly gave attention to the matter. His first step was to find an influential manufacturer and mill-owner who would take an interest in the scheme; and he made a happy choice in Mr. Henry Houldsworth, the chief partner in a large firm of cotton spinners in Manchester. Some other gentlemen were spoken to, and a preliminary meeting was held on August 15 ; the general feeling was found to be favourable to the formation of such a society, and Mr. Fairbairn was deputed to sketch out its objects and rules, with the view of submitting them to a larger and more general meeting to be called for the purpose.

Meantime the attention of the public was attracted to the proposal. A notice of the first meeting had appeared in the 'Manchester Guardian' of August 16, and the same paper, on September 16, devoted a leading article to a further explanation of the nature and objects of the proposed association, warmly recommending it to the attention of engineers and manufacturers.

The 'Mining Journal' of September 9, 1854, recorded the verdict of the coroner's jury on a fearful boiler explosion at Rochdale, which concluded with the following paragraph :—

The jury cannot separate without pressing on the consideration of the owners and users of steam-boilers throughout the
kingdom the necessity there is that measures should be taken
by them to ensure a thorough and frequent inspection of boilers,
so as to prevent, as far as human foresight can, the recurrence
of explosions.

In giving his evidence on this tragic case (where ten
persons were blown to atoms and an immense deal of
property was destroyed), Mr. Fairbairn

Suggested it was possible, and indeed quite practicable, to
establish associations in the several districts, the members of
which should appoint inspectors to take cognizance of the
boilers within their respective precincts, and to report to the
association weekly in what state they found them, and the causes
which prevented them from being in working order, if the inspectors should consider such to be the case. He did not conceive that it would be any tax on the proprietors of boilers to
pay a trifling sum yearly to meet the expense of such an association, for it struck him forcibly that, in addition to preventing
those very serious accidents, it would be productive of benefit to
the proprietors themselves, and save a great deal of money.

The 'Journal' added :—

Since the above observations were written, we perceive that
Mr. Fairbairn's earnest recommendation has been adopted, and
that an association has been formed in the district for the
inspection of steam-boilers and the prevention of boiler explosions. We cannot avoid anticipating from it the best
results.

On the 19th of September a second meeting, convened by circular, was held in the Manchester Town Hall,
the Mayor in the chair, when a committee was appointed
for making arrangements for the formation of the association. They set vigorously to work, and for some time
met every week, the minutes being usually signed either
by William Fairbairn or Joseph Whitworth, or both.

They succeeded in enrolling 271 steam-users as members, and on Jan. 23, 1855, they called another public meeting at which the Society was formally established.

Mr. Houldsworth was the first president, but in April 1858, he retired, and Mr. Fairbairn was elected in his place, a position which he held till his death. He was ever one of the most active and persevering supporters of the association, always accessible to the chief engineer when seeking his advice, and always one of the most regular in his attendance at the meetings of the executive committee. He always advocated the view that steam-boiler explosions arose simply from a greater pressure of steam than the boiler was able to withstand, and never afforded any countenance to those fanciful and visionary theories that would have attributed them to mysterious causes. He maintained that periodical inspection was adequate to prevent the greater number of explosions, and he wished inspection to be the fundamental principle of safety.

The institution is now in a most flourishing condition. Its full title is, The Manchester Steam Users' Association, for the Prevention of Steam-boiler Explosions, and for the attainment of Economy in the Application of Steam.

Its objects and constitution are stated as follows:—

This association undertakes the periodical inspection of steam-boilers, and gives a pecuniary guarantee of the integrity and efficiency of its inspections to the amount of 300*l.* on each boiler enrolled, so that in the event of the explosion of an approved boiler, whether that explosion arise from collapse of the furnace tubes, or from rupture of the shell, or failure of any part of the boiler whatever, all damage done thereby, other than by fire, whether to the boiler itself or to the surrounding property, will be made good to the extent of 300*l.*

The association also assists its members by taking indicator diagrams when requested, as well as by affording competent engineering advice with regard to the working of boilers and engines, the prevention of smoke, the economy of fuel, and any other points calculated to prove of value to the members of the association as steam-users.

Its system of inspection is voluntary, and permissive on the part of its members. Its reports are suggestive and recommendatory on the part of its officers. Its benefits are mutually shared by all enrolled. There are no shareholders to whom dividends are paid out of the members' subscriptions, but the funds are devoted solely to promote the direct objects of the association. The executive committee are appointed by the general voice of the members of the association. They receive no remuneration for their services. They employ a considerable amount of steam-power themselves, and are thus interested in everything that affects its use.

The object of the guarantee is not so much to ensure the members against pecuniary loss in case of explosion, as to give a pledge of the *bonâ fide* intention of the association to prevent the occurrence of explosions by efficient supervision and careful periodical boiler inspection.

The number of members in 1874 was 768, and the annual income 5,236*l.* The number of boilers under regular inspection was 2,689.

Soon after the foundation of the Boiler Association, Mr. Fairbairn determined to follow out one of the ideas which had been present to his mind when he established the society. It was originally his intention that the association, in addition to the commonplace work of inspecting boilers and finding out faulty or weak places, should undertake the investigation of theoretical principles. The practical views of his coadjutors were opposed to this, and it was struck out of the programme; but Mr. Fairbairn, nothing daunted, resolved to effect the investigations in his own way.

At the meeting of the British Association at Glasgow, in 1858, he urged the subject upon many scientific friends, and as the importance of it was admitted, it was agreed that the Royal Society and the British Association should jointly authorise the enquiry, and should furnish a grant of money for the expenses.

The objects immediately named were to investigate certain doubtful points in the construction of boilers, and in the nature of steam. The former was first undertaken, and Mr. Fairbairn availed himself of the assistance of a practical mathematician, Mr. Thomas Tate (who had previously aided him in other labours) and Mr. Unwin, a young engineer, whom he had engaged as secretary.

The first result was a paper ' On the Resistance of Tubes to Collapse,' read before the Royal Society May 20, 1858, and afterwards published in the Philosophical Transactions. It has already been mentioned that the internal tubes, or fire flues, of high pressure boilers, are subject to a severe external pressure, tending to cause them to collapse or crush in ; in fact, they form the weakest and most dangerous element of the construction, inasmuch as the external crushing force is uncertain and obscure in its action, and the resistance to be provided against it is difficult to determine. When accidents have occurred with this kind of boiler, it is almost always the internal tube that has given way ; and some cases of collapse have occurred with a very moderate pressure.

No scientific or well-founded rule existed to guide the design or proportions of this part of a boiler, and hence it was desirable in the first place to make some experiments of a general nature to ascertain the resistance of tubes to strains acting in this way.

For this purpose, tubes of various dimensions, thicknesses, and lengths, were constructed, and were subjected, in a closed water bath, to external hydrostatic pressure till they collapsed, the pressures and the circumstances of collapse being carefully recorded.

The particulars were given in the paper, but the general result deduced from the whole was that the strength of the tubes diminished in an important degree as their length increased, a principle of much importance, on account of the great length steam-boilers were usually made.

It was always Mr. Fairbairn's principle to give, if he could, a practical value to his enquiries; and having discovered the defect, he set to work to find a remedy. It occurred to him that it would be possible effectively to shorten the tubes, without shortening the boiler. For this purpose he inserted stiff rings of iron at various points in the length, which served as supports to the tube in the places where they were fixed, so that the effective length of the tube was shortened to the distance between two of these rings. For example: in a boiler 24 feet long, by inserting two rings, the effective length of the tube became reduced from 24 feet to 8 feet, and the resistance to collapse was increased accordingly. He further suggested some improvements in the riveting, the advantages of which were described in the paper.

Mr. Fairbairn, in his Autobiography, thus alludes to this memoir :—

Shortly after the meeting of the British Association in Glasgow, I entered upon a long series of experiments on the law of the resistance of tubes to collapse. These investigations were the more interesting as they led to the establishment of the law of collapse from pressure on the external surfaces ; and the improvements deduced from this law led to the security of steam-boilers, by doubling or trebling their powers of resistance, and thus were the means of saving many valuable lives from violent death by explosion.

This was an important discovery, for in the case of steam-boilers with tubes it was found that the internal tubes were, in most cases, only one-third of the strength of the outer shell, and hence the fallacy of the ordinary belief, that the tubes from their reduced diameters were stronger than any other part of the boiler.

Another important feature in these investigations was, that by simply encircling the tube with two or more rigid rings, the resistance to collapse was increased in the inverse ratio of the distances between the rings.

The experiments were very expensive, as large and powerful apparatus had to be prepared to sustain a pressure of upwards of 300 lbs. per square inch. In this I was assisted by a grant from the Royal Society, out of the Government fund, and I had every facility for conducting them at the engine shed of the London and North Western Company at Longsight, Manchester, who were interested in the subject.

This essay was one of the most meritorious works of Mr. Fairbairn's scientific and professional career, and deserves more credit than it has generally received. The process of investigation was admirably philosophical; there was first the ascertaining of facts by careful and well-directed experiment and observation; then there was the deduction from them, by scientific reasoning, of a general theoretical law; and finally there was the invention and application of a measure founded on that law, which rendered the whole of practical utility and advantage. Mr. Fairbairn's anti-collapse flue rings, which arose out of this investigation, have been in constant use ever since, and have been the salvation of the high pressure stationary-engine boiler.

An abbreviated account of the investigation was published in the Report of the British Association for 1857.

On May 12, 1859, a second paper was read at the Royal Society, as a sequel to the former one, and in this Mr. Fairbairn connected Mr. Tate's name with his own.

It was entitled 'On the Resistance of Glass Globes and Cylinders to Collapse from Internal Pressure, and on the tensile and compressive Strength of various kinds of Glass,' and was published in the Philosophical Transactions for the year.

The novel results arising out of the first trials had suggested the propriety of carrying them farther, with a variation in the nature of the material; and glass was chosen, as a homogeneous crystalline and rigid substance, to contrast with the ductile and fibrous one at first employed. Moreover it was remarked that, much as glass was employed in philosophical experiments, there was a want of information as to its properties, which it was very desirable to supply.

Accordingly, the strength of glass to resist tensile and compressive forces was first experimented on; after which trials were made on the power of glass vessels to resist external crushing force. The law of their strength was found to correspond with that deduced for iron tubes.

An anticipatory notice of this series of experiments was communicated to the British Association at their Leeds meeting, September 1858.

A third paper, which arose out of the boiler enquiry, was presented to the Royal Society on May 10, 1860. It was entitled 'Experimental Researches to determine the Density of Steam at Different Temperatures; and to determine the Law of Expansion of Superheated Steam, by William Fairbairn, Esq., F.R.S., and Thomas Tate, Esq.' This paper was considered of such importance and merit that it was selected by the Society as the 'Bakerian Lecture' for the year, and it was published in the Phil. Trans., vol. cl.

The first object of the enquiry was to determine by direct experiment the law of the density and expansion

T

of steam and other condensible vapours at all temperatures. Theoretical laws had been propounded and extensively adopted, but no trustworthy direct experiments had been made to test their truth. The paper gave full details of a large number of carefully conducted observations made with this object, with a deduction of generalised formulæ from the results obtained.

The second part of the paper was devoted to an investigation of the laws of what is called *superheated* steam. A plan had been coming into use, for steam-engines, of heating the steam after it had left the boiler, with the object of evaporating any water it might contain, and rendering it *dry*. This process, which was called superheating, was supposed to offer practical advantages, but no sufficient investigation had previously been made of the properties of steam so treated. The paper supplied, to a certain extent, this deficiency.

The authors were assisted by Mr. Unwin, and Mr. Fairbairn testified to the great precision and care with which the experiments were conducted. The substance of the enquiry was laid before the mechanical section of the British Association at their Aberdeen meeting in September 1859.

In this paper Mr. Fairbairn had occasion to refer to the great researches on vapours by the eminent French philosopher, Regnault. From the wide reputation of these researches and of their author, the following letter may be placed on record :—

Mon cher Mr. Fairbairn,—J'ai reçu votre lettre, et je m'empresse d'y répondre par écrit, afin de pouvoir vous l'envoyer de Paris, car lundi prochain je pars pour Londres, et j'espère bien que j'aurai l'occasion de discuter oralement avec vous les questions importantes que vous avez traitées.

Vous pouvez faire l'usage que vous voudrez du tableau

numérique que je vous ai donné sur les forces élastiques des vapeurs. Grâce au Ciel, le gros volume qui contient l'ensemble de mes expériences est enfin terminé. Voici sept ans que l'imprimeur a commencé ; vous jugerez facilement que le volume réprésente une énorme labeur.

J'espère apporter ce volume moi-même à la Société Royale de Londres. Il ne manque que la planche qui renferme les courbes graphiques et qui n'est pas entièrement terminé à la gravure.

J'aurai l'honneur de vous en offrir aussi un exemplaire quand le tirage sera terminé.

Veuillez me croire
Votre serviteur dévoué,
V. REGNAULT.

Some years before Mr. Fairbairn's death the question was much agitated whether it would be advisable to introduce any legislative measures to ensure the safety of boilers, or to prevent or diminish the danger of explosion. Mr. Fairbairn took much interest in the controversy. It seems that the matter had also excited interest in France, for in 1863 the eminent French mechanical engineer, M. Chas. Combes, wrote to ask Mr. Fairbairn's opinion, which was given as follows :—

Manchester: March 28, 1863.

My dear Sir,—In this country we are always jealous of Government interference, in matters relating to the industrial projects of individuals in their single or collective capacity, and that for two reasons ; firstly, that official inspection is not always judicious ; and, secondly, that it removes the responsibility off the shoulders of those that ought to bear it.

I am quite aware of the regulations which exist in France as regards the construction of boilers, but in this country we prefer that the owners of boilers should be responsible for their own actions, and the Government holds them responsible in every instance where loss of life or injury to the person arises from any neglect on their part. This is the extent of the

English law, and every man is at liberty to make any description of boiler he pleases, but he must be answerable for the results. It is true, and we admit it to be the duty of every Government to afford protection to life and property, but not to interfere so as to cramp the energies and enterprise of individuals in their pursuit of knowledge, and the advancement of industrial resources.

In this country, as in France, but at a later period, there was a transfer from the low-pressure system, as adopted by Watt, to that of high pressure, working the steam expansively, by which a considerable saving of fuel was effected. During the time of this change, which spread over a series of years, many serious accidents, attended with loss of life, occurred, and the public in this district became alarmed to such a degree, that we found it necessary, in order to prevent Government interference, to establish the association of which I send you the rules. Being the founder of this association, I have never ceased to advocate its efficiency, and the principles on which it is founded. Out of an average of 1,600 boilers under the inspection of the association only three accidents, with the loss of two lives, have occurred during the eight years of its existence.

This association takes cognizance of the construction, form, and quality of material used, and the monthly reports point out, in every case, but without mentioning names, the defects that require attention, and of which a written statement is immediately forwarded to the proprietor, leaving it to his option to apply the remedies or not as he may deem expedient.

I have now to reply to your queries as follow, viz. :—

1. *Is it desirable to fix by law, under penalty of fines, the thickness of plates, &c.*

Answer.—It is not desirable, as there is a great difference in the quality of plates. These points are left to the makers, and the association make no recommendations. They simply inspect *existing* boilers, and point out the defects, if any, and suggest the remedies to be applied.

2. *Do you consider the previous testing necessary ?*

Answer.—We consider a hydraulic test necessary up to one and a half times, or in some cases to double the pressure at which the boiler is worked.

3. (Question not quoted.)

4. *Is it desirable to prescribe, under penalty of fine, the combustion of smoke?*

Answer.—Yes, under local acts applied to towns, as the emission of smoke from furnaces may be prevented.

5. *Are there any rules in England respecting the condition of the boiler house, &c.?*

Answer.—There is no condition by law, but it is desirable in every case to have boilers in a separate building, distinct from the factory where a number of persons are employed.

Yours faithfully,
WILLIAM FAIRBAIRN.

M. CHARLES COMBES, Member of the Institute.

A little later the subject was taken up at the British Association, who, at their meeting at Norwich in 1868, appointed a committee, consisting of Messrs. Fairbairn, Whitworth, Penn, Hick, Bramwell, Webster, Fletcher, and others, to consider ' how far coroners' inquisitions are satisfactory tribunals for the investigation of boiler explosions, and how these tribunals may be improved.' The committee reported at the Exeter meeting in 1869, to the general effect that the inquests were unsatisfactory, and with a recommendation that coroners should get the assistance of skilled engineers. The report alluded to the fact that during the past session a bill had been introduced into Parliament for placing all steam-boilers under Government inspection; but the committee expressed a strong dread of any such legislative interference, in which the meeting of the Association concurred.

The next year, 1870, the bill was re-introduced, when Sir William personally exerted himself to procure its rejection, and to obtain instead the appointment of a select committee to investigate the question. His efforts were successful, and the committee was appointed on May 16.

They sat many days, and took evidence, but could not conclude their labours, and adjourned over the recess.

In the meantime the committee of the British Association, at their meeting at Liverpool in 1870, took up the matter again, and presented a long report, the gist of which was in the last paragraph :—

They are convinced that explosion might be, and ought to be, prevented; that competent inspection is adequate for the purpose; and that any well-organised system of inspection extended throughout the entire country would partially extinguish boiler explosions.

But they did not point out what was the best means of ensuring this inspection.

The House of Commons Committee met again in March 1871, and took more evidence; but Sir Wm. Fairbairn, conceiving that some of this was misleading, at once wrote an energetic letter to Mr. John Hick, the chairman, protesting against it, and showing its fallacy. The committee reported in June, but their report did not go farther than to recommend that the responsibility of explosion should remain upon the steam users; and that the efficiency of coroners' enquiries should be somewhat improved.

This left the question just where it was, and Sir William had the gratification of seeing that, although his favourite remedy of inspection had not received Parliamentary confirmation, he had at any rate succeeded in defeating the attempt to introduce Government interference.

In April 1871 he published an article in the 'Quarterly Journal of Science,' embodying his views on this subject.

Sir William, in his late years, again exercised his invention on the subject of boilers. In 1870 he took out

a patent (March 18, No. 810) for improvements in them.
He had long held the opinion that it would be advantageous to use a still higher pressure of steam.
It had already been much increased in locomotives,
and he believed it might be also increased with benefit
in stationary engines, if the boilers could be made
strong enough to bear the requisite strain with safety.
He had, in his two-flued boiler with the stiffening
rings, added greatly to the strength; but still, when

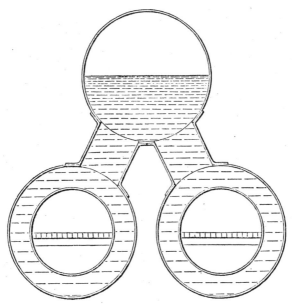

FAIRBAIRN'S IMPROVED BOILER FOR HIGH-PRESSURE STEAM.

any great power was required, it was necessary to have
the outside shell of a large diameter, which always
involved more or less danger, the risk being proportionate
to the size. He strove, therefore, to contrive a form of
boiler which, while retaining ample heating surface and
evaporating power, should enable him materially to
reduce the diameter of the vessels used; and the arrange-

ment he hit upon was to substitute three or more smaller vessels for one large one. He placed the fire or furnace tubes within external shells, not much larger than themselves (thus leaving merely annular water spaces round them) and he added above them other vessels for the purpose of obtaining the requisite water and steam room ; proper communication pipes being made to connect the various vessels together. The annexed figure will illustrate the nature of the new construction.

By this means he could make, he stated, boilers which would have a resistance equal to 750 lbs. pressure per square inch. He also added arrangements by which the examination, cleaning, and repair of the boilers might be much facilitated, knowing how much the safety and economy of working depended on these precautions.

In 1873 he took out another patent (January 23, No. 270), in conjunction with Mr. Thos. Beeley, a boiler-maker at Hyde, near Manchester, for improvements in the 1870 form of boiler, which rendered it more especially suitable for steam vessels ; and in February 1874, he sent to the Admiralty a design for the adaptation of the new boiler to one of Her Majesty's frigates, the 'Daring.'

At the beginning of 1874, a few months before his death, he expressed a wish to resign the chairmanship of the Boiler Association ; receiving the following letter in reply from one of his colleagues :—

Groby Lodge, Ashton-under-Lyne, March 10, 1874.

My dear Sir William,—Your letter of resignation was read at our meeting to-day, and there was evoked one united response expressive of the feelings which in every heart arose on the reading of it. A resolution was promptly adopted, which will be sent to you officially. It conveys a very inadequate and imperfect recognition of the honour and esteem in which you

Brighton 2 Courtney Terrace

The Polygon   June 8th 1874

Ardwick, Manchester.

Dear Sir

I must make use of what little power I have to answer your letter of the 6th I think it most desirable to have the experiments made as quick as possible but you will not require the 5-6 cylinder more than 4 or 5 feet long Thus

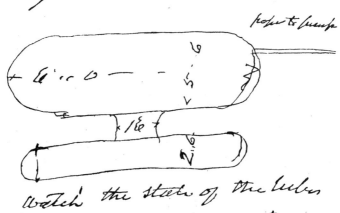

Watch the state of the tubes while writing on carefully at every increase of steam until it bursts

This I think will give you a
fair indication of the results
I am sorry to say I do not
improve I will however
give the clear coin which is
warm and excellent a trial
for another fortnight and if
I get no better I will return
and prepare for the change that
cannot be far distant
Ever sincerely
yours
W. Lambe...

Leavington E Fletcher Esqr

are held by your colleagues. We cannot let you break your official connection with us yet. So long as the Almighty is pleased to spare your valuable life, I earnestly hope we may have the great honour of your presidency. Your name and high character are a tower of strength to the Association of which you are the founder. Your services can never be realised. You have been the instrument of saving very many valuable lives by means of the Association. Allow us to continue to receive the lustre of your great name. For your sake we will do our best to uphold the reputation of the society. I feel it a very great honour to have been associated with you. May the years of your declining life be blessed with every mercy.

With great respect, I remain,
My dear Sir William, yours sincerely,
HUGH MASON.

Sir WILLIAM FAIRBAIRN, Bart.

The last letter he wrote on engineering matters was one dated June 8, 1874, to Mr. Fletcher, the engineer of the Association, referring to a proposed test of one of his new boilers by hydraulic pressure up to the bursting point. The Association had a fac-simile taken and distributed, as a memorial of their respected founder ; a copy is inserted on the opposite page.

Mr. Fletcher has favoured the editor with the following remarks on the subject of boiler explosions, which, in consideration of the importance of this subject, and the great interest Sir William Fairbairn took in it, may be inserted here.

Manchester, July 5, 1876.

Dear Sir,—In addition to the information already furnished with regard to the Manchester Steam Users' Association, it may perhaps be of further assistance if I add a few lines thereto.

When the association first started its operations, a good

deal of mystery was attached to the subject of steam boiler explosions, and they were apt to be attributed to very recondite causes. The association has been at the expense, however, of investigating the cause of every boiler explosion which has occurred for many years in any part of the country, carefully recording the results, and circulating amongst the members and the public generally, by means of its printed monthly reports, an abridged account of the cause of each of these catastrophes.

The association has always advocated the view that explosions are not mysterious and not accidental, but that they arise from simple causes, the cause being, in the great majority of cases, merely that the boiler is too weak for the pressure at which it is worked, the weakness in some cases resulting from original malconstruction, such as the want of encircling hoops round the flues, &c., and in others from wear and tear, wasting of the thickness of the plate by corrosion, &c. All our investigations go to support the simple statement of the late Joshua Field, when President of the Institute of Civil Engineers, viz., that ' boilers burst because they are not strong enough.' That we find to be the whole secret. The association does not take credit to itself for having arrived at this conclusion, but it has endeavoured persistently to keep this view before the public, and those not brought face to face with the circumstances of the case will scarcely believe how difficult it is to get this view accepted after an explosion has occurred. The boiler owner and the boiler maker have both an interest in throwing the blame on the attendant, so that they always attempt to show that the explosion was due to shortness of water, through the attendant's failing to keep up the regular supply. In some cases the most absurd and fanciful theories have been suggested to account for explosions. They have been attributed to the formation of gases inside the boiler, ignited by the fire outside through cracks in the plates. In some cases they have been attributed to a sudden accession of pressure through the mixture of two steams flowing from different boilers. They have been sometimes attributed to magnetism or, in fact, to any cause but unscientific construction or the bad condition of the boiler. In Cornwall we find it most difficult to induce boiler owners to strengthen the furnace tubes with hoops. They cannot be persuaded that a boiler can burst unless short of water.

Sir William Fairbairn and the members of the executive committee, as steam users, always entertained a very wholesome dread of Governmental interference with private industries, and therefore hoped, by taking up the system of periodical boiler inspection, to render Governmental inspection unnecessary, so that they had in view a double object—one, to prevent the sacrifice of life by steam-boiler explosions; the other, to prevent Governmental interference, which it was feared this loss of life would provoke. It is interesting to trace how the working of the association for years has somewhat led to a modification of the view with regard to Governmental interference, and this is a point to which I would call attention. It was found that, in spite of all the association could do, steam users still persisted in working old and dangerous boilers, and continued year after year to incur on an average fifty explosions, killing between sixty and seventy persons, and injuring about 100 others. Seeing that inspection was competent to prevent these disasters, the association felt at length compelled to urge on the Government to interfere in the interest of the public safety, and to take some measures to stimulate steam users to a due sense of their responsibility. What the association recommends is that the Government should institute an impartial and thoroughly competent tribunal to make a most searching investigation in the event of every explosion, so as to bring the blame home to the right party, the tribunal being empowered to institute a prosecution. The association has twice waited on the Home Secretary with memorials to this effect; the first time in June, 1875, and the second in June, 1876. The deputation was favourably received on each occasion (the memorials are published in our proceedings). Prior to this, the association had presented a memorial to the Home Secretary, in April, 1869, very much to the same effect as those referred to, the primary difference being that in the memorial of 1869 we proposed that the investigation should be conducted by the coroner's court, aided by scientific assessors, and in the memorials of 1875–76 it was to be conducted by another and more competent court, entirely independent of the coroner's.

Between the presentation of the memorial of 1869 and the one of 1875, public opinion seemed to set in favour of a direct compulsory system of enforced inspection, and Mr. Henry B. Sheridan, then member for Dudley, brought in a Bill for placing all the boilers in the country under the inspection of the Board of Trade. To this measure the association strongly objected, and instigated the appointment of a Select Committee to enquire into the whole question of steam-boiler explosions. Evidence was given before the committee by Sir William Fairbairn, by Mr. Hugh Mason, our present president, by the late Mr. Charles F. Beyer, member of our executive committee, and by myself.

The association has now fallen back from any system of compulsory inspection of boilers when in use, to a searching investigation of boilers after explosion, with a view of increasing the owner's responsibility. The question, like many others, has assumed different phases in different stages.

I have troubled you with this little history of the association's movement with regard to steam-boiler legislation, as it seems to me to open a very interesting and important question, and one that is being raised with reference to the conduct of other of the world's industries, such as mining, shipping, &c., the problem being how to control the careless without hampering the careful, and how to save human life and check recklessness without hampering progress. That questions of such interest should spring out of the simple subject of boiler inspection might not perhaps at first be anticipated.

We have at these offices very full illustrated reports of all the explosions the association has investigated, and which form a most valuable record.

LAVINGTON E. FLETCHER, Chief Engineer.

CHAPTER XVII.

MR. HOPKINS'S EARTH EXPERIMENTS

1851—1857

CHAPTER XVII.

Mr. Fairbairn was engaged for some years on an experimental investigation of great scientific interest, in regard to which, although the results were not published in his own name, he was entitled to much credit. This was an enquiry into certain physical properties of the materials of the earth's crust, undertaken at the instance of the late Mr. William Hopkins, of Cambridge.

Mr. Hopkins was an eminent mathematician and physicist; but he had chiefly made himself celebrated for studies of a novel and peculiar character, involving the application of high mathematical and mechanical principles to the science of geology.

The study of the structure of the earth, although from the time of Hutton and Werner it had occupied the earnest attention of scientific men, had involved only deductions and reasonings of a comparatively simple character. Mr. Hopkins had set himself to investigate, in a much deeper and more comprehensive manner, the nature of the mechanical forces and conditions which had been at work in order to produce the observed appearances; and he had shown that they were as capable of being reduced to rule and law as the phenomena of astronomy, although of course the processes were more obscure and the demonstrations more difficult to obtain. He had published many papers, for example, on the mechanism of glacier motion; on the influence of mechanical forces on the conformation of rocks, their elevation, denudation,

&c. ; on the theories of volcanoes and earthquakes; on the temperature of the earth; on climate; and many other subjects involving mathematical reasoning.

In the course of investigation it occurred to him that it would be possible to extend mathematical enquiry to the problem of the share that igneous action had had in the formation of the crust of the earth. There had always been a leaning in the minds of cosmical philosophers to the hypothesis that our planet had originally been a globe of matter in a state of fusion, on which a crust had become formed by the gradual cooling of the exterior, leaving the interior in all probability still a molten igneous mass. In support of this hypothesis were brought the well-known phenomena of volcanoes, earthquakes, and hot springs, as well as the established fact of the gradual increase of temperature in descending below the surface of the ground.

In January and March 1839, Mr. Hopkins laid before the Royal Society two papers, ' On the Phenomena of Precession and Nutation, assuming the Fluidity of the Interior of the Earth,' in which were some profound speculations and calculations as to the refrigeration and internal heat of the globe, and their effects on astronomical phenomena. These were followed by another paper in January 1842, on the ' Thickness and Constitution of the Earth's Crust,' in which he pointed out that the problems would be materially affected by the *effect of pressure on the temperature of fusion* of the different matters forming the earth's crust, which were supposed to have been in a liquid state. He added, ' With the aid of a proper series of experiments on this point, a direct method of arriving at an approximation to the thickness of the crust of the globe, or rather to its least limit, might be easily explained.'

At the meeting of the British Association at Oxford,

in June 1847, Mr. Hopkins presented a long and elaborate report ' On the Geological Theories of Elevation and Earthquakes,' in which the problems of the fluidity, solidi-- fication, form, and thickness of the earth's crust, were largely treated of, and he again urged (p. 52) the importance of the experimental determination of the influence of pressure in the process of solidification. To show in what a remarkable manner this would bear on the theory of the earth, he said :—

If this influence can be detected at all by experiment, it is probably considerably greater than stated above, as sufficient to justify the conclusion of the earth's solidity to a great depth; and there could, I conceive, in such case be little doubt as to the earth's entire solidity. If, on the contrary, it should appear that pressure exerts no such influence, or that it tends to retard solidification, we must conclude that the interior temperature of the earth cannot be due to its original heat. Whatever, then, may be the results of experiment on this subject, they must probably lead us, should they be sufficiently determinate, to conclusions of the first importance in speculative geology respecting the state of the interior of the globe.

To obtain these data by experiment, it became necessary to consult a mechanical engineer; for the means of producing and resisting the enormous pressures required were far beyond the scope of any ordinary laboratory arrangements. Mr. Fairbairn was known to Mr. Hopkins, not only as a practical engineer, but as a man devoted to science, and Mr. Hopkins, early in 1851, wrote to him as follows :—

Cambridge, April 25, 1851.

My dear Sir,—I am very anxious to get some experiments made for the purpose of determining whether great pressure has any sensible effect on the *temperature of fusion* of any proposed substance (a metallic substance for instance), or what will

U

probably be found to be the same thing, on the temperature at which any substance, in a previous state of fusion, will become solid.

For this purpose I want the means of producing an enormous pressure on a cylinder of perhaps an inch or rather more in diameter, such as Mr. Hodgkinson produced on similar cylinders in his experiments on the crushing forces for them. My friend, Professor Willis, informs me that the lever which Mr. Hodgkinson made use of for this purpose is still, as he believes, in your hands at Manchester. And my object in now writing to you is to ask whether you could allow me the use of it, supposing the experiments to be made under my own superintendence, at Manchester. I have no doubt of being able to procure considerable pecuniary assistance from the committee for disposing of the annual grant made by Government for scientific purposes, but I should not like to apply to them till I can see my way clearly to the means of performing the experiments effectively. With the exception of the lever, the apparatus required would be of very small magnitude.

If you would have the kindness to give me an answer as soon as may be perfectly convenient to you, I shall feel very much obliged to you, as my application for pecuniary aid must be made during the present year.

Yours very truly,

W. HOPKINS.

To this Mr. Fairbairn replied :—

Manchester, April 29, 1851.

My dear Sir,—I have a lever such as you describe, with all the requisite apparatus, the whole of which is very much at your service. The strength of the lever is computed to a pressure of about fifty tons, but this may be doubled by an additional apparatus if required.

It will afford me great pleasure to render any assistance towards the completion of your interesting experiments, and I shall be glad if you will inform me when you can visit Manchester for that purpose. In the interval you will perhaps inform me further of the nature of your experiments, and the preparations you will require to render them effective and satisfactory.

I am, My dear Sir,

Yours sincerely,

W. FAIRBAIRN.

Mr. Hopkins then applied for the Government grant, and obtained an allowance of 250*l*. ' for investigations on the effect of pressure on the temperature of fusion of certain substances.'

It was stipulated in the terms of the grant that the expenditure of the money should be under the superintendence of a committee, in which the name of Mr. Joule was inserted. This gentleman had, as is well known, identified himself especially with the study of the mechanical action of heat, and he took, thenceforward, an active share in the investigations.

In July Mr. Hopkins gave some further explanations, of which a few extracts may be inserted, as illustrating the nature of some of the difficulties Mr. Fairbairn had subsequently to overcome.

One of the most important, and perhaps difficult points, will be the determination of the time when the solidification of the matter experimented on (concealed from sight) takes place, and its temperature at that time. It has occurred to me that this may be done by carefully observing the change of temperature, as the matter is allowed to *cool* from a temperature which maintains it in a state of perfect fluidity. The temperature will decrease pretty uniformly till the solidification begins, but will remain nearly *stationary*, I conceive, till the solidification is completed, after which it will again regularly decrease. This is the first point I wish to have clearly tested, to ascertain with what degree of exactness the *stationary temperature* can be determined. If it can be done with accuracy I anticipate no serious difficulty in the experiments.

He then went on to describe certain preliminary experiments on easily fusible substances, and added suggestions as to how these might be extended further, recommending Mr. Fairbairn to consult with Mr. Joule on the subject generally.

After some further correspondence, Mr. Hopkins, in the middle of December, visited Manchester, and conferred fully with Mr. Fairbairn and Mr. Joule ; the nature of the apparatus was settled, and it was put in hand, Mr. Hopkins paying another visit in January 1852, to examine what was being done.

The construction appears to have occupied some months, for in April, Mr. Fairbairn, in writing an account of what he was doing to his friend Dr. Robinson, of Armagh, remarked that he had some difficulty in ' procuring vessels sufficiently strong at an increased temperature, to retain the substances on which the experiments were to be made.'

Constant discussions went on between the parties, and on May 8 Mr. Fairbairn wrote :—

I had a long conversation with Lord Rosse this morning, and he informed me he has written to you on the subject of a report as to what you are about. I think that report should be that we are only beginning ; that we shall want all the money, and that it will be well spent. I think your views on the subject are correct. I make no doubt that a new theory on the laws of solidification will be the result ; at all events we shall be able to show how nature works in the cooling of bodies under severe pressure.

On May 20, 1852, Mr. Hopkins wrote :—

I much approve of your latest suggestion respecting our apparatus. The idea of the arrangements which you propose was the first I recollect which occurred to me ; but the mechanical difficulties seemed to me so great that I at once abandoned it. If, however, you can overcome them, I believe it will be the best arrangement possible. [This was done.]

On June 26 Mr. Fairbairn wrote from London:—

I had no time to write you on the subject of our experiments, which in some respects were highly satisfactory, in others not so. The apparatus is now completely insulated and perfectly tight, but we had some difficulty in reading off the temperature, &c., &c.

The earlier experiments were directed to the behaviour of a substance easily fusible—namely, spermaceti, the object being to make very exact observations on the temperature of fusion; and for a long time the aim was simply to verify by careful observation the suggestions in Mr. Hopkins's letter of July 1851 as to the temperature remaining stationary for a time at the point of solidification. When this was settled the spermaceti was put under heavy pressure, with the object of observing what effect this had in varying the point at which the congelation occurred. The experiments appear to have been conducted by all three of the persons mentioned. Mr. Fairbairn and Mr. Joule were living at Manchester, but Mr. Hopkins paid, as appears from the papers, 'long and frequent visits,' during which he was generally a guest at Mr. Fairbairn's house.

Writing to Baron von Humboldt on August 23, 1852, Mr. Fairbairn said:—

I am at present engaged, in conjunction with Mr. Hopkins, of Cambridge, on a series of experiments to determine the laws of the solidification of bodies under severe pressure. It is a subject in which I am sure you take a deep interest, as it involves a question in physics most difficult to solve; namely, under what circumstances solidification is effected at great depths under the surface of the earth, and how nature works under superincumbent pressure. I have a powerful apparatus for the purpose, and can give a pressure of nearly 6,000 lbs. upon the square inch; but we have many difficulties to encounter, and considerable trouble in preventing the radiation of heat from the vessel which contains the substances under pressure. I have got the apparatus so far complete as to indicate with certainty the progressive changes of temperature during the progress of crystallisation in passing from the fluid to the solid state; nevertheless, we have still much to do.

In September Mr. Hopkins was again at Manchester, arranging further contrivances for increasing the accuracy of the experiments, which it still took two months to carry out; and on November 23 Mr. Fairbairn wrote to Mr. Hopkins:—

Enclosed you have the results of our experiments on Saturday last, which on examination you will find a nearer approach to the stationary temperature than any of those yet made.

On a consultation with my friend, Mr. Joule, we have come to the decision to let the matter stand over for a time, till we hear from, or rather till we have the pleasure of seeing you either here or in London. At our next meeting something must be determined upon, and I think it may be desirable to vary the form and character of our proceedings, in order to arrive at conclusions that will enable you to deduce your laws.

Some further experiments were made, and Mr. Hopkins replied on December 21 :—

I thank you for the account of your last experiments. I have no doubt whatever of the temperature of solidification having been obtained *very* approximately in both of the last experiments under pressure. We are manifestly approximating to unquestionable results.

After this, new apparatus was prepared according to the plans jointly agreed on.

In March 1853, Professor (now Sir) William Thomson,

who had been previously consulted on the subject by Mr. Hopkins and Mr. Joule, devised an improvement in the apparatus, so elegant and ingenious as to deserve a brief mention. It had been difficult to find out, while the heat was increasing, the exact point of time at which the fusion took place. As the only feasible mode thought of, the spermaceti was enclosed in a glass tube, through which it could be observed, and the fusion determined by its loss of opacity. Professor Thomson suggested that a small piece of magnetised steel wire should be put into the spermaceti before it was enclosed in the tube, and so placed as to be at the upper part of it when operated on. A small compass was then placed *outside* the vessel, in such a position that its needle might be acted on by the magnetised wire inside. When fusion took place, the wire, being no longer supported by the solid material, fell to the bottom, and the moment of its doing so was made evident by the motion of the compass outside. This was tried in July, and answered admirably, allowing the containing tube to be made of brass, and so avoiding the danger of the use of glass under such great heat and pressure.

On August 12, 1853, Mr. Joule wrote to Mr. Fairbairn :—

Salford, August 12, 1853.

My dear Sir,—Our experiment this morning was satisfactory, the needle having fallen at 373, the exact temperature expected by Mr. Hopkins, and which shows that the temperature of fusion rises with the pressure in arithmetic progression. The lead box answered capitally. I have sent a line to Mr. H. to communicate the result.

I am yours truly,

James P. Joule.

Wm. Fairbairn, Esq.

Mr. Hopkins, remarking on this in a letter dated August 22, said :—

I had previously heard from Mr. Joule of his completely successful experiment, for such it has manifestly been. Its agreement with my calculated result is most satisfactory. In this case the law is clear, that the increase of the temperature of the fusion is proportional to the pressure.

With respect to the conductive power of the substances pressed, we had better leave those experiments till my next visit to Manchester, or at least till after the meeting at Hull.

Could you send to Professor Phillips a drawing (it does not signify how rough) of our apparatus? It may be as small, too, as you please. He will get an enlarged drawing of it made for exhibition at Hull [British Association meeting] if I should find it expedient, as I think I shall, to exhibit it at the time of my address.

The subject was brought forward at the Hull meeting, and the nature of the experiments and apparatus was explained; but no written paper upon it was presented, and therefore no record of it appeared in the published report for the year.

The following letter may be put on record on scientific grounds:—

Salford, August 24, 1853.

My dear Sir,—I transmitted to Mr. Hopkins yesterday, an account of some experiments on the physical properties of beeswax, which may perhaps serve to throw some light on the experiments on the alteration of the point of liquefaction by pressure. The results arrived at are as follow:—

Specific heat between 48·88° Centigrade and 18·74° = ·991
      ,,   ,,   ,,   39·8° and 19·1°   = ·923
      ,,   ,,   ,,   32° and 18·34°   = ·647.

The wax softened gradually until the point of absolute fluidity, 54° Cent., was reached. The increase of the specific heat at high temperatures was owing to the heat due to a change of state being mixed therewith.

I find the specific heat of wax in the perfect fluid condition to be ·506, and another experiment gave ·509.

Taking the specific heat both at perfect solidity and perfect fluidity to be ·5, I find the heat absorbed in changing the state of one grain of wax from perfect solidity to perfect fluidity to be 33·2° Cent. per one grain of water.

I find the expansion of beeswax weighing 61·828 grains to be

From 16·6° to 26·8° = 0·793 gr. of water volume,
  ,,   26·8° to 37·4° = 2·739 ,,   ,,   ,,
  ,,   37·4° to 49° = 4·255 ,,   ,,   ,,
  ,,   49° to 53·4° = 1·609 ,,   ,,   ,,
  ,,   53·4° to 67·4° = 0·578 ,,   ,,   ,,

The total expansion of 61·828 grs. of wax between 26·8° and 53·4° Cent. being equal in volume to 8·603 grs. of water. The volume of 61·828 grs. of wax at

26·8° being 64·795,
and at 53·4° ,,   73·398.

Professor Thomson's formula gives, with the above data, 96 divisions of the thermometer used in the pressure experiments, or 24° Cent. as the theoretical elevation for our greatest pressure, the actual result being 68 divisions, or 17° Cent. The difference is not great under the circumstances.

I am afraid I shall not be able to get to Hull, unless, indeed, I contrive to get off for one day.

Believe me, dear Sir,
Yours very truly,
J. P. JOULE.

W. FAIRBAIRN, Esq.

To this time the experiments had only been preliminary —*i.e.*, on substances which had no immediate connection with the enquiry, but were used to obtain general laws. But, emboldened by the success of these trials, Mr. Hopkins now proposed to carry them out on a large scale, to apply them to other substances, and to make use of greater pressures and higher temperatures. He accordingly, on November 7, 1853, gave Mr. Fairbairn suggestions for the necessary alterations and additions to the apparatus, and requested his advice and co-operation thereon. At the beginning of 1854 he again spent some days at Manchester, but the new arrangements took some time. In April thermometers were still in construction (extending to 640° Fahr.), and it was the middle of the year before Mr. Hopkins could get the new experiments fairly in hand.

The following letter, written by Mr. Hopkins to Mr. Joule, has not much bearing on Mr. Fairbairn's share of the work, but it will be interesting to scientific men as an important part of the investigation, and as a specimen of the author's able reasoning; and as it does not appear to have been already published, it is inserted entire :—

Cambridge, June 6, 1854.

My dear Sir,—I have been lately considering the formula given by Thomson.

$$\delta p = \frac{\mu L}{\gamma - \tau} \cdot \delta t.$$

I think I some time ago expressed my doubts as to its applicability to the case in which a mass passes from a solid to a fluid state, or the converse, by slow gradations extending through a considerable range of temperature, as was the case in your experiments with wax. At all events the mode of investigating the formula, as given in Thomson's memoir, does not seem to be founded sufficiently on the physical conditions of the problem, in this case of gradual solidification, to *prove* the formula to be strictly applicable to it. An infinitesimal portion of the fluid is supposed by Thomson to pass into the gaseous state, or if a solid into a fluid state *instantaneously* on an indefinitely small increase of heat, the physical state of the remaining portion of the fluid in one case and that of the solid in the other being supposed unaltered, as in the case of water passing into steam or ice into water. In the case, on the contrary, of a gradual change, it would seem that the *whole* solid mass undergoes an infinitesimal change in its physical state, by an increase δt of temperature, instead of an infinitesimal portion of it undergoing its whole change, leaving the rest unaffected.

We have by this theory, you will recollect,

$$\delta p = \mu M . \delta t.$$

With respect to any particular substance, M has of course to be determined experimentally. Now if a mass whose volume $= v_0$ be compressed till its volume $= v$, the temperature being constant, $M(v_0 - v)$ or $M\delta v =$ the *quantity of heat* which must be given out by the mass when thus compressed. Let Q be this quantity of heat, then

$$M(v_0 - v) = Q,$$

or if $q =$ the quantity of heat thus given out by a *unit* of *volume*, $Q = qv_0$ and

$$M(v_0 - v) = qv_0$$

$$\therefore \quad M \frac{v_0 - v}{v_0} = q.$$

This is easily put under another form. Let Q be such as will raise a unit of the *volume* V of water τ°. Then

$$Q = V\tau,$$

$$q = \frac{V}{v_0} . \tau,$$

$$= \frac{W}{\omega} . \frac{\sigma}{s} . \tau.$$

When W and ω are the weights of the water whose volume $= V$, and of the mass experimented on, s and σ being the specific gravities of water, and the substance. Here

$$M = \frac{v_0}{v_0 - v} q,$$

$$= \frac{v_0}{v_0 - v} \frac{W}{\omega} . \frac{\sigma}{s} . \tau.$$

τ might, I suppose, be determined as you have done in many of your experiments, provided a compression can be at once produced to develop a sufficient quantity of heat to make τ large enough to be accurately observed. The *compression*, I imagine, might be produced by means of a piston worked by a screw, the motion of which might be measured by its having a graduated head. But you could manage all this better than any way I can suggest.

It would be necessary to repeat the experiment on any proposed substance at several different temperatures *between* those of *perfect solidity* and *perfect fluidity,* for it would seem probable that the values of M may be different for different physical states of the substance. We should thus get

$$p_1 - p_0 = \mu \{ M_1 \overline{t' - t_0} + M_2 (t'' - t') + \&c. + M_n t^{(n)} - t^{(n-1)} \}.$$

M_1 being supposed constant for the difference of temperature $t' - t_0$, M_2 for the difference $t'' - t'$, and so on, and μ being supposed the same between the temperatures of solidity and fluidity.

That the values of M for different values of t between the temperatures of solidity and fluidity are different, would seem perhaps probable from the following reasoning. The quantity q may be supposed to consist of two parts, q_1 and q_2, the former being the value which q would have supposing no physical change to take place in the substance in its compression from v_0 to v; and q_2 to be that part which is due to such physical change. It seems not improbable that q_1 may be constant or nearly so, while q_2 may be very different for different values of t between the above-mentioned limits. q_1 is probably always *positive,* while q_2 may be positive or *negative,* and greater or less also than q_1 so that M may be positive or negative according to the substance operated on.

The reason why pressure affects the temperature of fusion may, I conceive, be thus explained. Conceive a substance to be retained at a given volume. Then a general theorem asserts that if a quantity of heat be added which shall raise the temperature δt we must have

$$\delta p = \mu M . \delta t.$$

Now the pressure must generally be affected by the change of physical state (as well as by the mere fact of adding a quantity of heat) by the expansion or contraction superinduced by that change. But the whole change of pressure must be consistent with the condition expressed by the above equation; and therefore if the physical change tends to produce a value of δp different from the above for an increase δt of temperature, the physical change must be arrested. Hence the dependence of the temperature of fusion on the pressure.

The formula above given for $p_1 - p_0$ is that which corresponds to the extreme case in which every part of the substance is supposed to pass simultaneously and gradually from a state of solidity to that of fluidity or the converse, the corresponding limiting temperatures being different from each other. Thomson's formula applies to the other extreme case, in which the passage of any infinitesimal portion of the substance from solidity to fluidity is instantaneous, but takes place at consecutive times for consecutive portions. To these latter cases belong (very approximately) those of ice and water, and water and steam ; to the former the case of wax would seem, from your experiments, to approximate much more nearly. The actual cases in nature are, I doubt not, really *between* these extreme limits, and formulæ for *intermediate hypotheses* might be easily investigated should it be found that those for the two extreme hypotheses give considerably different results. The formulæ for . these hypotheses are not derivable, as far as I see, the one from the other, though each may be derived from a more general formula, founded on the union of both extreme hypotheses.

These experiments ought to be made, and assuredly *you* are the man to make them. I expect to be at Manchester next Wednesday, and should then like to have some talk with you on the subject. I send this sketch beforehand, that you may have time to give it a little previous consideration. I will bring your results obtained for wax with me.

Some of our magnetised needles have been lost or broken. Will you have the kindness to have five or six more prepared for us by Wednesday. I have procured the requisite thermometers. They go up to above 600° Fahr., I believe (I have not yet seen them). Oil, I believe, can be elevated to that temperature without difficulty.

Believe me, yours truly,
W. HOPKINS.

At this time the second element was brought into the investigation. Mr. Hopkins desired to ascertain the capabilities of the various substances for the conduction of heat, and the influence of compression on this property. Mr. Fairbairn had accordingly to prepare specimens, in the form of small cubes, which were compressed under pressures sometimes reaching to 80,000 lbs. on the square inch.

At the meeting of the British Association at Liverpool, in September 1854, Mr. Hopkins presented to the Physical Section ' An Account of some Experiments on the Effect of Pressure on the Temperature of Fusion of different Substances.' [1] In this he stated ' his great obligations to Mr. Fairbairn for the promptitude with which, in the first instance, he proffered his assistance and cooperation ; and the manner in which he had since afforded the aid of his great practical knowledge, and the ample means which his establishment afforded for conducting experiments of this nature.'

Mr. Hopkins described the apparatus, and the causes of the failures which had occurred successively, till by degrees apparatus had been devised and constructed which was likely to prove successful. He then gave the results obtained, which showed that the temperature of fusion increased in regular ratio with the pressure. The following were the substances tried, and the melting points (Fahrenheit) at different pressures :—

	At Atmospheric Pressure	At 7,790 lbs. per square in.	At 11,880 lbs. per square in.
	°	°	°
Spermaceti . .	124	140	176·5
Wax . .	148·5	166·5	176·5
Sulphur . .	255	275·5	285
Stearine . .	138	155	165

On October 20, 1854, Mr. Fairbairn wrote to Mr. Hopkins :—

[1] Report for 1854. *Transactions of the Sections*, p. 57. Mr. Fairbairn also gave, at the same meeting, some account of the experiments and apparatus ; pp. 56, 140.

The tubes, cylinder and furnace, and other parts of the apparatus for the compression of substances, are now complete, excepting only the electric wires and the float for measuring the amount of compression. Altogether it is a complete apparatus, and may be used in a laboratory or elsewhere, with tolerable certainty as to the results. It is rather an expensive piece of machinery, something above 20*l.*, but it is very complete, and I make no doubt will effect good and satisfactory results. The only difficulty will be the working of the wires and the float, but that can only be determined by a few experiments.

It was decided to make the first trial of the new machine at Manchester; but Mr. Hopkins could not get there till the Easter vacation of 1855.

On June 16 of that year, Mr. Fairbairn, writing to Sir David Brewster, said :—

I am the more anxious to see you, as I wish to consult you upon the experiments on densities, which I mentioned to you some time since. Some of them are very curious and interesting, and I make no doubt, with the powerful apparatus I have at command, that some new facts are almost sure to present themselves. You shall see them, and at the same time give me your advice, when you come down.

Mr. Hopkins spent some further time at Manchester in the long vacation, and afterwards, on October 8, 1855, he wrote Mr. Fairbairn a letter from which the following are extracts :—

I was prevented writing to you as I had intended, at Glasgow, by the difficulties which continued to beset me in my experiments till the last moment of my being at Manchester. It was only on the last day of my sojourn there that I considered myself to have overcome, as I believe, the *last difficulty*, and to have obtained results which I could rely upon with the more difficult substances, such as tin and bismuth. With respect to the latter, there is clearly *no increase*, but probably a *decrease* of the temperature of fusion resulting from *pressure*. According to our new theory of heat, this ought to be the case, provided there be no increase of volume while the substance passes from the solid to the fluid state. I had just time before I left to try the experiment, and assure myself that bismuth in a fluid state probably occupies *less volume* than in its solid state, while such substances as wax, spermaceti, &c., of which the temperature of fusion is so much increased by pressure, occupy much *larger* space in a fluid than in a solid state. This is all accordant with theory ; but requires still to be worked out with accuracy, which there will be no difficulty now in doing. This, with some other things, must remain for my Christmas visit.

But this Christmas visit never took place; Mr. Hopkins's health began to fail, and he was obliged to give up any further active labour in the experiments. In August, 1864, he wrote to Mr. Fairbairn as follows :—

During the winter I have repeatedly formed the intention of writing to you. My old enemy, the bronchial cough, attacked me again in the summer of 1863. . . . . I became very feeble and ill. I was sure also that my memory for abstractions, and my power of continued application to that kind of mental effort which, during the latter and best part of my life has afforded me the most intellectually active and agreeable employment, was in danger of being affected.

I understand that there is 100*l.* with which the Royal Society has accredited me over and above what I have drawn on account of our experiments. I will see, whatever it may be, that it be paid to yourself. I wish you also to keep all the instruments, about which I think I spent myself some 50*l.* or 60*l.* All this, in addition to what the Royal Society has advanced to you before, will, I fear, be but a very poor compensation for all the expense and trouble you have undertaken for me. My age now numbers too many years to allow me to *work* as I have done, and for the last eighteen months or more I believe that I have injured my health by too close application. I am not strong enough at present to carry on the experiments, and from what I have stated above you will understand that I am not sanguine of ever being able to do so. They have already enabled me to produce two memoirs, which perhaps will hereafter be found of some value to those interested in the subject; but I fear now that I shall not have sufficient strength to finish the final memoir which I had contemplated, though I have obtained a certain amount of materials for it. But it would require still much labour to make it complete enough for publication, except as an abstract.

Mr. Hopkins's prognostications were but too well founded. Soon after this, his powerful mind succumbed to the great strain he had put upon it, and he died in October 1866.

In December, 1865, the Royal Society wrote to Mr. Fairbairn on the subject of the balance of money ; but he declined to receive anything further.

The results of the whole matter were given, in a scientific form, in a paper read by Mr. Hopkins before the Royal Society, June 18, 1857,[1] entitled ' Experimental Researches on the Conductive Powers of various Substances, with the Application of the Results to the Problem of Terrestrial Temperature.'

In the opening paragraph he says :—

I am likewise bound to express in the strongest terms my obligations to my friends Mr. Fairbairn and Mr. Joule. Without the aid of the former of these gentlemen I should have been unable even to commence the series of experiments which I have now nearly concluded ; and among the many ways in which this assistance has been so promptly rendered, I may mention his having constantly placed at my disposal the invaluable services of one of his principal workmen, William Ward, without whose

[1] *Phil. Trans.* 1857, p. 805.

untiring activity and mechanical resources I should have utterly despaired of bringing my experiments to any successful issue.

This paper contains an elaborate mathematical discussion of the subject; but a more popular account of the results arrived at may be gathered from a lecture given by Mr. Hopkins before the Royal Institution, on May 13, 1859.[1]

After stating the facts, showing a gradual increase of temperature in descending below the surface of the earth, which (excluding local anomalies) he estimates at 1° Fahr. for every sixty feet depth, he formulates the inference from it as follows :—

If a sphere of very large dimensions, like the earth, were heated, and left to cool in surrounding space, it is shown by accurate investigation, that after a sufficient and very great length of time, the law according to which the temperature would increase in descending beneath the earth's surface, would be that the increase of temperature would be proportional to the increase of depth, which coincides with the observed law. Now, according to this law, the temperature at the depth of sixty or seventy miles would probably be sufficient to reduce to fusion nearly all the materials which constitute the earth's external solid envelope; and hence it had been concluded that the earth probably consists of a central molten mass, or a fluid nucleus, and an external solid shell, of not more than sixty or seventy miles in thickness, or even less.

This has been the ordinary supposition, not only popularly, but also generally among scientific men. But Mr. Hopkins goes on to show that the experiments, of which it has been the object of this chapter to give an account, throw doubt on the conclusiveness of the reasoning on which this opinion is founded.

He points out that an important element of the argument is wanting. It involves the hypothesis that the *conductive power* of the rocks which constitute the lower portions of the earth's crust is the same as that of the rocks which form its upper portion. For if the conductive power of the lower portions of the earth's solid crust be greater than that of the thin upper portion of it through which man has been able to penetrate, the depth to which we must proceed to arrive at a certain temperature (as that of fusion for the lower rocks) will be proportionately greater.

He then shows that the experiments in question lead to the conclusion that the conductivity of the inferior portions of the earth's solid crust, which are consolidated under very heavy pressure, must be much greater, and may be very much greater, than that of the less consolidated and more superficial sedimentary beds.

Moreover, the temperature of fusion under heavy pressure is another element in the argument. The experiments show that in regard to certain substances that also is much increased by great pressure; and by analogy, it may be concluded that such will, at least in some considerable degree, be the case with the mineral matter of the earth's crust.

Judging by the data obtained, Mr. Hopkins infers that the actual thickness of the solid crust of the earth must probably be at least about 200 miles, and may be considerably greater, even if we admit no other source of terrestrial heat than the central heat here contemplated.

Mr. Hopkins then goes on to explain another kind of argument, of a mathematical nature, bearing on the same subject, derived from the phenomenon of the precession of the equinoxes, which brings out a similar result; and he concludes :—

Thus, both the modes of investigation described lead to

like conclusions respecting the least thickness which can be assigned to the solid envelope of our globe. It must be much greater than geologists have frequently imagined it to be.

The following paragraph from the Royal Society paper may be added :—

After the preceding investigations, it appears to me extremely difficult, if not impossible, to avoid the conclusion that a part at least of the heat now existing in the superficial crust of our globe is due to superficial and not to central causes. It should be remarked, however, that the argument thus afforded is not directly against the theory of a *primitive* heat, but only against the manifestation of the remains of such heat as the sole cause of the existing terrestrial temperature at depths beyond the direct influence of solar heat.

.   .   .   .

The conclusion that the earth's solid crust is so thin as many geologists have believed it to be, as well as those theories resting on that conclusion, whether of volcanic action or of elevation or depression of the earth's surface, at least in more recent geological times, must be in a great degree invalidated.

Mr. Hopkins stated in this paper his intention of following it with another, in which a further portion of the experiments, not included here, would be given and reasoned on ; but this he had not strength to do.

It will be gathered from the above account what great and difficult questions these experiments were directed to ; and although of course it is not intended to claim for Mr. Fairbairn any of the more abstruse portions of the researches, there is no doubt that his excellent practical skill contributed largely to the success of the investigation.

CHAPTER XVIII.

THE MANCHESTER MANUFACTURING BUSINESS

CHAPTER XVIII.

ALTHOUGH it is the object of this biography to record the work of Mr. Fairbairn, during his long career, in many different capacities, as consulting engineer, as scientific investigator, as writer on mechanical subjects, and so on, it must not be forgotten that the principal occupation of his life was that of an engineering manufacturer. It was by this he earned his livelihood in his early years, and acquired his fortune at a later time; and it was by his mechanical constructive skill that his widest reputation was obtained.

For this reason it is desirable to give a somewhat more connected account of the Fairbairn manufacturing establishments, which have been occasionally referred to in various parts of this work.

There were two establishments of this kind, namely, the shops for general engineering work in Manchester, and the ship-building yard and marine engine factory at Millwall, on the Thames. These were so distinct in their character that they may occupy separate chapters in the description.

The account of the origin of Mr. Fairbairn's manufactory at Manchester is given by himself in Chap. VII. Having resolved to free himself, at the age of twenty-eight, from the bondage of employment as a hired workman, he succeeded in obtaining some small orders to be executed on his own responsibility, and this led to the formation of the firm of Fairbairn and Lillie, manufacturing engineers, in 1817.

The establishment at first consisted only of a 'miserable shed,' in High Street, containing a single lathe, which the two partners made with their own hands, and which was turned by their one workman, a muscular Irish labourer. With these small means, however, aided by willing hearts and clever hands, they contrived to execute their work so creditably as to obtain a much larger order, namely, the construction and erection of the driving machinery for a new cotton-mill of considerable size.

But the rough shed and the single lathe were not sufficient to carry out this work, and it was necessary to remove to a better building, to engage a few more workmen, and to add a few more tools; and so, with an improved establishment fixed in Mather Street, they succeeded in making a thoroughly good job of the new mill.

It was in this work that Mr. Fairbairn's true character began to appear. He stepped out of the ranks of the mere manufacturer, the workman carrying out the designs of others; he became really an engineer, studying the principles of mechanics, and applying those principles in original mechanical conceptions of his own.

In the execution of his first orders, small though they were, he had the acuteness to perceive important defects in the machinery used for driving the cotton spinning mills. This branch of industry was new, and the mechanical arrangements had been usually carried out by millwrights in a rough and clumsy way, without the application of anything like scientific design. Mr. Fairbairn perceived how the defects could be remedied; he predicted, with admirable foresight, the advantages that would arise from the change; and he carried out the improvements in the new mill with perfect success.

The advantages of the new system of driving machinery were so obvious that the author of it suddenly found himself famous as a mechanical engineer, and the character of the firm became established as manufacturers possessing more than ordinary skill and intelligence. The result was a large accession of orders, among which came, in the year 1824, that for the water-wheels at Catrine Bank, an account of which is given by Mr. Fairbairn in Chap. VIII.

This was of such magnitude and importance that the firm considered it justified them in making a further extension of their manufacturing means. With this view they took a small plot of land in Canal Street, Ancoats, purchased a steam-engine to drive their tools, and laid out a manufactory in a more complete and perfect form. This was the foundation of the Canal Street Works, which, subsequently much extended, were carried on under the name of Fairbairn for half a century.

The water-wheels and machinery were constructed and remodelled with the same ability and mechanical skill that had been shown in former cases; new improvements were introduced; the whole work was efficiently done, and the proprietors were thoroughly satisfied and pleased. Writing to Mr. Fairbairn in July 1828, Mr. Buchanan said :—

We are very sensible of your valuable assistance. What you have done for us equals every expectation, and the *Muckle wheels* continue the admiration of all who see them. *Nout o' th' sort* can do better.

Their satisfaction, however, was manifested in a way more to the purpose by another large order immediately following, from the same firm, for other works belonging to them at Deanston.

Mr. Fairbairn, speaking of these works some years afterwards, said :—

The constructions at the Deanston Works were commenced in the year following those at Catrine. They consisted of eight wheels of 100 horse power each. Two of these were completed in 1827 and two in 1832, the others subsequently. These are perhaps the largest hydraulic machines in existence.

In this way, by perseverance and industry, the partners continued to thrive, gradually increasing their shops and plant by the profits they made, until, by the year 1830, they had amassed property to the amount of 30,000*l.*, and were masters of an establishment employing 300 hands.

Soon after this the circumstances took place (detailed in Chap. IX.) which led to the dissolution of the partnership, and the lapse of the Canal Street Works into Mr. Fairbairn's sole hands. This change was effected in the year 1832.

During the partnership the work undertaken had consisted almost entirely of mill machinery, including waterwheels ; such work in fact as the old millwrights used to undertake, but done in much better style, both as to design and manufacture. The firm had never made steamengines, which are generally looked upon in the trade as a specialty, requiring a superior class of workmanship, and more extensive tool arrangements.

But no sooner did Mr. Fairbairn find himself free from the obligation to consult a partner in his proceedings, than he began to give more scope to his natural ambition by launching out into new branches of manufacture. The object of this was not merely to extend his transactions

and increase his profits. Nothing could be more remunerative than the kind of business he was already doing,
and he could obtain as much of it as he liked; but he
wished to get more exercise for his skill in the art of
mechanical design.

Probably also he may have been influenced, in some
measure, by the fact of his late partner setting up business
in competition with him, close in the same neighbourhood.
Lillie was a good mechanic; he had done his fair
share in the manufacturing business, and was no doubt
quite competent to continue successfully the construction
of such work as that the firm had been engaged in; but
Mr. Fairbairn felt his own superiority in the higher gifts
of design and invention, and generally in the true qualifications of an engineer, and he anticipated that by applying
these to new subjects he would soon raise himself above
all rivalry.

He accordingly directed his attention to two new
branches of manufacture, in which he hoped to distinguish
himself as an engineer as well as a manufacturer, namely,
iron ship-building and the construction of steam-engines.

The iron ship-building business arose, as explained in
Chap. X., out of the professional investigation made by
him on the Forth and Clyde Canal. The little iron steamer
he had built, the 'Lord Dundas,' although she did not
enable the canals to compete with the railways in speed,
did him much credit, and excited much attention, and he
at once received an order to build another, the ' Manchester,' of a larger size, 100 tons. She was also successful, and in the two succeeding years several more
were built, when the prospects of the trade appeared so
promising that Mr. Fairbairn decided to remove this
branch altogether to a more convenient place, as will be
described in the next chapter.

The Canal Street Works were much enlarged and improved, with considerable increase of plant and tools; and here the manufacture of the other new description of work, namely, steam-engines, was taken up energetically. Mr. Fairbairn did not immediately introduce any striking novelties, for the general design of the machine had been well thought out by Watt and his successors, and there were already many good firms engaged in its manufacture; but he paid great attention to the details and to the quality of workmanship, and the engines erected by him were noted for efficiency and for economy of fuel.

He also made his own boilers. Boiler-making is usually considered a separate trade, and many manufacturers of steam-engines are content to order their boilers from others, rather than introduce into their factories a rough branch of the business, requiring great room, and causing a great deal of inconvenience. But Mr. Fairbairn entertained a strong opinion of the importance of this fundamental part of the steam-engine, and would not trust either its design or its manufacture out of his own hands. He had, in fact, a great partiality for boiler-engineering all through his life, as has been sufficiently explained in Chapter XVI.

Boiler-making therefore formed, after 1832, a large and important branch of the manufacture carried on at the Canal Street Works; and it was on the occasion of a strike among the workmen employed in this department in 1837, that Mr. Fairbairn introduced, with the help of his foreman, Robert Smith, the ingenious and useful invention of the riveting machine.

About 1837 or 1838 Mr. Fairbairn further extended his business to the construction of locomotive engines. The London and Birmingham railway was just completed, and many more lines were in progress in various parts of the country. The locomotive was a new invention, and there were, down to that time, only two or three firms who had paid attention to its peculiarities. Mr. Fairbairn saw that there was an opening, not only for a large business in the manufacture, but for engineering skill in the design, and he seized the opportunity promptly and successfully. He became a large and celebrated locomotive maker. More than 600 locomotives were built at his shops, and this branch of the business furnished much occupation for them for many years. It is believed that he was the first designer of the *tank* engine, in which the fuel and water are carried on the engine itself, dispensing with the separate tender;—a form now become perhaps the most useful known.

In 1839 came the large Turkish orders for woollen-mills, silk and cotton-mills, engineering workshops, iron-making establishments and machinery, iron houses, and mechanical work, in great variety. These occupied him in the designs, and the manufactory in the execution, for some years, and were very profitable.

About this time, however, he began to get into difficulty with the management of the Millwall establishment; and this led, as will be explained in the next chapter, to the introduction into the business of his son Thomas, who joined him as a partner about 1841. A few years later, in 1846, another son, William Andrew, joined, and the business was thenceforward carried on under the name of William Fairbairn and Sons.

Both sons actively exerted themselves in aid of their father, and this accession of strength led to the further extension of the manufactory, and to increased energy in the prosecution of the Manchester business, which from that date forward became highly prosperous. The work done was so large in its quantity, and so multifarious and varied in its character, that it would be impossible, as indeed it is unnecessary, here to give any account of it at all approaching completeness. It must suffice to mention a few of the most important things that were done.

In 1846 the firm made, in conjunction with Mr. (afterwards Sir) William Cubitt, the iron arrangements for the large landing stage at St. George's Pier, Liverpool. This was by far the largest thing of the kind that had been projected; the two movable girder bridges, for connecting the floating stage to the shore, were each 150 feet long; they had to rise and fall with the tide, and the general arrangements, to give stability and strength combined with convenience, were laid out with great skill.

In 1846 Mr. Fairbairn took out the Tubular Bridge Patent, mentioned at the end of Chapter XIII., and soon afterwards began the manufacture of wrought-iron bridges on that plan.

That was about the time of the great railway mania, when, although numbers of railway schemes were abortions, yet the actual construction of *bonâ-fide* lines was pushed energetically. These lines required bridges in large numbers, and Mr. Fairbairn's invention was most opportune, as the kind of bridge it introduced was strong, convenient, reasonable in cost, and easy and expeditious in erection.

He was at that time the person who best understood its design, and, consequently, as soon as the merits of the invention became known, he was inundated with orders; he had, in fact, a complete monopoly at high and remunerative prices; and the manufacture of these alone realised a fortune. Before 1851, he had erected more than a hundred of them, from 40 to 180 feet span, and subsequently the number was augmented tenfold, extending to much larger sizes. It is estimated that the total quantity of this work executed cannot have been less than 100,000 tons.

In the course of his large practice in steam-engine construction, he made, as already stated, many improvements in detail; but he seldom gave to the world any special description of them. In the middle of 1849, however, he communicated to the Institution of Mechanical Engineers, at Birmingham, a paper ' On the Expansive Action of Steam, and a new Construction of Expansion Valves for Condensing Steam Engines.' He had seen the advantage of the well-known principle of expanding the steam, introduced by Watt and Hornblower in the last century, and with his usual skill and practical judgment, he introduced modifications in the form and arrangement of the valve apparatus, by which this principle might be more effectually carried out; and these novelties it was the chief object of the paper to describe.

About 1850 Mr. Fairbairn was engaged in a large work at Keyham Dockyard, near Plymouth, namely, the construction of a huge wrought-iron caisson for closing the entrance to one of the docks.

The Keyham docks extend for some distance along the Eastern shore of the Hamoaze, and early in 1844 it was determined by the Admiralty to form an establishment there, of sufficient capacity and extent to admit simultaneously, to the basins and docks, the largest ships and steamers of the navy. For this purpose, two large basins, communicating with each other, but having separate entrances from the sea, were laid out. In one of these entrances it was resolved to adopt a modification of the ordinary floating caisson, and as it involved a structure of great size, and subject to peculiar strains, Mr. Fairbairn (who had shortly before built a caisson for Portsmouth, of a smaller kind) was requested to consider the subject and to undertake the construction of the caisson. It was 80 feet long and 43 feet high, and its total weight was 290 tons. It was finished in 1850, and was tested by careful experiment in July of that year. A description of the work was presented to the Institution of Civil Engineers on May 9, 1854, and was published in their Minutes of Proceedings for that year.

The same year, an attempt was made to quicken the speed of the express passenger trains on some of the great railways of the country. The recent battle of the gauges had brought out the claims of the broad gauge for superiority of speed and power, and the narrow gauge companies desired to show that they could also do great things in this way if they pleased. Messrs. Fairbairn accordingly built, for Mr. MacConnell, the locomotive engineer of the North Western, a locomotive of hitherto unparalleled power, intended to run from London to Birmingham (112 miles) in two hours. It was a fine specimen of design and construction, and it was no doubt capable of performing a large duty; but the company found that such high speed might be bought too dearly, and the time of the transit between the two places has remained at three hours.

In November 1850, Mr. Fairbairn took out a patent for an invention which was very successful, namely an improvement in the instrument called a crane, for hoisting and lifting purposes. Ordinary cranes are usually

constructed on one of the plans shown in the two first
of the following figures:—

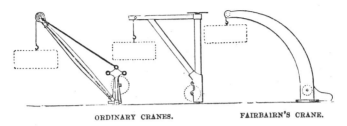

ORDINARY CRANES.   FAIRBAIRN'S CRANE.

In these the inclined strut, called the 'jib,' is placed
at an angle of about 40 or 45 degrees with the vertical, so as to obtain the greatest strength. But if the
article to be raised be at all bulky, this position of the
jib will interfere with the height to which it may be
raised.

Mr. Fairbairn's improvement consisted in making the
projecting arm of the crane of iron plates riveted together
so as to form a hollow tubular girder of curved form, as
shown in the third figure. It allowed the article to be
raised to a greater height, and at the same time offered
greater strength and security.

Six large cranes were soon afterwards made on this
plan by Messrs. Fairbairn and Sons for Keyham Dockyard. A description of them was given by Mr. Fairbairn to the Institution of Mechanical Engineers, and was
published in their Proceedings for 1857. Each crane
was calculated to lift 12 tons to a height of 30 feet from
the ground, and to sweep a circle 65 feet in diameter.
These answered so well that a few years afterwards a still
larger one was ordered for the same place to lift 60 tons
60 feet high, with a circle of 106 feet diameter. Cranes
of this kind were soon appreciated by the public for their
convenience and strength, and became largely used.

The following figure represents a crane of this descrip-

tion erected at one of the Royal Dock Yards, and worked
by steam power.

LARGE STEAM CRANE ON FAIRBAIRN'S PRINCIPLE.

In 1851–2 occurred the great strike of the engineering
workmen. It originated in Lancashire, and was the first
of those contests between capital and labour which commanded the marked attention of the general public, and
have since spread with such rapidity and fierceness that
not only all trades, but all countries have been embraced
in the struggle.

The Amalgamated Society of Engineers, through
its Council, made demands upon some of the mechanical firms in Manchester and Oldham, which appeared
to the employers incompatible with freedom of action
in the control of their affairs. After protracted but vain

efforts to adjust the differences, on December 17, 1851, the leading engineering and machinist firms in Lancashire gave notice that they would simultaneously close all their establishments at the close of the year, if a threatened 'turn-out' of the workpeople of one of their number should be persisted in. No compromise was listened to, and the first week of the new year 1852 saw the gates closed against 10,000 skilled workmen, involving the forced idleness of at least 40,000 persons. Immediately the Metropolitan and other employers, seeing the dangers involved, followed the example of the Lancashire masters, and during the bitter fight of four months, not less than 100,000 hands went without wages. Of course there could be but one result to such a contest; but it may be well to observe that public opinion at a very early period sided with the masters and against the men. It was seen almost instinctively, and expressed unhesitatingly, that a movement, to dictate to employers what men they should employ, how long they should work, and in what way they should work, was not to be encouraged. But when an exposure of the secret workings and intentions of the 'Executive Council' of the Amalgamated Society was made public; when it became known that this irresponsible body had proclaimed that 'If our recommendations be adhered to, and our members are active and energetic in their trade proceedings, we shall soon still further improve our condition, and *make our Society the real ruler of the destinies of our trade,*'—a general indignation was aroused, and it was felt that the masters could not yield without permitting an entire social revolution.

Mr. Fairbairn did not take any active part in the proceedings of the Committee of Associated Employers; but his son and partner (the present Sir Thomas Fairbairn) was one of the most prominent figures in the contest. Under the well-known signature of 'Amicus,' he contributed to the 'Times' a long series of letters, which excited great interest and curiosity. The social and political consequences of the labour question were argued at great length, and these letters created a discussion of the strike by the press, so comprehensive and exhaustive that a reproduction of the newspaper articles would fill volumes. Lords Shaftesbury and Ashburton, and other well-known 'friends of the working classes,' used all their influence to wean the workmen from their folly. Lord Ashburton sought the arbitration of the then Lord Chancellor, Lord Cranworth, who replied in a long letter of admirable temper and argument. Writing to. Lord Ashburton, he said :—

I have been thinking more and more of the unfortunate matter to which our conversation referred. I confess it is one which gives me great pain, and the more so because I cannot but come to the conclusion that these men are in the wrong. The masters have greater wealth, and perhaps therefore, greater instruction, if not greater intelligence, on their sides. I wish therefore, not unnaturally, that, in talking over the matter with you, I could take the part of the weaker body ; but I really cannot. . . . . The masters ought, surely, to be at liberty to employ whomsoever they may please, for each and every portion of the work. If it is work only to be done well by skilled workmen, they must employ skilled workmen ; and unless they do so, the work will be badly done, and the masters will be the sufferers. If it is not work requiring skilled workmen, on what possible principle can the masters be called on to employ them ? The master ought to be at liberty to employ whom he may choose. Of course the workman would equally be left at liberty to accept the terms offered by the master, and work, or to reject those terms, and abstain from working. Both parties ought to be left at liberty to do what they think most for their own interest. So as to piece-work or overtime—all the relations between employer and employed are, or ought to be, those of contract between perfectly free agents. The master may propose whatever terms he chooses; the workman may accept or reject those terms. . . . . I cannot wonder that the masters refuse to agree to any arbitration that is to impose on them any restriction whatever as to the terms on which they are to contract with their men. . . . . I should have been very glad if we could have seen our way to suggest any sort of arbitration which would solve the difficulty; but I really cannot.

Lord Cranworth's kindly expressed, but decided opinion, the arguments of the press, and the entreaty of friends were all in vain. The blood was up; and the fight went on until all available funds were exhausted, and the savings of years and household treasures were parted with. Then the inevitable conclusion took place, after much misery had been endured on the one side, and heavy losses sustained on the other.

The authorship of the 'Amicus' letters was hotly disputed; they had been attributed to Mr. W. J. Fox, M.P. for Oldham, who in seeking his re-election had to challenge the direct avowal of the 'Times,' to protect him, as he said, from a persevering report which had been made to damage his chances at the poll. For many years afterwards 'Amicus' was a constant contributor to the columns of the leading journal on many topics of social and political interest.

The following letters on this subject have been found among Mr. Fairbairn's papers :—

December 29, 1851.

My dear Mr. Fairbairn,—You have taken, I see, the bold, manly, and righteous course of resistance to this Louis Blanc conspiracy of the mechanics and engineers.

It is very sad; all was looking so well, and, were it not for some evil-disposed men, would continue to look so well! But we are fallen on troublous times; and I much fear that, in the language of Scripture, 'there will be wrath' on this our country.

God forgive us, for we are a very thankless people!

I rejoice that none of *my* operatives, as I regard them, are connected with this movement of wickedness and folly.

Now let me thank you and Mrs. Fairbairn for your agreeable hospitality during my manufacturing tour. I am very happy that I have been introduced into the interior of your family.

May God prosper you all.

Yours truly,
SHAFTESBURY.

W. FAIRBAIRN, Esq.

Manchester, December 31, 1851.

My dear Lord Shaftesbury,— I needed not the assurance contained in your note to satisfy me that your lordship could never approve the arbitrary demands made by the Amalgamated Society upon their employers, and that you would yourself emphatically condemn the agitation got up by a few dangerous demagogues who form the Executive Council. The whole course of your public life, and your unwearied and most disinterested labours for the amelioration of the moral and physical condition of helpless children, women, and all the working class, were to my mind a sure guarantee that the promulgation of socialist doctrines would receive your resistance, from whatever quarter they might spring. From your conversations I have further gathered that it was never your lordship's intention to interfere with adult labour.

It appears, however, that the leaders of the Amalgamated Society drag in your lordship's name to give colouring or a kind of sanction to their dangerous proceedings, and such a remark as the following is by no means uncommon in this district, from unthinking but perhaps well-meaning persons : ' Oh ! you see what Lord Shaftesbury has brought upon you !'

I had intended writing to your lordship on this very important subject, and suggesting that it might have a desirable effect were your lordship to address a letter embodying your views on the subject, either to myself or direct to the ' Times.'

Your lordship's faithful servant,
WM. FAIRBAIRN.

Exactly a year after this date Mr. Fairbairn says, in a letter to General Morin :—

We have at last got over our troubles and effected a settlement in the establishment with our workmen. It has taken us nearly twelve months to restore matters to their regular routine state, but we are now all right again, and I make no doubt we shall continue to be so for many years to come.

About 1852 the Government called in Mr. Fairbairn's aid in the establishment of the now well-known Small Arms Factory at Enfield. In conjunction with the officials of the Ordnance Department, he laid out the works, arranged the general design of the mechanical provisions, and constructed most of the machinery and ironwork, with the exception of the wood-working machines. This order was a large and important one; it occupied much of his careful attention, and the successful working of the establishment has proved how well he fulfilled the trust reposed in him.

About 1852 or 1853 he finished the largest work he had undertaken in mill construction, the great woollen works of Mr. (afterwards Sir Titus) Salt, at Saltaire, near Bradford, Yorkshire.

This kind of work was peculiarly his own; it was by it that he first acquired his fame; his practice in it was exceedingly large, and he kept up his interest in it during the whole of his manufacturing career. In addition to the improvements originally introduced by him in the re-arrangement of the driving machinery, he had continued to add other beneficial changes from time to time; and among others he was the first to take the driving power from the rim of the fly-wheel of the steam-engine, by providing it with teeth working into an adjoining pinion of smaller size, which he considered had much advantage in the directness of the action and the convenience of the mechanical arrangements.

But it was not only the machinery of mills that he improved ; at a later period he devoted considerable attention to the design and construction of the buildings in which the machinery was placed, more particularly as to their strength and the preservation of them from fire. Many accidents from malconstruction had come under his notice, and he had turned every opportunity of this kind to account in the improvement of his designs. Iron was largely used in these structures, and he made it his business to perfect the experimental knowledge of the strength of the material in its different forms, and of the best modes of applying it to the purposes in question.

The Saltaire mill was remarkable not only for its great extent, but for the perfection of its design. It was entirely planned by him, except the architectural features. A description of it, with plates, is given in Mr. Fairbairn's book ' On the application of cast and wrought iron to building purposes,' published in 1854.

The mills and dependencies extend over $6\frac{1}{2}$ acres of ground. The main range of buildings, or the mill proper, is 550 feet in length, 50 feet in width, and about 72 feet (6 storeys) in height. The loom-shed, one storey high, is nearly 300 feet long by 200 feet wide ; and another, the combing shed, is a little smaller.

The engines are 1,250 horse-power, and the length of shafting is very nearly 2 miles, weighing upwards of 60 tons, and making from 60 to 250 revolutions per minute. The mills contain within themselves every means of preparing from the raw material the supply for 1,200 power looms, the yield of which is 30,000 yards of alpaca per day, or upwards of 5,000 miles per annum.

From the commencement of the new partnership in 1846, for many years onward, the Manchester business enjoyed very great prosperity. The managers were able and energetic, and the circumstances of the time were eminently favourable.

During the railway mania immense orders were given for railway work of various kinds, at very high prices, yielding large profits ; and large contracts were undertaken for locomotives, the execution of which extended over many years. But these formed only a portion of the work done. Mr. Fairbairn's reputation was so great that he was consulted from all parts of the world, and the consultation almost always led to large orders for works, which were professionally designed in the offices and executed in the manufactory. He was the person, *par excellence*, applied to when any great mechanical works of novel or unusual character had to be undertaken, and his scientific investigations, which were so frequently before the world, drew attention to his position in a manufacturing capacity. The firm, with him at their head, undertook all sorts of engineering work, and in the manufacture of bridges, girders, cranes, caissons, &c., and in fact all the novel applications of wrought iron to structural and mechanical purposes, they had absolutely their own way.

Between 1848 and 1860, the large loss at Millwall (100,000*l.*) was not only all made good by the Manchester works, but considerable fortunes were amassed by all the partners.

In December 1853, Mr. Fairbairn having realised a competency, resolved to give up his more active part in the business, which was thenceforward conducted by his two sons.

He did not however on that account relinquish his engineering occupations ; for he was afterwards constantly engaged in giving advice on engineering and mechanical matters, and he afforded active assistance to the manufacturing firm whenever he found it would be useful to them.

During the siege of Sebastopol it was determined to supply the troops daily with new bread and fresh flour from the grain of the surrounding country, by providing the means of converting the wheat into flour, and baking it upon the spot.

Mr. Fairbairn was consulted as to the best means of carrying out this proposal, and he at once prepared designs for a floating flour mill and bakery. Two iron screw steamers were purchased by Government and placed in his hands for adaptation to the purpose; the firm prepared the machinery with all expedition, and the whole apparatus was fitted and completed in less than three months.

An interesting description of this arrangement was communicated by Mr. Fairbairn to the meeting of the Institute of Mechanical Engineers at Newcastle-on-Tyne, August 24 and 25, 1858, and is published in their Transactions for that year.

The flour mill machinery was similar to that ordinarily used on shore, with such modifications only as were necessary to adapt it to its novel position, and fit it to sustain the constant and varying motion of a ship at sea. These difficulties were overcome, and the mill was found to answer admirably, grinding in almost all weathers at the rate of 20 bushels, or 1,120 lbs. of flour per hour, and that at a time when the vessel was steaming at seven and a half knots; both the mill machinery and the ship being propelled by the same engines. From the official reports sent home, it appeared that important advantages were gained by the introduction of this machinery, and it is calculated that great numbers of lives were saved by the abundant supply of wholesome bread and flour furnished to the camp during the latter part of the siege.

In 1859 William Fairbairn, Junior, retired, leaving

Thomas the sole proprietor, after which the works were carried on under the title of Fairbairn and Company.

About 1860 the firm undertook, under Mr. Fairbairn's direction, a work of considerable difficulty, namely, the rebuilding of two large viaducts on the Manchester and Sheffield Railway. These had been originally built about 1844, of wood, each was some hundreds of feet long and 100 to 120 feet high above the valley below. After a few years the wooden ribs became distorted, and the entire structure of one of them was so unsafe, that it had to be trussed with iron rods to keep it in form. Within ten or twelve years after erection the timber in both became so much decayed as to endanger their security, and Mr. Fairbairn was consulted as to the best mode of reconstructing them in iron. The difficulty and expense, however, frightened the directors, and temporary repairs were resorted to. But these did not last long, and in 1858 the viaducts were again in such a state as to alarm the passengers and the people in the neighbourhood, who drove and travelled several miles to avoid crossing either bridge. Under these circumstances it was finally resolved to renew them with iron, and Mr. Fairbairn being again referred to, designs were made and carried out.

The timber arches had to be removed and iron girders substituted, under however a stringent condition by the directors that the railway traffic on the viaducts should not be interrupted during the progress of the works. This was agreed to, and Mr. Fairbairn states that in carrying it out he incurred heavy responsibilities, and much anxiety ; but the works were completed without accident ; and although there were about seventy trains per day passing over the bridges, no stoppage, even of a single minute, occurred with any one of them.

The mode of executing this difficult work is too

technical to be stated here ; it was fully described by Mr. Fairbairn in a paper read before the Institution of Civil Engineers, February 24, 1863, and published in their Proceedings for that year.

About 1864 the business was transferred to a Limited Liability Company, who thenceforth traded under the title of ' The Fairbairn Engineering Company.'   Mr. Fairbairn and his family retained, however, a considerable pecuniary interest in the concern, and Mr. Fairbairn himself still kept an office on the works, and gave much personal attention to them.   The firm undertook several large contracts, among which was the construction of some forts for the Government to be erected at Spithead ; the roof of the Royal Albert Hall ; many large bridges and roofs for railways, &c., &c.   But about the time of Sir William's death, the tide of a long continued prosperity seemed to have turned, and in the face of a serious depression in the iron trade, which was obviously coming on, it was considered expedient not to risk further losses, but to wind up the concern.   The shops were accordingly dismantled, the plant was sold, and probably by the time this biography reaches the public, the Canal Street Engineering Works will have altogether disappeared.

CHAPTER XIX.

THE MILLWALL SHIP-BUILDING FACTORY

CONTRAST WITH THE MANCHESTER BUSINESS—EARLY HISTORY OF IRON SHIP-BUILDING—THE 'AARON MANBY' AND SIR CHARLES NAPIER—MR. FAIRBAIRN'S EARLY EXPERIMENTS—CHOICE OF A LOCALITY FOR THE SHIP-BUILDING MANUFACTURE—MILLWALL—OUTLAY—MANAGEMENT—ORDERS—WORK FOR THE ADMIRALTY, THE EAST INDIA COMPANY, AND THE MERCANTILE MARINE—ROYAL PLEASURE YACHTS—PATENTS—DIFFICULTIES—COMPETITION—WANT OF EXPERIENCE—UNFAVOURABLE REPORTS AS TO MR. FAIRBAIRN'S CREDIT—DEPRESSION AND ANXIETY—RESOLUTION TO GET RID OF THE WORKS—THEIR SALE—MR. FAIRBAIRN'S SONS—LARGE AMOUNT OF LOSS BY THESE WORKS.

CHAPTER XIX.

THE great prosperity which attended the Manchester business was considerably marred by results of an opposite character arising from the other manufacturing establishment with which Mr. Fairbairn was connected, the ship-building yard at Millwall. It was in existence about twelve years; it was never in a paying condition, it absorbed capital to a large amount; it was an incessant source of anxiety and annoyance to everybody concerned, and it ended with a loss which, if not met by the Manchester profits, would have sent Mr. Fairbairn into the Bankruptcy Court, and ruined his prospects for ever.

The origin of the Millwall establishment has been explained by Mr. Fairbairn in that portion of his autobiography given in Chap. X. He entered upon it soon after his separation from Lillie in 1832.

The application of iron to ship-building was then almost new. Some few canal boats made of iron appear to have been in use on the Midland Canals about 1812 or 1813, but the first iron boat that ever put to sea was a small steamer, built in 1821 at the Horseley Iron Works, Staffordshire, by Mr. Aaron Manby, whose name she was given. She was 120 feet long and 18 feet beam, and was propelled by an engine of 80 horse-power. She was sent to London in parts, and having been put together there was navigated, down the Thames, across the Channel, and

up the Seine to Paris. This unique voyage was performed under the command of Captain (afterwards Admi-
ral Sir Charles) Napier, R.N., who was largely interested
in the undertaking, and devoted much time, and his usual
skill and energy, to the enterprise.

Other iron boats of small size were made at the same
works, and shortly afterwards Mr. John Laird, of Birken-
head, and another ship-builder in Scotland took up their
construction; but the manufacture had made but little
progress, when in 1830, Mr. Fairbairn directed his attention to the use of steam-power on the Forth and Clyde
canal, and built the famous little iron steamer the 'Lord
Dundas.' This was succeeded by others, built at his
works at Manchester, and he may be said to have been
among the first to show the superior strength and security
of the new material. He found that the resisting power
of an iron vessel, when properly constructed, could be
depended on for navigating the open sea; and, moreover,
that she was much better calculated for lightness, and
capacity for cargo, than one composed of timber.

These results were so good as to promise a great and
profitable field for the exercise of his designing and
manufacturing skill. But it was immediately apparent
that this manufacture could not be successfully carried on
in an inland town, and he determined to set up another
establishment at a seaport. He was undecided for some
time between Liverpool and London, but at last fixed on
the latter, for the reason, as he says, that he believed it
offered more encouraging prospects for the new business.
But it is very probable that, as he began to feel a desire
to make himself more known in the world, his preference for the metropolitan situation may have partly
arisen from the better opportunity it would give him in
this respect. The choice no doubt was right in a personal,
though wrong in a commercial point of view. It was the

London situation that caused, or at least magnified, the financial difficulties (for almost all iron ship-building enterprises have been unsuccessful on the Thames), and if he had chosen Liverpool, he might have made the business pay, but the course of his life would have been changed; he would have been less before the world, and would, in all probability never have gained the honour and celebrity that attended his actual career.

In accordance with this decision Mr. Fairbairn selected a plot of land on the north bank of the Thames, at Millwall, in the Isle of Dogs, and entered on it early in the year 1835. Here he laid out complete arrangements for building iron ships of considerable size, and, as these might be expected for the most part to be steamers, he had also to erect workshops and tools for the manufacture of their engines and machinery.

The first outlay was heavy, and it was provided entirely by borrowed money. It was afterwards much increased as the necessities arose, and this capital outlay was one of the causes that hampered the concern, and contributed to the trouble it gave.

The mode of managing two large establishments two hundred miles apart, each requiring constant attention, was a difficulty very early seen; but Mr. Fairbairn hoped, by frequent journeys backwards and forwards, to give so much of his personal attention to each as would keep both in order.

He found no difficulty in getting work for the new factory. The fame he had acquired in his Manchester business told favourably in this, and orders came in plentifully. In the first year the firm had made contracts for twelve vessels, and the demand went on year after year at about the same rate, upwards of a hundred vessels

z

having been made at Millwall during the thirteen years the works were in operation.

It will suffice to notice some of the larger and more important orders undertaken.

The Admiralty patronised the firm, by giving them a frigate to build, the 'Megæra,' 2,000 tons, with engines of 600 horse-power; and they also constructed large engines for several other frigates, among which were the 'Dragon,' the 'Vulture,' the 'Odin,' and the 'Cormorant.'

For the East India Company they built twelve iron vessels for navigating the Ganges, each about 240 tons; and for the Peninsular and Oriental Company the 'Pottinger,' 1,700 tons.

Many others were constructed for the mercantile marine service, among which were the 'Rose' and the 'Thistle,' for Australian lines; eight steamers for the Baltic, and four for the Black Sea, &c.

The firm also built iron steam yachts for the Emperor of Russia and the King of Denmark.

Mr. Fairbairn took out two patents for improvements in marine steam machinery. The first was in September 1841 (No. 9,072), for 'Certain Improvements in the Construction and Arrangement of Steam-engines.' The invention consisted of making the engines direct acting, and applying a novel disposition and construction of some of the working parts, particularly the parallel motion; by means of which the necessary motions of the air-pump, force-pump, and other working parts of the engine were brought into a smaller compass than in the ordinary construction of marine engines.

The second patent of this kind, dated March 7, 1846, was for an improvement in the mode of driving the screw propeller, by the application of a large wheel with internal teeth. It is believed that a pair of engines were constructed on this plan, but it never came into general use.

But though there was plenty of work at the Millwall yard, it was done in the face of a host of difficulties, and from various causes it produced no profit, but the contrary. In the first place, there arose, at an early period, a formidable competition. Other people saw that iron ship-building was likely to be an increasing trade, and, jealous of the interloper from the North, they opened an energetic opposition to him, which kept prices down. Moreover, the business was new, the construction of large iron ships was at first tentative, and much experience had to be gained; and this, in the face of sharp competition, was necessarily very costly.

When, four years after the works had been in operation, Mr. Fairbairn was requested to go to Turkey, he consented with considerable hesitation, fearing that his business might suffer in his absence. His fears were but too well founded; for when he returned from Constantinople, he found affairs at both his works (which then together employed more than 2,000 hands) in great confusion. In regard to Millwall, he says:—

A short time previous to my departure for Turkey, I was engaged in negotiating with the Admiralty for an iron frigate; and under the impression that the order was confirmed, a large proportion of the plates were ordered by Mr. Murray, and most of them delivered at the works. On my return, I found that a change had been made in the dimensions of the vessel, which rendered the material next to useless, or little better than old iron. I will not recount the mortification I endured when I found the firm indebted to a large amount for material that was not wanted. There was, however, no alternative but submission.

z 2

Other difficulties also stood in his way; he had realised a good deal of property, but it was all invested in buildings, plant, and machinery; he had little or no ready money; and this fact, becoming known, gave rise to unfavourable reports as to his circumstances, which, though unfounded, tended to affect his mercantile credit. He says, speaking of this :—

In the philosophy of trade and commerce there appear to be the same fixed and definite laws regulating the transactions between man and man as exist in the physical and moral world. A merchant cannot well afford to be poor. He must never own it if he is; otherwise it is more than probable the most serious consequences may arise injurious to his credit, as all the commercial gossips, of whatever grade, will set upon him, and a hundred to one but he is devoured. Such was nearly my own case at the time I refer to.

He speaks feelingly of the depression he suffered in consequence of these adverse circumstances.

In this contest with the world I suffered many heartburnings and mortifications. Mrs. Fairbairn was confined of her last child. My sons were all at school, my daughter was nearly of age, and a numerous family were entirely dependent on me. These considerations pressed upon me with a force that was almost past endurance. In the fits of melancholy which sometimes overtook me I pictured to myself every possible contingency.

It is pleasant, however, to read the expressions of the determination and energy which he brought to bear on his affairs, and which enabled him, almost unaided, to right himself, and to overcome all his difficulties.

I never thought of bankruptcy. I never relaxed in my exertions, and, above all, I met the difficulties which multiplied around me with a determination which nothing could conquer, and which was sure to mitigate if not entirely to remove their effects. It was this determined perseverance that enabled me to keep the wolf from the door.

In another place he says :—

Such was the buoyancy of my spirits, and such my determination to overcome the difficulties of my position, that I resolved to stem, with an energy that nothing could crush, the tide which set in against me, and I set to work with redoubled energy to secure a respectable independence for my family.

To meet the want of ready money, Mr. R. Smith, the former manager of the Manchester works, put into the business two or three thousand pounds, as an equivalent for a small share in the profits ; and, in addition, a few thousands more were borrowed on the security of the fixed property.

The Millwall works proved, however, too onerous to be retained ; and after much hesitation and consideration, Mr. Fairbairn, about 1844, came to the conclusion that it would be to his interest to get rid of them, even at a large loss. He accordingly determined to wind up that branch of his business, and the works, which had cost upwards of 50,000*l.*, were sold for 12,000*l.*

The place, however, could not be got rid of all at once, as large orders were in hand for iron vessels, which it was necessary to complete. For this reason one-half the freehold and the ship-building yard were retained. One of the ships thus finished was the ' Megæra,' a vessel which was afterwards converted into a troop-ship, and ultimately wrecked in the South Seas. Two or three years were occupied in finishing this vessel, and some other orders in hand from the Peninsular and Oriental and other Companies.

During the years 1845, 1846, and 1847 the factory was used for the experiments on the great tubular bridges, described in Chapter XIII. This was the last work done there.

The whole premises were dismantled and given up in 1848. They were purchased by Messrs. Robinson & Co., and subsequently came, with adjacent lands, into the hands of Mr. Scott Russell, by whom they were used, among other purposes, for the construction of that mighty monster of iron ship-building, the 'Great Eastern.'

It was a great relief to Mr. Fairbairn to get rid of the Millwall establishment, as it enabled him to concentrate the whole of his business in Manchester. And one reason why he wished to do this was, as he states :—

I should have the assistance of my sons, then on the point of leaving school, and likely in a few years to render that support which was then so much wanted, and which I have since had the happiness to experience.

The present Sir Thomas Fairbairn has given the editor the following memorandum respecting these transactions :—

Eight years of my own time and devoted attention were taken up in bringing the disastrous Millwall concern to a close. I was taken away from an intended university career in 1840, and was engaged at Millwall until the final close in 1848, excepting some ten months in 1841–42, which I spent in Italy.

The loss sustained at Millwall altogether was over 100,000*l.*, the whole of which had to be made good from the profits of the business in Manchester.

CHAPTER XX

IRON ARMOUR

AGE 73-79

1861—1867

CHAPTER XX.

FROM 1861 to 1865 Mr. Fairbairn was engaged in aiding the Government on an official investigation respecting the *application of iron to defensive purposes in warfare.* The present construction of the iron armoured vessels of our navy has all arisen out of this enquiry; and on account of the great public interest and importance of the question, it demands a notice at some length.

It is necessary to give a short preliminary account of the circumstances which led to the investigation.

Some twenty years ago it began to be perceived that a great change must be made in the construction of ships of war, in consequence of the introduction into heavy artillery of rifled shell. The ' Wooden Walls of Old England,' which had done such good service from the time of the Spanish Armada to that of Trafalgar, were powerless against the long range, the accurate aim, the penetrating power, and the destructive effect, of these deadly missiles; and it was seen that unless something could be done to meet the difficulty, the efficiency of our navy must be seriously endangered.

The use of iron was one of the most obvious modes of resisting the penetration of shells; but hitherto the application of this material had not found favour with the naval authorities of the country.

It has been mentioned in earlier parts of this work how actively Mr. Fairbairn had exerted himself in intro-

ducing iron ship-building. The first application of this
material had been for mercantile purposes, but in 1835-6
he had arrived at the conclusion that wrought iron was
the safest and most durable material for naval constructions
also, and he was anxious to impress on the Government
the advisability of its being employed for vessels of war.
He was, at an early stage of the manufacture, in communication with the Admiralty,[1] and he urged that iron
ships, if applied to war purposes, would be not only superior in power, but safe under all the circumstances of
attack and defence.

There was at that time a great deal of ignorance and
prejudice in regard to the use of the new material.
Many people (among them persons of influence in naval
matters) conceived that the flotation of a timber ship was
due to the fact of wood being lighter than water, and
seriously argued that if a heavy material, like iron, were
substituted, the ship must inevitably go to the bottom.
This argument was of course met in a simple way by the
direct logic of facts, inasmuch as iron ships, which did
really float, were in existence ; but there were other
objections less easily disposed of, and one of the most
formidable was the great damage likely to be done to
the iron plates by heavy projectiles. In a ship with
wooden sides, a shot hole was not a very serious matter ;
it seldom made a great leak, and the hole could easily be
plugged up. But a shot blow on iron plates rent them
open with a fearful gash incapable of stoppage. It was
suggested that this evil might be diminished by backing
the plates with soft or elastic substances, and some
experiments were tried, in 1840, by the Admiralty at
Portsmouth with this view ; but the results were so unfavourable that they were deemed conclusive against the

---

[1] Paper read before Inst. Nav. Arch., March 1869.

adoption of iron vessels for war purposes, and the Government stood aloof from the general movement, deciding to limit the construction of iron vessels to the mail and packet services.

Still, however, in regard to wooden ships, the awkward difficulty remained of their destructibility by the new rifled shell. With solid shot the improved artillery would have been much less formidable. The entrance of a solid shot into a ship, was an event always expected in action ; and though it often did much damage, it did not destroy the ship, which was capable, in brave hands, of holding out for a long defence, even though ' riddled,' as the expression was, by the fire of the enemy. But large shells, bursting out like fierce volcanoes among the timbers of the structure, or scattering between the decks showers of fragments of jagged iron, every piece dealing destruction in its path, made such havoc as no bravery or skill could hold out against; and a wooden ship efficiently attacked in this way must, in a very short time, either blow up, or sink, or surrender.

Shells, in themselves, were no novelties ; they had, long before the introduction of rifled guns, been used for bombardment with mortars, and had even been introduced as projectiles from ordinary cannon ; but from the uncertainty of aim and want of force when fired from a distance, and from the imperfect construction of the missiles themselves, they were not much more effective against ships than ordinary cannon balls. It was only when rifling enabled them to be fired at long range, with great accuracy and powerful impact, and when the improvements of their construction gave full scope to their destructive capabilities, that they became so formidable.

The use of timber ships being retained, there remained

the alternative of casing them with an armour of iron plate, of a thickness which shells could not penetrate. There were many difficulties in the way of this, and the first person who made any successful efforts to overcome them, was the late Emperor of the French. At the time of the Russian War, when rifled guns were first beginning to assume importance, Napoleon III. saw the necessity of an impenetrable armour, and quietly pursued experiments and investigations on the subject till he had succeeded in building three floating batteries, which were protected by thick plates of iron. These were sent out to the Black Sea, where they arrived shortly before the conclusion of the war, and they were employed by the French in the allied attack upon Kinburn, on October 17, 1855.

These batteries were exposed to a heavy fire, at a distance of 700 yards, for about three hours, unsupported by the fleet ; and though some casualties occurred from shell and shot entering the large old-fashioned port-holes, yet the vessels themselves were comparatively uninjured. This success, so creditable to the skill and perseverance of our ally, settled the question of the practicability of defending ships of war by iron armour ; and in France the further development of the principle was soon rapidly pushed forward.

In England, however, the authorities were loth to distrust their time-hallowed wooden walls ; and although the subject was looked into, very little was seriously done. In 1858, two floating batteries were experimentally cased in iron plates, in imitation of the French batteries at Kinburn, and were fired at for trial. Iron plates were also, about the same time, placed experimentally on the sides of some of Her Majesty's ships, and Mr. Whitworth's new rifled ordnance, with steel projectiles, were used against them. The result demonstrated the value of the protection, though it showed much imperfection through want of experimental knowledge.

In the mean time the French, profiting by their experience at Kinburn, pushed on vigorously, and, a year or two after the Crimean War, had completed a frigate plated with iron armour, which was named 'La Gloire,' and was launched about 1859. She was timber-built, resembling one of our line-of-battle ships cut down, and was cased from end to end with iron plates $4\frac{1}{2}$ inches thick; she was 250 feet long, and was propelled by a screw, with engines of 900 horse-power.

When the news of the construction of 'La Gloire' reached this country, our Government became alarmed, and naturally so; for she was a formidable challenge to our navy. Accordingly, early in 1859, the Admiralty determined, in great haste, to build a ship to oppose her, and they laid down the celebrated iron-plated frigate the 'Warrior,' which was built with great celerity, and was launched in December 1860. This ship was much larger than her opponent, being 380 feet long, 6,000 tons burthen, and having engines of 1,250 horse-power. Her armament was much heavier than that of 'La Gloire,' and her speed much faster. She differed also materially from the French ship, in that she was built of iron instead of timber. The Government had, as already stated, arrived, twenty years before, at the conclusion, that iron was an unfit material for ships of war; but the subject had since been much discussed, and the opinions of scientific naval constructors in its favour had been urged so strongly, in opposition to the prejudices of the Admiralty, that they were induced, almost against their own will, to fall in with Mr. Fairbairn's original recommendation. This has since become universally adopted, and wooden ships of war are now things of the past.

Although, however, there was no timber hull to set on fire, yet the thin plates were easily penetrable both by shot and shell, and hence it was as necessary to protect an iron as a wooden ship. But nothing was known experimentally as to how the iron armour could be applied, our authorities having wasted, in indecision, the time that the French Government had employed in investigation and experiment.

In this state of ignorance our designers considered they could not do better than repeat the plan they had followed with the floating batteries, namely, copy from the French as nearly as they could. They, therefore, first made the hull of the 'Warrior' represent that of 'La Gloire,' by fastening, on the outside of the iron skin, a thick cushion of timber, on which they proceeded to fix the plates by bolting. They introduced certain novelties into the details, which, however, were afterwards found to be no improvement, but rather inferior to the French designs.

On the finishing of the 'Warrior,' the Government bethought themselves that it would be desirable to do what they ought to have done five years before, namely, to ascertain something about the principles which should guide the design of iron armour. In other words, having already built the ship, they began to enquire how they ought to have built her (a curious line of policy which, it will be seen, was repeated in an analogous case a few years later). It was apparent that the use of iron for such a novel purpose was so complicated by considerations of a mechanical and metallurgical character as to demand a more searching technical investigation than it could receive at the hands of purely military or naval authorities; and at the end of 1860 the Government wisely determined to submit the whole matter to a mixed special committee. The Secretary-at-War, Mr. Herbert (afterwards Lord Herbert) therefore selected six gentlemen, and, having obtained their consent to act, the Committee, called the 'Special Committee on Iron,' was formally appointed on January 12, 1861. The members were :—

Captain (afterwards Sir John) Dalrymple Hay, R.N., chairman, to represent the Navy.
Major Jervois, R.E., to represent the Royal Engineers.
Col. W. Henderson, R.A., to represent the Royal Artillery.
Dr. John Percy, F.R.S., the eminent metallurgist.
Mr. William Fairbairn, F.R.S.} Civil Engineers, specially
Mr. William Pole, F.R.S.,
experienced in the uses and properties of iron.

The Committee were actively at work four years, during which time they presented to the Government four Annual Reports, each accompanied with a large volume of minutes of experiments and proceedings. The information contained in these volumes was of the greatest value, but unfortunately they were never published. The Government, although no particular secresy had been observed in the proceedings (foreigners having been often admitted freely to them), were reluctant to make the mass of knowledge gained public property, and accordingly only extracts and abstracts were made known from time to time.

It is, however, no breach of confidence, after this lapse of time, to give a summary of the principal matters that occupied the Committee's attention.

Their first duty was to collect and classify all the meagre information that existed, and the results of all the experiments that had been made on the use of iron for resisting shot.

They then called before them various persons whom they considered likely to have knowledge of the subject, military and naval officers, engineers, ship-builders, and iron manufacturers ; and their evidence, given very fully, was recorded and considered. But the great diversity of the opinions thus gathered showed the obscurity in which this novel application of the material was involved.

The Committee then commenced an elaborate series of investigations and experiments systematically carried out ; first on a small scale on single plates of various sizes and thicknesses ; and then on targets of large size, made to represent actual ships' sides, of a great variety of constructions. These enquiries extended over several years, and led to the establishment of many important principles as to the nature of the material best adapted to the purpose ; the arrangement and dimensions of the armour ; the mode of fastening to the ship ; the effect of the form and material of the shot ; and so on. It may be interesting to give an account of some of the trials made and the results arrived at on these points.

One of the most important considerations was as to the nature of the material best fitted to be used for armour ; for as this was capable of being given many varieties of character, according to the mode of its preparation, it was desirable to ascertain which was best for the purpose in view. On this point the opinions of the witnesses had varied a good deal, but there had been a general impression that one of the most important qualities to give was *hardness*. It was urged that the harder the armour was made the better would it resist the shot, and that in fact the best material, if it could be made and applied conveniently, would be hard steel, or at least a combination of steel and iron.

This was a plausible idea, but it was not borne out by

investigation and experiment. It was found that hard plates were brittle, and were broken up by the blows, when the detaching of the fragments exposed the vessel to penetration ; soft plates, on the contrary, gave way, and became dented, bruised, and distorted, but still held together and formed an efficient protection.

Both theoretical considerations and practical experiments showed that the best principle of defence was not to attempt to resist the blow, but to receive it in such a way as would do the least mischief. The obvious mode of accomplishing this with iron armour was to make it of *soft, tough* plates, which would allow the energy of the shot to be expended in indenting and battering them without producing fracture.

The Committee, therefore, came to the conclusion that the best material for armour was wrought-iron, free from hardness and brittleness, but as soft and tough as could be procured. This opinion, though it was arrived at in opposition to the ideas generally prevalent, has been fully confirmed by subsequent experience.

The mode of making the plates also engaged the attention of the Committee. It was a new thing in the iron trade to fabricate plates of this enormous size ; and the first attempts were imperfect, the iron being of inferior quality. The Committee requested the principal houses to produce plates for trial, invited them to witness the experiments, and gave them every aid in their endeavour to perfect the manufacture ; and the result was a marked improvement and a much better approach to the quality required.

Two processes were used for making the plates— hammering and rolling. In the former, large lumps of iron, previously prepared from ' scrap ' or from ' puddled

A A

bars,' were brought to a welding heat, and being laid together, were placed under heavy steam hammers, the repeated blows of which welded the masses together, and shaped them to the required form and dimensions. This process was the first adopted for the manufacture of armour plates; it was used by the Thames Iron Company, who built the ' Warrior,' and the plates of that ship were made in that way.

Shortly afterwards a firm in Yorkshire adopted another plan, namely, by *rolling*—a process in fact the same as that used for ordinary boiler-plates, but on a much larger scale. The masses of iron, first prepared, were flat in shape, and several of these, being laid one on the other, were heated to the welding point in a furnace, and then passed between large rollers, which rolled them out into one solid plate of the required size. The process was a difficult one, from all the apparatus requiring to be of such great size, and the machinery of such immense power.

The Iron Committee tried extensive experiments on plates made by both these systems. They found the hammered plates had a tendency to be hard and unequal. The repeated blows of the hammer hardened the material, and this effect was not always the same in different parts, some receiving more action than others. Moreover, from the irregular form of the primitive masses, the parts were not always perfectly welded together. The rolled plates, on the other hand, from the more uniform and less sudden action of the compressing force, were softer and more uniform in quality, but they still had the defect of what was called ' lamination,' *i.e.* a want of perfect welding between the different layers. The Committee, on the whole, preferred the rolled plates, and this mode of manufacture has now superseded the other almost entirely.

Another point investigated by the Committee was the effect of the form and material of the shot. They considered, however, that too much importance had been attached to these particulars. The shot was merely a means of transferring to the plate a certain amount of mechanical energy generated at a distance by the powder ; and the only way in which form and material influenced the result was by causing a greater or less proportion of this energy to be absorbed by the shot itself, and so wasted, or diverted from its intended purpose.

It was attempted by a very ingenious process to ascertain the amount of work absorbed by the shot. It was found that, after striking the plates, the shot, or the fragments of them, became highly heated, and, according to the recently established thermo-dynamic law, by measuring the rise of temperature, an approximate estimate could be given of the work absorbed. It was thus found that with a hard-tempered steel shot, the energy expended upon the projectile was about one-tenth of that stored up in it at the moment of striking; while with softer steel it was two-tenths ; with soft wrought-iron it amounted to above one-half of the whole ; and with cast-iron to probably still more.

These results, which were fully corroborated by the effects produced on the plates, pointed to hard steel as the best kind of shot to be used against iron armour ; but this expensive material was afterwards superseded, in consequence of a discovery made by Capt. Palliser, that cast-iron shot would answer, if made of a particular quality, and in a particular form. In the ordinary shapes, shot of cast-iron, whatever the quality of metal, broke up with great facility ; but Capt. Palliser showed that if the head were made pointed and the metal were very hard, the shot would penetrate the plate before breaking, and the minimum amount of work would be lost on the projectile. The shot so designed was accordingly adopted in the service.

The Committee further investigated the laws of resistance offered by plates of different thicknesses to projectiles of different natures and weights, and with different velocities. Reverting to the principle that the damage to the iron plate was proportional to the work in the shot, or to the charge of powder, it was assumed that some definite estimate might be made of the thickness of plate necessary to resist certain artillery. As far as could be made out, there appeared reason to believe that, within certain limits, the resisting power of a plate bore a tolerably near ratio to the square of its thickness; but there was so much difficulty in estimating the amount of damage done, and the quality of the plates tried was so variable,. that no trustworthy relation could be fixed. In heavy plates, moreover, practical effects came in which disturbed the application of any general law.

Another question that occupied the attention of the Committee was what *form* it was most advantageous to give to the defensive material. Several forms were proposed, such as bars, superposed thin plates, corrugations, ribs, bosses, and many other ingenious contrivances. More than four hundred of such plans were submitted to the Committee; and a great many were fully considered and tried; but, through all these complications, they arrived at the simple result that the best application of the material was a single plate of uniform thickness, with the surface perfectly plane.

Great interest and importance were attached to the mode of applying the iron armour-plates upon the hull of the vessel. In the 'Warrior,' as already explained, a cushion or bed of timber about eighteen inches thick had been interposed between the armour-plates and the iron skin of the vessel, a plan followed, probably, more for the purpose of imitating the construction of 'La Gloire,' than with any very definite idea of what object the wood was to serve.

Many objections were raised to this by persons of considerable authority in ship-building and mechanical science. It was said that the plates had better be fastened at once upon the iron skin, and that the wood backing was not only unnecessary, but was absolutely prejudicial, as liable to decay, and to destruction by fire and shells. It was necessary to test this, and no less than three expensive targets were constructed for the purpose.

The result of these trials was to convince the Committee that the wood backing performed several important functions, which, though they had not been foreseen, were of much advantage.

In the first place, by its softness, it deadened the jar and vibration caused by the blow of the shot. In the iron targets this was severely felt, breaking the bolts and rivets, and shaking and damaging the structure generally ; but with the interposition of the soft cushion these evils were much reduced, and the structure was greatly preserved.

Secondly, it had the advantage of distributing the effect of the blow over a much larger area of the skin plate. When the armour was fastened directly upon the skin the shot acted upon a small area, which gave it a better chance of penetrating ; but with the large thickness of wood between, the area of operation enlarged backwards, like a cone, thereby increasing materially the power of the thin skin to resist the damaging effect.

Thirdly, if, under heavy fire, the armour-plate became broken, the pieces did not fall off, but became imbedded

in the wood, and were thereby held in their places, retaining their utility of defence in a considerable degree.
Fourthly, the wood was useful in catching what is called 'langrage,' or pieces of shot and shell, and preventing their entering the ship. For these reasons the Committee recommended the retention of the wood backing to the armour, and it has ever since formed an essential feature of naval defence.

The best sizes of armour plates, the process of bending them and adapting them to the form of the ship, and the modes of fastening them to the hull, and securing them in their places, also received the consideration of the Committee, and were fully reported on.

The Committee wished to carry their experimental investigations so far as to put the ' Warrior ' herself under the fire of heavy guns. This was thought too expensive and troublesome a proceeding, but the case was met by the construction of a target, about 20 feet long and 10 feet high, which was made exactly a counterpart of a portion of the ship's side. This target was erected at Shoeburyness in 1861, and was fired at with the old 68-pounder gun, and with the Armstrong rifled 110 and 120-pounders, the maximum charge of powder being 20 lbs. It received altogether, from these guns, twenty-nine rounds, the combined weight of the shot being 3,229 lbs.

It was, of course, a good deal damaged at the front, but it was not penetrated, and would still have afforded efficient protection. This result, considering how small an area the fire was concentrated upon, was very favourable, and showed that the ship's armour was strong enough to resist guns of the size then used.

The Committee also experimented on many other

targets of different kinds, made to represent ships' sides defended by different iron constructions. One of these was designed specially by Mr. Fairbairn, for the purpose of testing certain views held by him.

The experiments were carried on for the most part at Shoeburyness, where it was possible to get a large area of free ground, and where the artillery depôts enabled the Committee to obtain the most powerful guns and the most skilled gunners. The trials involved a great deal of risk, but by admirable precautionary arrangements no accident ever occurred.

Mr. Fairbairn, in addition to a frequent attendance at the meetings and experiments of the Committee, undertook, at their request, some special investigations for them, reports of which were published in their proceedings. These were :—

In 1861 :—

On the Mechanical Properties of Specimens of the Iron and Steel Plates subjected to Experiments with Ordnance, their Strength, Ductility, Resistance to Punching Force, &c.

In 1862 :—

On the Resistance of different kinds of Shot to a Force tending to crush them, and the forms they assume under Pressure.
Experiments on Punching.

In 1863 :—

On the Mechanical Properties of Iron Plates.
On the Manufacture of Armour Plates.
Experiments to test the value of annealing Armour Plates.
On the Tenacity of Cast-Iron Shot.

In 1864 :—

On the Mechanical Properties of Iron Plates.
On the Manufacture of Armour Plates.
General Summary of Results.

In these investigations he was ably assisted by Mr. Unwin, whose services in the matter were specially acknowledged by the Committee.

Mr. Fairbairn communicated information on this subject in two papers read before the British Association in 1861 and 1862 ; at a lecture at the Royal Institution in 1862 ; and in a memoir to the Institution of Naval Architects in 1869.

In December 1867, the War Office called the Iron Armour Committee together again, with the addition of some other members, for the purpose of investigating the construction and properties of certain large iron shields for land defences which had been sent out to the forts at Gibraltar and Malta.

As in the case of the ' Warrior,' previously mentioned, the Government had first made the shields, and afterwards begun to consider how they ought to be constructed. To enlighten themselves on this point, they had one of the shields fired at, and it proved so weak that, in alarm, they appealed to the Committee, who, after due examination, reported unfavourably of the strength and construction of the shield.

Mr. Fairbairn attended some of the meetings, but his great age and infirm health prevented his taking a very active part in their proceedings.

CHAPTER XXI.

MISCELLANEOUS MATTERS

AGE 61–80

1850—1869

CHAPTER XXI.

In this and the following chapter it is intended to collect brief notices of a great variety of matters in which Mr. Fairbairn was engaged during the later years of his life, all of more or less importance, but not of sufficient magnitude to be recorded under special heads. These notices will serve to show the extraordinary activity, both mental and bodily, that he possessed at a period of life when most men feel inclined to relax their energies and rest from their labours. He had no motive for continuing to work but love of the work itself, for he had already acquired both wealth and fame, and if he had ambition, it was only to show that his heart was in his profession, and to render himself useful to mechanical science.

Visit to Northern Europe.—About the middle of 1850 Mr. Fairbairn, accompanied by his son Peter, visited Northern Europe. He had occasion to go to Sweden, to examine some mills and machinery the firm were erecting there, and he extended his tour to Russia, with the object of negotiating for the construction of some large bridges over the Neva and other rivers.

The following extracts from some of his letters to his family will give sufficient information as to the events of his journey and the impression they made upon him.

Stockholm, June 17, 1850.

I thought to have written you from Gefle, but I was uncertain as to the time we should have a vessel for Russia, and I purposely deferred it until our return to this city. We have travelled through nearly the whole of Sweden. Two days after our arrival at Copenhagen we had to proceed to Gottenburg, and then embark in a steamer which traverses the line of the great lakes, and after a voyage of nearly 400 miles we again entered the Baltic at a town called Soderkoping, esteemed as a famous watering-place by the citizens of Stockholm.

The tour through the interior has been so exceedingly interesting, that I must endeavour to describe it. It commenced at Gottenburg by ascending the river Gotta, which is navigable for nearly 100 miles from the sea, where it terminates by a series of picturesque falls, over which the water pours and thunders from a height of 120 feet. These falls are surmounted by a series of twelve locks, which land the vessel on the surface of the great lake Wenner. Here we commence a new voyage to Carlstad, at the extreme end of the lake, 100 miles distant. This lake—the largest in Sweden—is 100 miles long and 50 miles wide, and, like most of the Swedish lakes, is covered with a number of small islands, wooded down to the water's edge.

At Carlstad we remained all night, and next morning crossed the lake, where we entered the canal which unites the great lake with another of half the size. This brought us to Motala, where we found a large engineering establishment in a flourishing condition. Some distance below Motala we entered the lake Roxen, and from thence through another series of lakes reached Soderkoping, where we entered the Baltic, on the opposite side of the kingdom.

From Soderkoping a sea voyage amidst innumerable islands, with which the coast is studded, carried us to the entrance of the Mälar lake, at a place called Sodertelge. From this little town, a short voyage of only thirty miles opened out some of the finest views in Sweden. The lake contains upwards of 130 islands beautifully covered with oak, birch, and pine, and the romantic rocks and sylvan dells which mark the surface of those enchanting spots are scarcely to be equalled in any other country, Norway alone excepted.

On reaching Stockholm, I found that the objects of my

journey and other particulars had been announced before my arrival. I was, therefore, at no loss for introductions; but, unfortunately for our visit as a matter of business, there is nothing to be done, as the King and the whole of the administration are incessantly occupied with arrangements for the grand ceremony of the marriage of the Prince Royal to the Princess of the Netherlands, whom I dined with at Potsdam, and who landed here yesterday under the firing of cannon and the greatest rejoicings. I cannot, therefore, do anything at present with the authorities, excepting only with some members of the university and some of the leading men connected with the public works. To them I have communicated all the information required, and we must wait the result.

After a couple of days' sojourn in Stockholm we proceeded by sea to Gefle, about 150 miles north of Stockholm. At this town we are building the large factory; and after having given the necessary instructions and made the requisite arrangements for the buildings, I was presented with 100*l*. for my trouble, and, having been feasted for two days, we hired carriages and travelled overland and through almost interminable forests to Upsala, the ancient capital of Sweden. Here I was received by the students as if I had been the friend of Linnæus or Berzelius. Our arrival, they told me, had been announced in the papers, and they welcomed me to Sweden as if I had been a great man. I was introduced to the Governor and the Archbishop of Sweden, who is well known in England from his writings.

Before reaching Upsala we crossed the river Elfertilge, and visited the falls, which are about the same height as those of Trollhatta. They are, however, still more magnificent from the greater quantity of water which plunges all at once over a precipice of rock, and dashes forward at an astounding rate till it is lost in the deep water below. From the falls to Upsala the road passes through interminable forests of pine, with here and there a cultivated patch to mark an occasional habitation. From Upsala to Stockholm the journey is made by water on a lake which presents the same picturesque features as described in the former route.

I am this moment called off to dine with a party made up for us, and must bring this letter to a close. We sail to-morrow at six in the morning, and hope to reach Abo, in Friedland, on Wednesday night, and Petersburgh on Saturday or Sunday.

St. Petersburgh, July 22, 1850.

I have this moment returned from Peterhoff, where we have had a kind and most gracious reception from the Emperor, the Empress, and the Grand Duke Alexander. The Emperor met me like an old schoolfellow, shook me cordially by the hand, and listened with great interest to everything I had to say about the bridges. The audience lasted nearly an hour, and I found myself in familiar conversation not only with a sovereign of the highest rank in Europe, but with a gentleman of sound judgment and great good sense. His Majesty at once placed me perfectly at ease, and received with attention all the information I was able to communicate. At parting he again took me by the hand, thanked me for the presentation of the book, and, without pledging himself to any ulterior measures, said he hoped I would occupy myself on my return to England with plans and drawings for a bridge across the Neva.

On board the ' Nicholas,' July 25.

Now that I have finished the object of my journey to Russia, I cannot but feel highly gratified with my reception in every quarter. My name had reached Petersburgh before me ; and I may not probably be accused of too much vanity if I state that I was received with marked attention, and particularly by the members of my own profession. Generals . . . and . . . all of them at the head of the civil as well as military engineering, were most kind and attentive ; and during the whole of my professional career I never spent a month more gratifying to my feelings or more flattering to my self-esteem. I have often put the question to myself, Do I merit all this distinction ? I always get alarmed on this subject, as I have more than once seen the ill effects of undue presumption. I hope and pray that a just sense of the value of what I have done, and what I might have done had I been more industrious and persevering, will keep me equally safe in the height of prosperity, as it would nerve me with resolution in the depths of adversity. I write thus my feelings and sentiments freely, in order that you [this was to his sons] may benefit from them. I have had some experience in the world, and I think it is safer in an estimate of one's own abilities to be within than beyond the bounds of moderation.

I believe we may calculate upon some good orders for cranes and other work at Petersburgh and Cronstadt. At the latter place a great deal has to be done. Large engineering works, double the extent of those at Woolwich, are in progress of erection. I spent the whole of yesterday with the different officers in command, and, as at Petersburgh, was most kindly received.

Last night we sailed for Lubeck ; and I am now completing the letter ready for the post when we reach Hamburg.

As a result of Mr. Fairbairn's visit to Sweden, he was honoured with a distinction by King Oscar, as the following letter will explain :—

Stockholm, le 19 Juillet, 1850.

Monsieur,—Le Roi ayant daigné décerner à M. William Fairbairn une médaille en or à l'effigie de sa Majesté, en témoignage de la haute satisfaction avec laquelle sa Majesté a reçu l'ouvrage scientifique que cet ingénieur distingué lui a offert, j'ai reçu l'ordre de vous transmettre ci-près, Monsieur, cette médaille, et de reclamer vos soins obligeans pour la faire parvenir à M. Fairbairn, dont l'adresse est inconnue ici.

Je profite de cette occasion, &c. &c.

L. MANDERSTRÖM.

Monsieur GORDON, Chargé d'Affaires de S.M. Britannique.

Inventors.—It was the lot of Mr. Fairbairn, as it is that of all eminent engineers, to be pestered by inventors, often with the most absurd and trumpery schemes. The following letter, introducing one of these worthies, is worth preserving:—

London, Feb. 3, 1851.

Dear Sir,—You have, I dare say, frequently to endure the misery of listening to an enthusiast who dreams that he has discovered the perpetual motion. Perhaps I am going to add one more to this class of tormentors.

I got a letter from a person at Ilchester some time ago, saying that a friend of his, a mechanic, who had previously invented a glove-cutting machine, had discovered a new engine which was likely to supersede steam; and, as he was a Free Trader, he had pitched upon me as the only person to whom he would impart his secret. I wrote, in reply to this complimentary epistle, to say that I had no technical knowledge in such matters, but offered to name a trustworthy engineer; and in reply to the enclosed letter I have taken the liberty of referring the writer to yourself. Should the genius in question present himself to you, you will, I am sure, be kind enough to give him a courteous hearing. I have no doubt it will turn out a waste of time for him and yourself.

Do not take the trouble to reply, but believe me,

Ever faithfully yours,

RICH. COBDEN.

W. FAIRBAIRN, Esq.

Exhibition of 1851.—Mr. Fairbairn acted as a juror in the machinery department of the Great Exhibition of 1851.

At the close of the work he received the following letter from the Rev. Professor Moseley, who wrote the official Reports on the department to which he was attached :—

Wandsworth, Feb. 11, 1852.

My dear Sir,—The reports are about, I believe, to be struck off at length. It has been a tedious affair ; but in completing it, and thus bringing to a close my own labours in connection with Jury V., I am reminded of its special obligations, and of my own personally to some of its members, and among others to yourself.

We are indebted to you in a great measure, I believe, for the report on which we acted as to Sections E, F, G, than which in the compilation of my own report I found none more full, complete, and satisfactory. Your guidance and judgment in matters of which you have so extensive an experience was of the utmost value to the jury; and considering how many and important are your other occupations, it has great obligations to you for the time and labour you devoted to the work it had undertaken.

I beg of you also to accept my own thanks for the support and assistance I, as chairman, always received from you, and to subscribe myself

Yours, my dear Sir, truly,

HENRY MOSELEY.

British Association at Hull.—In 1853 Mr. Fairbairn was appointed President of the Mechanical Section of the British Association, at their meeting at Hull, and he delivered, on the opening of the business, an address ' On the Progress of Mechanical Science.' He alluded to the improvements that had taken place, and to the progress going on in the same direction, referring particularly to the great advance in naval architecture and steam navigation, as exemplified in the ' Duke of Wellington ' and the ' Great Eastern ' steam-ships; the extension of the scale of manufacturing industry by the erection of gigantic manufactories, and other improvements in various departments of the mechanical art.

Cooling Air in Tropical Climates.—In 1853 and 1854, Mr. Fairbairn formed one of a committee of the British Association appointed to consider a matter of much sanitary importance to the European residents in India. The purport of it may be shown by the following copy of a memorial, which was drawn up by another member of the committee, the late Professor Macquorn Rankine :—

B B

*To the Honourable the Board of Directors of the East
India Company.*

The Memorial of the British Association for the Advancement of Science, showeth :

That your memorialists are deeply impressed by the well-known pernicious effects upon the health of Europeans produced by the high temperature of the air in tropical climates.

That they are convinced that if the means existed in tropical climates of furnishing for the ventilation of buildings —especially hospitals for the sick—large supplies of cool air, much disease and mortality would be prevented, and the comfort and health, and consequent vigour and efficiency in thought and action, of Europeans in such climates greatly promoted.

That the means of cooling air at present employed depend upon the evaporation of water, and are not only uncertain and imperfect in their action, but, even while depriving the air of its heat, tend to make it pernicious in another way, by loading it with moisture.

That your memorialists have had submitted to them the descriptions of proposed machines whereby the property which elastic substances possess of causing heat to disappear when they expand, may be made available for the cooling of air in tropical climates.

That the proposed method of cooling air is founded on correct scientific principles, and that there appears to be no reason to doubt its practical efficiency.

That it could be applied to large volumes of air without affecting the dryness or purity, and at a moderate expense.

Your memorialists, therefore, beg leave respectfully to submit for the consideration of your Honourable Board the description of the proposed method of cooling air, and to suggest the expediency of a trial of its efficiency being made in some large building containing many inmates, such as a hospital.

In respect whereof this memorial is subscribed, and the seal of the British Association for the Advancement of Science appended hereto.

The design of the machine in question was suggested by Professor Piazzi Smith (now Astronomer Royal for Scotland), and a grant was made by the Association for experiments; but the sum was too small for any efficient trial, and for want of further encouragement the proposal fell to the ground; but the idea is a good and laudable one, and the fact of its having been thought practicable by such eminent men, deserves to be put on record.

The Institution of Mechanical Engineers.—In 1854 Mr. Fairbairn was elected President of the Institution of Mechanical Engineers. This society was founded in 1847, for the study and encouragement of the mechanical branch of engineering, particular attention being devoted to the details of that department of the profession. The head-quarters of the society were fixed in Birmingham, for the sake of being near the more important iron manufacturing districts, and many eminent mechanical engineers gave it their active support. Mr. Fairbairn joined it in October 1847. He took a warm interest in the proceedings of the society, and communicated many papers to the Transactions. He retained the presidency during the years 1854 and 1855.

Business in France.—During the year 1854 Mr. Fairbairn went, with his son Adam, to Paris, where he remained a few days. During this time he was introduced to the Academy of Sciences, and visited many objects of scientific and engineering interest. He was also honoured, through the mediation of Lord Cowley, by an interview with the Emperor Louis Napoleon, who received him in a flattering manner, and on taking leave of him presented him with a handsome gold snuff-box set with diamonds.

As a sequel to this he was chosen one of the jurors sent from this country to the Paris Exhibition of 1855, and was nominated by the French Imperial Commission as chairman of one of the mechanical sections.[1]

After the conclusion of the Exhibition, he made an elaborate report to the Right Hon. Lord Stanley of Alderley, President of the Board of Trade, 'On the Machinery of the Paris Universal Exhibition, 1855.' It was afterwards published in his 'Useful Information for Engineers,' Third Series, 1866, and it contains some remarks on the comparative merits of British and Continental manufactures which are of permanent interest. Mr. Fairbairn says :—

> I am of opinion that the locomotive engines of Great Britain are superior to most others ; and although they may not have the same amount of polish, there is nevertheless a simplicity of form and a soundness of workmanship which give character and stability to these important constructions.

---

[1] The following letter from an eminent friend of Mr. Fairbairn's, now deceased, who did *not* serve as a juror, is highly characteristic of the man :—

Dorset Place, July 9, 1855.

My dear Sir,—On my return home after a few days' absence, I found your very kind letter, enclosing an opinion which is the more valuable because it is founded on the most extensive personal experience of one who has himself contributed so large a share to the present advanced state of constructive engineering. It is gratifying to me to acknowledge the strong support I have ever received from practical engineers, and it is curious that the warmest supporter of the analytical engine, Lord Rosse, has also himself a claim to a high place in that class. I wish, when you are in Paris, you would explain on fit occasions why I was not on the list of jurors of the French Exhibition. I declined the recommendation which came to me *through the English Government*, and it was on that ground *alone* that I declined it. You who know with what injustice I have been treated will not be surprised at my decision.

I am, my dear Sir,
Yours sincerely,
C. BABBAGE.

To WM. FAIRBAIRN, Esq., Manchester.

The marine engines will not bear a comparison with those that were exhibited at the Great Exhibition of 1851.

The French *ouvriers* are active, intelligent, and well employed; the Germans swift, and Belgians patient and enduring; and although foreigners may take a longer time in executing works than English workmen, they are nevertheless expert, and, in many cases, better educated, and therefore better able to cope with the difficulties and surmount the obstacles in the way of a successful progress.

I do not mean to intimate that the mass of the workmen abroad are better informed in the practice of their respective callings than in England; but I firmly believe, from what I have seen, that the French and Germans are in advance of us in theoretical knowledge of the principles of the higher branches of industrial art; and I think this arises from the greater facilities afforded by the institutions of those countries for instruction in chemical and mechanical science.

When reporting on the manufacture of iron, I endeavoured to show that, notwithstanding the natural resources placed at our disposal, the quality of our cast-iron is not to be depended on; that under the powerful stimulus of self-aggrandisement we have perseveringly advanced the quantity, whilst other nations, less favoured and less bountifully supplied, have been studying with much more care than ourselves the numerous uses to which the material may be applied, and are in many cases in advance of us in quality.

In regard to machinery for the manufacture of textile fabrics, Great Britain has assuredly every reason to be proud of the position she holds.

In regard to steam-engines, iron bridges, and machinery, our superiority is not so strongly marked; and although we still take the lead, we are not so much in advance of others, as the engines exhibited at Paris fully proved. In marine construction we are still superior to all other nations, but abroad rapid advances are making in that direction also.

In the construction of mill-work this country stands unrivalled; our millwrights stand alone for neatness of design and judicious proportion of parts. In tools for workshops we are also unequalled.

With the exception of reaping machines, in which America excels, our agricultural implements, including those for working plastic materials, are superior to those of most countries; and this superiority appears to be due to the variable nature of our climate, which necessitates an improved system of culture and the use of machines calculated to save time and to ensure success in the labour of the farm.

But although Mr. Fairbairn thus gave, on the whole, the superiority to Great Britain in machinery, he was not blind to the deficiency of our countrymen in regard to such portions of manufacture as were dependent on the fine arts. In a letter to Lord Overstone, written January 16, 1856, he expressed the idea, that had occurred to many careful observers, of the superiority of continental over English designs. He said, alluding to a proposition that had been made :—

I am glad to find you approve of the proposal of Lord Ashburton to move for a committee.

I quite agree with you that there is no reason for alarm; but it is nevertheless good policy, on the part of a nation as well as a general, never to despise the strength of an enemy.

As an observer and a juror at the Paris Exhibition, I had opportunities of noticing in what we appeared to excel and in what we were inferior to our competitors; and it is rather mortifying to find that in matters of taste and design in our own manufactures we are indebted to the intellect of others. In our porcelain, silversmiths', calico printing, and some other trades, the [best] results are from foreign and not from native talent; and the same defects are observable in architecture, which, by the bye, is now improving, as in some other of the useful and industrial arts. Altogether I think the enquiry will do good, and I am glad to find we shall have the benefit of your lordship's valuable assistance.

Shortly after this Mr. Fairbairn had some correspondence on the subject with Lord Ashburton himself; and received from his lordship the following letter, the opinions in which are of public and enduring importance :—

Grange, Jan. 27, 1856.

My dear Mr. Fairbairn,—Were it not for prolonged illness, I should have proposed to have met you at Manchester on your return from abroad, so anxious am I to state in person to those who might possibly co-operate in the proposed enquiry, the spirit in which it may be worked, and the precise nature of the evil which it is calculated to remedy. We cannot but be proud as Englishmen of the lead we have taken in scientific discovery, as well as in the ingenious applications of those discoveries to the most extensive development of industry that has ever existed.

This has been due to the instinctive genius of great minds, who have made their own way upward in spite of all their disadvantages. They had no Polytechnic School, no systematic instruction to level half the ascent for them. They had to win the whole way for themselves.

Perhaps they were the greater for this ; but the mass was left behind in hopeless ignorance ; and it is to the condition of that mass that I wish to draw general attention.

England possesses special advantages, such as are not enjoyed, such as will never possibly be compassed by any other nation.

We have the most accessible coal and iron, the cheapest system of transit ; we have operatives superior in physical strength, in constancy of application to labour, in the conscientious execution of their work ; but our greatest superiority consists in that habit of self-reliance and independent effort which will now right this mischief of which I have to complain, as it has uniformly righted other similar mischiefs, as soon as the public mind has been convinced of their existence.

The mischief consists, as I have said before, in the ignorance of the masses, in which masses I include our peers, gentry, tradesmen and mechanics, as well as our manufacturers and operatives. As for our peers and gentry and tradesmen, no evidence is wanting. They plead guilty; I trust that I may obtain such evidence with regard to the manufacturing classes as will show not only the existence among them of this general ignorance, but evidence also of the evils consequent upon it.

If you ask me my present private opinion of the cause of this ignorance, I feel disposed to impute it to the monastic teaching of our universities, which impart to all the special instruction required for the Church. It is from the universities that have been drawn the masters of our principal middle and commercial schools, and their fashion has been followed elsewhere. As for teaching the workman before you have enlightened his employer, as for teaching the tradesman before you have enlightened the customer, we may set up a thousand benevolent schools and institutes, we shall only lose our labour. The course of nature is that the demand should precede the supply, and we may as well seek to persuade water uphill as attempt to reverse this course.

But I am now launching into the field of speculation. Such opinions may or may not result from the enquiry.

The enquiry is into the ignorance of the masses with regard to science, and the evils resulting therefrom.

2ndly. The conditions of our present system of education, which permit the continuance of such ignorance.

3rdly. The remedies, and those remedies will be designated by better heads than mine.

I have written you this that you may show it and obtain opinions, and, if possible, secure co-operation.

I believe this move to be capable of working great good; but for that good I look not to the Government, but to the combined efforts of all classes of the nation.

I remain, dear Sir,

Yours truly,

ASHBURTON.

In the same year Mr. Fairbairn was applied to by the Emperor of the French to give advice in regard to some bridges proposed to be erected in France, one an ornamental one in the Bois de Boulogne, and others at Brest and elsewhere. He had an audience of his Majesty, and submitted some suggestions and drawings, but it does not appear that any of his proposals were carried into execution. As an acknowledgment of the services he had rendered in this and other matters concerning France, he was, on November 13, 1855, awarded by the decree of the Emperor, the distinction of the Legion of Honour.

Watt.—The inhabitants of Manchester have, with much public spirit, ornamented their city with statues of many eminent men. The esplanade in front of the Infirmary contains statues of Wellington, Peel, and Dalton, the discoverer of the atomic theory. To these it was determined to add a statue of the great engineer, Watt, to whom the town was so much indebted for its mechanical advantages.

The statue, an enlarged copy in bronze of Chantrey's marble one in Westminster Abbey, was inaugurated on June 26, 1857, Mr. Fairbairn, as the most eminent mechanic in the city, being deputed to take the lead in the ceremony. He said, addressing the Mayor and Corporation :—

It is my pleasing duty, as President of the Literary and Philosophical Society and Chairman of the Watt Memorial Committee, to transfer from our hands to your superior keeping and to that of your successors this statue and memorial of the inventor of the steam-engine, James Watt.

The character of the statue and its position render it an appropriate and fitting companion to that of our distinguished townsman, the late Dr. Dalton. It will show, though late, that Manchester has not been ungrateful, but remembers and deeply appreciates the services of Watt to her and all mankind ; and this day I trust will show that among her other art treasures [alluding to the ' Exhibition of Art Treasures ' then open in Manchester] she numbers this as a most precious memorial of a great and good man.

It would be superfluous for me to attempt to eulogise the inventions and discoveries of Watt; the world knows and feels them, and is now living by them. The steam-engine is the pioneer and promoter of civilisation. By its agency the weak become strong, and time and distance become short. It gives employment to thousands, and transports with the same celerity, on land as on water, the products of industry of every clime to any part of the globe.

The smallest honour we can do to the great benefactors of mankind is occasionally to bring them to our recollection ; and I trust that this statue will stimulate in the minds of future generations a spirit of emulation to excel, and will cherish a desire in every right-minded person to treasure up in his memory the honour and obligations ever due to the virtues of our great men.

This statue is the property of the mayor, aldermen, and citizens of Manchester.

In 1857 Mr. Fairbairn contributed a note on the merits of James Watt, to a memoir of him by Arago, published in a translation of Arago's ' Biographies of Distinguished Scientific Men.' He conceived that sufficient justice had not been done to Watt by the French author, and he endeavoured to correct the error.

Henry Cort.—About the same time, Mr. Fairbairn interested himself warmly in the case of the family of an inventor, Henry Cort, who had contributed largely to the improvement of the iron manufacture, but who had been ruined in the carrying out of his inventions (see Chap. II., pages 31, 32). In the article on Iron, written in 1856 for the Encyclopædia Britannica, Mr. Fairbairn had said :—

It would be a difficult task to enumerate all the services rendered by Mr. Cort to the industry of this country, or sufficiently to express our sympathy with the descendants of a man to whose mechanical inventions we owe so much of our national greatness.

As a sequel to this Mr. Fairbairn, in February 1857, made a powerful appeal directly and personally to Lord Palmerston on behalf of certain descendants of Henry Cort who were in distress. Lord Derby had kindly relieved them temporarily from the royal bounty fund, and had held out a hope that a pension should be granted; but for two years nothing was done.

In July 1859 Mr. Fairbairn brought the case to public notice by a letter to the *Times*, and got up a memorial to the Government, which was signed by 130 iron manufacturers, and was presented to Lord Palmerston by a deputation including many men of the first eminence in the mechanical world. These measures resulted in a grant of 100*l*. per annum to the only surviving son, and of 50*l*. each to the three surviving daughters.

In addition to this, Mr. Fairbairn exerted himself to get up a private subscription among persons interested in the iron manufacture; but this was not taken up by the iron masters with a liberality at all corresponding to his zeal or their own means; and the total sum raised for the family was only a little over 500*l*., of which 100*l*. was contributed by Mr. Fairbairn himself.

Manchester Art Treasures Exhibition.—In 1857 the ' Art Treasures Exhibition ' was held in Manchester. It was got up with great expense and trouble, and brought much credit to the town. Mr. Fairbairn aided the committee in regard to the arrangements of the building (which was very large, chiefly composed of iron, and erected for the express purpose), but otherwise did not take a prominent part in the management. His son Thomas was the chairman of the Committee of the exhibition, and its principal promoter.

Journey to Italy.—In the latter part of 1857, Mr. Fairbairn suffered from a slight rheumatic attack, and as it lasted some months he determined to endeavour to cure it by a visit to the warmer climate of the south of Europe. He accordingly left England with his son George on December 11, 1857, and went through Paris to Marseilles. From thence they took the steamer to Nice, and travelled by land along the beautiful Cornice Road to Genoa. The journey was then extended to the most important cities of Italy, including Naples, Rome, Florence, Bologna, Milan, and Turin. The whole journey occupied two months and eight days, during which he derived, as he states, 'unmixed pleasure and gratification.'

His powers of observation were in active exercise the whole time, for he wrote, for the benefit of his family, a diary of the whole journey, in which he gave animated descriptions of the novel scenes he passed through, interspersed with many philosophical reflections and remarks on the habits and customs of the people. It is unnecessary to reproduce any portions of this diary, for there were no incidents in his journey much differing from those ordinarily met with; and descriptions of the routes, the places, and the objects of interest are now common enough in all sorts of forms.

But there was one element of the journey which especially interested him, namely, the change of climate ; and as he conceived the general information on this topic was imperfect, he wrote, soon after his return, a paper ' On the Comparative Temperature of the Climates of England and some parts of Italy.'

This he read before the Manchester Literary and Philosophical Society on April 6, 1858, and it was published in their Proceedings, vol. i. p. 45. The object was to point out that although Italy had usually the credit of possessing a warm and agreeable climate in the winter season, this really only applied to those parts which lay south of the Apennines. In the northern districts, including the cities of Milan, Venice, Turin, Bologna, and in fact the whole of Lombardy and the depression lying between the Alps and the Apennines, the cold in winter was generally intense, sometimes almost Russian in its character. In January, when he was there, the thermometer was usually below freezing, and on arriving at Milan it descended as low as 19°. On the 13th the minimum had touched −12·5° Reaumur, or nearly our zero.

The Atlantic Cable.—From 1859 to 1865 Mr. Fairbairn interested himself actively in regard to the grand enterprise of carrying electric telegraph communication to America.

The Atlantic Telegraph Company was formed in 1856, and the first cable was laid in 1858, but after a few days' working it became useless, partly from imperfect construction, and partly from want of care in laying. The Company, however, nothing daunted, appealed to the Government to assist them in an undertaking of such great public importance, and in 1859 the Board of Trade appointed a commission, consisting of Captain Galton, R.E., Professor Wheatstone, Mr. Fairbairn, and Mr. G. P. Bidder, to join with the engineers and the secretary of the Company in holding an enquiry into the ' best form for the composition and outer covering of submarine telegraph cables.' This joint committee sat for nearly two years ; they took a great amount of evidence from all those who had most experience on the subject, and made many important investigations of their own. In April 1861 they laid before Government a full report, embodying their views and recommendations, which was afterwards published, with the evidence and many valuable documents, as a Parliamentary paper. In the course of

the enquiry Mr. Fairbairn undertook personally a series of
experiments 'on the permeability of various kinds of
insulators,' an account of which, written by him, was
appended to the report.

The result of the enquiry was to lead the committee
to the following statement:—

We are clearly of opinion that the failures of the existing
submarine lines have been due to causes which might have been
guarded against, had adequate preliminary investigation been
made into the question. And we are convinced that if regard
be had to the principles we have enunciated in devising, manufacturing, laying, and maintaining submarine cables, this class
of enterprise may prove as successful as it has hitherto been
disastrous.

To this able report we owe probably the establishment
of public confidence in the undertaking, and the prompt
measures that were taken to re-organise the arrangements
for another cable. But the Company wisely resolved that
they would not risk a second failure for want of advice,
and they accordingly appointed a 'Permanent Consulting
Scientific Committee,' consisting of Captain Galton, Mr.
Fairbairn, Professor Wheatstone, Mr. Whitworth, and
Professor Wm. Thomson, to whom mechanical questions
as to the construction and laying of the cable might be
referred to from time to time. Mr. Fairbairn was asked
to give more immediate aid by joining the Company, but
he declined to do so, on the ground of his advancing
years.

In 1863 he wrote a long report giving a strong opinion
on the practicability of the scheme ; on the tests for insulation ; on the strength, the laying, &c. He also aided
in the negotiations with the Government on the matter,
and was in constant communication with various parties
on the subject. At the British Association meetings in

1864 and 1865 he presented papers descriptive of the investigations in which he had taken part.

In 1865 the second cable was laid by the 'Great Eastern' steamer, and during that year Mr. Fairbairn was still in active correspondence on various matters connected with the undertaking; always expressing great confidence as to its ultimate success. The operation failed by the fracture of the cable, and some discouragement was again felt for a time ; but in the following year a new cable was successfully laid, and ultimately that of 1865 was picked up and repaired, thus giving a duplicate communication which has been in almost constant work to the present time.

In the third series of 'Useful Information for Engineers,' 1866, Mr. Fairbairn republished his papers on this subject.

Manchester Literary and Philosophical Society.—Mr. Fairbairn was long connected with this Institution. It was founded in 1781 as a weekly club, but was more formally established, with the present name, in 1789. The second president was the celebrated Dr. Henry, and the still more eminent Dr. Dalton became secretary in 1800. In 1817 he was chosen president, and remained so till his death in 1844. A few years afterwards the same office was filled by Mr. Eaton Hodgkinson. The Society has held the first rank among provincial associations of the kind, and its proceedings have been highly esteemed.

From about 1820 Mr. Fairbairn had been a constant and active member of this society, and he states, ' when he was young, in the pursuit of knowledge, how delightful and instructive it was to listen, on the days of meeting, to the plain, straightforward style of Dalton ; the polished periods of Henry, and the animated remarks of Dr.

Holme and other members who used to lighten up the conversation, and render the meetings attractive.'

Mr. Fairbairn was elected President of the society in 1855, and remained in that office till 1860, working zealously to maintain its character and promote its interests. At the opening meeting of the session of 1859-60 he gave a presidential address, which began as follows :—

In most societies having for their object the advancement of science, it is the custom for the president to open the session with an address. This, although not hitherto practised in this society, is nevertheless a salutary custom, as it affords an opportunity for taking in review the discoveries and improvements of the past, and of giving encouragement to the members in the production of papers for the future. Under the impression that such a retrospect might be useful, I venture to lay before you such a statement, showing what has already been done and what, in my opinion, remains to be accomplished in the present session.

The address consisted of an able review of the history of the society, and of its connection with the progress of different branches of science.

Royal Society Gold Medal.—In 1860 a further distinction was paid him by the Royal Society. The Society have the power of distributing annually four medals— one 'Copley Medal,' from a legacy in 1709 by Sir Godfrey Copley, Bart., for great general eminence in science; one 'Rumford Medal,' founded in 1796 by Count Rumford, specially to reward discoveries in regard to heat and light ; and two ' Royal Medals,' established by George IV., and continued by the sovereigns ever since, for any important recent scientific investigations.

This year Mr. Fairbairn was awarded one of the Royal medals. In the annual address, the President said :—

A Royal Medal has been awarded to Mr. William Fairbairn, for his various experimental enquiries on the properties of the materials employed in mechanical construction, contained in the 'Philosophical Transactions,' and in the publications of other scientific societies.

He then enumerated several of Mr. Fairbairn's most important works and papers, and concluded :—

Perhaps it may be said with truth, that there is no single individual living who has done so much for practical science, who has made so many careful experimental enquiries on subjects of primary importance to the commercial and manufacturing interests of this country, or who has so liberally contributed them to the world.

MR. FAIRBAIRN,

In presenting this medal to you from this chair, I will venture to say that the award of the *Royal* medal,—the medal which Her Majesty the Queen has been graciously pleased to place at the disposal of the President and Council, for scientific services such as yours, so eminently conducive to the general good, is even peculiarly appropriate.

British Association at Manchester.—In 1861 the meeting of the British Association was held at Manchester, and Mr. Fairbairn, as one of the most eminent scientific celebrities of the town, was appropriately chosen as President.

The opening meeting was held on September 4, when Lord Wrottesley, the retiring President, said :—

In retiring from the office I have had the honour to hold, it is a great pleasure to me to know that I am to be succeeded by one who is so well worthy of your support. We may derive important instruction from the career of Mr. Fairbairn, whether we view him as the successful engineer or as the distinguished man of science. In the former capacity he is one who has by perseverance, combined with talent, risen from small beginnings to the summit of his profession, and he forms one of that noble class of men, the Stephensons, the Brunels, the Whitworths, the Armstrongs, which have conferred such important services on their country, and some of whom, unfortunately for that country, have perished, alas, too soon, exhausted by their arduous toils. Mr. Fairbairn, therefore, is one of the many examples of what can be done in England by such men who resolve, undaunted by the difficulties and obstructions that beset their path, to struggle gallantly onward till success crown their efforts.

Again, if we look at Mr. Fairbairn's claims to scientific distinction, they read to us an important lesson; for they show what can be done by zeal and energy, and the exercise of a strong and resolute will, fully determined to carry out objects in which the public is deeply interested. It is extraordinary that any man should have been able, during the few leisure hours that can be snatched from an important and engrossing business, to accomplish for science what Mr. Fairbairn has done ; and not only has he been a most successful contributor to mechanical science, but his liberality has been unbounded in placing all his great mechanical resources at the disposal of his fellow-labourers in the same field.

Such a man is one whom all should delight to honour, and to such a man I resign with great satisfaction the chair which I now vacate.

Mr. Fairbairn then took the chair, and gave his inaugural address, which opened with the following remarks :—

A careful perusal of the history of this Association will demonstrate that it was the first, and for a long time the only institution which brought together for a common object the learned professors of our universities and the workers in practical science. These periodical reunions have been of incalculable benefit in giving to practice that soundness of principle and certainty of progressive improvement which can only be obtained by the accurate study of science and its application to the arts. On the other hand, the men of actual practice have reciprocated the benefits thus received from theory, in testing by actual experiment deductions which were doubtful, and ratifying those which were erroneous. Guided by an extended experience, and exercising a sound and disciplined judgment, they have often corrected theories apparently accurate, but, nevertheless, founded on incomplete data, or on false assumptions inadvertently introduced. If the British Association had effected nothing more than the removal of the anomalous separation of theory and practice, it would have gained imperishable renown in the benefit thus conferred.

Were I to enlarge on the relation of the achievements of science to the comforts and enjoyments of man, I should have to refer to the present epoch as one of the most important in the history of the world. At no former period did science contribute so much to the uses of life and the wants of society; and in doing this, it has been only fulfilling that mission which Bacon, the great father of modern science, appointed for it when he wrote that 'the legitimate goal of the sciences is the endowment of human life with new inventions and riches;' and when he sought for a natural philosophy which, not spending its energy on barren disquisitions, should be operative for the benefit and endowment of mankind.

Looking, then, to the fact that whilst in our time all the sciences have yielded this fruit, engineering science, with which I have been most intimately connected, has pre-eminently advanced the power, the wealth, and the comforts of mankind. I shall probably best discharge the duties of the office I have the honour to fill, by stating as briefly as possible the more recent scientific discoveries which have so influenced the relations of social life. I shall therefore not dwell so much on the progress of abstract science, important as that is, but shall rather endeavour briefly to examine the applications of science to the useful arts, and the results which have followed, and are likely to follow, in the improvement of the condition of society.

Mr. Fairbairn then went on to trace the applications of astronomy, magnetism, chemistry, geology, botany, zoology, &c., and devoted the latter part of his address to a retrospect of the progress of his own science, mechanics, as applied to engineering and to machinery, closing with some observations on the patent laws.

He had asked Mr. Hopkins to look over the address previously to his delivering it, and Mr. Hopkins, in returning it, said :—

I think the address will do extremely well, and has the great merit of individuality. Your historical sketch of engineering is very good and very appropriate. It illustrates well the advantage of having men of different pursuits and habits of thought to occupy the presidential chair of the Association. Engineering has scarcely been touched upon before by our presidents, for the obvious reason that they have not been engineers.

The meeting was very successful, and, as was appropriate to the President and the place of meeting, mechanical science had a large share of attention, the presidency of that section being taken by Mr. Fairbairn's son-in-law, Mr. J. F. Bateman.

Mr. Fairbairn was highly complimented by many distinguished friends, as the following letters will show :—

Brougham, Penrith, September 6, 1861.

My dear Mr. Fairbairn,—I hope you will excuse the liberty I take in congratulating you upon your most admirable and most useful address, which I have read with the greatest satisfaction, and I believe that it will most effectually serve to convince all classes of the practical tendency of the sciences and their beneficial effects in promoting the business of society.

Believe me to be most sincerely yours,
H. BROUGHAM.

The following was from one of the most eminent scientific engineers of his day :—

The Priory, Hatcham, Newbury, Berks, September 10, 1861.

My dear Sir,—I have read, in my retreat at this place, the daily proceedings of the British Association at Manchester, so ably presided over by you, and so creditable to our order. I was particularly struck with your able address, not only on matters of physical science, but in the department of applied mechanics in which you were, as the French say, *au fait.* But it is the steam-engine and its labours, whether administering to our necessities, comforts, or luxuries, or for the purpose of aggression or defence, and the wonderful changes it has produced in our social and political existence, that has contributed so much to the interest of your address. It recalls to my mind an occasion when old Mr. Watt and Mr. Lovell Edgeworth were sitting before dinner, when my father, not having made his appearance, and I being alone with them, ventured to remark that ' it was the steam-engine that carried on the war.' When asked why? I replied, ' it made things so much cheaper than making them by hand,' for which answer I was commended by Mr. Edgeworth.

Your observations comprised under science applied to manufactures were particularly applicable at Manchester.

GEORGE RENNIE.

In one passage of the address Mr. Fairbairn had alluded to the great invention of the multitubular boiler for the locomotive, without which the railway system of transit, as now known, could hardly have existed. The inventor, not an engineer, but the secretary of the Liverpool and Manchester Railway, said of this, in a letter to a friend:—

Princes Park, September 6, 1861.

Thanks to you for Mr. Fairbairn's address, and your reference to page 17. It is pleasant to see recognised, now and then, my claim (which has never been denied) to be the inventor of the modern tubular boiler, though neither George Stephenson nor I knew the importance of it at the time.

When you see Mr. Fairbairn, my respects to him, with my thanks.   Truly yours,

H. BOOTH.

During the meeting, Mr. Fairbairn received, as guests in his house, many eminent scientific men from all parts of the kingdom. Dr. Whewell was invited, but wrote from Vevey, September 2:—

Your kind letter has followed me hither. As you will see from the date of this, I shall not be able to attend the meeting over which you are so worthily elected to preside, and I cannot help writing a line to thank you, on my own part and Lady Affleck's, for your still giving me an opening to join your party if it had been possible. You are very kind in wishing for my presence, but I am sure that I shall be very little missed.

I am glad to hear from the Astronomer Royal that he is to preside over Section A, a post which I have several times filled with great interest. He tells me now that he is to give an evening lecture on the eclipse which we, as well as he, witnessed last year in Spain. He will, I know, try to convey to his audience the wonderful impression which is produced by seeing the sun blotted out from the heavens and the stars coming into view. It is not easy to exaggerate the striking effect of this phenomenon.

Lady Affleck joins me in very kind regards to you and Mrs. Fairbairn, and I am, my dear sir,

Yours very truly,
W. WHEWELL.

W. FAIRBAIRN, Esq.

Another Cambridge celebrity, then at a very advanced age, attended the meeting, and afterwards wrote on November 5, 1861 :—

I ought not to write any letters. The attacks of giddiness still return upon me occasionally, and sometimes bring me to the ground. My Cambridge doctor, almost every time he has called, has commanded me to abstain sternly from all letter-writing.

I remain, dear Sir,
Very faithfully yours,
A. SEDGWICK.

Offer of Knighthood.—The following gracious offer from Her Majesty arose out of this meeting :—

Balmoral, October 18, 1861.

Sir,—I have much satisfaction in informing you that I have

received Her Majesty's command to signify to you her pleasure that, if you are willing to accept the honour, the dignity of Knighthood should be conferred upon you in consideration of your distinguished services to engineering science, and of your able presidency of the British Association.

I have the honour to be, Sir,
Your obedient servant,
G. GREY.

W. FAIRBAIRN, Esq.

Mr. Fairbairn returned the following reply :—

Athenæum, London, October 23, 1861.

Sir,—I shall ever retain a lively sense of gratitude for Her Majesty's consideration in offering to me the dignity of Knighthood for the services I have rendered to science. My thanks to the Queen could not be more hearty in accepting the proffered honour than they are now felt by me in respectfully declining it.

During a long life I have tried above all things to make myself useful. For more than seventy years I have found the plain names I bear sufficient for the furtherance of the great object of my life, and I pray Her Majesty to permit me to retain them in their simplicity to the end. Thanking you for the courteous terms of your communication,

I have the honour to be, Sir,
Your faithful servant,
W. FAIRBAIRN.

The Right Hon. Sir GEORGE GREY, Bart., M.P.

Richard Roberts.—At the end of 1861 he interested himself warmly in endeavouring to obtain a pension for Mr. Richard Roberts, one of his fellow-townsmen and brother-engineers. Mr. Roberts was a man of great mechanical ability, and was particularly noted for his elegant and useful invention of the self-acting mule, and for many other ingenious contrivances, he being in fact ' one of the most prolific and useful inventors of his time.' He had been a partner in the great and flourishing locomotive and manufacturing firm of Sharp, Roberts & Co., Manchester, but had fallen into poverty.

Mr. Fairbairn applied directly to Lord Palmerston, armed with the force of his position as President of the British Association, and obtained the following characteristic and truthful reply :—

94 Piccadilly, Dec. 3, 1861.

My dear Mr. Fairbairn,—I will give due consideration to the case of Mr. Roberts, in connection with those of other candidates for a civil list pension. But I rather fear that it will scarcely fall within the limits of the rules by which the grants of civil list pensions are governed.

Moreover, the whole amount disposable is very small, and it is scarcely ever possible to give to any person more than a hundred pounds a year; and one should think that if the invention of Mr. Roberts has been greatly advantageous to the manufacturers of cotton, those who have grown rich by the use of his invention might, among them, well be able to give him a better annuity than the civil list could afford.

Yours sincerely,

PALMERSTON.

He continued his aid, for in 1864 we find him still agitating for a private subscription to be got up in the same cause.

Honorary Degrees.—Mr. Fairbairn received honorary degrees from two British Universities.

In 1860 his old and distinguished friend, Lord Brougham, was elected Chancellor of the University of Edinburgh; and Mr. Fairbairn received the following letter :—

Edinburgh, May 11, 1860.

My dear Mr. Fairbairn,—Lord Brougham is to be installed as Chancellor of our University on Friday, the 18th inst.; and it is proposed on that occasion to confer the degree of LL.D. on a few individuals distinguished in science.

I am authorised to enquire if it would be convenient for you to be present on that day to receive the degree?

Ever most truly yours,

D. BREWSTER.

The degree of LL.D. was accordingly given. The following letter of congratulation from the late Right Rev. Prince Lee, then Bishop of Manchester, was much prized by its recipient :—

Manchester, May 26, 1860.

My dear Dr. Fairbairn,—No one can rejoice more sincerely than both Mrs. Lee and myself at any recognition of services like yours, or any circumstance which can cause happiness to you, Mrs. Fairbairn, and your family. During the twelve years I have been in Manchester, I have seen your utterly unselfish pursuit of what was calculated to advance the moral and temporal advantage of others, combined with a thorough devotion to the investigation of scientific truth.

In the present case this recognition has come from the highest scientific body of your own countrymen, to you most gratifying, but to those who see how Government honours are given a proof that our rulers are not acting as they ought to do.

That you may long enjoy the honour and happiness you so richly and truly merit is, my dear friend, the sincere hope and prayer of

Your most attached and obliged,

J. P. MANCHESTER.

W. FAIRBAIRN, Esq., LL.D.

The following letters relate to a degree from the University of Cambridge:—

Devonshire House, May 16, 1862.

Sir,—According to ancient usage, a considerable number of honorary degrees will be conferred on the occasion of my first visit to Cambridge as Chancellor of the University.

If it would be agreeable to you to accept this compliment

from the University, I should have great pleasure in adding your name to the list which I have been invited to draw up.

I am, Sir,

Your obedient Servant,

DEVONSHIRE.

W. FAIRBAIRN, Esq.

The Lodge, May 16, 1862.

My dear Mr. Fairbairn,—I find that at the Chancellor's suggestion you are to receive an honorary degree on the occasion of his installation. I hope when you come to Cambridge you will consider yourself my guest. If I am not able to give you a room in the lodge you can have one in the college near to us, and will be our guest in all other respects.

Believe me,

Yours very truly,

W. WHEWELL.

W. FAIRBAIRN, Esq.

The honorary degree of D.C.L. was conferred in due course.

British Association, 1862.—At the meeting of the British Association at Cambridge, in October 1862, Mr. Fairbairn occupied, for the second time, the position of President to the Mechanical Section ; and he opened the proceedings with an address on the progress of mechanical science generally, on the International Exhibition of that year, and on the iron plate armour experiments in which he was then engaged.

International Exhibition of 1862.—In the Great International Exhibition of 1862 his son Thomas had been nominated one of the five Royal Commissioners, and Mr. Fairbairn himself was appointed President of the Jury for machines and tools employed in the manufacture of wood and iron.

No communication from him was published in the

official documents of the Exhibition, but he appears to
have written an elaborate Report on the Department of
Machinery generally. With what object this was done,
or to whom the Report was addressed, does not appear,
but an abstract of it is given in his ' Useful Information
for Engineers,' Third Series, 1866. It concludes with
the following passage :—

Having thus glanced, however imperfectly, at some of the
leading objects in the machinery department of the great International Exhibition recently closed, we may safely state in
conclusion that more splendid and more instructive examples of
the useful arts were never at any previous time brought under
the inspection of the public. There is no department of
practical science which has remained unrepresented, and the
student, mechanic, or engineer had only to read in his own
department of study the great page of nature and art which at
this Exhibition was laid open for his perusal. It is a great
privilege for the present generation to have had before their
eyes the finest specimens of the manufacturing machines in
operation in their day, and in the construction of which it is
their ambition to excel. This is an advantage of which few
countries can boast, and it is of a character that will leave its
impress upon the public mind, and will raise the thinking and
industrial position of the community of this and of all other
nations much higher in the scale of civilisation.

Work for the Admiralty.—Owing to the great experience he had had in iron ship-building, his opinion
and judgment were highly esteemed by the Admiralty,
and during the last twelve or fifteen years of his life,
he was frequently consulted by them, and was, indeed,
almost in constant communication with them on matters
affecting naval construction.

In July 1863, he gave, in answer to the request of
Mr. Reed (then chief constructor of the Navy), a long
Report on the general design of a proposed new ship of

war; which was followed by other reports and communications. These however were considered confidential documents, and have not been made public.

Baronetcy.—It was in 1869, when Mr. Fairbairn had arrived at the 80th year of his age, that the crowning honour of his life was conferred on him, the dignity of the baronetage.

The following is a copy of the letter communicating the offer to him:—

Raby Castle, Darlington, Sept. 9, 1869.

Dear Mr. Fairbairn,—I am empowered by Her Majesty to signify her desire to confer on you the honour of the baronetage, and if I may anticipate your acceptance of a distinction so well earned by your scientific eminence and services, I am sure that the public will unanimously recognise the marked propriety of the selection.

It is extremely agreeable to me to convey to you this intimation.

I remain, faithfully yours,

W. E. GLADSTONE.

W. FAIRBAIRN, Esq.

Mr. Fairbairn, as in duty bound, intimated his grateful acceptance of the favour, and the patent was issued soon afterwards.

He was overwhelmed with congratulations, among which was one from a nobleman with whom Mr. Fairbairn and his family were often in friendly communication:—

Knowsley, Prescot, Nov. 10, 1869.

Dear Sir William Fairbairn,—Let me congratulate you on a well-earned honour, which I only regret that the Government of which I was a member did not gain the credit of conferring upon you.

Very truly yours,

DERBY.

SIR W. FAIRBAIRN, Bart.

In writing to a relation Mr. Fairbairn said :—

April 16, 1870.

Your kind congratulations have been very gratifying to both my wife and myself : and although I may not value these titles to the same extent as some others do, I am nevertheless very much gratified with this recognition of the services I have rendered to science. These were the conditions on which the distinction was granted by Her Majesty and the Government, and I ought to be very thankful.

As regards the name, I liked the old one ' William Fairbairn, of Manchester,' better ; I am well known by it, and I fear both my friends and the public will be slow to recognise me by any other. But be this as it may, I am becoming every day more reconciled to the new title, and ' My Lady ' takes to it with more grace and dignity than her husband.

CHAPTER XXII.

LITERARY WORK

1850—1873

MR. FAIRBAIRN A VOLUMINOUS WRITER — TUBULAR GIRDER BRIDGES—PAPER FOR THE ROYAL SOCIETY—EFFECT OF REPEATED MELTINGS ON CAST-IRON—APPLICATION OF IRON TO BUILDING PURPOSES—ARTICLE 'IRON' IN THE 'ENCYCLOPÆDIA BRITANNICA'—'USEFUL INFORMATION FOR ENGINEERS'—SELF-ACTING BRAKES—THE STRENGTH OF IRON SHIPS—SECOND SERIES OF 'USEFUL INFORMATION'—EFFECT OF VIBRATORY ACTION ON GIRDERS—MILLS AND MILLWORK—IRON SHIP-BUILDING—THIRD SERIES OF 'USEFUL INFORMATION'—CONTRIBUTION TO BAINES'S 'LANCASHIRE AND CHESHIRE'—ON THE DURABILITY OF IRON SHIPS—MR. FAIRBAIRN AS A LECTURER—HIS LAST ADDRESS—MR. W. C. UNWIN.

CHAPTER XXII.

AMONG the voluntary labours of the latter portion of Mr. Fairbairn's life, one of the most prominent was the use of his pen. He was naturally fond of writing, and whenever he undertook a mechanical investigation, or studied a scientific subject, it seemed natural to him to ' fix his ideas ' (to use the French expression) by putting them into a written form. His earlier books and papers had been well received, and when he found himself relieved from his arduous occupations at the manufactory, he began to write for publication more frequently.

A list of his writings, so far as can be ascertained, is given at the end of this volume, and it will show how prolific a writer he was. It consists in all of about eighty publications, including several large books, and many elaborate memoirs in scientific periodicals of high character. The greater number of these were written after he had passed his 60th year ; several of them have already been mentioned under special heads, and it is intended in this chapter to give brief notices of the more important books and memoirs among the remainder.

In March 1850, Mr. Fairbairn contributed a paper to the Institution of Civil Engineers, on ' Tubular Girder Bridges.' The subject was not, however, so general as the title would make it appear. It had happened that a bridge which had been designed by Mr. John Fowler, to cross the Trent at Torksey, in Lincolnshire, and which had been made by Messrs. Fairbairn, was objected to by the Government Inspector as too weak. The subject was brought before the Institution of Civil Engineers, and the strength was discussed at much length, the discussion involving some curious points that required novel mathematical treatment. Mr. Fairbairn's paper gave his own views on the subject, and many other engineers took part in the investigation; the result being that the sufficient strength of the bridge was declared to be proved, and the objection to it was withdrawn.

Immediately after Mr. Fairbairn's election as a Fellow of the Royal Society, he presented to that body a paper entitled 'An Experimental Enquiry into the Strength of Wrought-iron Plates and their Riveted Joints, as applied to ship-building and vessels exposed to severe strains.' It was read on June 13, 1850.

The following extract will give a general idea of the nature and objects of the investigation :—

At the commencement of iron ship-building, in which I took an active part, the absence of acknowledged facts relative to the strength and varied conditions under which the material was applied, was the principal reason which induced me to enter upon this enquiry. I have extended the investigation into the best methods of riveting, and the proportional strength of rivets, joints, &c., as compared with the plates and the uses for which they are intended. The latter is a practical and highly important enquiry; as great difference of opinion exists among engineers and others as to the form, strength, and proportions of rivets, and the joints of which they form an essential part. I therefore considered an experimental investigation much wanted, not only on account of its important practical bearing, but what was probably of equal value, in order to remove existing discrepancies, and to establish a sounder principle of construction founded upon the unerring basis of experiment. From these considerations I bestowed increased attention upon the enquiry, and endeavoured to render it practically useful.

The paper was divided into four parts.

The first part was on the strength of wrought-iron plates to resist tearing asunder by direct tensile strains. This was illustrated by an account of twenty experiments on plates made of iron of different qualities.

The second part treated of the strength of the joints of iron plates when united by rivets, and on the best modes of riveting. A number of experiments were tried on riveted joints, formed in many varieties of ways, and the general mean result was that, considering the strength of the solid plate itself to be 100, that of a single-riveted joint (*i.e.* having the rivets disposed in one row), might be taken at 56, while if the joint were double-riveted (*i.e.* if the rivets were disposed in two rows), the strength would be 70, showing, in any case, a considerable loss of strength.

The third part of the paper treated of the strength of wrought-iron plates to withstand a force applied perpendicularly to one point in their surface, tending to indent or bulge them in, or if great, to burst them open ; as, for example, in the case where the hull of an iron ship would strike against a projecting rock.

The fourth part was an investigation of the strength and value of the wrought-iron frames or ribs used in ship-building. The strengths of these, when in different shapes, were shown, and inferences were drawn as to the best forms and modes of construction.

In the course of the paper Mr. Fairbairn took occasion frequently to speak of the comparison between wood and iron as a material for ship-building. He said:—

In conclusion, I would venture a few remarks on the value and judicious use of iron in its adaptation to ship-building. It appears from the facts already recorded, that iron is very superior in its powers of resistance to strain; it is [1] highly ductile in its character, and easily moulded into any required form without impairing its strength. It is also stronger in combination than timber, arising from the nature of the construction ; and the materials composing the iron ship become a homogeneous mass when united together, forming as it were a solid, without joints, and presenting as a whole the most formidable powers of resistance. These are some of the properties which cannot be obtained in the union of timber, however ingeniously contrived. It moreover possesses the property of lightness along with strength ; in fact its buoyancy, strength, and durability constitute the elements of its utility in the innumerable cases to which it may be applied. In ship-building it possesses other advantages over timber. Its hull is free from the risk of fire ; and in case of shipwreck, either on rocks or sandbanks, it will resist the heaviest sea, endure the severest concussion, and with proper attention to the construction it may be the means of saving the lives of all on board. It moreover has the advantage of bulkheads, which, made perfectly watertight, not only strengthen the vessel, but give greater security to it, and by a judicious arrangement in the divisions will float the ship under the adverse circumstance of a leak occurring in any one of the compartments.

These are the qualities and the powers of the iron ship ; and I trust the present research into the strength and proportions of the material of which it is composed, will not only give increased confidence in its security, but will lead to an extension of its application in every branch of marine and mechanical architecture.

There was also added a mathematical investigation relative to the experiments, contributed, at Mr. Fairbairn's request, by Mr. Tate.

The paper was selected by the Council of the Royal Society for publication in the quarto ' Philosophical

---

[1] When of good quality. Of late years, unfortunately, much iron has been used for common boat work, to which this description does not apply. —ED.

Transactions' (an honour awarded only to those papers that are considered of special scientific merit), and it accordingly appeared in the volume for 1850, page 677. It occupies 50 pages, and is illustrated with many tables and with five engraved plates.

Mr. Fairbairn, in his autobiographical notes, speaks of this paper as one of the most important he had ever undertaken. He says :—

These experiments were of great value, as they not only determined the strength and other properties of the iron, but they exhibited what was of greater importance, namely, that the riveted joint was little more than one-half the strength of the plate itself. These discoveries led to further experiments, which resulted in the single, double, and chain riveting joints being subsequently used in all well-proportioned and well-constructed iron ships. The principles they disclosed have been adopted in her Majesty's dockyards, and for many years have been in use throughout the kingdom.

At the meeting of the British Association in 1853, at Hull, he read a paper ' On the Mechanical Properties of Metals as derived from repeated Meltings, exhibiting the Maximum Point of Strength, and the Causes of Deterioration.'

This paper was written in pursuance of a request from the Association passed at the meeting of 1850. The object was to throw light on certain anomalous conditions observed by practical ironfounders in regard to the use of their material. It is the habit frequently to melt iron, for casting purposes, again and again, and it had been observed, or rather conjectured by certain appearances, that remelting improved the quality. The object of Mr. Fairbairn's enquiries was to determine this, and to ascertain with precision the conditions of the problem. Numerous elaborate experiments were made, and the result seemed to be a gradual improvement, both in strength and elas-

ticity, up to about the twelfth melting, beyond which a
sudden and rapid deterioration set in.

In regard to this, Dr. Robinson, of Armagh, wrote to
Mr. Fairbairn, as follows, dated May 28, 1855:—

I have only recently got the report of the Hull meeting of
the British Association, and have just read your interesting report on the effect of repeated fusion on the strength of cast-iron.
I was greatly struck by the abrupt loss of strength and the
silvery grain assumed by the iron, and fear you have not kept
the fragments; but if they are to be found, it would be very
desirable to have a chemical analysis made of the iron so
changed, and another of the original quality.

My reason is this: Many years ago, while working at chemistry, I reduced mixtures of lime and oxide of iron in charcoal
crucibles at an extremely intense heat. The buttons sometimes contained the metallic basis of lime; they were exces-
sively hard, and their fracture was fine and silvery. Now the repeated fusion with lime and coke seems not unlikely to alloy
the iron with calcium. We want greatly, by the way, a well-
arranged set of experiments on the combination of the metals
of the earths with iron, which I suspect play an important part,
especially in steel.

In 1854 Mr. Fairbairn published his second book,
the title of which was, ' On the Application of Cast and
Wrought Iron to Building Purposes.' It was originally
intended to be an essay on ' Beams and Bridges,' more
general in its scope than the former work on the Menai
structures, and containing fuller information resulting
from the large experience the firm had had in the manufacture of such works. But it was afterwards extended
to other applications of iron.

The author says in his preface:—

In the following pages I have endeavoured to collect the
sum of our practical knowledge on the use of iron, in its combination with other materials, in the construction of fire-proof

buildings. The subject is one of vast public importance. It
is undeniable that great want of judgment has been displayed
in many examples of buildings even of very recent date, and
it is to be lamented that so much ignorance of those unde-
viating laws which govern the strength of materials should still
prevail. Experimentalists and mathematicians have provided
the knowledge, but practitioners I fear have, in a great degree,
failed to avail themselves of it.

Part I. treats of cast-iron beams for supporting the
floors of buildings, giving many experiments on their form
and strength, and the influence on them of various dis-
turbing causes.

Part II. treats, in the same manner, of beams of the
lighter and stronger material, wrought-iron.

Part III. refers to the construction of fire-proof warehouses, and the work concludes with a general description
of the mill at Saltaire.

The book is dedicated to Sir David Brewster, and the
following letter, from a well-known literary man, refers to
a presentation copy sent to the writer :—

58 Lincoln's Inn Fields, May 19, 1854.

My dear Sir,—I have received with the greatest pleasure
the volume you have kindly sent me, of which I mean to read
every word. So far from connecting you with 'plain matter of
fact,' I regard you, and men like you, as the great enchanters
of modern time. What we mere bookmen used in old days to
do with fiction and fancy, you now more nobly accomplish with
fact and philosophy, and are properly become the leaders of the
world. May your Government last long, and be as beneficently
administered as it has been justly obtained.

Always, my dear sir,
Most sincerely yours,
JOHN FORSTER.

WM. FAIRBAIRN, Esq.

A second edition of the work was brought out in

1857, incorporating a new part of considerable length,
on the construction of bridges formed of malleable iron
beams or girders. A third edition appeared in 1864,
containing a few further additions.

It was also translated into French, by M. L. Perret,
in 1855.

In 1856, Messrs. Black, of Edinburgh, the publishers
of the ' Encyclopædia Britannica,' applied to Mr. Fairbairn
to re-write the article ' Iron ' for the eighth edition of that
work, which was then in process of publication. The
publishers felt it was desirable to introduce into this
edition a notice of the many improvements that had been
effected in the iron manufacture ; and knowing how completely Mr. Fairbairn had identified himself with the use
of the material, they selected him as the best qualified
person to undertake what they desired. It was soon
found that it would be scarcely possible to alter satisfactorily the former article, and it was accordingly determined
that he should write an entirely new essay.[1]

The article contains twelve chapters, and is copiously
illustrated with woodcuts, not the vague imperfect things
publishers too often produce in scientific works, but prepared, as might be expected, from accurate engineering
drawings.

Mr. Fairbairn acknowledged, in this article, the assistance he had received from many friends, who had
furnished him with novel information on special points.
Among these was his old friend Mr. James Nasmyth, who
sent him complete descriptions of his steam hammer, an

[1] The succeeding article, on ' Iron Bridges,' was written by Mr. Robert
Stephenson, and it was interesting to see side by side the writings of the
two men who had been engaged together on the largest applications of iron
that had ever been made. Both articles were, however, brought out in a
somewhat imperfect state through haste in their preparation.

invention which was then only recent, but which may be said to have almost revolutionised the iron manufacture, by increasing to an enormous extent the magnitude of its operations.

Mr. Nasmyth, in forwarding the particulars to Mr. Fairbairn, said:—

I am very happy to know that the article ' Iron ' has fallen into such able and authentic hands; and I am sure you will not only render it worthy of the theme, but also worthy of yourself, which is saying everything.

With respect to the description of the steam hammer, would fain that you gave it in your own words, as I don't like to do anything that savours of the ' Use Warren's Blacking ' system. The steam hammer is so well known and so simple, that a mere figure of it is description enough. I am but a poor tool in the literary line; had I but the powers that you so happily possess, wouldn't I hold forth on things in general, and steam hammers in particular! The steam hammer has really been a great help in the mechanical arts, and will do more and more yet. I am at No. 489; they are making them by the thousand on the Continent and in America, but I am well satisfied with my share.

The article was so much approved that, a few years after it appeared, the publishers reprinted it as a separate book, Mr. Fairbairn having the opportunity of correcting the imperfections in the ' Encyclopædia ' copy, and of adding some new matter.

It was afterwards translated into French, with additions, by M. Gustave Maurier.

In 1856, Mr. Fairbairn brought out another work, entitled:—' Useful Information for Engineers, being a series of lectures delivered to the working engineers of Yorkshire and Lancashire. Together with a series of appendices containing the results of experimental enquiries into the strength of materials, the causes of boiler explosions, &c.'

The title will explain pretty clearly what the work consists of. Mr. Fairbairn had frequently delivered lectures to Mechanics' Associations and other similar institutions in the manufacturing districts. These had sometimes been printed in ephemeral pamphlets, or abstracts had been given of them in still more ephemeral local journals ; but they were inaccessible to engineers in general, and the author reaped no profit from them, and but little fame. He consequently determined to collect and publish them in a volume.

In the preface he says, in his justification :—

In presuming to offer useful information to the members of an important profession, I would especially guard myself against an undue assumption of personal merit, and rather rest the justification of the title given to the present volume upon the well-grounded opinion that the elementary principles of science are too much neglected in the study and practice of engineering.

It is generally admitted that one of the most popular and useful forms of imparting knowledge to others is that of public and entertaining lectures, and I may therefore state that the lectures which I have now the opportunity of publishing were mostly prepared at the request of the directors of the various educational institutions of the north of England, and delivered to the mixed assemblies of their members. The circumstances of passing events gave to some of the addresses considerable local and temporary interest ; but it does not by any means follow that, thus hastily conceived, the subjects of which they treated were wanting in permanent value and importance to the mechanical student. . . . . My object was to impart to working engineers, in intelligible and simple terms, all I myself knew of the varied branches of practical science which their calling embraces ; and hence my main reliance was on the results of my own practice and experience.

The volume contains ten lectures, chiefly on steam and steam boilers. It was so well received by the public that it went through several editions, and the author was induced afterwards to follow it up with further collections of the same kind.

In 1859 Mr. Fairbairn presented a short memoir to the British Association, entitled 'Experiments to determine the efficiency of continuous and self-acting Brakes for Railway Trains;' but he afterwards re-wrote the paper in a more elaborated form, and submitted it to the Institution of Civil Engineers, where it was read on April 17, 1860.

In March 1860 he read an important paper before the Institution of Naval Architects, on 'The Strength of Iron Ships.'

He said that former investigations had related principally either to the strength of the material itself, or to the detailed arrangements of its use, riveted joints, &c. Nothing, however, had been done in determining the strength of an iron ship as a great whole, and this it was the object of the paper to do.

It explained the cases in which large iron ships might become strained in actual use. A ship might, for example, get on two rocks, one at each end, and so be without support in the middle; or she might lodge upon a single rock in the middle of her length, leaving the two ends overhanging. He pointed out that of late years it had been found convenient to increase the length of iron vessels to as much as eight or nine times their breadth of beam, partly to obtain an increase of speed by giving fine sharp lines to the bow and stern, and partly to secure an increase of capacity for the same midship section. This, he pointed out, seriously compromised the strength of the ship if she ever got into circumstances of the kind alluded to. And he remarked that even independently of the possibility of being stranded, the ordinary circumstances of floating under the swell of a heavy rolling sea would subject a ship to strains similar in nature, although less in amount.

Reasoning from the known laws established in regard to large iron tubes, he went on to determine the nature of the strains, and to compare them with the strength actually put into ships as ordinarily built; and he showed how insufficient was the resistance of the fabric.

He then proceeded to explain how the defect might be remedied, by adding to the strength in certain ways which he pointed out and illustrated by diagrams and calculations.

In 1860 he brought out a second series of 'Useful Information for Engineers,' containing reprints of four scientific papers contributed by him to scientific societies, and of eight lectures he had delivered at various places and times.

This volume was dedicated to General (now Sir) Edward Sabine, President of the Royal Society, who, in acknowledging the compliment, said :—

August 17, 1860.

This morning's post brought me your kind present, and I have read its inscription to myself with a gratification which I shall not attempt to describe. . . . .

I regard the honour this inscription confers as one of the greatest which I have ever received ; and on which I may reflect with confidence, should I ever be tempted to think that my life has been passed in vain.

At the Oxford meeting of the British Association in 1860, Mr. Fairbairn contributed a Report of :—Experiments to determine the effect of vibratory actions and long-continued changes of load on wrought-iron girders.

The frequent occurrence of accidents to railway trains by the fracture of wheel tyres and axles, and other iron parts of the engines or carriages, had raised an important question, whether the material suffered in its molecular structure by the repeated and long-continued blows, vibrations, and jarrings to which it was subject during the working of the trains. It had often been noticed that the parts so fractured exhibited a structure not favourable for strength and toughness, but it had been difficult to determine whether this was so originally, or whether such a condition had been induced by use. As is generally the case in difficult problems, all sorts of recondite explanations were volunteered ; electrical, magnetic, and chemical agencies were supposed to be at work, and it was often assumed that either by these, or by purely mechanical influences, the structure of the iron really underwent some deteriorating change.

There had, however, always been a want of positive proof of the fact ; and it therefore occurred to engineers of a more practical mind that it might be possible to get, by direct experiment, some conclusive evidence whether the change was real or only imaginary. The Iron Structure Commission of 1849 had tried some experiments, but Mr. Fairbairn considered they were incomplete, and he therefore instituted others on a more comprehensive scale. He directed attention chiefly to bridge girders of wrought-iron, with the view of testing whether the repeated passage of trains would produce any injury, and he contrived an apparatus by which a load could be alternately applied and removed for a great number of times. This was continued till the changes had reached a million and a half, and the results were thus expressed :—

It would appear, therefore, that with a load equal to one-fourth the breaking weight, the structure undergoes no deterioration in the molecular structure; and, provided a sufficient margin of strength is given, say from five to six times the working load, there is every reason to believe from the results of the above experiments that girders composed of good material and of sound workmanship are indestructible, so far as regards mere vibratory action.

At the Manchester meeting the next year, he reported a continuation of the experiments, confirming the results in the former paper.

In 1864 he embodied the foregoing results in a paper which was read before the Royal Society on February 4 in that year, and was published in the 'Philosophical Transactions,' vol. cliv.

About this time Mr. Fairbairn brought out an important work on a subject peculiarly his own, namely, a 'Treatise on Mills and Millwork.' It was in two volumes or parts. Part I. appeared in 1861, and Part II. in 1863.

The editor of the present biography had occasion to review Mr. Fairbairn's book for a scientific periodical soon after its publication, and ventures to insert here some extracts from the opinions on it then expressed:—

It has often been remarked that, although the English have been in advance of all other nations in the practice of engineering, they have been sadly behindhand in its literature. Indeed, it has become a proverb that we have executed works for others to describe; and the students of engineering know well that the best accounts of many of our most important engineering operations must be sought for in the publications of France and Germany.

In regard to the great branch of the profession comprehended under the name of mechanical engineering, the want of correspondence between our literature and our progress is most striking. We need not dwell on the fact that we are, and have long been, the first mechanicians in the world; but it is no less true that the evidence of this fact which will go down to posterity on the shelves of our libraries will be meagre in the extreme.[1]

It is, therefore, with much satisfaction, that we greet the production of the veteran mechanic whose name appears at the head of our article. He had founded, at an early part of his life, a firm in Manchester who have since become celebrated for the designs and manufacture of machinery in great variety, and on a very extensive scale; and it is more especially to the illustrations of modern machinery, derived from the archives of this firm, that the present work owes its value.

The first volume is devoted to the general principles of mechanism and to prime movers. After a chapter of ten pages (which might have been much extended with advantage) on the history of mills, a discourse follows on the theory of mechanism, and the remainder of the book is occupied with notices of the modes by which water, steam, and wind are made available as sources of mechanical power. In regard to the former of these, Mr. Fairbairn has not confined himself, as previous authors have done, to the treatment of the machines for making use of the power, but he has traced the moving agent back to its source in the clouds, and followed in detail the circumstances of its fall, its distribution, its storage, and its conveyance to the point where it is to become useful. The construction of water wheels and other hydraulic machines is also given very fully—it is a department to which the author has evidently devoted much attention; and this division of the book forms the best and most comprehensive essay on water power we have seen. We are the more pleased with this, because, since the general introduction of steam, water-power has been far too lightly esteemed.

The second part of the work is still more technical than the former, consisting, first, of chapters on wheels, straps, shafts, and couplings; and, secondly, information on the arrangement

---

[1] This was written in 1863; since that date the advanced education which has spread among the engineering profession has induced a much more copious literature, as well as a higher tone of thought.

of mills of various kinds—for corn, cotton, woollen fabrics, flax, silk, oil, paper, gunpowder, and iron. This latter division is, if we mistake not, almost entirely a novelty in engineering literature—the only similar attempt we remember being contained in an old work, called ' Nicholson's Operative Mechanic,' which, though popular in its day, is now quite obsolete. We could find much in these essays to remark on, if we were writing a technical review; but we must here content ourselves with recommending the work as supplying a want of long standing, and as calculated to be of much practical utility. It is illustrated profusely with woodcuts, and contains also several plates, well drawn and engraved.

In 1865 Mr. Fairbairn brought out a ' Treatise on Iron Shipbuilding ; ' which he dedicated to the Duke of Somerset, then First Lord of the Admiralty.

It is an octavo volume of 300 pages ; the earlier chapters treat of the laws of strains, the properties of iron, and the modes of jointing ; the later portions refer to iron armour and the effect of projectiles, with remarks generally on ships of war. The book contains also a theoretical essay on the strength of materials, contributed by Mr. Tate.

In 1866 appeared a Third Series of the ' Useful Information for Engineers,' containing, as before, several lectures and papers on miscellaneous subjects.

This volume was dedicated to Lord Brougham.

In 1869 Mr. Fairbairn gave his aid in the preparation of a work entitled ' Lancashire and Cheshire, Past and Present,' by Mr. Thomas Baines. The book was a large and handsome one, in four volumes quarto, giving a full history and topographical description of the two counties, and it was illustrated by many engravings of the scenery, buildings, and worthies of the locality.

Mr. Baines wisely saw that as subjects of a technical

and industrial character entered so largely into the interest attaching to the county 'of Lancashire, it would be well to get some expert to write the portion of the book treating of these matters; and he accordingly applied to Mr. Fairbairn, who responded with his usual public spirit.

His contribution to the work was a very important feature of it, forming of itself one quarto volume of 260 pages, and it was probably the largest book he ever wrote. It had a separate title—'The Rise and Progress of Manufactures and Commerce, and of Civil and Mechanical Engineering, in Lancashire and Cheshire.'

He says in his preface :—

When I was invited to write this work I entertained grave doubts of my own competency. The task seemed to require rather the descriptive powers of the historian than the bare matter of fact views of the engineer ; and I must, therefore, crave the indulgence of the reader for the imperfections which will doubtless be found in my treatment of a large subject. If I have failed to make the essay as attractive as a more fluent writer might have done, I have, at least, endeavoured to bring together a mass of information which will be useful to the student who may desire to weigh and appreciate the wonderful development of this great centre of manufacturing industry.

· · · · · · ·

I have endeavoured to trace the influence which the progress of manufacturing enterprise has had upon national character. The rapid growth and present high state of perfection of the trades touched upon in the following pages have raised the mechanics and artisans from mere labourers into a class remarkable for their intelligence, skill, and perseverance. They are now a great power in the state—one to be guided by wise laws and liberal encouragement, to the exercise of infinite good, but also capable of producing great evil to themselves and others, if their association and organisation are not regulated by high principles and sound judgment.

E E

The book is (like the main body of the work to which it is attached) somewhat desultory and ill-arranged, and it is difficult to give a precise summary of its contents; but it contains a great deal of valuable information, historical and descriptive. Among the subjects treated of are the scientific institutions of Liverpool and Manchester, and the engineering works of the district, such as the canals, the railways, the water supply, the docks, and the landing stages : the engineering and iron trades, and the cotton manufacture, are also fully described.

Mr. Fairbairn was engaged on this work from August 1867 to July 1869, but he received no remuneration for his labour, charging only a trifling sum for the expenses of drawings. We do not even see, in the preface to the main work, any acknowledgment of the service he had rendered.

Sir William's last literary production was a paper read before the Royal Society on April 26, 1873, ' On the Durability and Preservation of Iron Ships, and on Riveted Joints.'

The author, as an experienced iron ship-builder, discussed the liability of such structures to injury by corrosion, which he believed might be entirely prevented by proper care and watchfulness; and he recommended the same measure which he had found so beneficial in the case of boilers, namely, periodical inspection.

He further treated various questions in regard to riveted joints, such as the relative merits of machine and hand riveting, the comparative effect of drilling and punching in forming the holes; and the paper was accompanied by various tables and theoretical investigations.

Mr. Fairbairn was in great request as a lecturer, and

received frequent invitations to deliver lectures at scientific societies, mechanics' institutions, and the like, which
he generally complied with if he could. Some of these
lectures were printed at the time in separate pamphlets,
and some were republished by him in the ' Useful Information for Engineers.'

Independently, however, of regular lecturing, he had
many calls upon him to take the chair at anniversary
meetings, distribution of prizes, &c., and he generally gave
at each meeting an address appropriate to the object.
On all these occasions his great popularity never failed
to attract large audiences, and to give *éclat* to the institutions that asked his aid.

His last address was on October 28, 1873, at a
meeting of the Manchester Scientific and Mechanical
Society, of which he was president. Although suffering
from severe illness and very weak, he contrived to write
the address; but when the day came he was unable to
leave his bed, and it was read by the secretary. A few
extracts will show that age had done nothing to diminish
the sound practical sense he had always manifested on
such occasions :—

It is a source of pride to bear witness to the inventions and
discoveries that have been effected in machine making in every
department of industry. In the beauty, exactitude, and mathematical accuracy of these constructions, we stand unequalled ;
and we have only to refer to the International Exhibition of
1851 and its successors to be assured that rapid strides and improvements have been silently but progressively going on, not
only in the machinery then in use, but the introduction of the
self-acting principle, so much wanted and so eagerly looked
for in every manufacturing process where it could be introduced.

And here it is only just to state that the introduction of new
machinery and the self-acting principle owed much of their
efficacy and ingenuity to the system of strikes, which compelled

the employers of labour to fall back upon their own resources, and to execute, by machinery and new inventions, work which was formerly done by hand. Let me give an example which strikingly illustrates the benefits as well as the inconveniences of a sudden cessation of labour. Some forty years ago, when I undertook the manufacture of boilers, I had large orders on hand, and being unwilling to allow the men to dictate the terms on which I should engage apprentices and conduct the work, I received notice of a turn out, which immediately took place, and the works were suspended for a number of weeks. In this dilemma, with impatient customers, I was driven to the necessity of supplying the place of riveters by a passive and unerring machine, which from that day to this has never complained, and did as much work in one day as was formerly accomplished by twelve of our best riveters and assistants in the same time, and executing the work with greater perfection than could possibly be done by the hammer. This is not the only example of the effects of strikes that may be quoted, as I might instance the late Mr. Roberts, with his self-acting mule and other inventions, which produced much benefit.

I have stated that we have reason to be proud of the numerous inventions and discoveries that have been made in the machinery for the manufacture of the textile fabrics. We must not, however, run off with the idea that we are the only improvers and inventors ; on the contrary, we are on many occasions far behind, and I am anxious to impress upon the Society the necessity for exertion in every scientific pursuit, if we are to maintain our position and cope with the natives of other countries who have equal opportunities and are better educated than ourselves. This is actually the case in France, Switzerland, and Germany, and in the United States we have to contend with intelligent and very powerful rivals in both the scientific and the industrial arts.

I have dealt largely on the necessity of our members having a knowledge of first principles, and that all their designs and constructions must be founded on the unalterable laws of scientific truth. I intended to have said that the age of the rule of thumb was at an end, and that any design, however perfect and however ingenious in its development, is utterly useless unless it is also a work of science. It is true that great works have been sometimes accomplished by the master minds of men without education, but how much more certain and how much more perfect are the emanations and works of such men as James Watt, Smeaton, and others who have combined science with their discoveries.

As compared with many other professions, engineering has been in a dormant state within a period in my own recollection. In the year 1804, when I first entered business as an apprentice, there were not in the whole kingdom above half a dozen persons deserving the name of engineer. I recollect quite well when I first entered Manchester, in 1813, that the only important tools then in vogue were a few common lathes, a screw-cutter, and a boring machine for steam engine cylinders. These facts show the low ebb at which mechanical science was fifty years ago, and how much we are indebted to the late Mr. Roberts and our talented friend Sir Joseph Whitworth and others for the introduction of new and more perfect tool machinery, which has given not only mathematical precision, but almost a creative power—as one machine creates another.

In Mr. Fairbairn's more important writings, and in the experimental investigations they related to, he availed himself freely of such assistance as he felt would be useful to him, and this he always honourably acknowledged. He was not a deep mathematician, and mathematical reasoning was often necessary for the reduction and generalisation of his experiments, and for the clear exposition of the results obtained.

In his earlier publications he was assisted in this way by Mr. Thomas Tate, mathematical master of Battersea Training School. But at a later period, when he began to devote himself more earnestly to scientific work, he engaged as secretary a young engineer, Mr. W. C. Unwin, who, having had a good theoretical training, was able to take this work permanently for him. Mr. Unwin was with him from 1855 to 1863, during which time he gave

active aid in the many important investigations undertaken by Mr. Fairbairn, and in the publications recording
them, particularly those referring to boilers, the properties of steam, the strength of materials, submarine cables,
railway brakes, and iron armour. Mr. Fairbairn always
expressed a high opinion of Mr. Unwin's ability and the
value of his assistance, and he now occupies an eminent
position as one of the professors of engineering at the
Royal East Indian Engineering College, Cooper's Hill.

CHAPTER XXIII.

ILLNESS AND DEATH

THE FAIRBAIRNS A LONG-LIVED FAMILY—WILLIAM'S ROBUST CON-
STITUTION— FIRST SERIOUS ILLNESS—REACHES HIS SEVENTY-EIGHTH
YEAR—LOSS OF HIS ELDEST SON—LETTERS FROM SIR DAVID BREWSTER
AND DR. ROBINSON—COMPLAINTS—OBLIGED TO GIVE UP ROMPING
AND OTHER JUVENILE PROPENSITIES—OWEN'S COLLEGE—BRONCHIAL
ATTACK—VISITS TO BRIGHTON AND TO HOLLAND PARK—MARRIAGE OF
HIS GRAND-DAUGHTER—' GIVE HER A ROUND '—VISITS TO MR. BATE-
MAN—LAST DAYS AT MOOR PARK—DEATH—BISHOP SUMNER—FUNERAL
—OBITUARY NOTICES—MEMORIAL BY THE CITY OF MANCHESTER.

CHAPTER XXIII.

WE now approach the close of this long life, so actively and so usefully employed.

William Fairbairn came from a long-lived family. His grandfather, John Fairbairn, died in 1797, at the ripe age of eighty-one, and his grandmother also lived to a great age. His father, Andrew, died in 1844, aged eighty-six, and his mother lived to her sixtieth year. William himself inherited a robust constitution, and enjoyed generally good health for the greater part of his life. It was not till between his fiftieth and sixtieth years that he had any serious illness. Owing to some irregularity or other exciting cause during a journey, he was seized, somewhere about 1845, with an obstruction of the bowels, and was for some time considered in danger, powerful remedies being applied. He recovered from this attack, but it left evil consequences behind, from which he suffered more or less during the remainder of his life. He was obliged frequently, and often continuously, to take medicine for the purpose of ensuring proper digestive action, and he was subject at intervals to attacks of spasms in the stomach and intestines, which were very painful and troublesome.

Still he had nearly reached his eightieth year before he began to feel the approach of the last enemy. At the beginning of 1867 he lost his eldest son, John; he

felt this affliction deeply, and an aggravated recurrence
of his spasmcdic attacks at the same time brought him
very low.

Two of his oldest and most valued friends, both eminent in science, and both, like himself, well advanced in
years, wrote to him as follows :—

Brae Lodge, Murrayfield, March 4, 1867.

My dear Mr. Fairbairn,—My wife and I grieve to hear of
your illness, and of the severe domestic affliction which you and
Mrs. Fairbairn have suffered. We hope that the genial air of
the south will hasten your convalescence, and that the hope of
rejoining the son you have lost will alleviate a dispensation
which would otherwise be difficult to bear.

Since I had the pleasure of seeing you, I have suffered a
severe loss in the death of the widow of my eldest son; a beautiful woman, worshipped by everybody that knew her.

I have also been an invalid like yourself, but from a different cause. When on a visit to my daughter in autumn, I
caught *whooping cough,* a horrid complaint, from the effects of
which I am not yet free.

Time, too, has begun to tell upon limbs that have been
doing duty for more than 85 years, and the brainwork which
I have gone through has begun to tamper with the upper part
of the machine, so that I am burning the candle of life at both
ends.

Having been unable to get a house in Edinburgh this winter,
we are living in a charming villa in the immediate neighbourhood, and if business should bring you northwards, we have a
spare room at your service.

Notwithstanding my ailments, I have written *three* papers
for the Royal Society, of which I hope soon to have the pleasure
of sending you copies.

My wife joins me in kindest regards to Mrs. Fairbairn and
yourself, and to Mr. and Mrs. Bateman, and I am,

My dear Mr. Fairbairn,

Ever most truly yours,

D. BREWSTER.

Observatory, Armagh, February 22, 1867.

My dear Friend,—We are greatly grieved at learning through Miss Holland of your severe illness, and the subsequent death of your son. But I trust you are fully recovered in health, and I know that one so good and wise will bear the bereavement, however painful, as coming from God and therefore appointed for the best. I know how precious your time is, but I entreat you to spare so much of it as to tell us how you are, and how Mrs. Fairbairn has borne her affliction.

Of myself and mine I have little to tell, except that my sight is failing fast. If deprived of it, I shall feel the loss very heavily, but I hope I shall bear it in a proper spirit. I have at least this consolation— that during my long life I have used it not unprofitably.

Ever yours affectionately,

T. R. ROBINSON.

W. FAIRBAIRN, Esq.

Early in 1868 he wrote to an old friend :—

I have had a second attack of my painful and troublesome complaint.

The approach of winter seizes on me in the shape of spasms in the chest, and I have suffered more or less ever since. The doctors say I must give up my juvenile propensities, and consider myself an old man. This I am unwilling to do, and although I entered my 80th year last month, I am still unable to realise the fact that I *am old*. I hope you will long continue to have the same feeling when you get to my age, and be free from the torments under which I almost daily labour.

In July 1869 he alluded to ' more spasmodic attacks ;' and in August of the same year he was, to his great disappointment, prevented by them from attending the British Association meeting at Exeter.

In April 1870 he was better. He wrote :—

I am glad to inform you I have got a reprieve from the spasmodic attacks under which I have laboured for nearly two

years; and, as an old man, I must not now romp.   I still go to
the works, and although a little stiff, I nevertheless endeavour
to keep the judgment sound and the mind clear.

On May 23, 1871, he wrote to Dr. Robinson :—

I still continue to do a little in the field of practical science
and improvement, but I find it difficult to keep up with the
present generation, whose minds are better prepared and better
instructed than they were in my time.   I, however, endeavour
to the best of my ability, even at the advanced age of 82, to
keep pace with them ; but it is difficult to keep the mind young
when the exterior casing becomes brittle and insecure.

In December 1872 he complained again of spasms,
but not so severe as a year or two before.

In April 1873, writing to Professor Rankine, he
said :—

I cannot work now as I used to do, not so much from
mental deficiency as from physical ailments and the wear and
tear of life.   I ought not, however, to forget that I entered my
84th year only six weeks ago, and might yet be useful for some
time longer but from severe spasmodic attacks, under which I
have been suffering for the last three years.

In October of the same year, the new buildings of
Owen's College, Manchester, were opened ; and he, somewhat imprudently, resolved to be present at the ceremo-
nial.   He, no doubt, felt himself compelled to do so,
because not only was the Duke of Devonshire, the president, his guest on the occasion, but in 1870 his Grace
had appointed him one of the three governors of the
Institution.   Here he caught a severe bronchial cold,
which prostrated him for some time, and from the effects
of which he never recovered.

About the middle of 1874 his strength began rapidly
to fail ; and being much troubled by the bronchial irrita-

tion, he was recommended to try to get relief by a change of air to the South Coast. A friend opportunely offered him the use of his house at Brighton, and it was during this visit he wrote, on June 8, the letter to Mr. Fletcher, mentioned in Chap. XVI., the following passage in which may be repeated here :—

I am sorry to say I do not improve. I will, however, give the clear air, which is warm and excellent, a trial for another fortnight, and if I get no better I will return and prepare for the change which cannot be far distant.

He did not get better, and he left Brighton to pay a short visit to his son William, at Holland Park, London. Here in July, he complained of frequent nausea, and consulted Sir William Gull, who (warning the family of his critical condition) recommended absolute rest, and great caution in avoiding all risk of increasing the bronchial irritation by taking fresh cold.

The middle of this month, one of his grand-daughters, the second daughter of Mr. Bateman, was married to Major Maxwell (since unhappily deceased) ; he was very desirous to be present at the wedding at Moor Park, but was too ill to go. He sent, however, to the bridegroom the following letter, which was the last he wrote. It will show that although so ill, his exuberant animal spirits had not yet forsaken him :—

My dear Major Maxwell,—I would have written to Maggie, but she is busy. She will never have patience to read anything on such an occasion from such an old scratch as myself. I therefore address you on so momentous an occasion as the present to express Lady Fairbairn's and my own deep regret that the extremely infirm state of my health prevents us being present. Let me, however, recommend you, like all experienced and prudent husbands, to follow a piece of advice which I received from an old friend on a similar occasion, namely—
‘ Be sure, on every occasion of difference (and where is the

family that have not differences), that you and the wife are never in a passion at the same time.'

He added, however, in a half-whisper, ' But when she is done, 'gad, you may then give her a round.'

You will pardon me for adding more, as I am scarcely able either to read or write, and can only add our united blessing, and prayer for your future happiness, and remain,

Your affectionate,

W. FAIRBAIRN.

[Date.—July 14, 1874.]

Immediately after the marriage he went down to Mr. Bateman's country seat at Moor Park, near Farnham, Surrey. There had always been a warm and reciprocal attachment between him and his daughter, Mrs. Bateman, and during the later years of his life, when he had given up the cares of business, although he retained to the last his home at the Polygon, Manchester (where his widow still resides), he had spent much time every year with Mr. and Mrs. Bateman and their family. The large works which Mr. Bateman had frequently been required to carry on in various parts of the kingdom had led him, partly for business convenience, and partly by a preference for country scenery, to occupy from time to time residences in picturesque districts; Morecambe Bay, Ambleside, North Wales, and Perthshire, were some of the situations chosen; and it was a great delight to Mr. Fairbairn to visit at these places. The house at Cardross in Perthshire, was taken by Mr. Bateman when carrying out the great works of the Loch Katrine water supply to Glasgow; it was held several years, and here, or at a house in which he subsequently lived, Fern Tower, near Crieff, Mr. Fairbairn spent, with his wife, much of the summer and autumn of each year. He was fond of the neighbourhood, from his old Scotch associations, and he met here many friends who esteemed him for his talents and worth, and loved him for his estimable social qualities.

The Glasgow Water Works being finished, Mr. Bateman gave up his Scotch residence, and bought, in 1859, the Surrey estate, where Sir William Fairbairn was afterwards a frequent visitor. After his arrival there, about the middle of July, 1874, he was for a short time able to walk about and dine with the family. One day he walked round the grounds with Mrs. Bateman, after having visited, with her, the camp at Frensham, during the autumn manœuvres. He took great interest in military matters, and conversed freely on what they had seen; after which he spoke to her of his own state, and of what he felt was the approaching change. The walk was perhaps too much for him, for after it he took to his room, which he never again left alive. The windows of this room looked out on the flower garden, and on a beautiful rural prospect, which he often expressed himself as enjoying.

His last attack was a painful one, but he bore it with exemplary patience, no murmur ever escaping from his lips. He loved life and the exercise of his active mental power, but he looked upon death as an inevitable doom, and he was quite prepared to die. He spoke little of the probability of his own decease, beyond an expression of resignation to it. He gave few directions as to the future, and made no particular communications either to his wife or his children. He gradually sank, retaining to the last a silent consciousness, and he died quite peacefully on August 18, 1874.

His friend Bishop Sumner lay on his deathbed at Farnham Castle at the same time, and each took great interest in the state of the other. The bishop died two days before Sir William.

It was the wish of the family that the funeral should be strictly private, but it was desired by the authorities of the town of Manchester and many friends of the deceased that a demonstration of respect should be made. The following account is extracted from a Manchester paper :—

The mortal remains of the late Sir William Fairbairn, Baronet, were interred yesterday at Prestwich parish church. The distinguished position of the deceased, and the fact that, notwithstanding his Scotch birth, he was pre-eminently a Manchester man, combined to make the occasion one of a public character, and the result was a public demonstration of respect for the deceased and of sympathy with the bereaved family. The deceased Baronet died on Tuesday last at Farnham, in Surrey, and his body was brought to Manchester on Friday night. The funeral *cortége* left the residence of the deceased—the Polygon, Ardwick—about eleven o'clock, and, accompanied by bodies of the city police and fire brigade, proceeded by way of Ardwick Green, Piccadilly, Market Street, Strangeways, and Bury New Road to the place of interment. In Stockport Road and along the line of route large crowds collected to witness the procession, and to pay the last token of respect to an eminent citizen. The shops were partially closed, and the blinds of many private houses were drawn. The body of police consisted of twelve men from each division of the city constabulary ; and the fire brigade was represented by twelve men from the central station. The following was the order of procession :—

Two Mutes.
Police.
Fire Brigade.
Several private carriages.
Three carriages, containing a deputation from the Manchester Steam Users' Association.
Police.
The private carriages of the mayor and other members of the Corporation of Manchester.
Two Mutes.
The Hearse, drawn by four horses.

The private carriage of the deceased, closed.

Seven mourning coaches, containing relatives and friends of the deceased.

Private carriages.

Police.

As the procession passed through the town, several other private carriages and a number of gentlemen on foot joined it, and it was not until one o'clock that it reached Prestwich. The corpse was met at the church gates by the Rev. Canon Gibson and the Rev. Canon Birch, the officiating ministers, and the path from the gates to the porch was lined by workmen in the employ of the deceased, who stood uncovered as the coffin was borne by. The church was thronged by a large congregation. The service was brief but impressive. The coffin, which was covered with wreaths of choice flowers, was deposited in the family vault near the south-west corner of the burialground, where three sons of the deceased are interred. A brass plate on the coffin bore the simple inscription,

WILLIAM FAIRBAIRN, BARONET :
Born 19th February, 1789 ;
Died 18th August, 1874.

The number of people present at the funeral was estimated at from 50,000 to 70,000.

The death was promptly announced in almost all the newspapers of the country, as that of a well-known public character, and memoirs of considerable length were given.

The *Times*, in the course of a biographical notice, said :—

It is almost useless to state here that no name stood higher than that of Fairbairn in the world of civil engineering ; and that although late in life he accepted a well-earned title, his reputation hereafter will date from a generation at least earlier than his patent as a baronet.

The *Daily News*, a journal always prominent in scientific matters, gave a leading article, containing such

F F

an admirable and truthful estimate of Sir William's position, character, and merits, that we may be pardoned for giving extracts from it at some length.

The death of Sir William Fairbairn, occurring as it does during the British Association week, breaks in upon the meeting of his scientific brothers almost as harshly as the death of the official in the Faroe Islands did upon the ceremonies at the reception of the King of Denmark. Of course Sir William Fairbairn's was not a premature end. He had lived to a good and even to a great old age. He had multiplied his years by intellectual activity and unceasing enterprise in the fields of industrial science. Nature could hardly have prolonged much farther his busy and fruitful career; and even in this age of longevity, when men turn to the real work of a public life at a time when their forefathers would have thought of retirement and rest, Sir William Fairbairn would be considered an old man. Still the death of such a colleague, occurring at the opening of the annual meeting of the British Association, must come upon its leading members with a painful shock. Sir William Fairbairn was one of the founders of the British Association, and he was one of its most distinguished presidents. He was a fitting representative of the spirit which made that Association a success, and of the age of industrial science, illustrated by literary intelligence, which allowed it to be successful. It used to be the habit at one time to sneer at the Association of 'philosophers.' But in the days when philosophy was a profession and a culture we should like to know what its teachers would have thought of an age when, even as a sneer, the title of philosopher could be conferred upon a maker of roads or a worker in iron. Sir William Fairbairn was emphatically a man who might be accredited with having helped to bring about the condition of things in England which proved that philosophy can enter into the building of bridges and the putting together of the hulls of ships. The career of him and of his like expounds the secret of modern England's greatness.

He was an indefatigable worker in what we may call the literary illustration of his enterprises and objects. Treatise after treatise, lecture after lecture, on all subjects in connection with this branch of industrial science, came from his active and unresting hand. He was associated with almost every society formed here or abroad to develop the true principles of engineering. Nothing that concerned in any way the interests of industrial science escaped his attention, or failed to enlist his sympathy. Thus he became known widely beyond the limits of his own profession. In every calling of life, as our social life is now constituted, there are men who acquire high reputation and enjoy entire confidence within the limits of that particular craft, but who are hardly known to the public outside. Every lawyer, every soldier, every engineer, every scholar, can tell of men in his vocation who rank, by common consent of its members, second to none there, and yet whose names, when told to an outsider, are spoken to unfamiliar ears. Sir William Fairbairn was not a man of this class. He always seems to have enjoyed a reputation with the general public as well as with those who were qualified to judge more accurately of the value of his career. That literary faculty, if we may so call it, in which the elder Stephenson was so entirely deficient, enabled Sir William Fairbairn to secure the whole public sometimes for his audience, and his death will therefore be felt as a national loss. The distinction which was conferred upon him at the recommendation of Mr. Gladstone, in 1869, was, we need not say, much better deserved than in nine cases out of ten in which a Prime Minister is the means of bestowing such an honour. It was a tribute to a very remarkable career, in which talents and perseverance fought their way from the lowliest rank and amid immense difficulties; and it is only to be regretted that such distinctions are not made of more genuine value by being less frequently conferred as the reward of plodding and brainless political partisanship. But Sir William Fairbairn was of all men the son of his own works. If he bore a title towards the close of his life we are glad of it, rather because it affirmed that the State acknowledges the dignity of industrial science than because we think it in any way ennobled him.

The *Engineer* said :—

A GREAT engineer in a past generation has departed. Sir William Fairbairn died a little after noon on Tuesday, at Moor

Park, Farnham, Surrey, full of years, and not without honours, hardly earned and very fully deserved. Fairbairn's *forte* lay in millwright work. It is not too much to say that he revolutionised the art of making mills, whether for grinding wheat or spinning cotton. He introduced, to begin with, most important improvements in water-wheels. Some of his Scotch wheels have never been excelled in efficiency by any water-power motor, except a very few turbines. He was not content with this. From end to end he remodelled the system on which mills were constructed. He gave the milling world new shafting, new couplings, new gear accurately made and properly proportioned to the work to be accomplished. No man, living or dead, has done so much to make mechanical engineering in two important branches so nearly perfect. Fairbairn found millwrighting a second-rate trade. He abolished the millwright, and introduced the mechanical engineer ; and for this achievement alone he would deserve to be honoured. In one word, it is difficult to discover a branch of the art of mechanical engineering to which Fairbairn has not contributed something. His footprints may be found on every path which the engineer can tread, and the sands of time will never efface them.

The Manchester papers especially made the occurrence their most prominent piece of news, and devoted many columns to obituary notices.

The *Manchester Examiner* said :—

A full account of Sir William Fairbairn's life would be to a large extent identical with a history of half a century of progress in mechanical science, in the development of the productive power of Manchester manufactures, in the application of iron to the building of ships, and in a wide range of invention and discovery connected with the strength of materials of construction and the economy of motive forces. Some of the greatest works of peace and war in our time are associated with Sir William Fairbairn's name.

In whatever way we seek to account for Fairbairn's remarkable success in life, compared with that of the mass of men who start from a similar station, it is a magnificent instance of the rewards that may attend such persistent endeavours directed to aims so honourable.

Another Manchester paper said :—

But the story of his life points a moral of the most valuable kind.

It was by the force of his will and the integrity of his character that Sir William Fairbairn won his position. He learned to labour and to wait, and, having a large faith in time, looked cheerfully forward to the ' perfect end.' No mere dreamer, he utilised every hour, and when disappointment came, as come it often did, if he retreated from what seemed to be an untenable position, it was only to gather strength for renewed effort and fresh enterprise. ' Something attempted, something done,' every day earned him physical and mental repose. Patient study enabled him to acquire that knowledge of first principles which resulted in the exercise of foresight akin to the marvellous, and the steady momentum imparted to his life by continuous application imparted an onward impetus to his fortunes, which resulted in the establishment of his reputation as the foremost mechanical engineer of his day. That branch of industry to which he devoted himself with so much zeal is now one of the most important in the world. Thousands owe their daily bread in a measure to the ardent mechanician who demonstrated with such telling effect the utility of iron, and the resources of the world have been augmented to an almost fabulous extent by his labours. It is natural, therefore, that Manchester should be proud of her foster-son, and fitting that honourable mention should be made of him by all who are capable of appreciating sterling worth and indomitable zeal. In an age replete with able men he held a prominent place, and his career serves to show that honesty of purpose, patient toil, unwavering integrity, while they tend to ensure material prosperity, are justly to be enumerated among those virtues which alone can give to nations a solid greatness, or to individuals an imperishable fame.

But it was not only in England that these manifestations of respect to his memory took place. One of the most important mechanical and industrial organs of Germany, the Berlin *Allgemeine Deutsche Polytechnische Zeitung*, published, on September 12, 1874, a biographical notice with a portrait, and a statement of his chief services to practical science, concluding with the words : 'Let all aspiring workers take Sir William Fairbairn as a model. He is no more ; but his name will ever live in what he has done.'

The Manchester Steam Users' Association took proceedings which are described in the following extracts from their annual report :—

The Committee of Management have now to refer with sincere and deep regret to the loss the Association has sustained by the death of its president and founder, the late Sir Wm. Fairbairn, Bart., which took place on the 18th of August last. At the institution of the Association, in 1854, Sir Wm. Fairbairn was elected a vice-president, and continued one for four years, when he was elected to the presidency, which office he continued to hold till the time of his decease, a period of sixteen years. The services rendered by him to the Association, and to steam users generally, the committee believe to be invaluable. His attendance at the committee and annual meetings of the Association was most regular, while his advice and service were at all other times freely placed at the disposal of the committee. The committee think it well to introduce the following copy of an address presented by them to Lady Fairbairn, together with a copy of Sir Thos. Fairbairn's acknowledgment of the same.

Copy of address to Lady Fairbairn, presented by the Vice-presidents and Executive Committee of the Manchester Steam Users' Association, on the death of Sir William Fairbairn, Bart., F.R.S., LL.D., &c.

'To LADY FAIRBAIRN,

'Dear Madam,—We, the colleagues of the late Sir William Fairbairn, on the board of the Steam Users' Association, desire very respectfully to express to your Ladyship our profound sympathy on the irreparable loss you have sustained by his deeply lamented death.

'We beg to assure you that so far as it may be possible to offer words of comfort and condolence to your afflicted mind and heart, we share in a very high degree those feelings of unfeigned regard and respect for the memory of Sir William Fairbairn, which we know are experienced by every one whose good fortune it has been to have enjoyed his friendship and acquaintance.

' It has been our happiness to have been associated with him for many years in the management of an Association of which he was the originator and founder, the object of which is one of practical regard for human suffering, and the safety of life to a large class of working men, no less than for the promotion of scientific enquiry on questions of vast public utility.

' Under Sir William's sagacious and able chairmanship, our Association has acquired a hold on the public mind which to him, its distinguished founder, must have been unspeakably gratifying.

' With your Ladyship's kind permission, we hope to have the honour and pleasure of placing in our board room a marble bust, by an eminent sculptor, of our late admirable president, and trust we may be allowed the favour of duplicating the bust which you possess.

' We will not multiply words in this brief record of our opinions and views. His important works are his enduring monument, and will ever live in the regard of his thoughtful fellow-countrymen.

' It is not enough for us to say that we respected and honoured him, for we loved him for his many fine qualities of heart, and shall never cease to revere his memory.

' We have the honour to be, dear Madam,
' Your Ladyship's very humble servants,
' (Signed)   *Vice-Presidents :*
JOSEPH WHITWORTH,   HUGH MASON,
THOMAS BAZLEY,   JOHN PENN.

Executive Committee :

JAMES PETRIE,   CHARLES F. BEYER,
JABEZ JOHNSON,   JAMES TAYLOR,
CHARLES HEATON,   ADAM DUGDALE,
THOMAS SCHOFIELD,   WRIGHT TURNER,
HENRY R. GREG,   LOUIS J. CROSSLEY,
WILLIAM ROBERTS,   EDWARD W. WRIGLEY.
SAMUEL RIGBY.'

Copy of reply from Sir Thomas Fairbairn.

Brambridge House, Bishopstoke, December 26, 1874.

' My dear Mr. Mason,

' I received on Thursday evening the case containing the beautiful volume, " In Memoriam," from the Vice-Presidents and Council of the Manchester Steam Users' Association, and yesterday I fulfilled your wishes by presenting it to the Dowager Lady Fairbairn. My dear mother desires me to assure you that no Christmas Day greeting could have been more consolatory to a widow's sorrowing heart than this most touching address. The distinguished men whose names are appended to it record not only their admiration of Sir William Fairbairn's career and public services, but they state that they " loved him for his many fine qualities of heart."

' The exquisite form in which this valuable testimony is enshrined will be retained and guarded by my family as one of its most precious heirlooms. I have always looked upon the foundation of the Steam Users' Association as one of my father's most useful and most honourable achievements. It was at all times a source of great joy to him that the persistent and unwearied support of yourself and colleagues had made the Association which he founded instrumental in saving hundreds of valuable lives.

' He advocated the system of inspection as against that of insurance with unswerving constancy ; and I cannot help thinking that there are some other branches of the world's enterprise to which such a system could be applied with great profit to human life and happiness. In connection, for instance, with the safe working of ships, how much fraud and wickedness might be avoided, how much property be preserved, and how many lives be saved, if the mercantile marine of this country were subjected to careful searching and periodical inspection.

' " Duty to others, and not gain to ourselves," has been the main-spring of your admirable Society, and a strict performance of this solemn obligation during a period of now many years has given your Association the reputation, authority, and power of usefulness which it now deservedly enjoys. I can

wish no more honourable association of merit with my father's
memory than that the sphere of your labours may be greatly
extended, and that you may reap the reward of public gratitude
for promoting an object of paramount utility upon the basis of
scientific truth.

'I am, my dear Mr. Mason,
'Yours very truly,
'(Signed)   THOMAS FAIRBAIRN.

'HUGH MASON, Esq.'

The marble bust, to which allusion is made in the address,
has been executed by Mr. T. Woolner, R.A., and is now to be
seen at the offices of the Association.

Almost all the other institutions with which he had
been connected followed the example.

The city of Manchester, in their corporate capacity,
were not backward in manifesting their sentiments of the
honour their departed townsman had been to them.

At the first meeting of the Council, the following
proceedings were reported:—

The Chairman:—Before proceeding with the remaining
business of the council this morning, it is my painful duty to
call attention to the fact that since we last met Manchester has
lost one of her most valued citizens. I allude to Sir William
Fairbairn, who was connected with the interests of our city for
a very long period. I will ask the town clerk to read a resolution of condolence with the family of the late baronet, and I
have no doubt it will be adopted by the council; I trust, also,
that the esteem in which Sir William was held in Manchester
will find still further expression. It would be a fitting thing
in this city to erect a monument on the area in front of the
Royal Infirmary, that may hand down to posterity the name of
a man who has done so much for the city in the particular
branch of business with which he was associated, namely, the
engineering trade. (Hear, hear.) Already Dalton and Watt are
commemorated by statues before the Infirmary, and for them a

statue to Sir William Fairbairn would be fit companion. (Hear,
hear.) Had his Worship the Mayor been here, he would have
been one of the first to express his willingness to assist in any
steps that may be thought desirable by his fellow-citizens to
carry out so desirable an object. (Hear, hear.)

The town clerk read the following resolution, which was
moved by the chairman, namely:—

'That this council has heard with deep sorrow of the removal
by death of their distinguished fellow-citizen, Sir William Fairbairn, Bart., who has for so many years been one of the most
useful and valuable members of this community, and who has
during the last half-century been actively and honourably associated with all movements having for their object the improvement of the intellectual, moral, or social condition of all classes
of his fellow-citizens. That the Mayor be respectfully requested
to communicate, through Sir Thomas Fairbairn, to Lady Fairbairn and the other members of the family the assurance of
the veneration and affectionate regard which is entertained by
this Council for the memory and character of the late Sir
William Fairbairn, and of sincere sympathy and condolence in
the irreparable loss which they have sustained.

Mr. Alderman Nicholls seconded the resolution.

The resolution was supported by Mr. Alderman Heywood,
and unanimously passed.

On October 19, a public meeting, convened by the
Mayor, Mr. Alderman Watkin, was held in the Town
Hall, ' for the purpose of considering what steps should
be taken to secure, as generally desired, some suitable
permanent memorial of their distinguished fellow-citizen.'
The Mayor presided; and there were also present the
Bishop and the Dean of Manchester, Sir Joseph Heron,
the Town Clerk; Sir Edward Watkin, M.P., and many
distinguished inhabitants of the town.

The Mayor said, being fully convinced that a general desire
existed in the city and the neighbourhood to commemorate in
some fitting way the greatness, goodness, and usefulness of their
departed friend, he had not waited for the usual and somewhat

tiresome method of organising in order to call this meeting, but had done it forthwith, so that what was to be done might be done without delay. He had called the meeting to receive suggestions as to the form which the memorial should take, and to organise means for carrying it out.

Sir Joseph Heron mentioned that he had received a great number of letters from gentlemen unable to attend, stating how fully they agreed in the object of the meeting, and that they would be prepared in any way to co-operate to carry out the object of the meeting.

The Bishop of Manchester said that he had much pleasure in moving the first resolution, which declared the desirability of obtaining a suitable permanent memorial of Sir William Fairbairn. He had not had the gratification of making the acquaintance of Sir William till he had passed the ordinary limit of life—he had passed the fourscore years. But since he had known him Sir William had been kind enough to admit him to a certain measure of personal intimacy and almost friendship, and he had certainly learned to feel his great qualities, his generosity, his largeness of heart, and those other qualities which seemed to have so much endeared him to the citizens of Manchester. His, certainly, was one of those names which Manchester people of this generation would desire should be held in respect and regard by generations yet to come. It was not the sum of money that was required, because he supposed that any sum could be raised that was reasonably required, but that an opportunity should be given to Manchester people to express their sense of the high qualities by which Sir William Fairbairn became the architect, he would not say of a very large fortune (but for his own part he did not care for that), but the architect of a reputation which ought to be dear to Manchester people, and which he believed would be an example to men of ability, who were conscious of intellectual gifts, of how those gifts might be best used to the advantage of the common wealth. Fairbairn's was a name which Manchester should delight to honour, and he had much pleasure therefore in proposing the resolution.

Mr. W. R. Callender, M.P., seconded the resolution. He said there were three causes why a testimonial should be adopted;

first of all, to commemorate the virtues of a departed fellow-citizen; secondly, to serve as an encouragement to those who might come after him; and, thirdly, to be of some practical use to the present and future generations. They ought, there-fore, in erecting this memorial to Sir William, with the primary object of perpetuating his memory, to give also to those whom they wished to stimulate some means of following in his foot-steps by providing for them some educational advantage either in connection with the Owens College or some other scientific society.

The Rev. Mr. Gaskell completely coincided with the remarks made by Mr. Callender, and read part of a letter which he had received from an old friend of Sir William Fairbairn, Mr. Ainsworth, of Cleator, who said, ' I cannot take the initiative— I am too old. But I shall be a liberal contributor for a statue and scholarship in the Owens College, or, better still, an en-dowment in his name as an adjunct to the professorship of practical mechanics.' He (the speaker) thought it would be very desirable indeed to have, as a memorial of Sir William, something which he himself would have wished : and they all knew the great interest he took in mechanics' institutes and kindred societies. He thought they could not do better than carry out such a suggestion as had been made by Mr. Ainsworth.

Dr. Pankhurst said he had not had the honour to know Sir Wm. Fairbairn in his private capacity, and it was not his province to speak of him with reference to his professional eminence, but he asked to say a few words of him as a public man. He had had the pleasure and honour of meeting him in many parts of the kingdom on great public occasions, and he had always found in him one of those men who were capable not only of exerting public influence themselves, but of inspiring the dis-position to exert it in others. Never was an appeal to follow his example in that respect more needed than it now was in our own city of Manchester. The public life of Manchester was very onerous and very exacting, and unless we could have a succession of men willing to devote time and thought to the public service, we should certainly not be able to keep up the great traditions of the city and district. Sir William Fairbairn being engaged in an industry which was very exacting in its claims upon him, and which could have given him enormous pecuniary returns, yet sacrificed much of his time and thought to the public service. He honoured him for so doing, and there could be no stronger reason given for cherishing his memory and for putting his effigy and figure in some public place.

Mr. Oliver Heywood asked to be allowed also to support the resolution. Sir William Fairbairn had been throughout his life a most kindly friend of his. He had had the pleasure of attending the same school with five of his sons. He had personally obtained from him the greatest assistance in the management of the Mechanics' Institution, of which Sir William had been the first secretary, and in which he had taken through life a very active interest.

The Rev. W. Gaskell also supported the resolution as one who had enjoyed the intimate friendship of Sir William Fairbairn for more than forty years.

The resolution was then unanimously agreed to.

A discussion then took place as to the form which the memorial should assume, it being felt, as pointed out by the Bishop of Manchester, that the amount of subscriptions must be regulated by the nature of the scheme submitted for adoption to the public.

Various opinions were expressed, some in favour of a statue, others in favour of the establishment of a scholarship; and after much discussion, the following resolution was adopted :—

That the permanent monument of Sir William Fairbairn be in the form of a statue of such character, and to be placed in such position as may be hereafter determined, and also of a scholarship or some other suitable endowment in connection with the Owen's College.

A committee was then appointed to raise subscriptions and carry out the resolution.

The Manchester papers all took interest in the discussion of the measure. One said :—

The prompt action taken by the Mayor of Manchester in organising a scheme to commemorate the name of the late Sir

Wm. Fairbairn, will commend itself to general approval. That this public duty will be well done, the enthusiasm which characterised the meeting held yesterday, and the influential and representative character of the committee then appointed, abundantly assure us. It remains for the thousands who in Lancashire owe direct advantage to the scientific labour of Sir Wm. Fairbairn, to assist the committee in seeing that the work is done with readiness. A public testimonial derives its value and its grace above all things from its spontaneity, and perhaps there never was a Manchester citizen who established a more substantial claim upon the respect of his neighbours far and wide.

The Committee, having collected about 2,700*l*., decided that the statue should be of marble, and placed in the new Town Hall; and after a good deal of discussion the commission was given for it, in December 1875, to Mr. G. E. Geflowski, of London.

No action has yet been taken with reference to the scholarship at Owen's College.

CHAPTER XXIV.

PERSONAL DETAILS

ILLUSTRATIONS OF CHARACTER

THE GOLDEN WEDDING DAY—SONS AND DAUGHTERS—THE PRESENT
BARONET—THE ROYAL FAMILY, THE PRINCE CONSORT, AND THE PRINCE
OF WALES—OFFERS OF RANK—HOUSE AT THE POLYGON, SOCIETY THERE
—MR. FAIRBAIRN'S CHARACTER—BUSINESS INTEGRITY—DOMESTIC LET-
TERS—NEW STOCK AND BARREL—TWO MOONS—OPINIONS ON WORTH-
LESS SCHEMES—RELIGIOUS FEELINGS, CROSS STREET CHAPEL, THE REV.
W. GASKELL, RIVAL HYMN-BOOKS—PECULIAR NOTIONS OF RELIGIOUS
TOLERATION—NOVEL READING—CORRESPONDENCE WITH MRS. GASKELL
—PROFESSIONAL AND SCIENTIFIC CHARACTER—PERSONAL AND PRIVATE
TRAITS—INDEFATIGABLE ACTIVITY—REGULAR AND PUNCTUAL HABITS—
LIBERALITY—POPULARITY—'THERE'S FAIRBAIRN!'—FONDNESS FOR
CHILDREN—REALITY OF SIR WILLIAM FAIRBAIRN'S MERITS—MORAL.

CHAPTER XXIV.

THIS chapter is intended to supply some personal details which it was not convenient to introduce elsewhere, and to give some illustrations of Sir William Fairbairn's character.

Mr. Fairbairn was, as already stated, married in 1816. The couple therefore lived together eight years beyond the date of the 'golden wedding day,' which is so seldom attained. He had nine children, seven sons and two daughters, of whom three sons and one daughter are now living.

The second and eldest surviving son Thomas, the present baronet, was born in 1823. He was the most active assistant to his father in his manufacturing business, and latterly had its sole management. He is a deputy lieutenant and magistrate for Lancashire and a magistrate for Hampshire, where he has a seat, at Brambridge, near Winchester, and he served as sheriff for that county in 1870. He has long and often been before the world on matters of science, art, and public policy. In 1860 he was elected by the Royal Commission for the Exhibition of 1851 a member of that Commission, and again was nominated by the Crown in a similar capacity for the International Exhibition of 1862. He was chairman of the Exhibition of Art Treasures at Manchester in 1857, and on the occasion of her Majesty's visit there was offered the honour of knighthood, which he declined.

Of the two other sons, the elder, William Andrew,

(formerly one of the partners,) still resides in London, and, the younger, the Rev. Adam Henderson Fairbairn, M.A., is vicar of Waltham St. Lawrence, Berks.

During the lifetime of the Prince Consort Mr. Fairbairn, as well as other members of his family, were honoured with frequent instances of the esteem and regard of various members of the Royal Family. Prince Albert on several occasions had conversations with Mr. Fairbairn on topics of scientific and educational interest ; these subjects engaging, as is well known, the Prince's thoughtful consideration and constant devotion.

General Knollys, writing to Mr. Fairbairn on December 9, 1865, to acknowledge the receipt of some volumes of his writings, which he had presented to the Prince of Wales, was desired by his Royal Highness

To return the Prince's best thanks, and to acquaint Mr. Fairbairn that it will always be a pleasure and instruction to him to receive the publications of so practical and scientific a writer, and one so highly esteemed by his Royal Highness's lamented father.

It ought further not to be unnoticed in this volume, as a circumstance probably without precedent, that this one family were honoured by one Sovereign, her present Majesty, with no fewer than five offers of rank :—the knighthood to Mr. Fairbairn in 1861 ; the baronetage to him in 1869 ; the knighthood to his son in 1857 ; a knighthood accepted by his brother Peter in 1858 ; and another also accepted by Sir Peter's son in 1868.

Mr. Fairbairn purchased his house at the Polygon, Ardwick, Manchester, in 1840, and was so attached to it that he continued it as his residence till his death—the long period of thirty-four years.

He was very hospitable. Nothing gave him more

pleasure than to receive his friends as guests. His letters
teemed with invitations to 'the Polygon,' and whenever
there was anything of public interest going on in Manchester his house was always full.

The society at the Polygon during the last fifteen or
twenty years of his life was of an unusually intellectual,
refined, and attractive character, and brought together
guests of singularly varied acquirements and talents.
Among them were the Chevalier Bunsen, Sir David
Brewster, Mr. Wm. Hopkins, Dr. Prince Lee, Bishop
of Manchester, Lord Rosse, Lord Wrottesley, the Rev.
Vernon Harcourt, Dr. Robinson of Armagh and his
gifted wife, Sir Edward and Lady Sabine, the Earl of
Derby, Earl Granville, Lord Brougham, Mr. Leonard
Horner, Mrs. Gaskell, Lord Houghton, Lord Shaftesbury,
the several eminent Professors of Owen's College, and
many others, whose names are well known in science,
literature, and the public service. It was his custom to
invite groups of visitors regularly every autumn ; his
invitations were gladly responded to, and these annual
pleasant gatherings of choice spirits were thoroughly
enjoyed by those who had the good fortune to be present
at them.

To offer an estimate of Sir William Fairbairn's character we may, in the first instance, gather some illustrative
traits from his correspondence, and then add the more
direct testimony of those who were best acquainted with
him.

The following extract of a letter to his partner Lillie,
written when he was quite young, first entering into business, gives an example of the high feeling of honour and
integrity that actuated his business transactions. The
italics are his own :—

London, December 12, 1827.

Mr. Cooke's wheel, Mr. Potter's work, and all the rest, we shall talk over together. In the meantime I shall look in at the watchmaker's and order both yourself and me a gold watch, *but on the condition that it is not to be delivered* until we have *paid for our buildings*, and are FAIRLY OUT OF DEBT.

His domestic letters had often a mixture of gaiety and jocularity with serious and good feeling.

The following are fair samples :—

February 19, 1858.

Many thanks for your kind and affectionate congratulations [on his 69th birthday]. By my letter to —— —— you will find I am a happy and contented old codger, and whether my doom is fixed for seventy or eighty, more or less, is a matter of little moment. Men only live while they are useful, and my hope is that my years will not be prolonged beyond that period.

The following was a new year's letter to one of his fellow-workers : —

January 2, 1856.

Many happy new years to you and your family, and I hope as long as I can keep up the steam that we shall always bring in the new year, not with some compliment, but with something useful to mankind.

I am an engine always ready for service, and although a little antiquated in construction, the working parts are never-- theless in pretty good repair. The boiler has a few patches upon it, but a little careful stoking will not only prevent an explosion, but maintain the old vessel in moderate condition and efficiency for a few years longer, when I make no doubt the repairs will terminate in a ' new stock and barrel.'

He had a quiet sense of humour which he could ex- hibit very effectively. On one occasion a friend asked him to present to the Royal Society a communication descriptive of some remarkable optical phenomena which the writer professed to have witnessed; and Mr. Fairbairn replied:—

I have read your paper which you are desirous of communicating to the Royal Society; but you will forgive me if I recommend you, in the present crude state of your observations, not to send it. If you could trace the appearance to its cause in some peculiar action of the organ of sight, it would be much more satisfactory.

I remember many years ago posting from Coventry to Birmingham on a clear moonlight evening, and the more I looked the more I was convinced that there were two moons! I saw them distinctly; but I afterwards accounted for the appearance by the fact of having previously dined with a jovial party. I am sure you will pardon me for this suggestion.

He could express himself strongly, too, when he considered himself aggrieved. On one page of his letter book is this note:—

These two letters were addressed to two scoundrels who repudiated payment for work ordered under an award where I was appointed sole arbitrator.—W. F.

One of the letters runs thus:—

Sir,—I have paid ——l. for your defective work and unprincipled character. I do not envy the saving you have effected when attained at the expense of equity and justice, and I offer no apology for remaining, with unqualified contempt, yours,   W. FAIRBAIRN.

The other is in similar tone.

It was one of the penalties of his position to be continually consulted on worthless schemes, often by personal friends; and all eminent engineers and men of science know how exceedingly difficult sometimes is the task of replying to such applications.

The following extracts of letters show how Mr. Fairbairn was in the habit of dealing with such cases:—

Manchester, November 24, 1853.

My dear Sir,—With a strong desire to render myself useful
to the undertaking in which you are engaged, I have arrived at
the conclusion, after a careful perusal of the Reports of ———,
that it would be premature, if not injurious, to allow my name
to appear in public as one of the promoters of this project. On
your account, and that of my respected friend Sir ———, I
would gladly do it; but until the invention is more matured,
and its practical effect more clearly developed, neither my name
nor that of any other person, however high in station, will advance—it may retard—its progress. In my opinion a great
deal has yet to be done in the way of perfecting the ingenious discovery of M. ———; but this is a work of time not unaccompanied
with experimental research. I am satisfied that the principle is
a happy idea; but from what I can see at present, its commercial value and utility, when compared with our best steam
engines, has not been satisfactorily established, and that it
still requires additional tests and experiments to satisfy the
public as to the superior advantages likely to accrue from the
change.

In the consideration of this subject I deem it essential that
I should speak plainly, and not attempt to raise expectations
which I might not at some future period be able to realise. The
question altogether is one of considerable importance, and I
shall deem it my duty to watch the progress of the invention,
and to encourage its ultimate success to the utmost of my power.
This I cannot, however, accomplish as a director of the company; and if my services are to be at all available in a practical
point of view, I must remain unfettered and with time to act,
as circumstances may require. Whenever you consider these
services requisite, you may command,

My dear Sir, yours sincerely,

W. FAIRBAIRN.

Manchester, February 11, 1850.

My dear Sir,—I have just received your note of Saturday
last. I much fear there is something wrong with your friend
in Belgium, otherwise he would not hesitate, but rather court,
investigation into the principle, as well as the practical working,
of his motive power.

I was in hopes I could have been of service to you, as well as to the projector, by a careful examination of his machinery, in case his ideas were sound and practical. I entertained hopes of being able to assist in bringing to maturity a well-digested scheme which had for its basis not a visionary but a permanent superstructure. On the other hand, should it prove to be one of those projects with no other foundation than that which exists in the imagination of the projector, I was then prepared, confidentially, to give to both an honest opinion as to the inutility of a scheme which could have no other result than loss of reputation and a useless expenditure of money. As it is, I most respectfully decline any interference with your friend and his scheme. I would be willing to do so on your account, but it is quite evident there is some screw loose in the principle, as well as the practice of the undertaking, otherwise a free and open explanation would not have been withheld.

Believe me, my dear Sir,
Very faithfully yours,
WM. FAIRBAIRN.

The following was to an eminent scientific professor, who had been stepping out of his way to meddle with practical mechanical inventions :—

Paris, July 24, 1855.

My dear Sir,—I have given your new project my best consideration, and I cannot better express my earnest desire to serve you than by advising you not to be too sanguine of success in this matter. I am sorry to differ from you in a question to which you attach so much importance, but I deem it my duty in projects which involve considerations of money as well as reputation, to be perfectly candid and perfectly honest in giving an opinion.

Under all the circumstances, whilst I admit the existence of the force, I must confess I do not see my way clearly to its practical application. There are difficulties to be encountered before the project, however good, can be realised. The great difficulty will be to induce capitalists to embark in undertakings of this kind unless they see their way clearly before them.

I mention all these things to show how much is to be done before your new invention comes into use, and the difficulties which will require to be surmounted before the improvements you suggest can be brought into useful application. I am sure you will pardon me for speaking thus plainly. I would not advise a patent for England, as we have no rivers on which it could be applied. It might be applicable in some parts of Europe or America, but I would not advise the expense of a patent until you have further experience of its utility.

Yours, &c.,

WM. FAIRBAIRN.

His religious feelings were often manifested in his correspondence. On his settlement in Manchester he became a member of the congregation at Cross Street Chapel, and remained so to the end of his life, ready on all occasions to show his interest in its welfare, and associating on terms of closest intimacy with its ministers, more especially with the Rev. J. G. Robberds and his colleague, the Rev. W. Gaskell, M.A.

The following letter will show the interest Mr. Fairbairn took in religious subjects :—

The Polygon, Sept. 15, 1861.

My dear Mr. Gaskell,—I almost regret that the printing of the sermon of last Sunday, so generously inscribed to myself, had not waited for the addition of your equally valuable and truly philosophical discourse of this morning. I look upon these two discourses as highly appropriate to the termination of the labours of the past week,[1] and I sincerely hope they may shortly be published (to which I would cheerfully contribute) for the benefit, not only of the Cross Street congregation, but of the general public.

I am sure Mrs. and Miss Gaskell and family were highly gratified to find the whole term of the meeting an ovation of the most gratifying description. Pray make our united regards acceptable to them, and believe me,

Ever faithfully yours,

W. FAIRBAIRN.

---

[1] Alluding to the meeting of the British Association ; see Chap. XXI.

On another occasion his interest in the chapel took the form of a sensible scolding to some of the trustees :—

Manchester, September 11, 1866.

Dear Sirs,—As one of the oldest pew-holders in Cross Street Chapel, I have witnessed with deep regret a tendency to dispute, if not a total disruption of the congregation, arising as I suppose from the desire of one party to establish new forms and conditions inimical to the other. I am totally at a loss to discover the cause of these differences. They cannot arise from the simple consideration of a change of hymn-books, and unless some other motives are at work, I am unable to account for the antagonisms which exist.

I am not sufficiently acquainted with the movements of parties to discover to whom we are indebted for all these unfortunate cavils, but I regret them, and should greatly deplore any attempt to carry out views by one party or another, contrary to the wishes of the congregation, and at variance with the harmony and good feeling which for a long series of years has been the pride and satisfaction of its members.

If the present unfortunate contest rested exclusively upon the choice of Kippis's or Martineau's hymns, the question might soon be settled by the decision of the majority. I am, from early associations, personally in favour of Kippis's, but I will sing from Martineau provided the congregation so wills it.

On these points I am, however, of opinion that nothing should be done without the aid and assistance of our Pastors. They of all others ought to be consulted. They have to conduct the services of the church, and it is fitting and right that they should have a voice in whatever changes may be considered necessary and expedient.

I offer these remarks under the impression that the present differences may be amicably settled without risk or danger of disruption, and that such may be the result,

I am, dear Sirs, sincerely and truly yours,

W. FAIRBAIRN.

The Trustees of Cross Street Chapel.

Above the pew in the chapel in which for so long a period he was accustomed to sit, a white marble tablet, exquisitely sculptured by T. Woolner, R.A., was erected by his son, the present baronet. It bears the following simple inscription between two stems of oak and thistle :—

THIS TABLET

IS PLACED HERE TO THE MEMORY OF

SIR

WILLIAM FAIRBAIRN

LL.D. D.C.L.

FIRST BARONET

OF ARDWICK

WHO WORSHIPPED IN THIS CHAPEL

FOR MORE THAN 50 YEARS.

HE WAS BORN

AT KELSO

18TH FEBRUARY 1789.

AND DIED

AT MOOR PARK

SURREY

18TH AUGUST 1874.

In a letter of 1854 to the daughter of an old friend, he says :—

Many thanks for the book of sermons, but I very much doubt whether they are at all likely to supplant Blair. Blair and I are old friends, and I have treasured up his benevolent and homely maxims from early life until they have become almost a part of my existence. Besides, they are very healthy discourses, and as I like my religious garments to sit easy upon myself, I am inclined to extend the same comfort to others. You must not therefore be alarmed about me, as in my endeavour to do my best in the faithful discharge of the duties of this life I hope, through God's mercy, to meet our dear friends in that which is to come.

At a later time an event occurred which tried his temper sorely. The young lady to whom the letter just mentioned was written had married, and Mr. Fairbairn invited the pair to pay him a visit; the invitation was accepted, but the husband (a Scotchman) having heard that Mr. Fairbairn attended a chapel where Unitarian views were held, was so shocked that, considering the residence of such a person as a pest house to be avoided, he wrote an angry letter putting an end to the arrangement. This letter cannot be found, or it might be printed as an example of Scotch notions of toleration; but Mr. Fairbairn's admirable answer to the young wife was as follows :—

My dear Mrs. ——, I do not wish to say a single word against the husband of your choice; but if I am to judge of his character by a letter received this morning, I should certainly arrive at conclusions anything but favourable to his discretion. He may be a good man, and have all the conditions you require, but he is assuredly devoid of the feeling of what is due from one gentleman to another. You may inform Mr. ——, that I do not envy his religious convictions, but I do most earnestly pray that *I may never possess them.* I may be wrong in this, but I am quite able to judge for myself in matters of faith without calling upon Mr. —— as my Father Confessor. I regret, my dear madam, that your promised visit to the Polygon should have had such a termination. Both Mrs. Fairbairn and myself retain a lively recollection of your *former self*, and with every good wish, believe me,

Most sincerely yours,
W. FAIRBAIRN.

P.S.—Mr. ——'s letter requires no answer.

In April 1874, a few months before his death, a lady friend, zealous to do good, wrote a long letter to him on his religious views. His answer is not preserved ; but he endorsed the letter 'I can think for myself,' and he remained in this tone of mind to the end.

The following remarks appended to an obituary notice in a Manchester paper are happily appropriate :—

It remains to say that in Sir William Fairbairn an urbane amiability of demeanour was united to intellectual strength, and that no man could be more deserving of the tributes of social esteem which he so constantly received.

He had the straightforward simplicity so characteristic of strong men, with a grave gentleness, neither rugged nor repellent.

The painter Haydon, visiting Manchester thirty-five years ago to lecture, to start a school of design, and to apprentice a son at Fairbairn's, is said to have made this entry in his journal after a dinner party at Mr. Darbishire's :—' Liked Fairbairn much ; a good, iron, steam-engine head. To see his expression when they talked of " Ernest Maltravers," made me inwardly rejoice. " I cannot get through novels," said he ; it showed his good sense. He has risen from a foundry labourer to be master of as great a manufactory as any in the world.' Haydon's observation, however true as far as it goes, prompts the addition that Fairbairn in his youth had been no ignorant clown. His mind was of finer mould, and had been better trained at home than is commonly to be looked for in the class of life to which Haydon referred him. Familiarity with hardships had no more roughening effect on him than would be expected from some of the sports of young gentlemen's playgrounds, or the experiences of a military campaign.

The expression quoted as his by Haydon that he ' could not read novels,' was, however, not literally true ; for when well written he read them with much interest, and when he happened to be on friendly terms with the authors he generally wrote to them his opinion of their works, sometimes indeed criticising pretty freely the parts which he did not approve.

He had a good deal of correspondence of this kind with Mrs. Gaskell, with whom, as the wife of his pastor, he was on terms of intimate friendship ; and his remarks were taken by that talented lady in very good part, as the following extracts from her letters will show :—

Plymouth Grove.

My dear Mr. Fairbairn,—I am ashamed that I have been so long in acknowledging your kind friendly note, and very just

criticisms on ' North and South.' Do you know I have half begun
to expect a note from you after the publication of every story
of mine, and I was beginning to feel a little disappointed that
none arrived on this occasion. You see how unreasonable
authors (as well as other people) become if they have once been
indulged.

Your kind and racy critiques both give me pleasure and do
me good ; that is to say, your praise gives me pleasure because
it is so sincere and judicious that I value it ; and your fault-
finding does me good, because it always makes me *think*, and
very often it convinces me that I am in error. This time I
believe you have hit upon a capital blunder . . . I don't think
a second edition will be called for ; but if it should be, you may
depend upon it I shall gladly and thoughtfully make use of your
suggestion.

I agree with you that there are a certain set of characters in
' North and South,' of no particular interest to any one in the tale,
any more than such people would be in real life ; but they were
wanted to fill up unimportant places in the story, when otherwise
there would have been unsightly gaps.

Mr. Hale is not a ' sceptic '; he has *doubts*, and can resolve
greatly about great things, and is capable of self-sacrifice in
theory; but in the details of practice he is weak and vacillating.
I know a character just like his, a clergyman who has left the
Church from principle, and in that did finely ; but his daily life
is a constant unspoken regret that he did so, although he would
do it again if need be.

But I am afraid I am taking up your time with what you
will not care to read. Thank you again, dear Mr. Fairbairn, for
your note, which I shall always value, and believe me,

I am yours most truly,

E. C. GASKELL.

The following relates to remarks of his on the work
by which this authoress is perhaps best known, the ' Life
of Charlotte Brontë.'

(Date probably June 1857.)

My dear Mr. Fairbairn,—I don't think you know how much
good your letter did me. In the first place I was really afraid

that you did not like my book, because I had never received
your usual letter of criticism; and in the second, it was the one
sweet little drop of honey that the postman had brought me for
some time, as, on the average, I had been receiving three letters
a day for above a fortnight, finding great fault with me (to
use a *mild* expression for the tone of their compliments) for my
chapter about the Cowan Bridge school.

So I gave your letter a great welcome, my dear Mr. Fairbairn, and I should have replied to it sooner, but that it has
seemed very difficult to catch you. No sooner did I hear you
were in Manchester than you wrote to Mary Holland, saying
that you were leaving; and, really, unless I had directed to
'Wm. Fairbairn, Esq., Railway Carriage,' I don't know where I
could have found you.

I have had a preface to my (forthcoming) third edition sent
to me, which I dare not insert there; but it is too good to be
lost, therefore I shall copy it out for you:—

'If anybody is displeased with any statement in this book,
they are requested to believe it withdrawn, and my deep regret
expressed for its insertion, as truth is too expensive an article to
be laid before the British public.'

But for the future I intend to confine myself to lies (*i.e.* fiction). It is safer.

We did so enjoy Rome. We often thought of you, and half considered if you would not turn up in the Holy Week, which you
hinted at as possible when we left. We came home by Florence,
Venice, Milan, Genoa, and Nice. I wonder if you are at home,
and if we could tempt you to come in to our 8 o'clock tea
to-morrow night. We have Miss Brontë's faithful friend E.
staying with us.

Yours ever most truly and gratefully,

E. C. GASKELL.

In regard to Sir William Fairbairn's professional and
scientific character, the following communications from
friends who had the best opportunity, as well as the best
capability of judging, speak for themselves:—

Royal Indian Engineering College, Cooper's Hill, Staines,
October 31, 1876.

You have asked me for an expression of my opinion in regard to the late Sir W. Fairbairn, especially with regard to his scientific position. I was, as you know, well acquainted with his scientific work during seven years, and assisted him in his researches. I am very glad, therefore, to state my impressions.

I would remark first of all that Sir W. Fairbairn's knowledge of science was not chiefly learned from books, and that his knowledge of mathematical methods was not extensive. He owed his extensive knowledge of the use of materials almost entirely to observation and experience. Interested in knowing what progress was making in different branches of science, and ready to accept any help from mathematicians, he still fought his own way to knowledge along a different path. He did not appear to me to accept with firmness anything which he had not confirmed by his own observations or experiment. His thorough reliance upon direct experiment made him willing to undertake any investigation likely to throw light on doubtful points of practical science, and when he had once formulated the results of his experiments he relied on them with a remarkable absence of doubt or hesitation, and applied his conclusions in practice with a courage which would have sometimes seemed rashness to anyone more conversant with theoretical considerations.

I do not think that anyone else would have ventured to apply the common plate girder formula to so different a construction as a ship. But after the wreck of the Royal Charter he investigated the strength of ships in that way, and was led to the conclusion that many ships were deficient in power of resisting bending strains. At the moment no more elaborate investigation was possible, and the rough result obtained by Sir W. Fairbairn was not only correct, but did good service. Later investigations of a much more elaborate character on the transverse strength of ships have been made; but so far as I know, Sir W. Fairbairn was the first to point out that an iron ship needs to be considered as a girder resisting transverse forces.

There can be no question that parallel with theoretical investigations in applied mechanics there is needed a series of

experimental investigations to check the results of theory, and to furnish the numerical data which are required. I suppose no one has done so much to supply such data as Sir W. Fairbairn. His experiments on the strength of materials and of structures involved a considerable expenditure of thought, of labour, and of money. Those experiments always were of a practical character, but they did not aim at any immediate commercial result. Sir W. Fairbairn was always ready to undertake researches which it appeared would increase practical knowledge, trusting that in time the results would prove to be of value. I may add that his experiments were always made in a truly scientific spirit, and with all the precautions which were known to be desirable. His experiments are therefore trustworthy, and free from any suspicion of bias.

As to Sir W. Fairbairn's position as an engineer, it would hardly be becoming in me to say very much. His reputation was so well established in so many different branches of engineering, and his works are so important and well known, that no testimony from me is needed. I can only say that a younger engineer could not help being struck with his sound and rapid judgment of practical questions.

Personally, it was extremely pleasant to be engaged under Sir W. Fairbairn. I found him uniformly kind and considerate. He made his influence strongly felt without exercising any direct pressure. He was very indefatigable in his own work, and very ready to recognise conscientious work in others. His memory was very accurate and retentive. In manner he was always calm, and free from hurry or irritation.

W. CAWTHORNE UNWIN.

Dr. Robinson, F.R.S., of Armagh, one of the ablest and most respected men of science of the present day, writes thus:—

Observatory, Armagh, November 8, 1876.

I would say that Sir William Fairbairn was among the noblest of the good and wise whom it has been my good fortune to know during my long life.

Through all our intimacy of more than forty years I never saw in him anything to cloud the high esteem in which I held him.

Kind, generous, and upright; prudent in forming resolutions, energetic in carrying them out, and gifted with rare experimental sagacity, he was one of the best types of a class of men to whom our nation owes so much of its greatness.

In one respect (at least so it seems to me) he was distinguished above the other great engineers of his time in the spirit of research which urged him to enquiries involving much expenditure of time, labour, and money, which, though of the highest importance to the science of mechanical engineering, brought with them no material remuneration. These he gave to the public without reserve; and it is not too much to say that his investigations on the strength of riveting, on the deterioration of cast-iron by long-continued strain, and as to the resistance of tubes to collapse under external pressure, were boons not merely to his profession, but to humanity itself.

Not less notable in him was the complete absence of affectation; he knew the exact measure of his attainments, and never pretended to anything beyond them.

Nor had he any of that jealousy of rivals which I regret to say is not very uncommon among men of science. Even in vexed questions where he considered he had been unfairly treated, he was never unjust to his opponents; and though more than one of his *protégés* repaid him with ingratitude, yet he spoke of this in no angry spirit.

T. R. ROBINSON.

The late Professor Macquorn Rankine, a high authority on mechanical science, spoke of Sir William's long series of experimental investigations as 'unparalleled for extent and for practical utility.'

Another friend, who knew him well in business, says:—

In a professional sense, no difficulty daunted him. He liked, as he said, 'to tackle a big job,' the more novel and daring the better; his energy and determination seemed to increase in proportion to the number and magnitude of the difficulties he had to overcome. He was for this reason very often consulted by the different departments of the Government, and by many of the

great civil engineers who, between 1830 and 1870, were developing and completing great industrial and national undertakings
with a rapidity and success which astonished the world. His
eagerness to associate himself with such enterprises, and his
desire to secure for his own manufacturing establishments some
portion of the constructive works, often led him into unprofitable bargains. He liked to secure a great order, and his one
anxiety, when such an opportunity presented itself, was to 'do
the work,' thinking little of the result, whether for profit or the
reverse. Fame with him was ever before money. He was
never, in the ordinary acceptation of the term, a 'good man of
business,' and thus we find that it was not till after 1845, when
his sons became associated with him as partners, and their influence began to predominate in the management of the concerns,
that he began to accumulate wealth, and make safe those profits
of business which he had constantly earned, but had allowed
to melt away again. He made several fortunes, but only kept
one.

In connection with his professional character and success,
one thing deserves especial mention. He had a wonderful eye
for *proportion* and the *mechanical fitness of things.* It was
the universal judgment and remark of the troops of eminent
scientific men whose friendship he enjoyed, that although he
made no pretensions to theoretical attainments, he had an eminently scientific and philosophic turn of mind and thought.
For this reason he almost intuitively went right in all his
designs of novel and original nature. I cannot call to mind a
single instance of failure, either from inadequate strength or
faulty proportions in any of his work; and his steam-engines,
water-wheels, mill-gearing, his boilers and bridges, were models
of symmetry, and were never disfigured, as is too often the case,
by the superfluous and injurious introduction of unnecessary
material.

He was frequently called in to satisfy public anxiety as
to the safety of large and important public structures. On
these occasions he seemed to take in at a glance the merits and
defects of any combination of parts, and he was never wrong in
the immediate opinion he expressed as to its security or insecu-
rity. He was presented with a gold snuff-box, by the council of

the famous Anti-Corn Law League, for the advice and assistance he gave in the construction of the roof which covered the vast area of the first great Free Trade Hall in Manchester ; and I remember his judgment and reports were at once accepted, as assuring the public safety, when he was asked to examine the galleries and passages of the buildings for the great International Exhibition in London, and the Exhibition of Art Treasures in Manchester. The weak points were detected in a moment, and the appropriate remedies and strengthenings were suggested at once.

His hand-sketching was admirably clear and clever. His business letters were frequently illustrated by neat drawings, and the draughtsmen who elaborated his plans never had any difficulty in rendering in full detail the original sketches he put in their hands. It was also a characteristic practice with him to order many of his mechanical contrivances to be drawn out full size on a large surface. For this purpose the floor of one large room nearly seventy feet long was kept free as a huge drawing-board; to these full-sized drawings the wooden patterns, when completed, were brought down and adjusted.

In addition to the above, the editor has been favoured by intimate friends of Sir William with many less formal memoranda, which enable him to give the following details of his personal and private traits of character :—

Perhaps the most remarkable feature was his indefatigable activity and his earnestness of purpose in work. With him work seemed a necessity of life, and he could not rest or be happy unless well employed. He was never heard to complain of hard toil ; indeed it was to him a pleasure.

The simple record of what he did as a school-boy, as an almost self-teaching student, as an engineer, as an experimentalist, and as a writer, shows that his favourite and oft-repeated assertions of 'indomitable perseverance' and 'determination to excel' were with him no idle phrases, but active guiding principles of conduct. His love for work lasted down to almost the very end of his long life. No hour of his day was ever unoccupied or passed in idleness. He never found ' dignity in leisure,' but was ever doing. In business he was unceasingly at work with his brain, his pen, and his draughtsmen, in scheming, inventing, or trying to improve something or other. Wherever he was he breakfasted early, and the meal over he at once set about a long day's work. When at Manchester, from nine to six o'clock of every day was spent in the office or the workshops; and during the height of his prosperity as a mechanical engineer he had seldom less than eight or ten draughtsmen constantly at work under his own personal direction.

His correspondence was prodigious, and he never failed to answer letters, however trivial their subject, and however obscure the writer, giving always the best advice and assistance to all he considered worthy of it. His reports and scientific writings were mostly done at night. When the family retired to rest he adjourned to his library at the Polygon; and at a little writing-desk in one corner of the room, with a shaded lamp by his side, and with the little picture of the *Arbeitszimmer* of his illustrious friend, the author of ' Cosmos,' before him, his pen might be heard scribbling away incessantly till the small hours of the morning. The quantity of matter he wrote was astounding; for the mass of his writings chronicled in the pages of this work, large as it is, only represents a small fraction of what proceeded from his hand.

The leisure moments he so fairly earned after a hard day's work, if not spent in writing, were devoted to reading. He was especially fond of history and biography. For works of fiction generally he had no particular taste, though he greatly enjoyed a novel which faithfully portrayed the scenes of home life. Goldsmith, Washington Irving, and Prescott were his favourite authors, and in later times he highly appreciated the works of George

Eliot, Mrs. Gaskell, and the authoress of 'John Halifax, Gentleman.'

His holidays, which seldom exceeded three weeks or a month, were spent either at the houses of friends, or in short trips abroad, or in revisiting in Scotland the scenes of his early days.

But long familiarity with the stir and activity of a large manufacturing town had disqualified him for enjoying the quiet and repose of country life. Nor had he any taste for field sports; he neither hunted, nor shot, nor fished; his only exercise was walking. Whenever business or inclination called him into the country, he would derive his chief interest from farming operations. Any time he could spare was usually spent in company with the nearest farmer, discussing the state of the markets and the different improvements in agriculture ; and it has been noticed how the farmers were struck with his sagacity and information on such matters.

Though he studied and thought much in solitude, he loved companionship, and on his long journeys, as well as on his visits to scientific gatherings, such as the British Association, he was generally accompanied either by one of his sons or by his son-in-law.

He was essentially a man of regular habits, always punctual to hours and in keeping appointments, and particularly neat and orderly in all he did. His friend Mr. Hopkins gave an amusing instance of the power of a long-continued habit. In his daily walk to and from Canal Street he was accustomed to cross the road at certain fixed points, and he would never allow anyone or anything to interfere with this practice. When these various stages in his walk were reached he would give Mr. Hopkins a gentle push from the causeway into the mud, and thus silently insist on crossing at the places he had been accustomed to.

All who were acquainted with Sir William Fairbairn will bear willing testimony to his high-mindedness and integrity. Strictly honourable and sincere in all his dealings, he had the greatest abhorrence of all meanness; and guiding his conduct by the high standard of truth and right, he was one who could be invariably trusted.

He was very liberal, not only with his purse, but in his feelings and behaviour to those with whom he came in contact. His activity in the cases of Cort and Roberts has already been noticed, and many other instances of his kindliness of feeling might have been cited. The following letter from one of his assistants only expresses what was a general sentiment among all who had served him :—

My dear Sir,—Your most generous present requires me to render again to you some imperfect acknowledgment of your kindness. I thank you much for that, but I value more the esteem you express in your letter. I have sometimes failed in doing what I might have done, but I am proud notwithstanding to have earned in some degree your respect.

I shall serve many masters and not find one who will treat me with so uniform a courtesy or such considerate trust.

I can only repeat that I shall always be glad, with such ability as I may have, and such opportunities as circumstances may permit, to assist you, or to preserve the record of your example as one of the most valuable heirlooms of all that you will leave for the benefit of men.

His sympathy with suffering and distress, together with his amiability and unsuspicious nature, made him sometimes an easy prey to impostors. This trustfulness, though no real loss to him, was often detrimental to his success as a man of business. Though fully alive to the value of money, he never made it an object of unworthy desire ; simple in his tastes and wants, he was amply satisfied as long as he obtained sufficient for the comfort and usefulness of himself and his family.

In the gatherings at the Polygon there were often earnest discussions, and sometimes long arguments, in which he willingly joined. But in these cases he was always calm; and whenever the combatants in dispute became heated or excited, his favourite exclamation, 'Stop a moment, now, let us consider,' would generally bring them to reason.

He had little appreciation of refined wit, and the most skilful play upon words and the most appropriate quotations would scarcely move him; but a good story, especially if it were a Scotch one, would of all things delight him, and he would recur to it again and again with fresh pleasure.

In private life Sir William Fairbairn was distinguished by a quiet dignity of manner, combined with a modesty, simplicity, courtesy, and gentleness, which won him all hearts, and made him a general favourite. Though without the advantage of early association with high-born people, he was by nature a gentleman in the best sense. He was a most faithful friend, never forgetting anyone who had shown him kindness or civility. He was thus known by thousands who were unknown to him, they having probably remembered some kindly word or act which he had forgotten. The people who sought his counsel were of all ranks and classes, and the very humblest of them never applied in vain. In Manchester especially his tall commanding figure and venerable white locks were known by everyone, and as he passed along the streets one heard constantly uttered, 'There's Fairbairn!' The universal esteem in which he was held was strikingly shown on the occasion of his funeral, of which an account has already been given.

As a parent he was most affectionate and indulgent. He always impressed on his children the necessity of independence of mind and action. ' Never play second fiddle to anyone' was his frequent advice to them. He would help them to the utmost of his power in any worthy pursuit they undertook, even when opposed to the course he had marked out for them and wished them to follow. His appreciation of his eldest son's sacrifice for his interests [1] was marked by his making him a partner in the profitable business before he came of age.

He was very fond of children. In the later years of his life he seemed to become quite young again in company with his grandchildren; and there was nothing he enjoyed more than a good romp with them, chasing them round the room amidst their screams of delight, singing them one of his songs, or giving the little ones a ride on his foot.

On the whole, most of his personal friends agree that his virtues were many and his faults few. He had perhaps an excessive ambition for popularity and fame; but this foible had one redeeming feature, namely, that he aimed not so much at obtaining the applause of the million as at standing well with the good and the wise.

Sir William Fairbairn was fond of drawing a moral from his own career. He would often, when lecturing to working men, or addressing students, allude, with pardonable pride, to the position he occupied, contrasting it with his humble origin. He would declare that it was by his own industry, perseverance, and determination that his

---

[1] See page 342.

success had been brought about, and he would urge on his hearers a like course of action.

He only consented to the publication of his biography on the ground that it might be 'for the benefit of those who have to encounter similar difficulties in life;' and it is earnestly hoped that the present work may fulfil the condition he so much desired.

APPENDIX

APPENDIX.

LIST OF SIR WILLIAM FAIRBAIRN'S PUBLISHED WORKS AND PAPERS.

In this Appendix is given a list, arranged in chronological order, of the various books, papers, and memoirs published by Sir William Fairbairn.

The list is complete so far as the editor has been able to ascertain; but it is quite possible that, considering the large mass of his writings, and the great variety of societies and publications to which he communicated them, some few may have escaped attention.

The more important writings in the list have been noticed in the biography, and reference is given, in each item, to the place where the notice will be found. In other cases a few words of explanation are appended.

1831.

'Remarks on Canal Navigation, illustrative of the advantages of the use of Steam as a Moving Power on Canals.' 8vo. pp. 93. With five plates. London: Longmans & Co.

See Chap. IX., p. 135.

1836.

'Reservoirs on the River Bann, in the county of Down, Ireland, for more effectually supplying the Mills with Water.' (Report) Tract, 4to. pp. 23. With large map. Manchester: Robinson.

See Chap. X., p. 158.

1837.

'An Experimental Enquiry into the Strength and other Properties of Cast Iron from various parts of the United Kingdom,' pp. 103.

Read March 7, 1837, before the Literary and Philosophical Society of Manchester, and published in their 'Transactions,' vol. vi. 1842.

See Chap. X., p. 161.

'On the Strength and other Properties of Cast Iron obtained from the Hot and Cold Blast,' pp. 39.

Report presented September 1837 to the British Association for the Advancement of Science, and printed in their 'General Report,' vol. vi. 1837.

See Chap. X., p. 162.

1840.

'An Experimental Enquiry into the Strength and other Properties of Anthracite Cast Iron,' being a continuation of a series of experiments on British irons from various parts of the United Kingdom.

Read November 1840 before the Literary and Philosophical Society of Manchester, and published in their 'Memoirs,' vol. vi. 1842.

See Chap. XII., p. 180.

'On the Economy of raising Water from Coal Mines on the Cornish Principle,' pp. 15. With two plates.

Transactions of the Manchester Geological Society, vol. i. 8vo. London: Simpkin & Marshall. 1841.

See Chap. XII., p. 180.

1843.

'Description of a Woollen Factory erected in Turkey.'

Min. Proc. Inst. C.E. vol. iii. 1843, p. 125.

See Chap. XI., p. 173.

1844.

'Experimental Researches into the Properties of the Iron Ores of Samakoff in Turkey,' &c. &c., pp. 20.

Min. Proc. Instit. C.E. vol. iii. p. 225.

See Chap. XI., p. 173.

' On the Consumption of Fuel and the Prevention of Smoke,' pp. 20.

Report of the 14th Meeting of the British Association, September 1844, p. 100.

See Chap. XII., p. 183.

' Report of William Fairbairn, Esq., C.E., on the Construction of Fireproof Buildings,' with introductory remarks by Samuel Holme.

Also ' Report of Mr. W. Fairbairn and Mr. D. Bellhouse, on the cause of the Falling of Messrs. Radcliffe's Mill at Oldham.' Tract, 8vo. pp. 39. Liverpool : Thomas Baines, Castle Street. 1844. See Chap. XII., p. 185.

1847.

' On some Defects in the Principle and Construction of Fireproof Buildings,' pp. 25. With a plate.

Min. Proc. Inst. C.E. vol. vii. p. 213.

See Chap. XII., p. 186.

Evidence and Documents on the subject of Iron Structures.

Report of the Commissioners appointed to enquire into the application of Iron to Railway Structures. Presented to Parliament 1849.

See Chap. XII., p. 188.

1849.

' An Account of the Construction of the Britannia and Conway Tubular Bridges, with a complete history of their progress,' &c. Large 8vo. pp. 291. With several plates. London : Weale & Longman. 1849.

See Chap. XIII., p. 197.

' On the Expansive Action of Steam, and a new Construction of Expansion Valves for Condensing Steam Engines.'

Civil Engineers and Architects' Journal, vol. xii. p. 315.

Dingler's Polytechnische Journale, vol. cxv. p. 1.

See Chap. XVIII., p. 319.

' On Water-wheels with Ventilated Buckets.'
Min. Proc. Inst. C.E. vol. viii. p. 45.
See Chap. XII., p. 188.

1850.

' An Experimental Enquiry into the Strength of Wrought
Iron Plates and their Riveted Joints, as applied to Shipbuilding
and vessels exposed to severe strain.'
Phil. Trans. 1850, p. 677.
See Chap. XXII., p. 402.

' On Tubular Girder Bridges.'
Min. Proc. Inst. C.E. vol. ix. p. 233.
See Chap. XXII., p. 401.

' An Experimental Enquiry into the Relative Power of the
Locomotive Engine, and the Resistance of Railway Gradients.'
Read before the Literary and Philosophical Society of Manchester, February 5, 1850, and published in vol. ix. of their
' Memoirs.'
This paper consists of a record of several series of experiments with locomotive engines on steep inclines on the Lancashire and Yorkshire and the East Lancashire railways, to determine the possibility of working such inclines with locomotive
engines instead of by fixed engines.
It is not clear what share Mr. Fairbairn had in these trials ;
but he reasoned upon them, and gave his opinion that ' the
locomotive engine of the present day is more than commensurate
for the attainment of these objects,' an opinion which has been
amply borne out by subsequent experience, as of late years
locomotive power has been used successfully for inclines much
steeper than those contemplated in the above paper.

' On the Security and Limit of Strength of Tubular Bridges
constructed of Wrought Iron.' Read April 2, 1850, before the
same Society, and published also in their vol. ix.
This was for the most part a reproduction of the paper
presented to the Institution of Civil Engineers about the same
time.

1851.

'Two Lectures on the Construction of Boilers, and on Boiler Explosions; with the Means of Prevention.' Delivered before the Leeds Mechanics' Institution April 23 and 24, 1851.

Tract, 8vo. London: Simpkin, Marshall & Co.; Weale. 1851.

(Also in Journal of the Franklin Institute, 1851.)
See Chap. XVI., p. 263.

1852.

'On Metallic Constructions.' Civ. Eng. and Arch. Journal, vol. xv. p. 145. Franklin Inst. Jour. vol. xxiv.

A paper containing matter for the most part published elsewhere.

'On a new Tubular Boiler' (Brit. Assoc.) C.E. and Arch. Jour. vol. xv. p. 330.

This was a description of a proposed modification of his original double flued boiler, but it involved some internal complexity, and did not come into general use.

'On the Minié Rifle' (Brit. Assoc.) C.E. and Arch. Jour. vol. xv. p. 331.

A description of the arm, then a novelty exciting much interest in this country.

1853.

'Experimental Researches to determine the Strength of Locomotive Boilers, and the Causes which lead to Explosion.'

Reports of the British Association. Hull Meeting, 1853.
See Chap. XVI., p. 264.

'On the Mechanical Properties of Metals as derived from repeated Meltings, exhibiting the Maximum Point of Strength and the Causes of Deterioration.'

Ibid.
See Chap. XXII., p. 405.

' On the Progress of Mechanical Science.' Address delivered by the President of the Mechanical Section on the opening of the business.

Ibid.

See Chap. XXI., p. 369.

' Experiments on the Strength of Cast Iron Smelted with Purified Coke.'

Min. Inst. C.E. vol. xii. p. 360.

This related to a proposed mode of purifying coke from sulphur by chemical means, and Mr. Fairbairn's experiments showed that the process improved the quality of the iron ; but it has not come into use.

' On a new Description of Winding Engine.'

Proceedings of the Institution of Mechanical Engineers, 1853.

This was an account of an engine erected by Messrs. Fairbairn and Sons at a colliery at Dukinfield near Manchester, 700 yards deep. The peculiarity of the engine was its large size, 400 to 450 horse power, and the fact that it had been modelled on the direct acting principle, similar to the marine engines which the same firm had put in Her Majesty's frigates, the ' Vulture,' ' Odin ' and ' Dragon.' The paper was accompanied by drawings of the engines.

' On the Retardation and Stoppage of Railway Trains.'

Ibid.

The object of this was chiefly to describe the continuous self-acting brake, invented shortly before by Mr. James Newall, of Bury, and which has since come largely into use both in England and abroad. The experiments quoted in the paper showed that a train weighing 88 tons, when running at 48 miles an hour down an incline of 1 in 40, could be stopped by this break in 371 yards ; when running on a level at 33 miles an hour it could be stopped in 100 yards.

1854.

' Description of an Improved Steam Travelling Crane.'

Read before the Institution of Mechanical Engineers, July 1854, and published in their ' Proceedings.'

This was an apparatus constructed for the purpose of lifting heavy weights and moving them about, chiefly applied to large stones during building operations. The hoisting machine was made to traverse a scaffold erected overhead, having motion both in the longitudinal and transverse directions; the novelty in this machine was that both the hoisting and the locomotion were effected by the power of a small steam engine attached to the machinery, and which moved about along with it; this application of power effecting a considerable saving both of labour and time.

'Description of the Sliding Caisson at Keyham Dockyard.' Min. Proc. Inst. C.E. vol. xiii. p. 444.
See Chap. XVIII., p. 320.

' On the Application of Cast and Wrought Iron to Building Purposes.' London: Weale. 1856. Large 8vo. pp. 183, with plates. Second edition, with additions. Weale, 1857. Third edition. Longmans, 1864.
See Chap. XXII., p. 406.

1855.

' Description of a New Construction of Pumping Engine.'
Proceedings of the Inst. of Mechanical Engineers, 1855, p. 177.
This was merely a description of a pumping engine erected by Messrs. Fairbairn at Dukinfield Colliery.

' Provisional Report of Committee of the British Association on the Properties of Metals used for Artillery.'
Brit. Assoc. Rep. vol. xxiv. p. 100.
This was the beginning of an enquiry that was not continued.

1856.

' On the Tensile Strength of Wrought Iron at various Temperatures.'
Brit. Assoc. Rep. vol. xxv. p. 405.
He had before investigated the same subject for cast-iron, and the Association had made him a grant for continuing the investigation. This paper was the result. It gave details of a large number of experiments on wrought-iron, and it appeared

that in a range from 0° to 500° or 600° Fahr. no perceptible variation in strength was caused by the alteration of temperature.

' Useful Information for Engineers.' Being a series of lectures, &c. London: Longmans. 1856. Large 8vo. Plates. Followed by other editions.

See Chap. XXII., p. 409.

1857.

' On Tubular Wrought Iron Cranes ;' with description of the 60-ton tubular crane recently erected at Keyham Dockyard, Devonport.

Proceedings of the Inst. Mechan. Eng., 1857, pp. 87 to 96. With four plates.

See Chap. XVIII., p. 321.

' On the Comparative Value of various kinds of Stone as exhibited by their Powers of resisting Compression.'

Read before the Literary and Philosophical Society of Manchester April 1, 1856, and published in their ' Transactions,' second series, vol. xiv. pp. 31–47.

This paper described a great number of experiments made in crushing small cubes of various kinds of stone, and a comparison of these with other materials, such as iron and timber. Drawings of the fractures were also given.

1857.

Note on the ' Life of James Watt.'

In Biographies of Distinguished Scientific Men. By Francois Arago. London: Longmans. 1857.

See Chap. XXI., p. 378.

1858.

' Experiments to determine the Strength of some Alloys of Nickel and Iron, similar in Composition to Meteoric Iron.'

Read before the Manchester Philosophical Society March 9, 1858. Published in their ' Transactions,' vol. xv. pp. 104–112. It had been supposed that such a mixture would be stronger and tougher than the simple iron, but these experiments proved the contrary.

'On the Comparative Temperature of the Climate of England and some parts of Italy.'
Ibid. pp. 45–48.
See Chap. XXI., p. 380.

'On the Resistance of Tubes to Collapse.'
Read before the Royal Society May 20, 1858.
Phil. Trans., 1858, pp. 389 to 413. With two plates.
See Chap. XVI., p. 270.
The same abbreviated.
Rep. Brit. Assoc. 1857, pp. 215–219.

'On the Collapse of Glass Globes and Cylinders.'
Rep. Brit. Assoc. 1858, pp. 174–176.
See Chap. XVI., p. 273.

'The Patent Laws.' Report of Committee. Presented by W. Fairbairn.
Rep. Brit. Assoc. 1858, pp. 164–167.
A summary of the effect of recent patent legislation.

'On Shipping Statistics,' Report of Committee. (W. Fairbairn, chairman.)
Rep. Brit. Assoc., 1858, pp. 239–260.
Having a view to the improvement of the character of statistical records, particularly as regards the definition of tonnage.

'Description of a Floating Steam Corn Mill and Bakery.'
'Proc. Inst. Mechanical Engineers,' 1858, pp. 155–158. Two plates.
See Chap. XVIII., p. 330.

'Notice of some Experimental Apparatus for determining the density of Steam at all Temperatures.'
Contributed by Mr. Fairbairn to the Manchester Literary and Philosophical Society on November 16, 1858, and published in their 'Transactions.' This consisted of a brief sketch of the apparatus with which he, in conjunction with Mr. Tate, was performing the investigation afterwards laid before the Royal Society.

'An Experimental Enquiry into the effect of Severe Pressure upon the Properties of Gunpowder.'
Read before the same society March 22, 1859. Published in their 'Proceedings.'

The Government had, during the late war, requested him to subject some samples of gunpowder to severe pressure, in order to ascertain the effect of close contact between the particles on its explosive properties ; and the effects are stated.

'Experiments to determine the effects of different Modes of Treatment on Cast Iron for the Manufacture of Cannon.'

Read before the same society May 3, 1859, and published in their 'Proceedings.'

This is an account of some experiments with certain peculiar modes of casting which were applied to some guns made by him and tried at Woolwich in 1855.

1859.

'Report of Committee on the Patent Laws.' Presented by W. Fairbairn.

Rep. Brit. Assoc. 1859, p. 191.

'Experimental Researches to determine the Density of Steam at various Temperatures.' By Wm. Fairbairn and Thomas Tate.

Rep. Brit. Assoc. 1859, p. 233.

See Chap. XVI., p. 273.

'Three Lectures on the Rise and Progress of Civil and Mechanical Engineering, and on Popular Education.' (Two delivered at Derby and one at Blackburn.) Derby: W. & W. Pike. 1859.

'On the Resistance of Glass Globes and Cylinders to Collapse from External Pressure, and on the Tensile and Compressive Strength of various kinds of Glass.' By W. Fairbairn and Thomas Tate.

Phil. Trans. 1859, pp. 213 to 247.

See Chap. XVI., p. 273.

1859-60.

'On the Efficiency of various kinds of Railway Brakes.'

Rep. Brit. Assoc. 1859, p. 76.

Also a more extended paper on the same subject in Min. Inst. C.E. vol. xix. pp. 490 to 517.

See Chap. XXII., p. 411.

'Experimental Researches to determine the Density of Steam at different Temperatures, and to determine the Law of Expansion of superheated Steam.' By Wm. Fairbairn and Thomas Tate. Phil. Trans. 1860, pp. 185 to 222. With three plates.

See Chap. XVI., p. 273.

'Useful Information for Engineers.' Second Series. London: Longmans. 1860. 8vo. pp. 330. Plates.

See Chap. XXII., p. 412.

'The Strength of Iron Ships.'
Transactions of the Institution of Naval Architects. Vol. i. 1860, pp. 71–81. Two plates.

See Chap. XXII., p. 411.

1860–61.

'Experiments to determine the effect of Vibratory Action and long-continued Changes of Load upon Wrought-iron Girders.'
Brit. Assoc. Rep. 1860, pp. 45–48 ; Ditto 1861, pp. 286–9.

See Chap. XXII., p. 413.

1861.

'Iron : its History, Properties, and Processes of Manufacture.' (Reprinted from the eighth edition of the 'Encyclopædia Britannica.') Edinburgh: Black. 1861. 8vo. pp. 236. Third edition 1869.

See Chap. XXII., p. 408.

'On the Mechanical Properties of Iron Armour Plates.'
Report of the Iron Armour Committee, 1861 (not published).

See Chap. XX., p. 359.

'Treatise on Mills and Millwork. Part I. On the Principle of Mechanism and on Prime Movers.' London: Longmans. 1861. 8vo. pp. 280. Plates.

See Chap. XXII., p. 414.

'Opening Address at the Meeting of the British Association at Manchester.'
Report for the year.

See Chap. XXI., p. 386.

'Remarks on the Temperature of the Earth's Crust, as exhibited in the Dukinfield Deep Mine.'

Brit. Assoc. Rep. 1861, p. 53–56. One plate.

This mine was sunk above 700 yards deep, and careful observations were made of the temperatures of the strata at various points in the descent. It increased from $62\frac{1}{2}°$ at 358 yards to 75° at 717 yards, and the experiments appeared to confirm the previous impression that the temperature increased directly as the depth.

'On the Permeability of various kinds of Insulation for Submarine Telegraph Cables.' Report of Joint Committee on the Construction of Submarine Telegraph Cables, 1861. Appendix No. 5.

See Chap. XXI., p. 382.

'On the Resistance of Iron Plates to Statical Pressure, and the Force of Impact by Projectiles at High Velocities.'

Brit. Assoc. Reports, 1861, pp. 280–286. 1862, pp. 178–184.

See Chap. XX.

1862.

'On the Resistance of different kinds of Shot.'

'On the Properties of Iron Armour Plates.'

Report of the Iron Armour Committee, 1862 (not published).

See Chap. XX., p. 408.

'Address at the Opening of the Section of Mechanical Science, British Association.'

Brit. Assoc. Rep., 1862, pp. 178-182.

See Chap. XXI., p. 394.

'On the Properties of Iron and its Resistance to Projectiles at High Velocities.'

Lecture at the Royal Institution, May 9, 1862. Proc. vol. iv. pp. 491–502.

See Chap. XX.

1863.

'Treatise on Mills and Millwork. Part II. On Machinery of Transmission and the Construction and Management of Mills.'

London: Longmans. 1863. 8vo. pp. 284. Plates.

See Chap. XXII., p. 414.

' On the Reconstruction of the Dinting and Mottram Viaducts.'

Min. of Proc. Inst. C. E., May 24, 1869.

See Chap. XVIII., p. 331.

' Four Papers on the Properties of Iron Armour Plates, and of Projectiles.'

Report of the Iron Armour Committee, 1863. (Not published.)

See Chap. XX., p. 408.

' Experiments to determine the effect of Impact, Vibratory Action, and long-continued Changes of Load on Wrought-iron Girders.'

Phil. Trans. 1864, pp. 311–325. Two plates.

See Chap. XXII., p. 414.

1864.

' Three Papers on the Properties of Iron Armour Plates.'

Report of the Iron Armour Committee, 1864. (Not pubished.)

See Chap. XX., p. 408.

1864–5.

' On the Atlantic Cable.'

Brit. Assoc. Rep. 1864, and 1865.

See Chap. XXI.

1865.

' Treatise on Iron Shipbuilding, its history and progress; as comprised in a series of experimental researches on the laws of strain; the strengths, forms and other conditions of the material, and an enquiry into the present and prospective state of the navy, including the experimental results on the resisting powers of armour plates and shot at high velocities.' 8vo. Plates and cuts. London: Longmans. 1865.

See Chap. XXII., p. 416.

1866.

' Description of the Removing and Replacing of the Iron Columns in a Cotton Mill.'

Read before the Institution of Mechanical Engineers August 1, 1866, and published in their 'Transactions' for the year, pp. 181–185. Three plates.

In consequence of the improvements in mule spinning it became necessary to widen the old mills, and to effect this in the case described a number of iron columns in a fire-proof building carrying iron and brick floors of a weight of 90 tons had to be removed while 300 persons were at work in the mill. The paper gives a description, with plates, explaining how this was successfully done.

'Useful Information for Engineers.' Third series. London: Longmans.
See Chap. XXII., p. 416.

1869.

'An Experimental Enquiry into the Strength, Elasticity, Ductility, and other Properties of Steel manufactured by the Barrow Hæmatite Steel Company.' London: Spottiswoode, 1869. 8vo, pp. 51. One plate.

'On the Law of Resistance of Armour Plates.'
Transactions of the Institution of Naval Architects, 1869.
See Chap. XX.

'The Rise and Progress of Manufactures and Commerce, and of Civil and Mechanical Engineering, in Lancashire and Cheshire.' Forming part of Baines's 'Lancashire and Cheshire, Past and Present.' London: Mackenzie.
See Chap. XXII., p. 416.

1870.

'On Governmental Boiler Inspection.' A letter to John Hick, Esq., M.P. (Tract.)
Manchester Guardian Office. 1870.
See Chap. XVI., p. 278.

1871.

'On Steam Boiler Legislation.'
Quarterly Journal of Science, April 1871, pp. 214–227.
See Chap. XVI., p. 278.

1873.

'On the Durability and Preservation of Iron Ships, and on Riveted Joints.'

Proceedings of the Royal Society, vol. xxi. pp. 259-263.

See Chap. XXII., p. 418.

INDEX

INDEX.